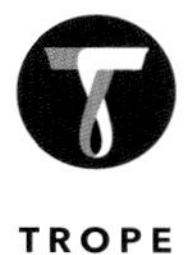

TROPE

ABOVE & ACROSS
TWIN CITIES

EDITED BY

MICHELLE FITZGERALD

KENDRA HUSPASKA

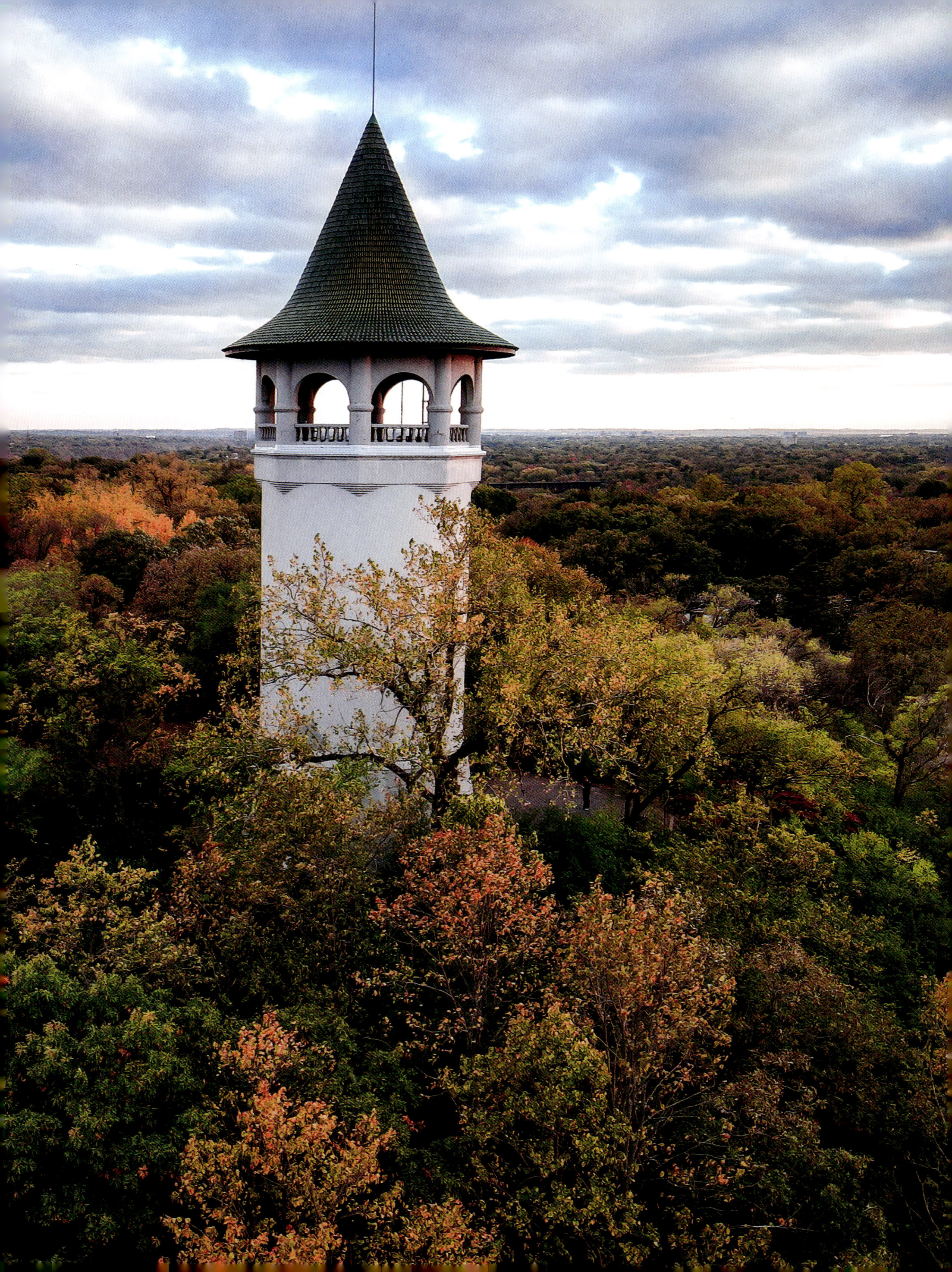

PHOTOGRAPHS BY

BRIAN JOHNSON

DAN ANDERSON

GREG SCHULZ

JAMIE HINER

MALIK BLAYLARK

MARK BERGERON

MICHAEL ANDERSON

OMAR GHRAYEB

ZACH BUTLER

FOREWORD BY

PEGGY FLANAGAN
Lt. Governor of Minnesota

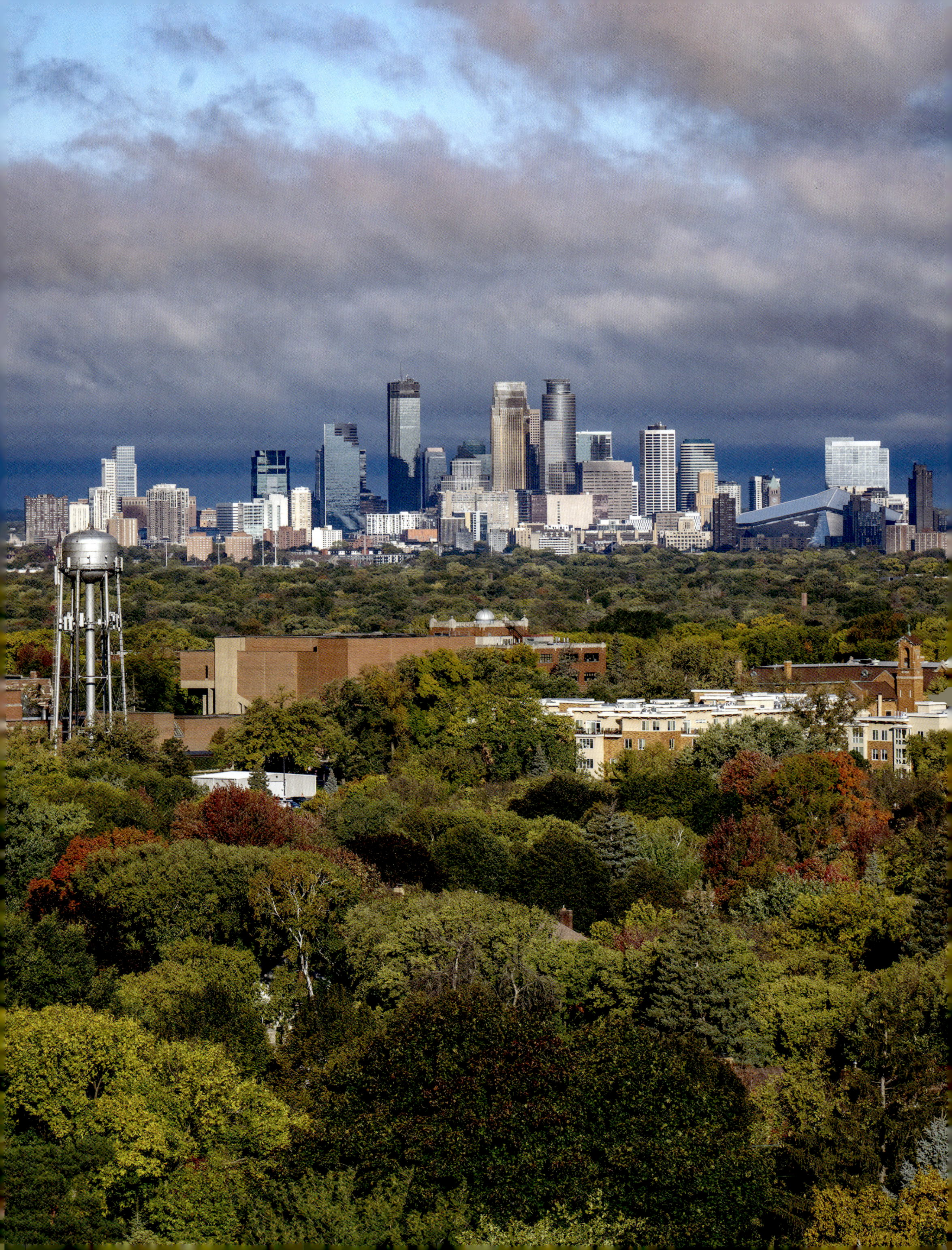

**"Every time I come back to the Twin Cities,
I feel like I'm coming back home."**
*– Rod Carew, former Major League
Baseball player*

Above & Across Twin Cities is a curated collection
of 140 aerial photographs of Minneapolis
and St. Paul from nine talented Minnesota-
based photographers.

Two distinct cities situated on opposite banks
of the Mississippi River, Minneapolis and St. Paul
have earned the nickname the "Twin Cities"
not only as a result of their geographical proximity,
but also their shared history and cultural and
economic interconnectedness. The images
in *Above & Across Twin Cities* represent
a contemporary view of the region.

Photographed in all weather conditions and times
of day, from the sunny days on Lake Harriet to
the snow-covered streets of downtown St. Paul,
each image captures a snapshot of the region.
The photographs in this collection, taken from
helicopters and observation decks, atop buildings
and hills, and with the use of drones, capture
the essence of the Twin Cities as seen by both
locals and visitors alike.

Let *Above & Across Twin Cities* transport you
to Minneapolis-St. Paul and experience the
breathtaking beauty of the region—from above
& across.

Michelle Fitzgerald & Kendra Huspaska
Editors

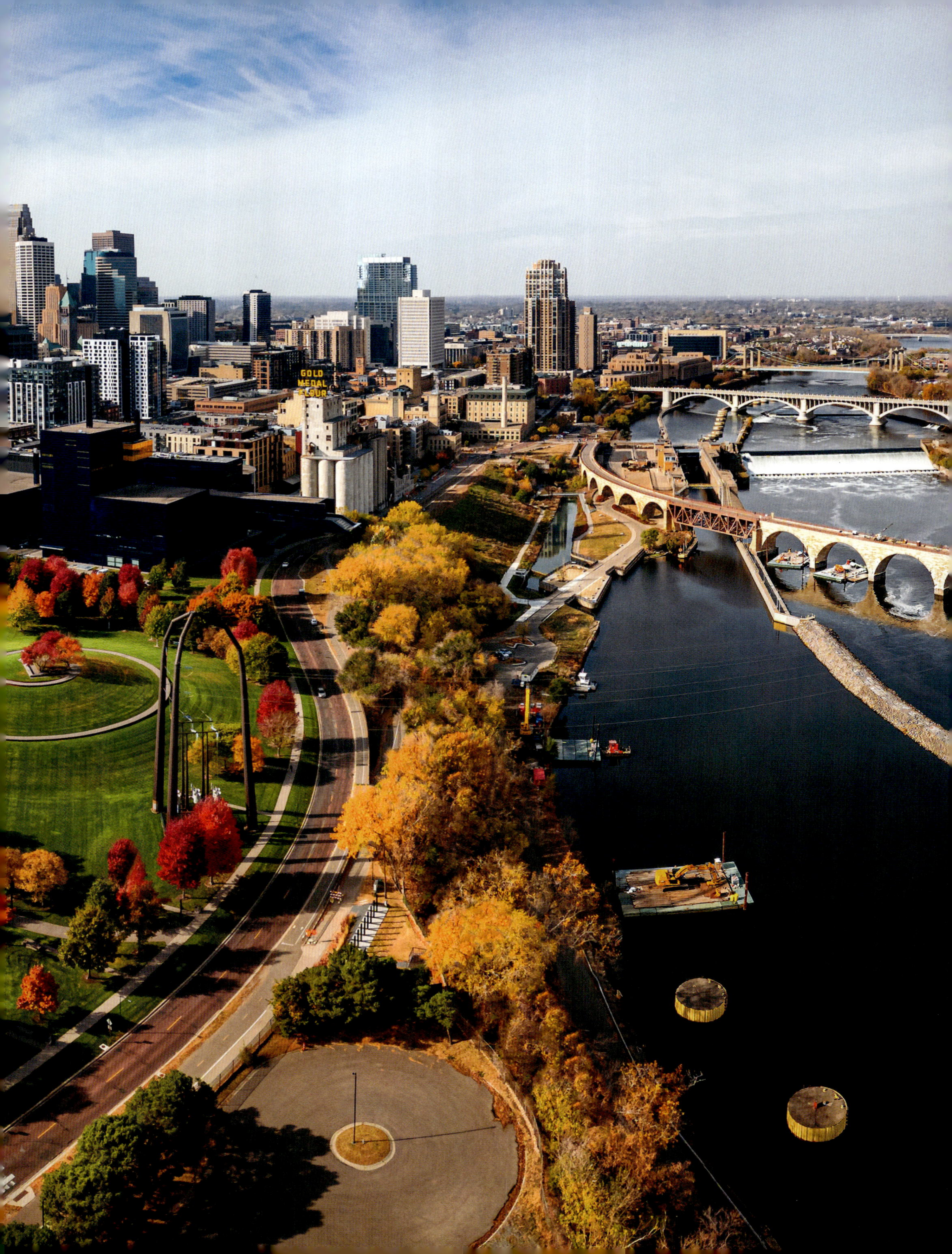

The reaction I kept having when I first paged through this book was, *look at all the places I love.*

Minnesota and the Twin Cities have been home my entire life, and *Above & Across Twin Cities* aims to showcase what I've always known: It's a special place. When people from other cities are asked where they're from, they'll answer "Chicago" or "London" or "San Francisco." But folks from Minneapolis, St. Paul, and the suburbs usually answer "Minnesota." Minnesota is an ethos, and the Twin Cities are its hub.

That hub is borne from the fact that the country's two longest rivers meet here. St. Paul is St. Paul because it was as far north as you could get on the Mississippi with goods to sell before the river became too treacherous for boats of yore. Minneapolis is Minneapolis because it's where the only waterfall on the Mississippi stands, and the power of those falls created important industries in timber and flour. But that history doesn't stop there.

What we know as the Twin Cities has been a hub for millennia. The confluence of these massive rivers is known as Bdote to the Dakota people who have lived here since time immemorial. The Dakota believe Bdote is a literal creation place for its people. And artifacts from centuries ago found here are now known to have been made by Indigenous people from as far away as present-day Florida. The idea of these rivers as highways for commerce and kinship long predates the United States. Even the word "Minnesota" is taken from the Dakota phrase Mni Sóta Makoce, which means "the land where the water reflects the skies."

As many cities, including the Twin Cities, have learned over the past century, a city suffers when it turns its back on those rivers. Fortunately, we're in an era of reconnecting with our waterways through redevelopment and cultural reconnection. One of the most important restaurants in the country for Native American and Indigenous cuisine is located near those falls in Minneapolis that were used and overused for commerce in the 19th and 20th centuries, but which have been another sacred space for millennia for our neighbors who were here long before all of that.

Rivers are an important artery for any nation or continent. But it's hard to appreciate their magnificence and importance in our daily lives. It's only when we can go above it all, as this book does, to get a better sense of the enormity. It brings up the mantra that seeing things from above makes our problems look smaller. We have to be careful with that because the problems that exist are real and need real solutions. But taking a moment to understand that we are part of something bigger than ourselves is critical in addressing those matters.

For me, being home reminds me of trick-or-treating during the Halloween Blizzard of 1991 (a true "where were you" moment for Minnesotans); going to see Santa at Dayton's in downtown Minneapolis; trying not to take for granted the grandeur of the State Capitol, where I work; and smiling every year when I enter my favorite place on earth—the Minnesota State Fair.

There's another mantra that says it's hard to get people to move to Minnesota (think about those long winters) but once they do, it's hard to get them to leave. My people came from other places, too. My Anishinabe ancestors came from the north and east, seeking a land where food grows on water. That food is manoomin, or wild rice. My Irish ancestors boarded boats for an unknown land, including my great-grandmother Katie Cooper, who was a teenager when she sailed and was solely responsible for multiple younger siblings. This is a hearty place with hearty people.

And when I fly back to the Twin Cities and am about to land, I try to find my house. It doesn't always happen as the plane zips towards the runway, but I don't need to see my house to know I'm home. It's one thing to see the forest for the trees. It's another to feel home from above.

Peggy Flanagan
Lt. Governor of Minnesota

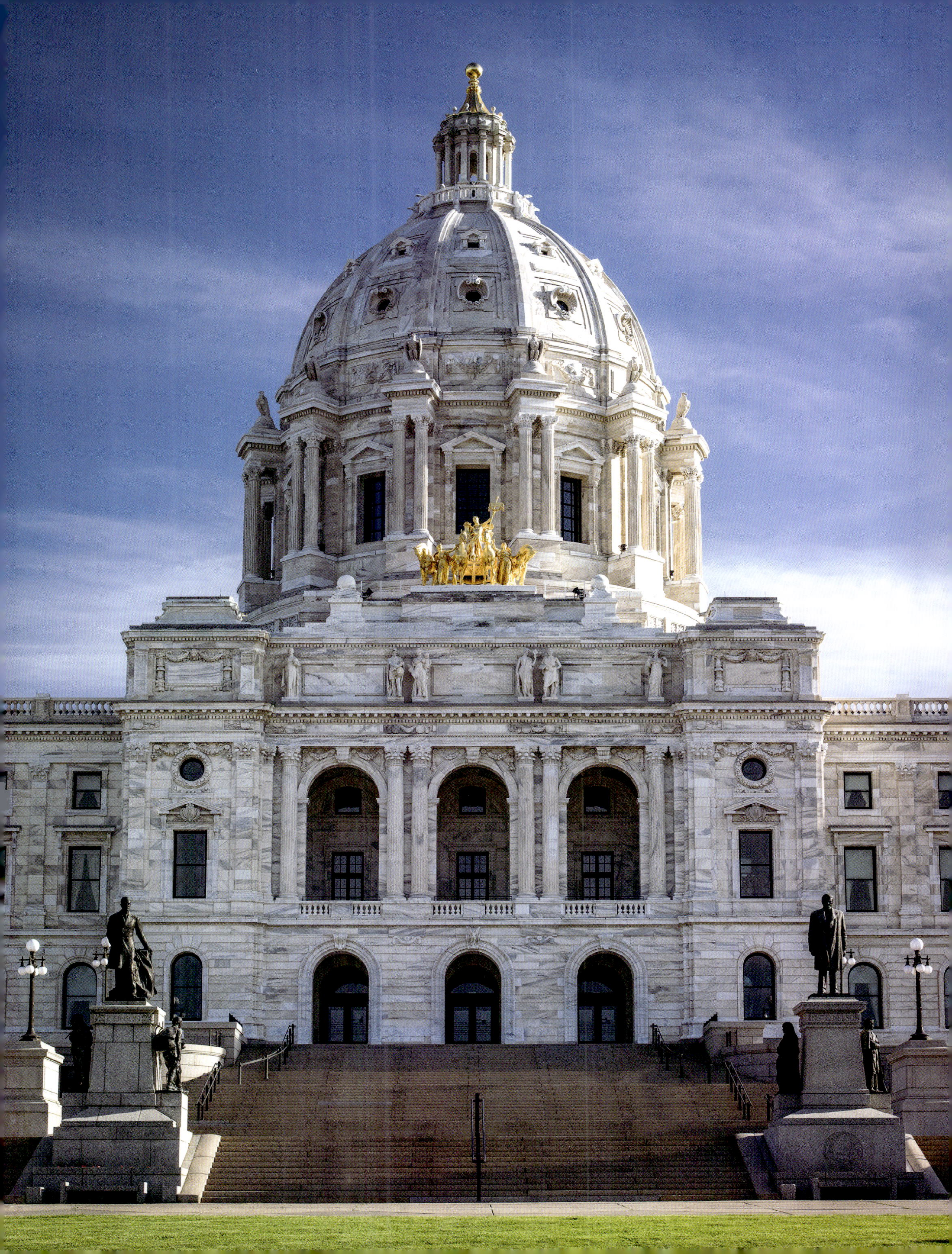

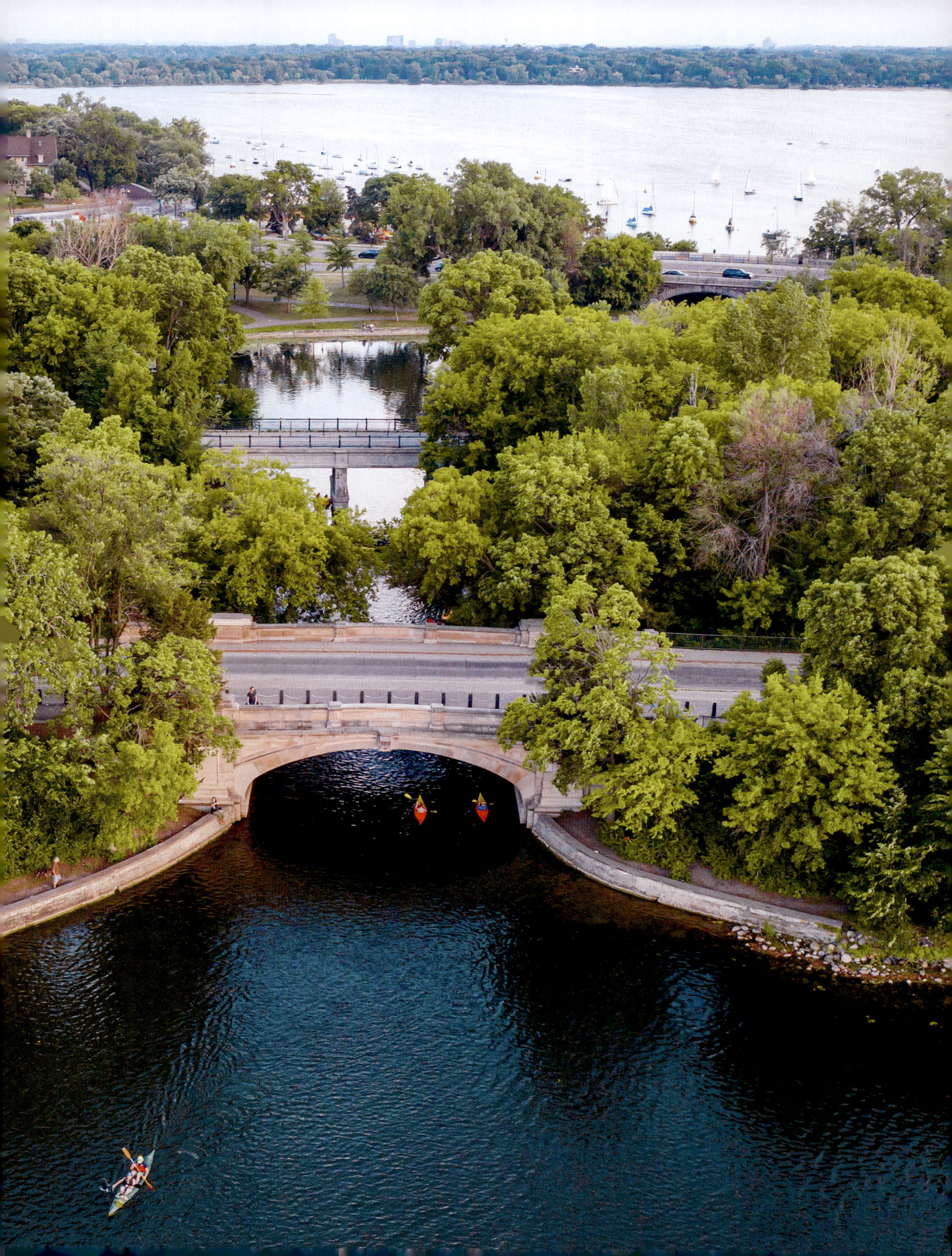

Lakes & Rivers ♦ The Twin Cities are often celebrated for their lakes and rivers, which shape both the geography and culture of the region. Minneapolis, famously known as the "City of Lakes," boasts a collection of more than a dozen major lakes within the city limits, with larger bodies like Lake Calhoun (Bde Maka Ska), Lake Harriet, and Lake of the Isles forming the core of its robust lake system. These lakes serve as hubs for recreation, community gatherings, and seasonal traditions. In summer, the lakes come alive as locals flock to the shores for swimming, kayaking, paddleboarding, and sailing, while well-maintained walking and biking paths encircle many of the lakes, providing scenic routes for walkers and joggers. ♦ The Mississippi River runs through both Minneapolis and St. Paul. In Minneapolis, it cuts through the city's center, historically powering mills and shaping the growth of the downtown area. Today, the river is a focal point for urban parks, trails, and cultural landmarks like the Stone Arch Bridge. St. Paul, lying further downstream, uses the river as a scenic backdrop for its historic riverfront and community events. Both cities celebrate the river's natural beauty while balancing environmental stewardship, with ongoing efforts to maintain water quality and restore native habitats along its banks. ♦ Beyond the Mississippi, smaller rivers and streams, such as the Minnesota and St. Croix Rivers, contribute to the Twin Cities' waterway network. These rivers provide opportunities for canoeing, fishing, and wildlife observation, connecting urban residents with Minnesota's rich natural heritage. Seasonal changes dramatically transform the lakes and rivers: summer's boating and swimming give way to frozen expanses in winter, when ice fishing, skating, and cross-country skiing become common.

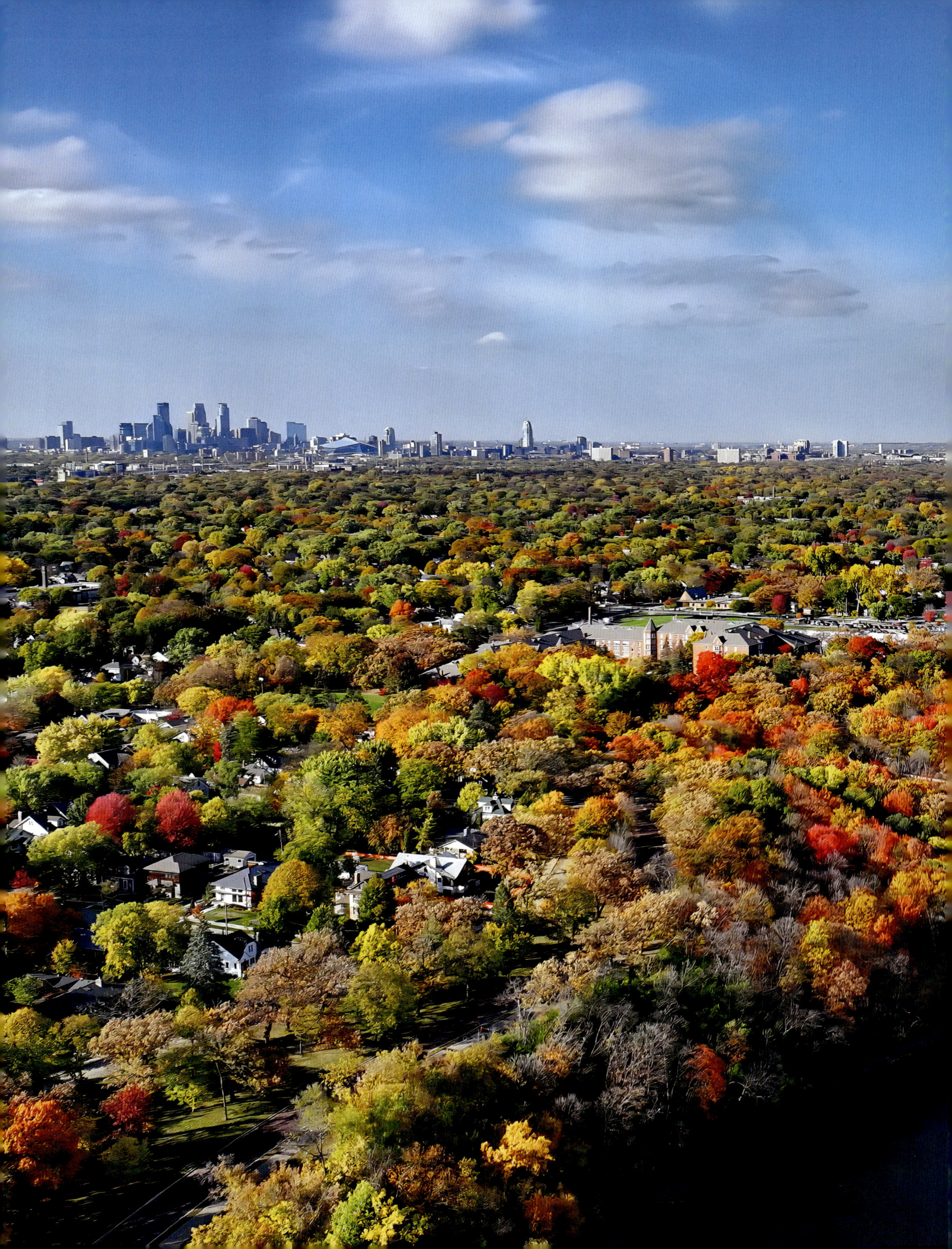

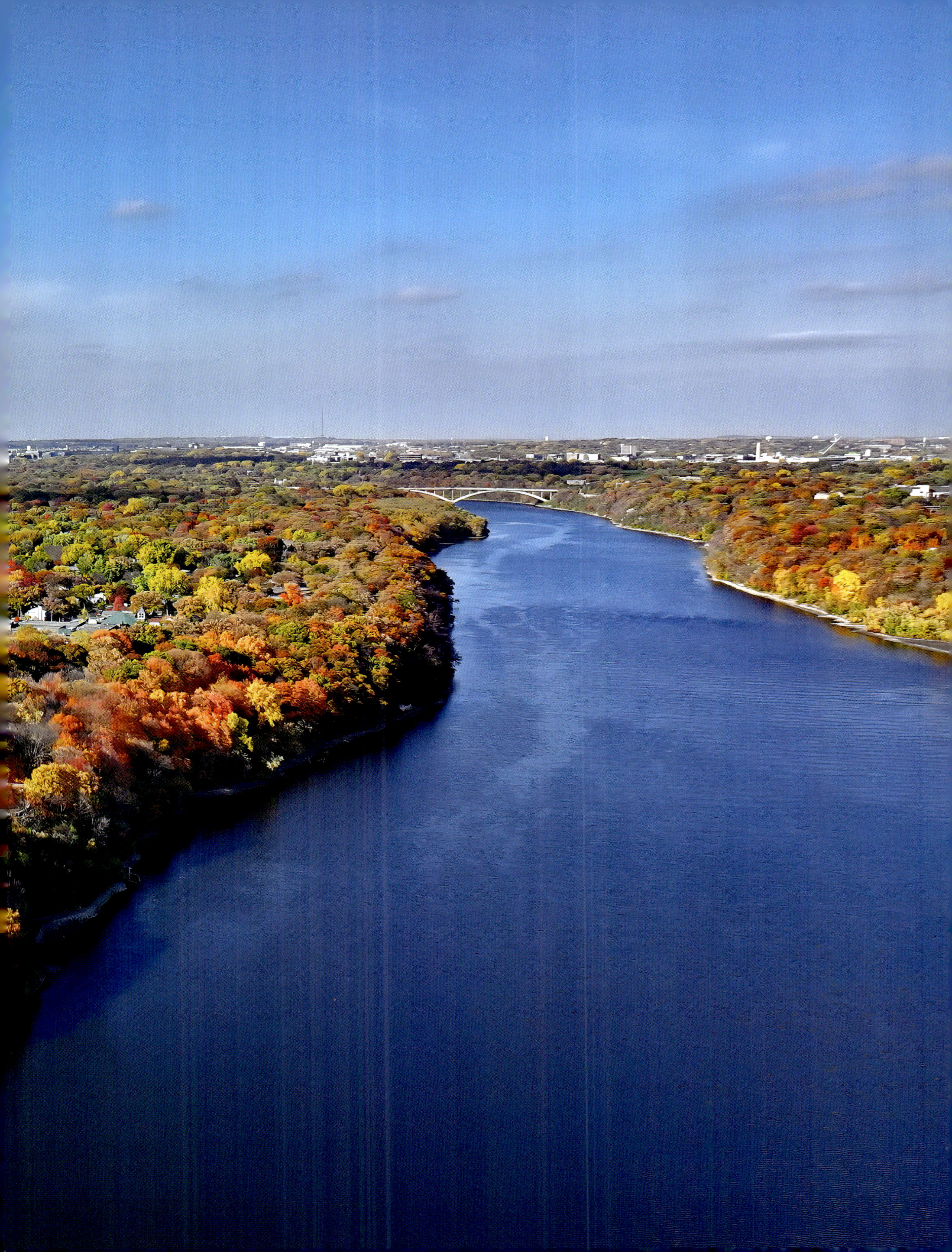

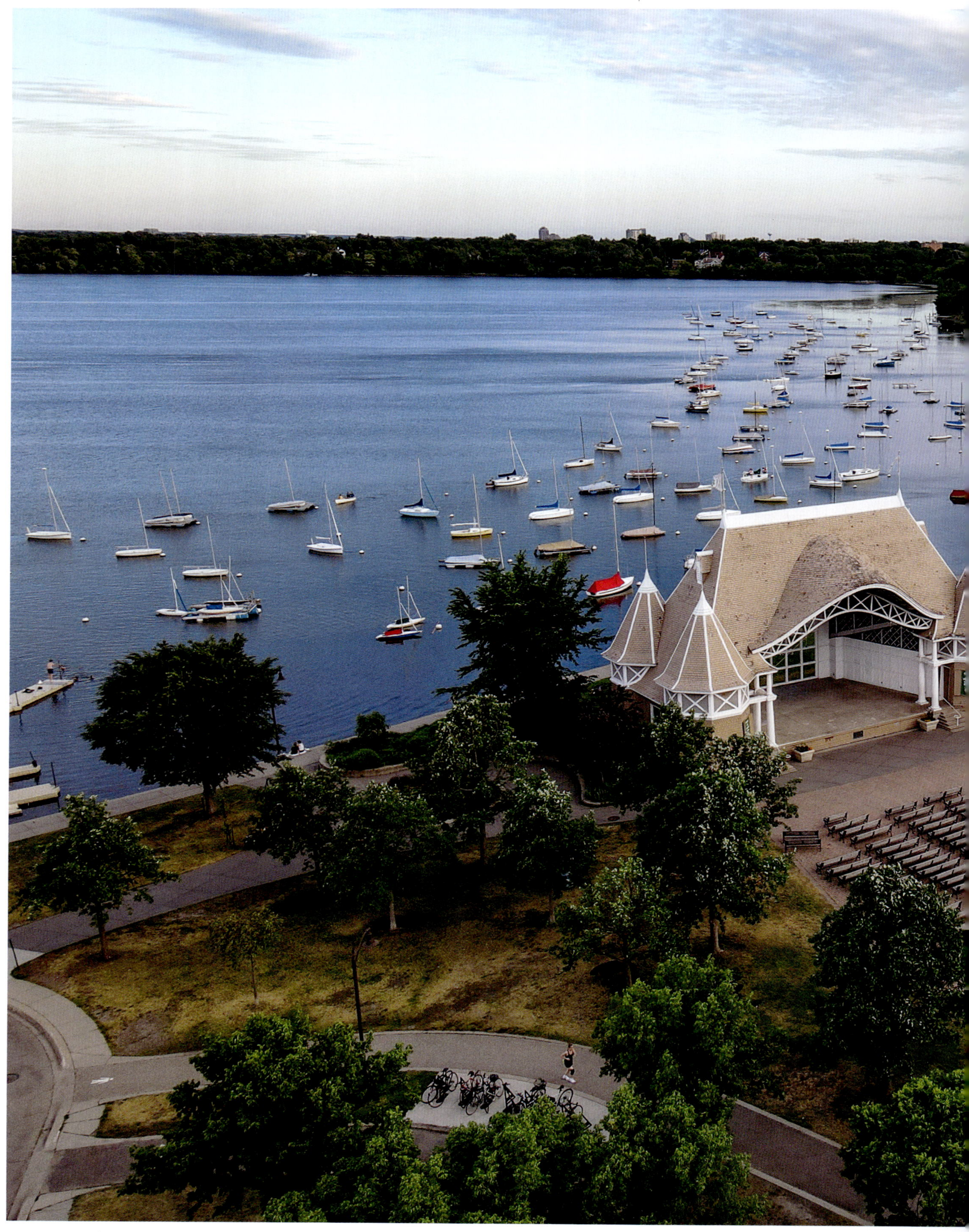

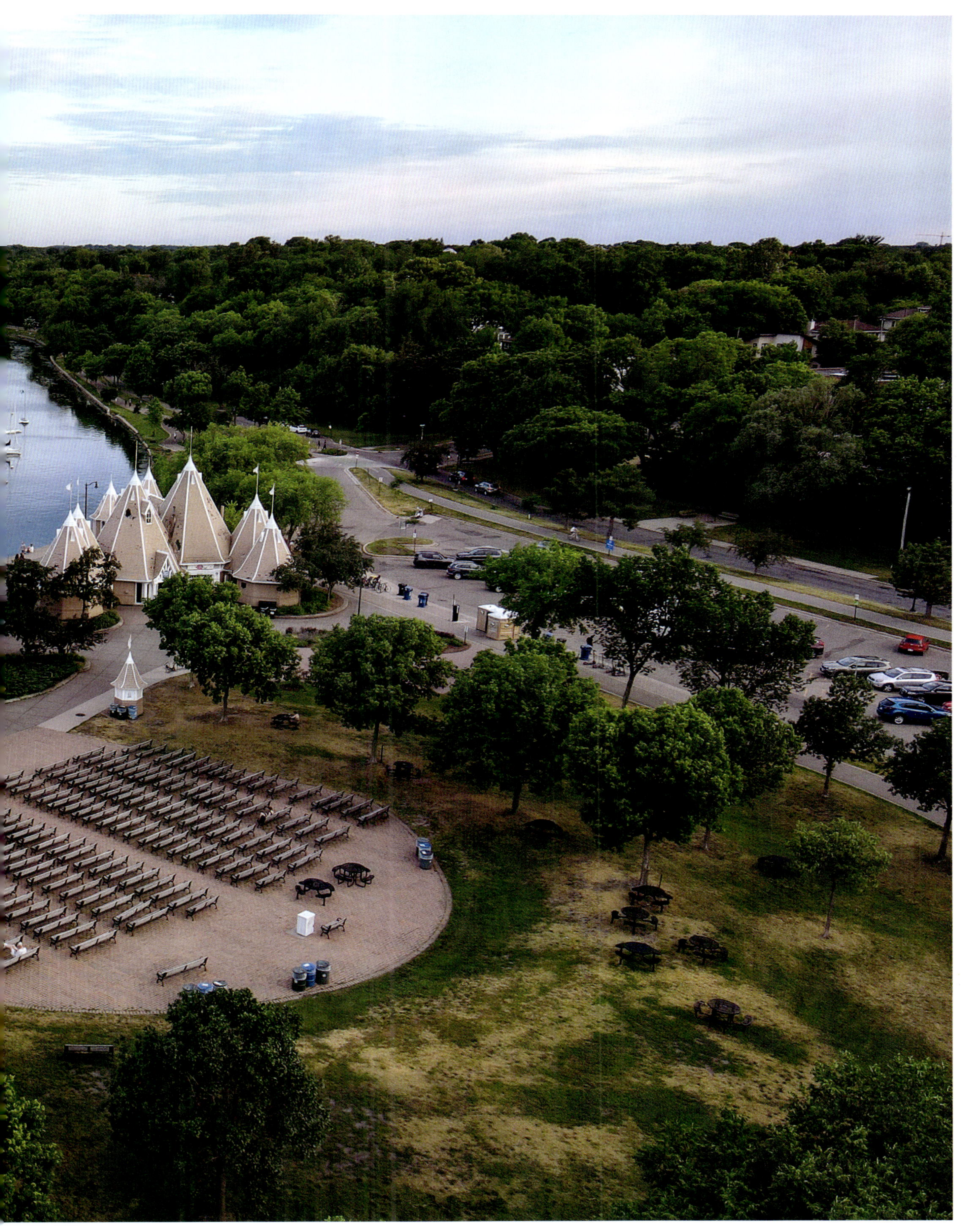

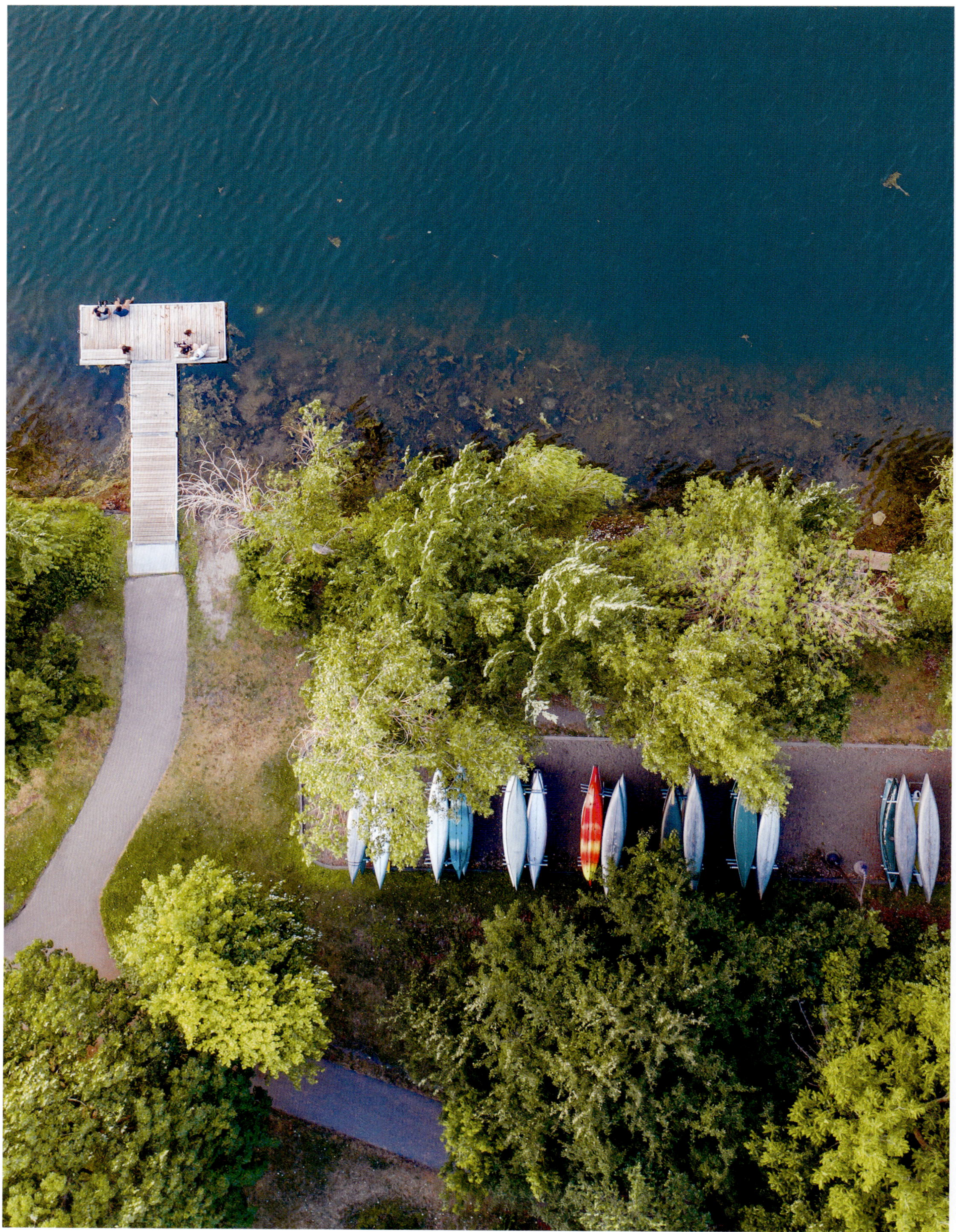

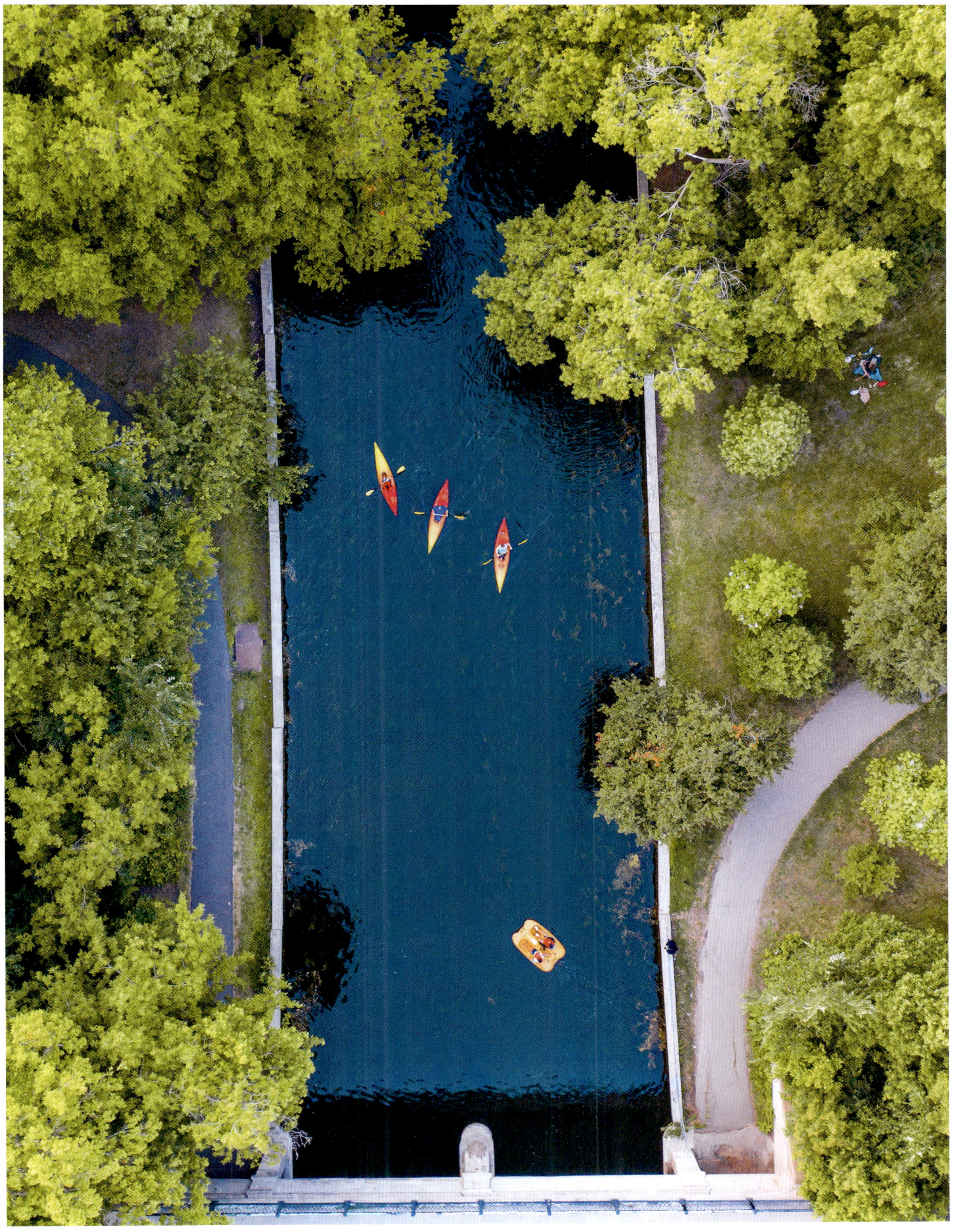

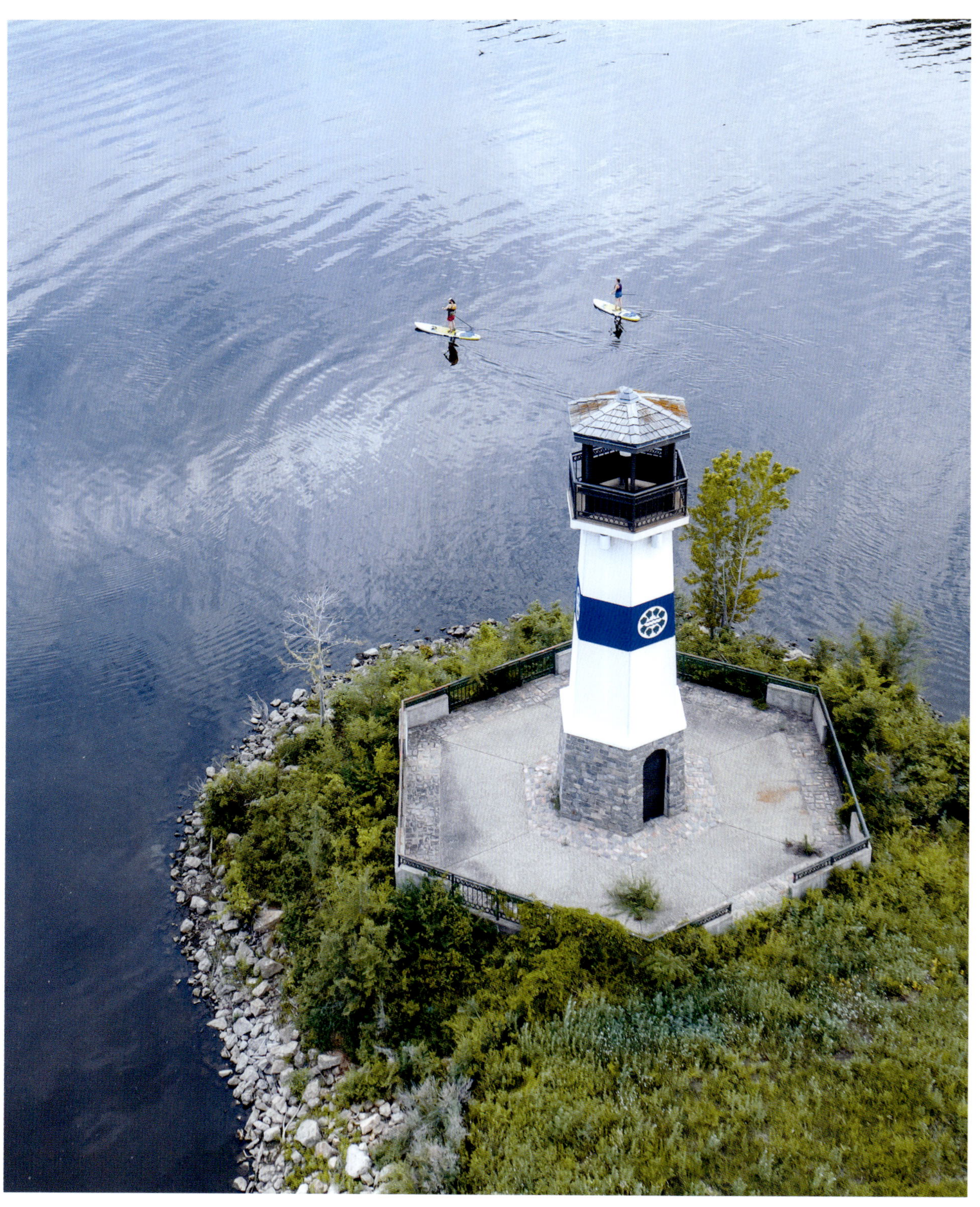

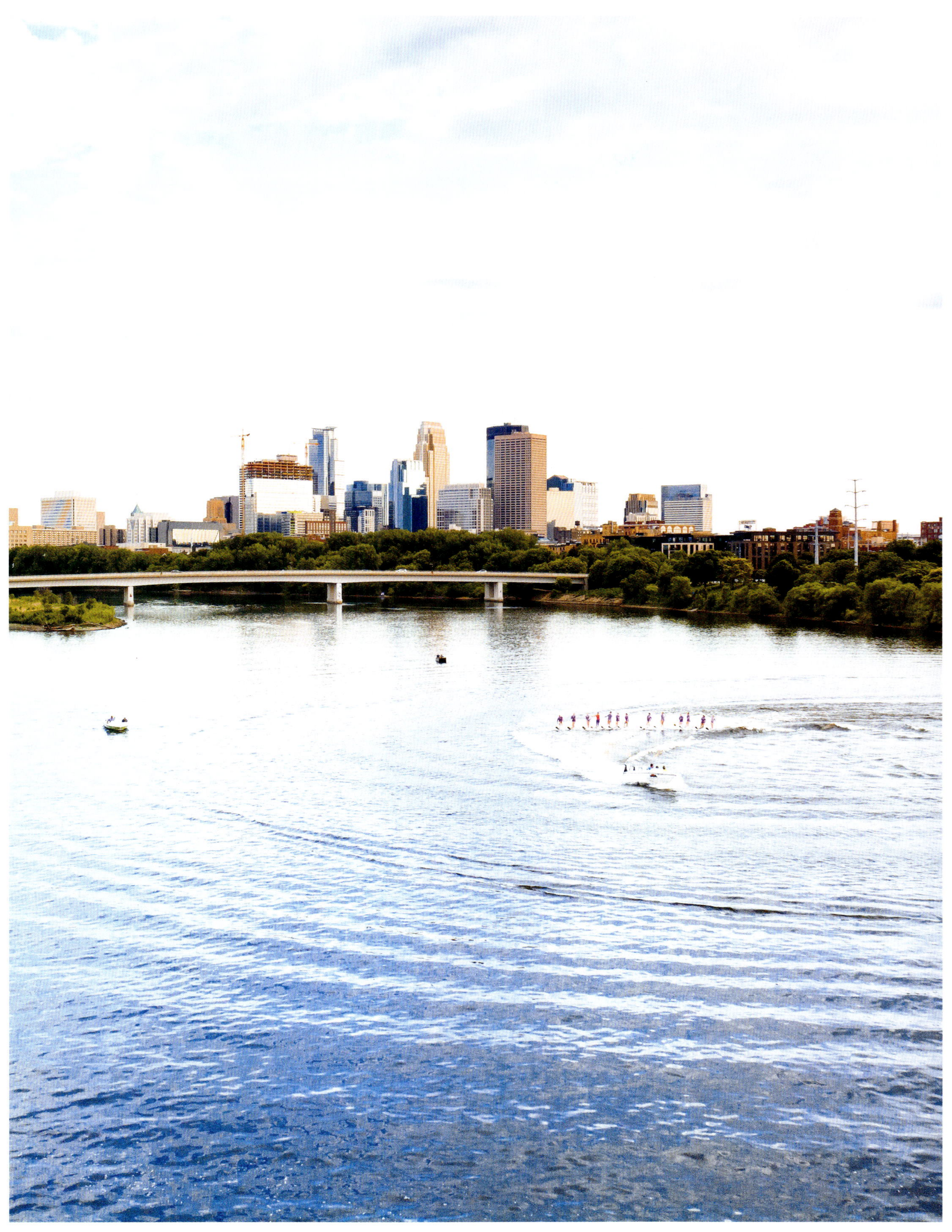

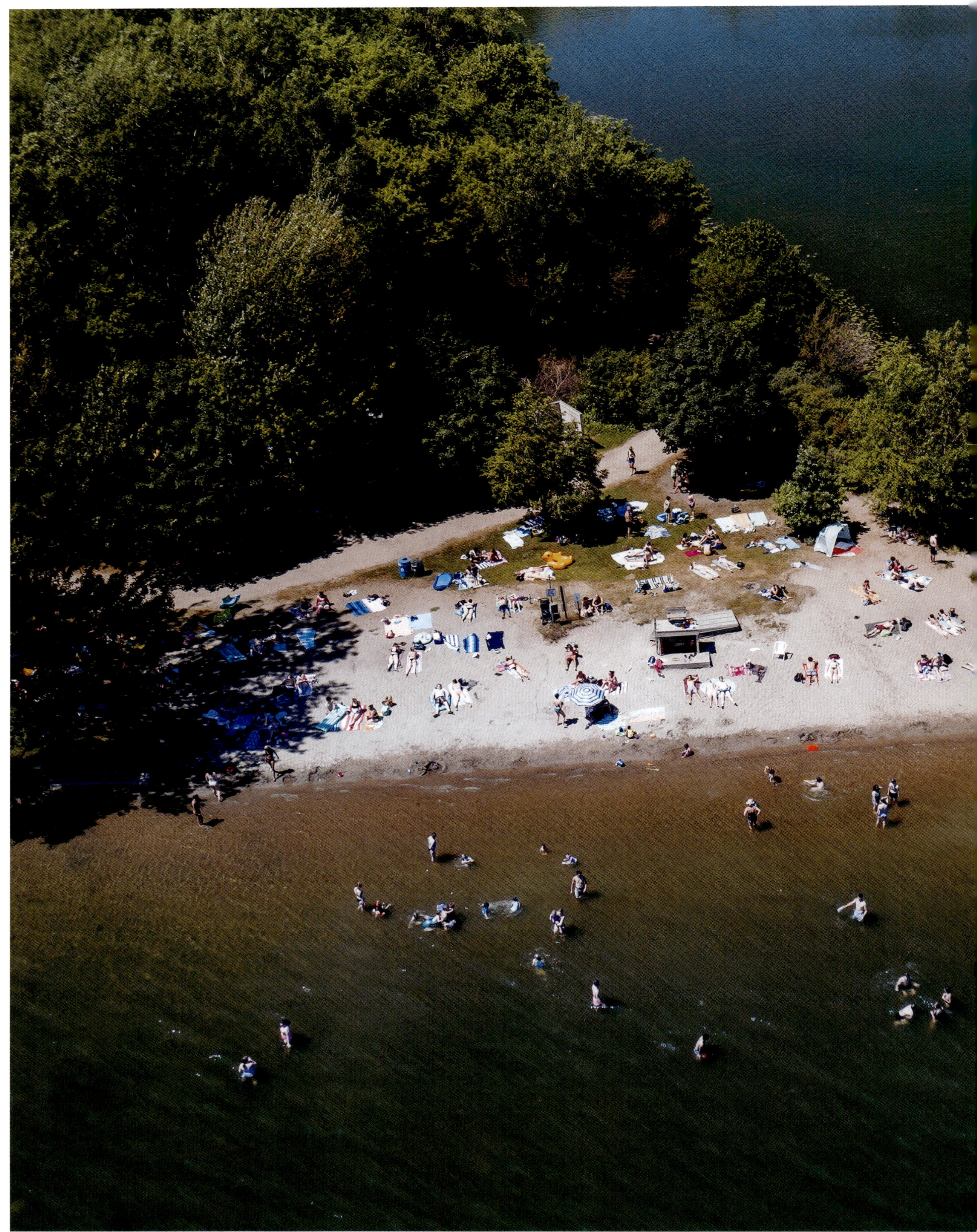

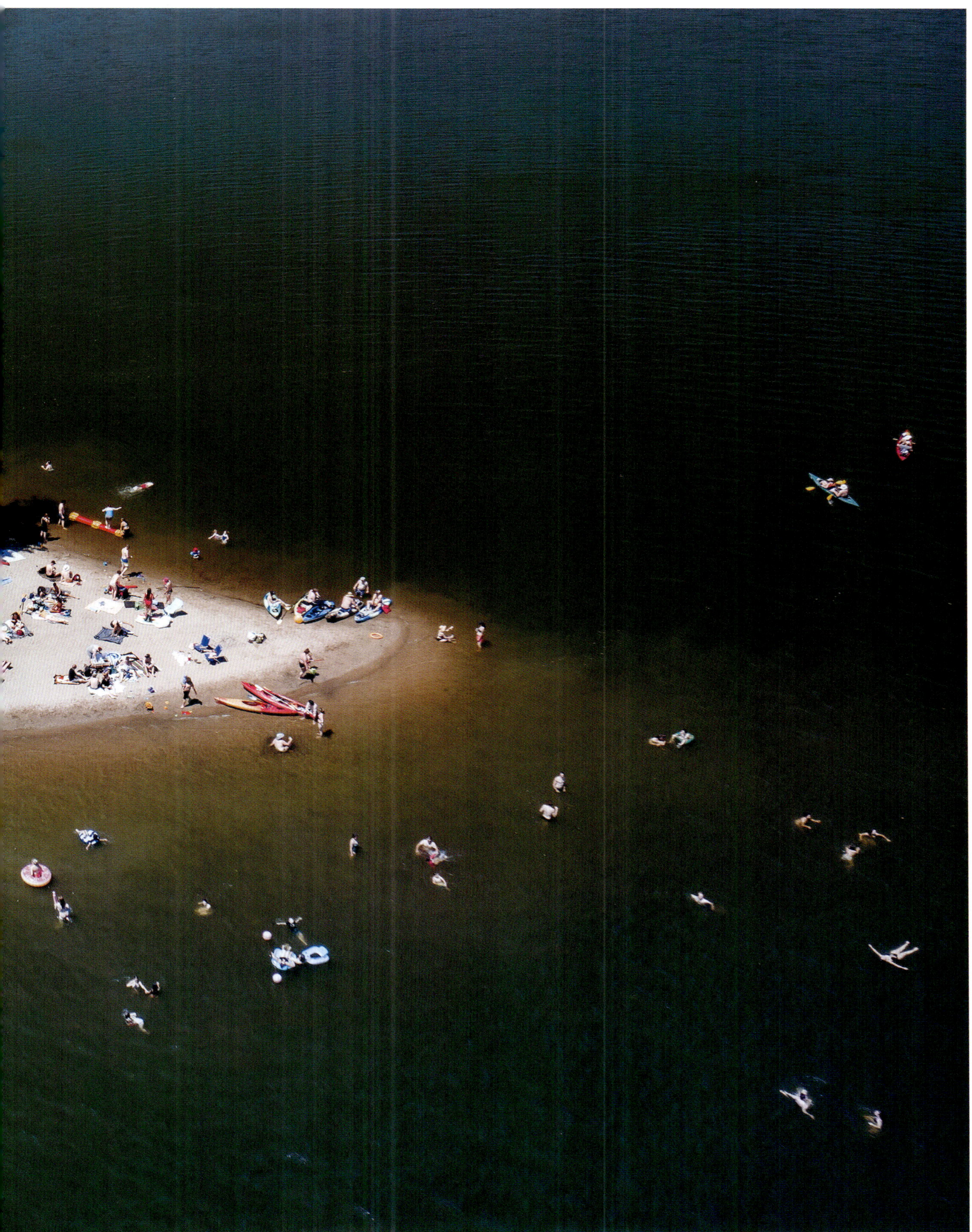

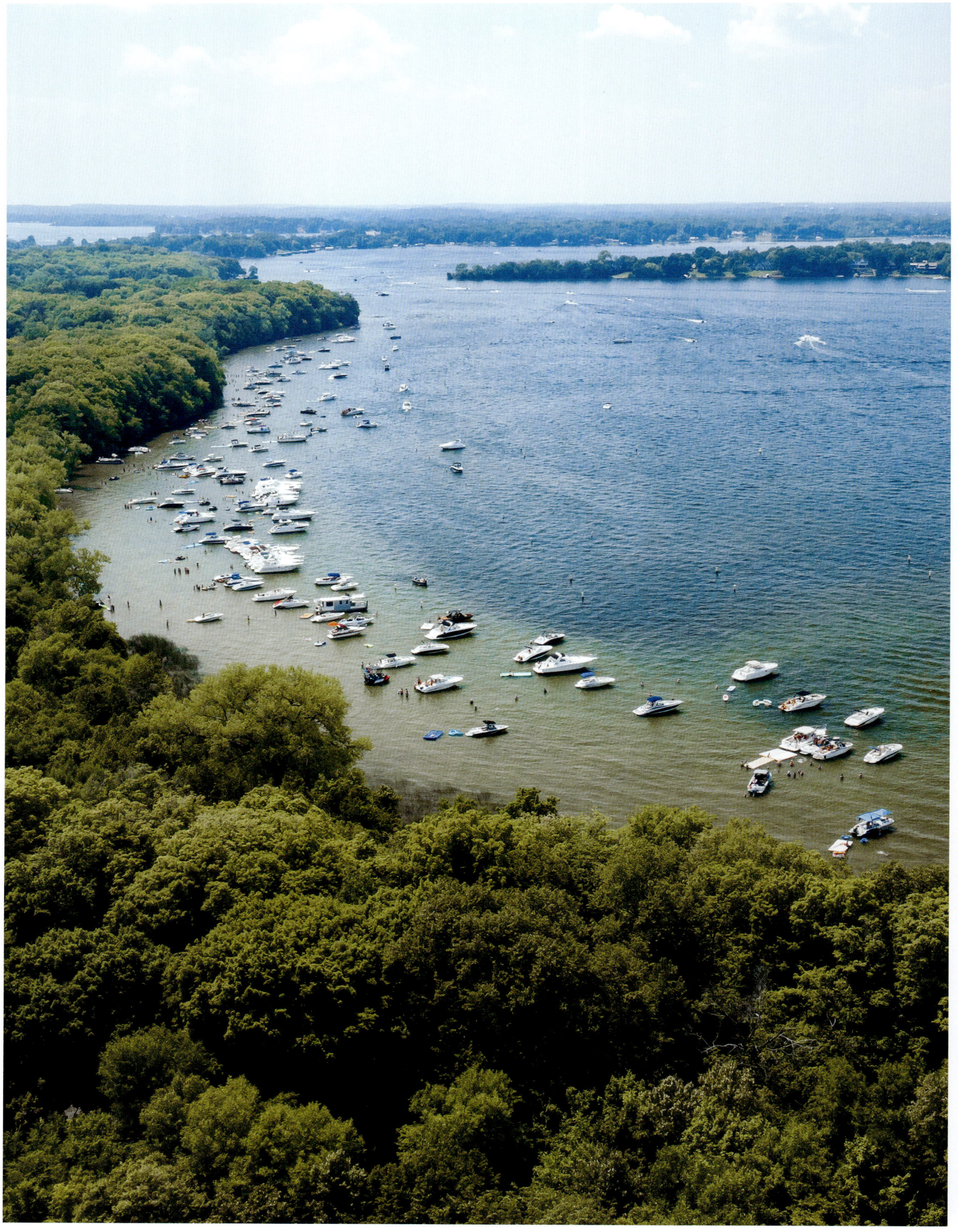

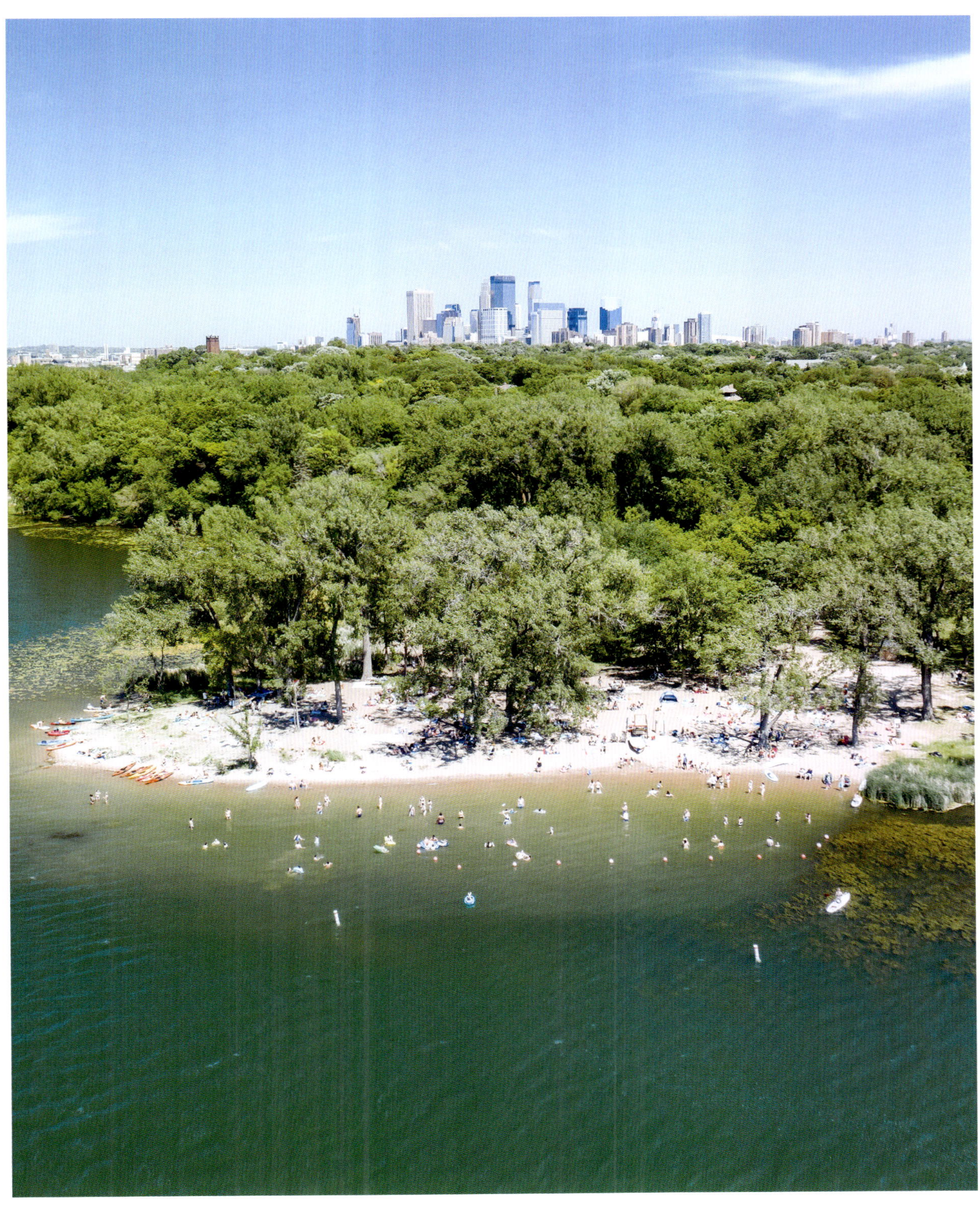

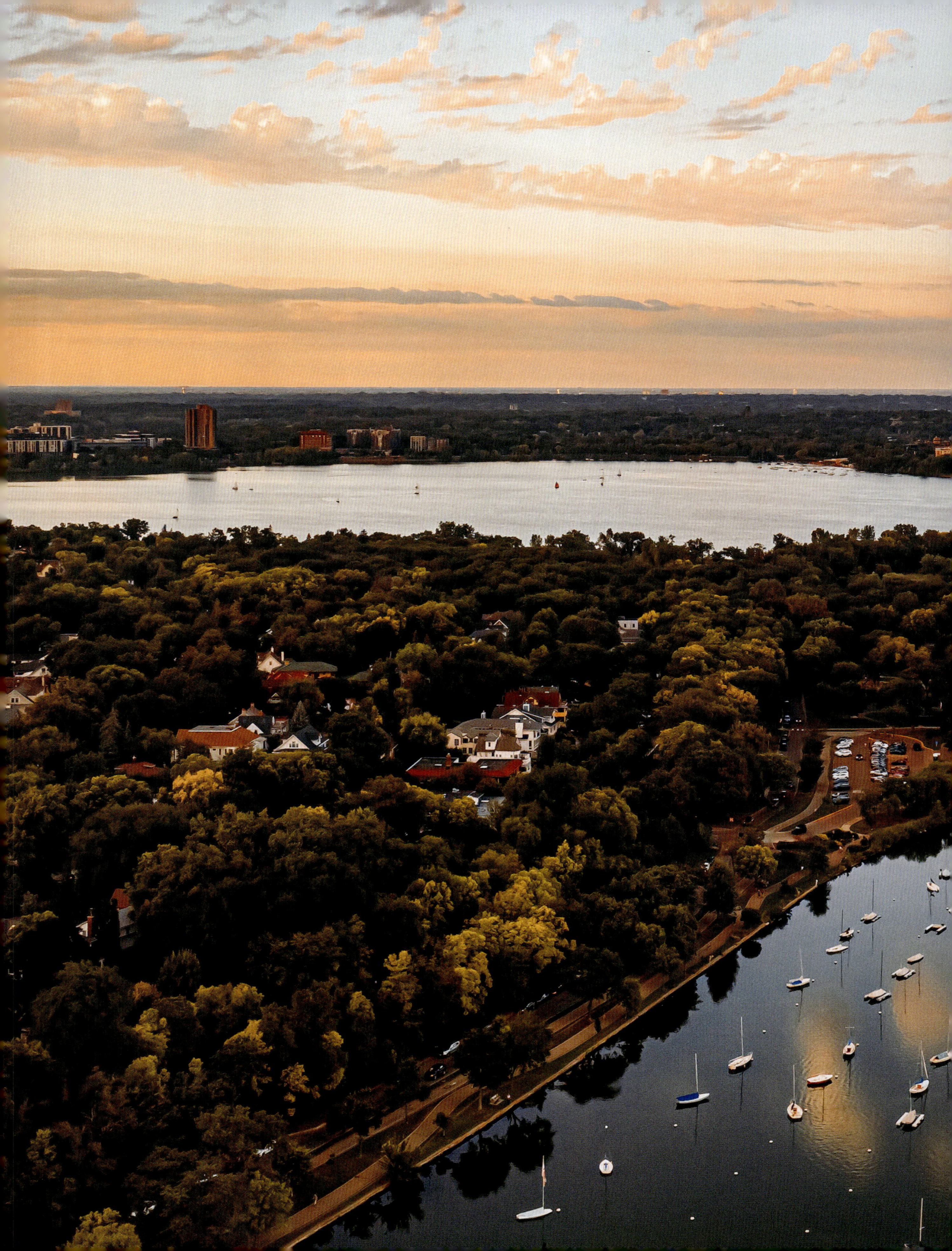

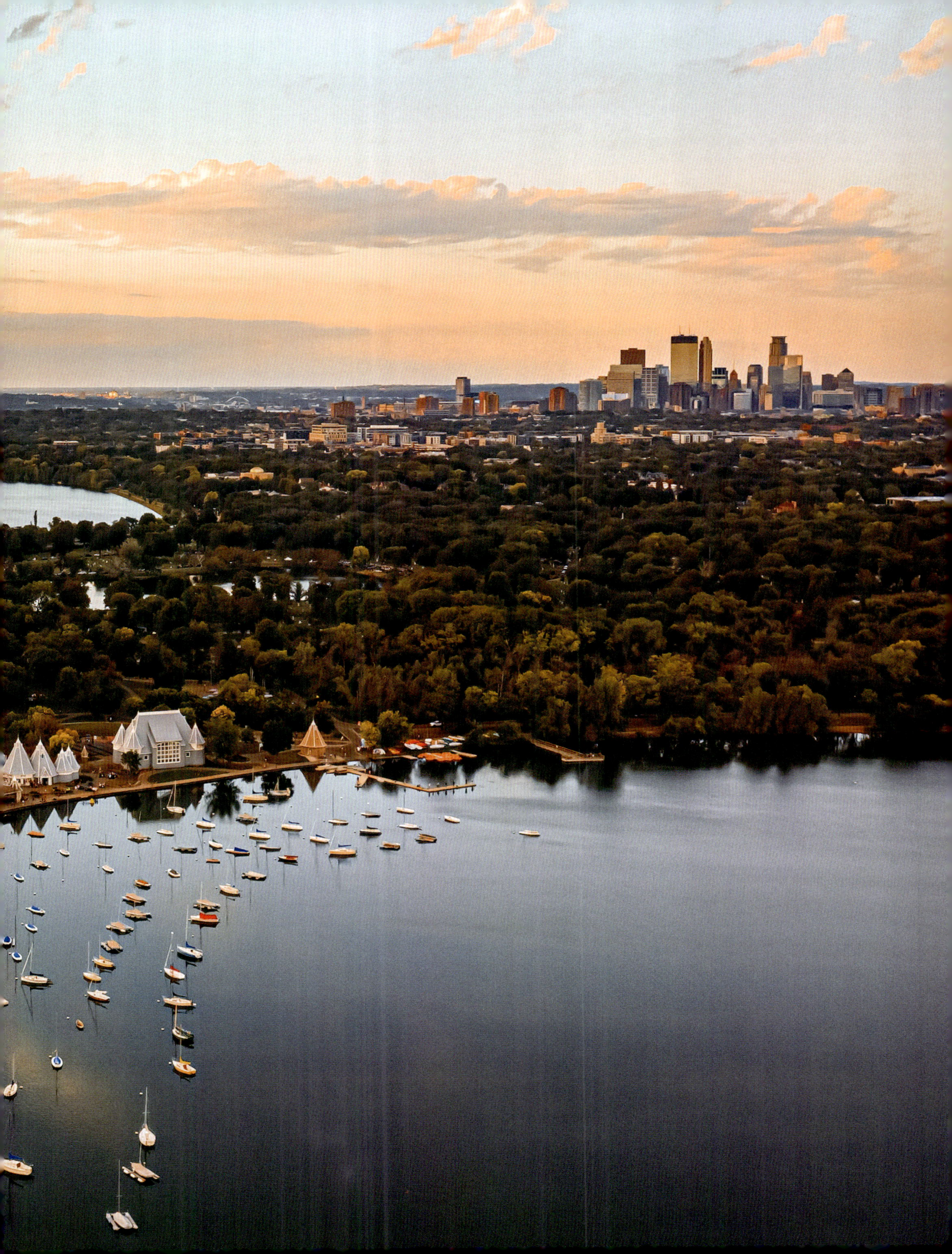

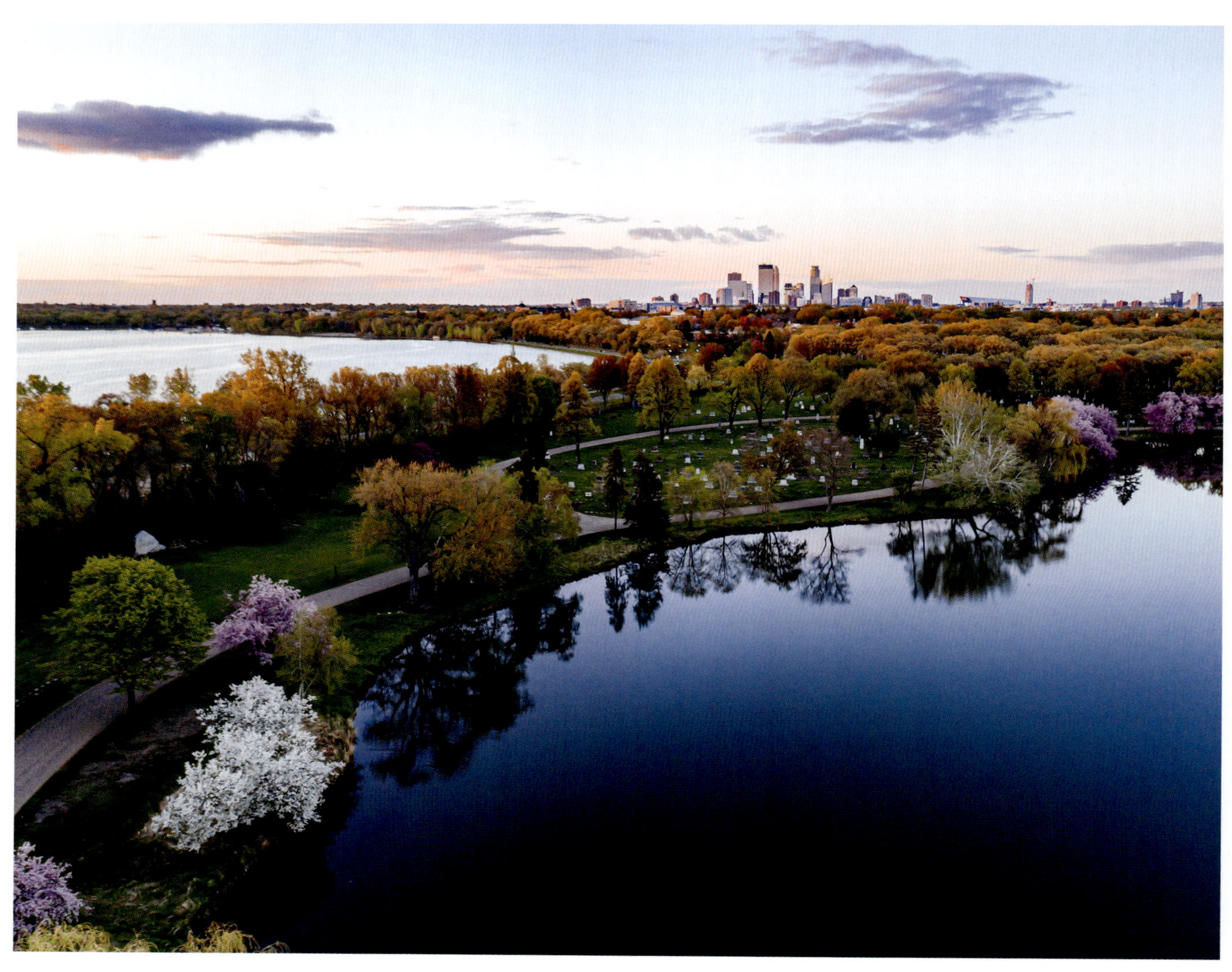

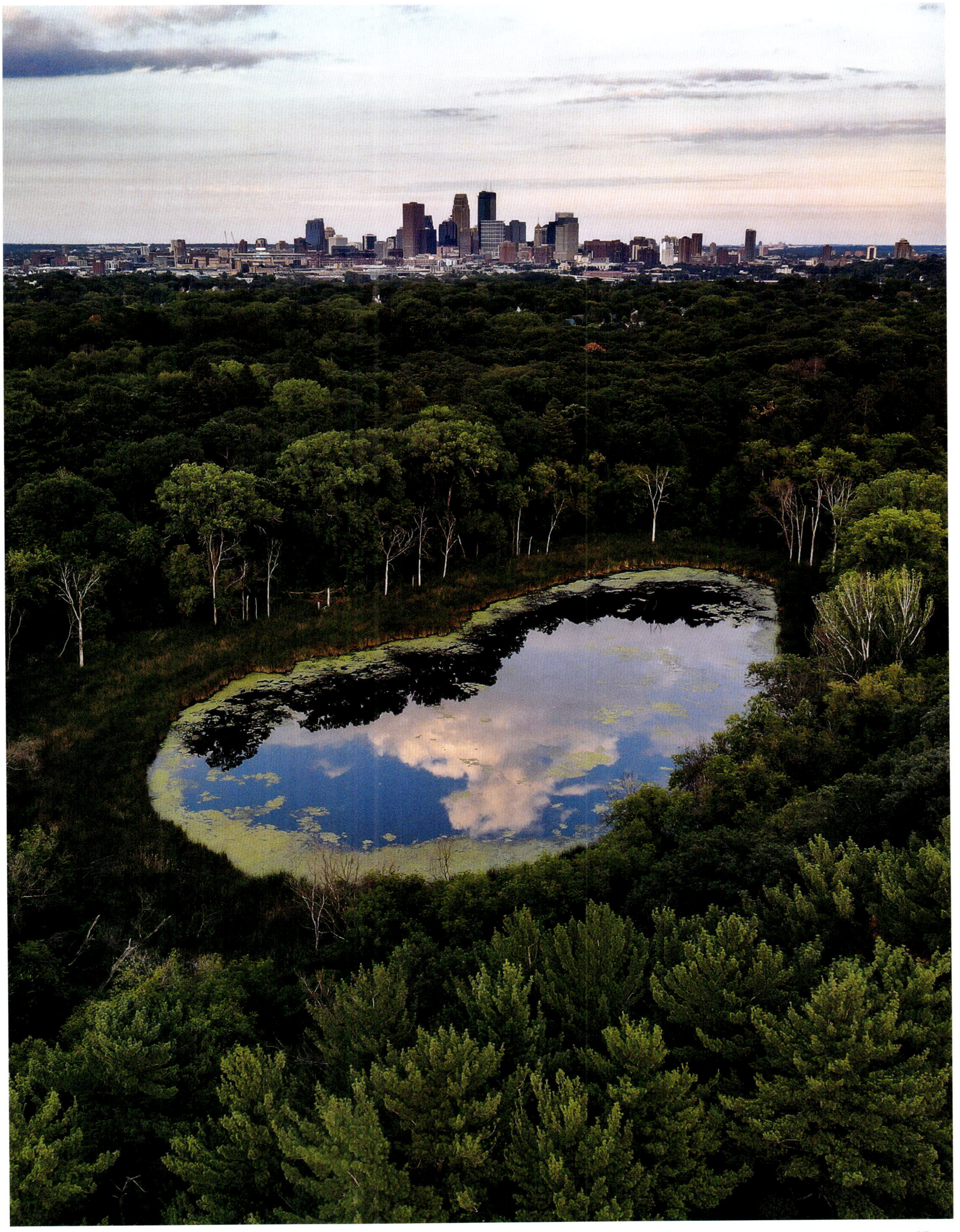

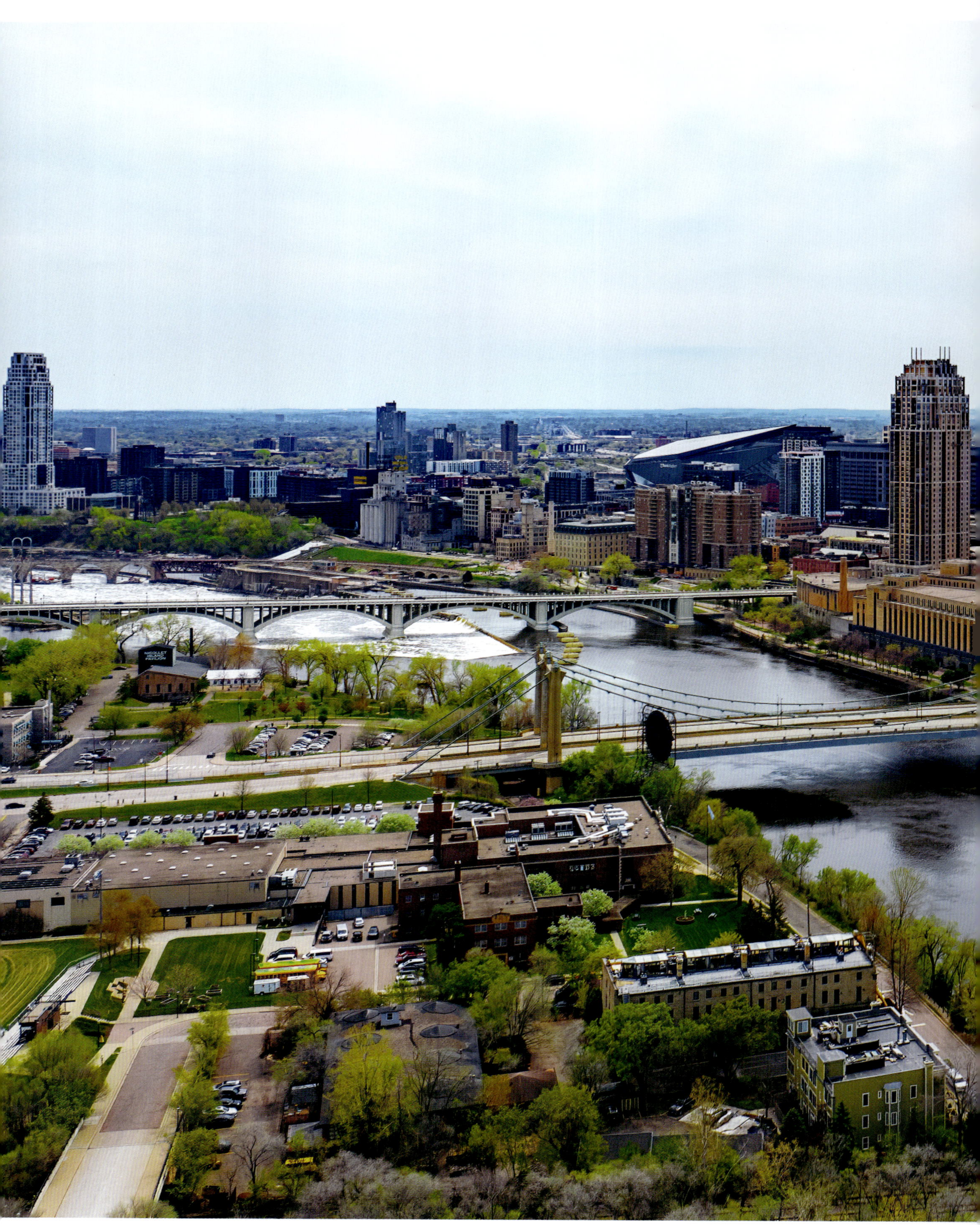

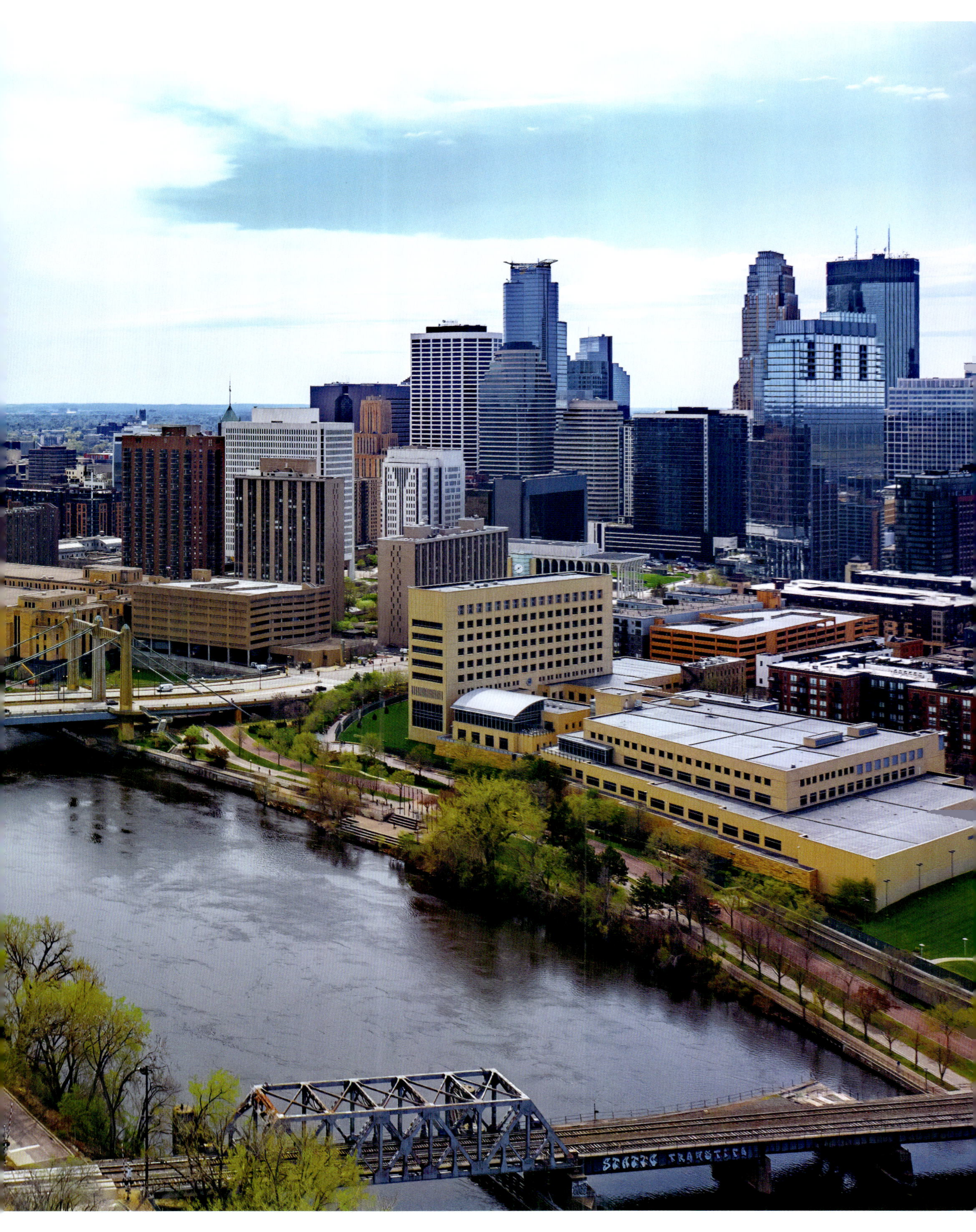

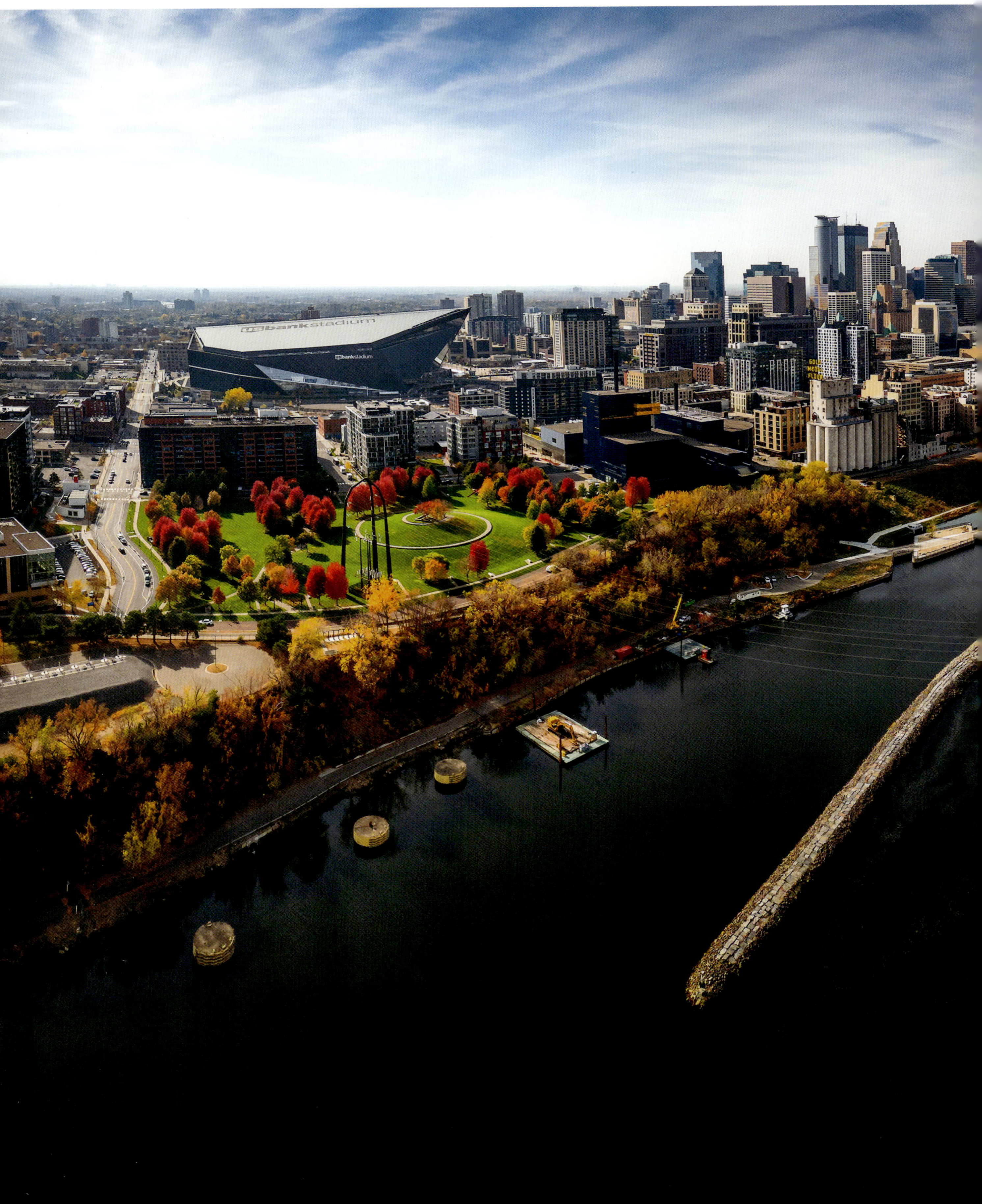

bankstadium
bankstadium

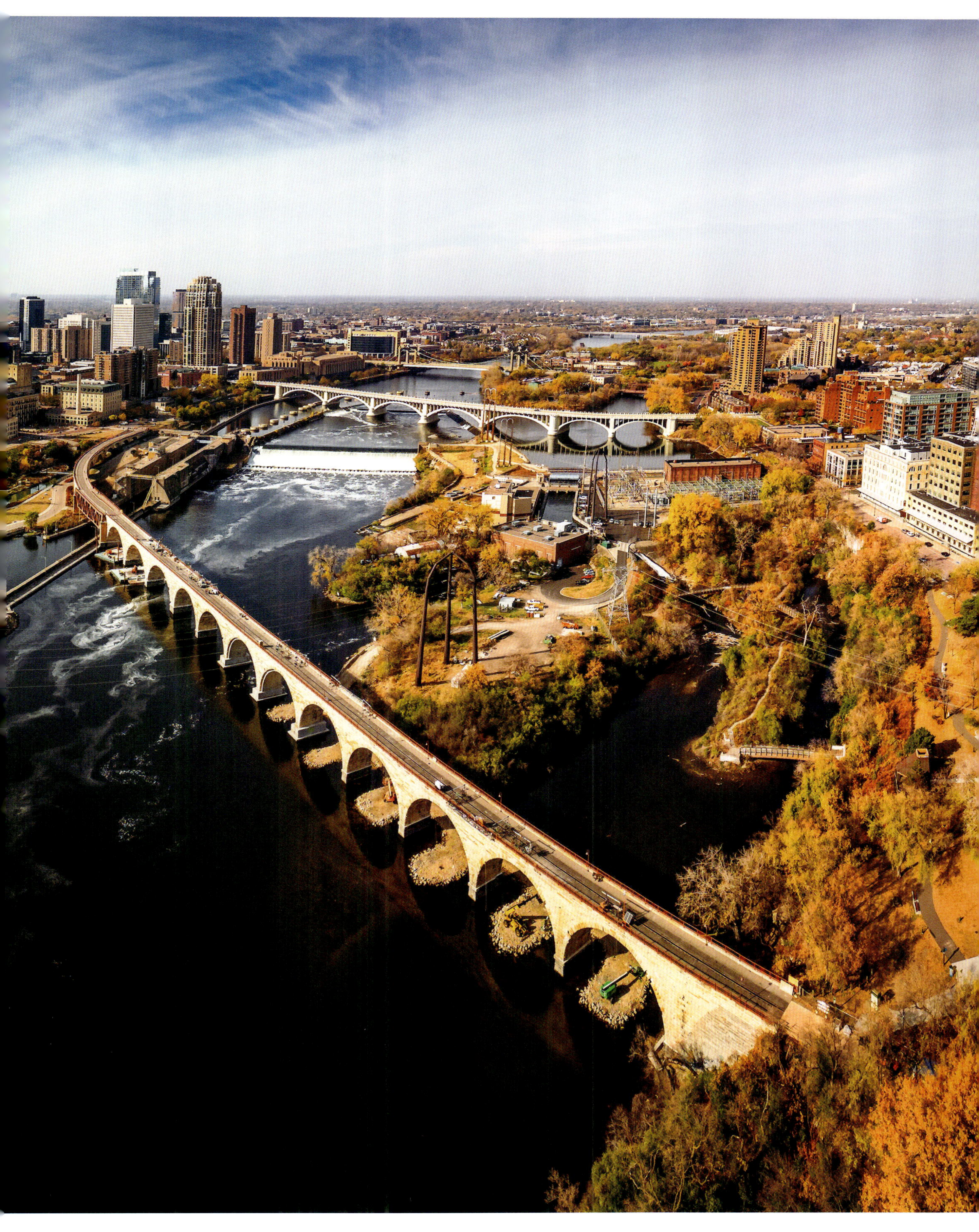

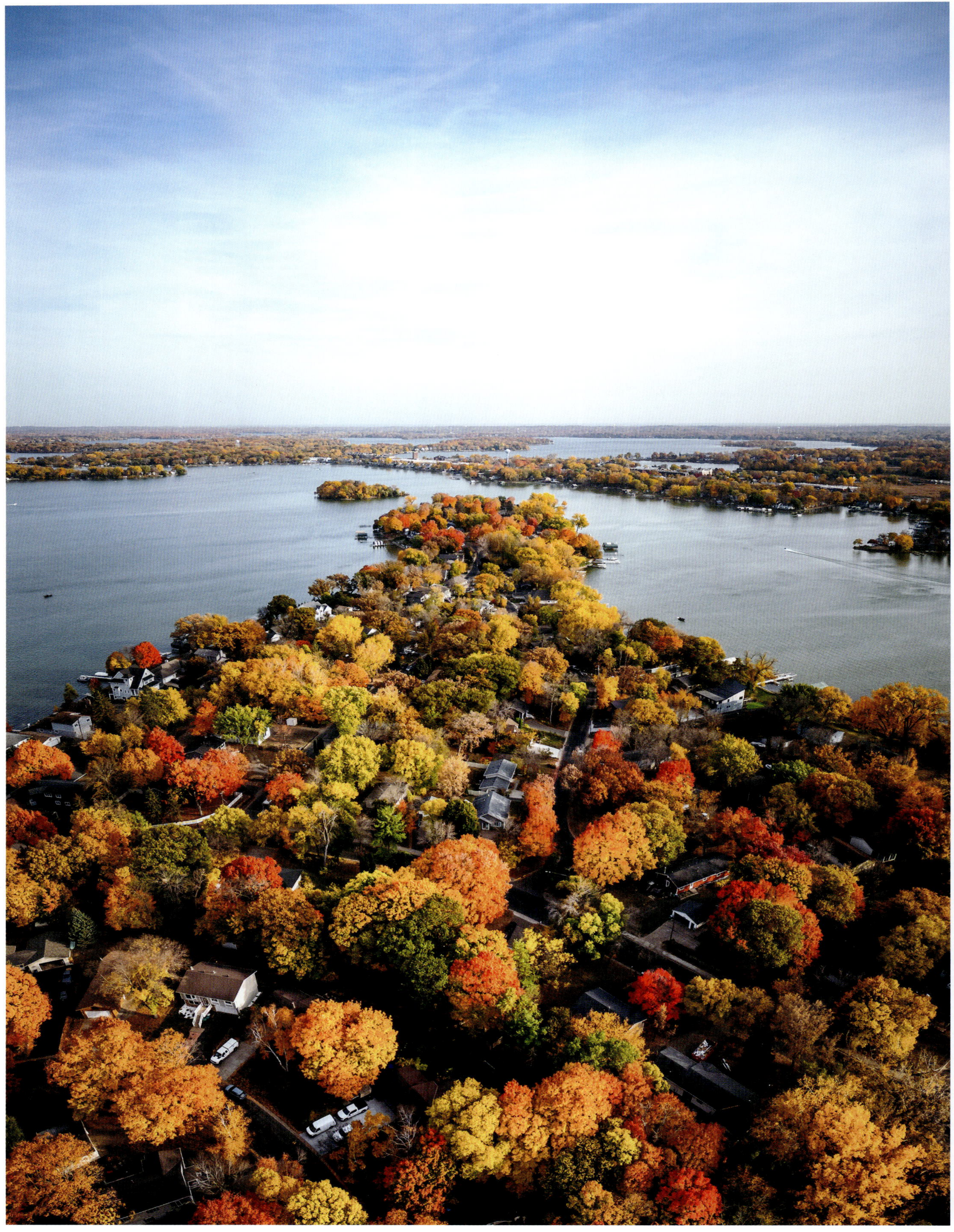

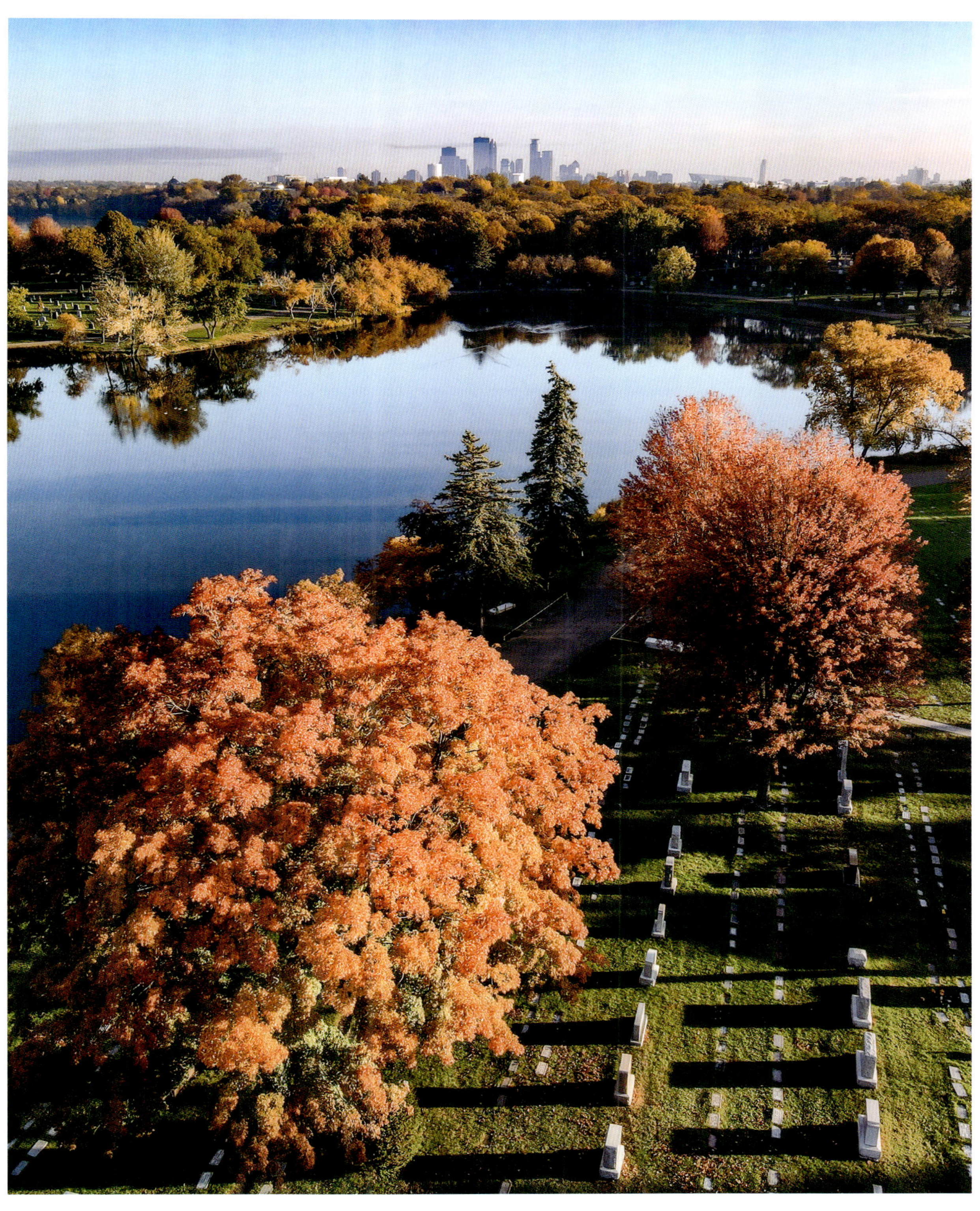

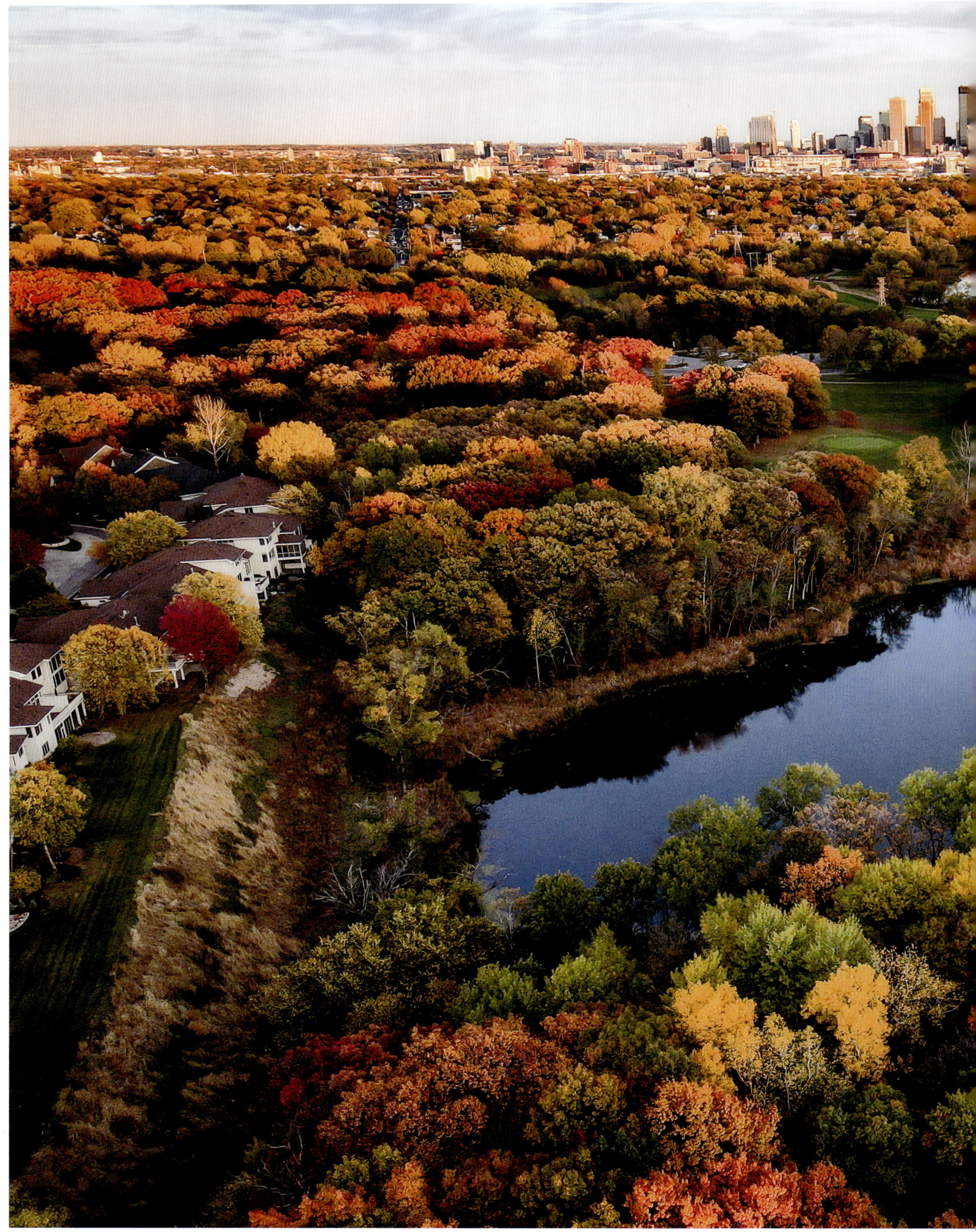

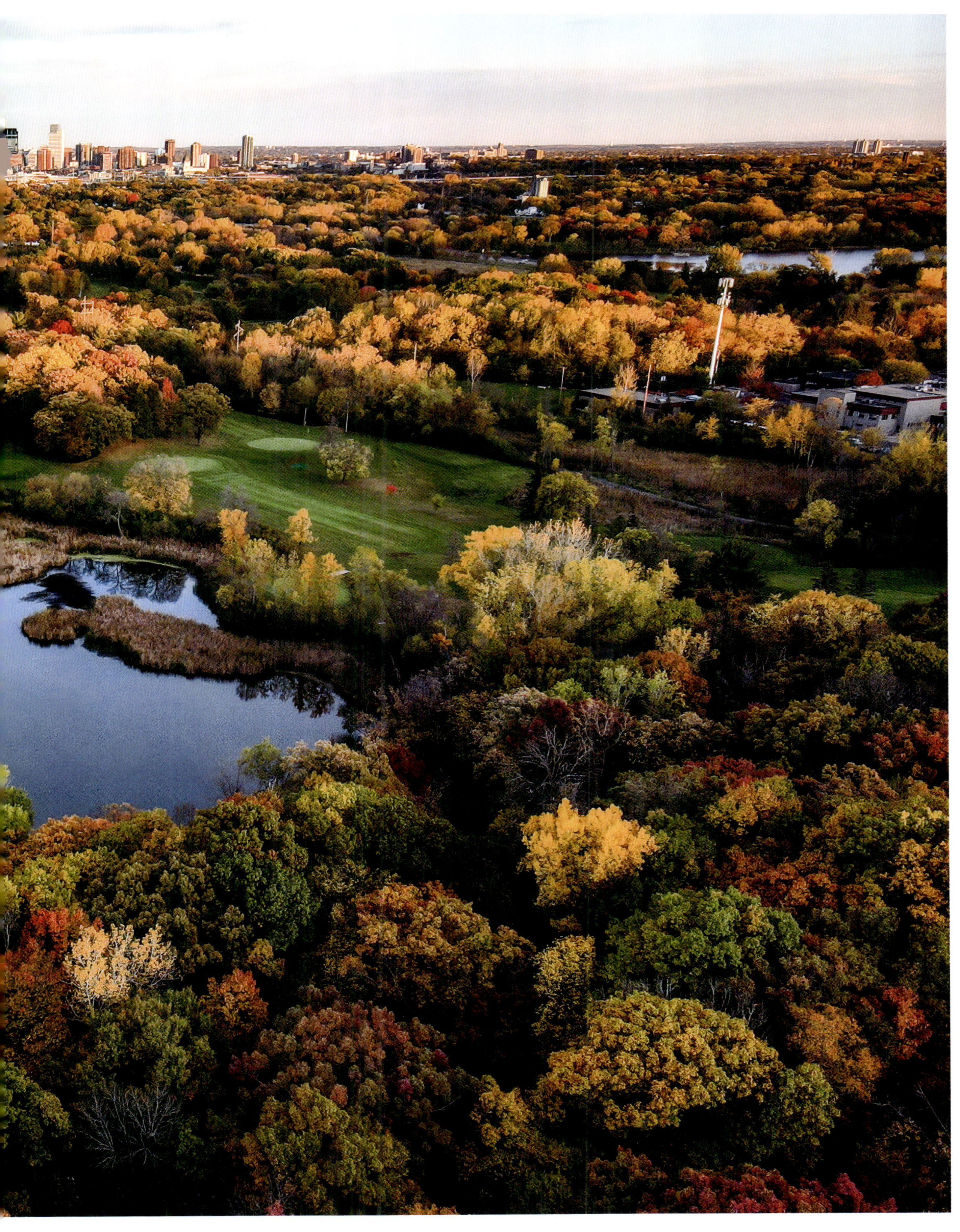

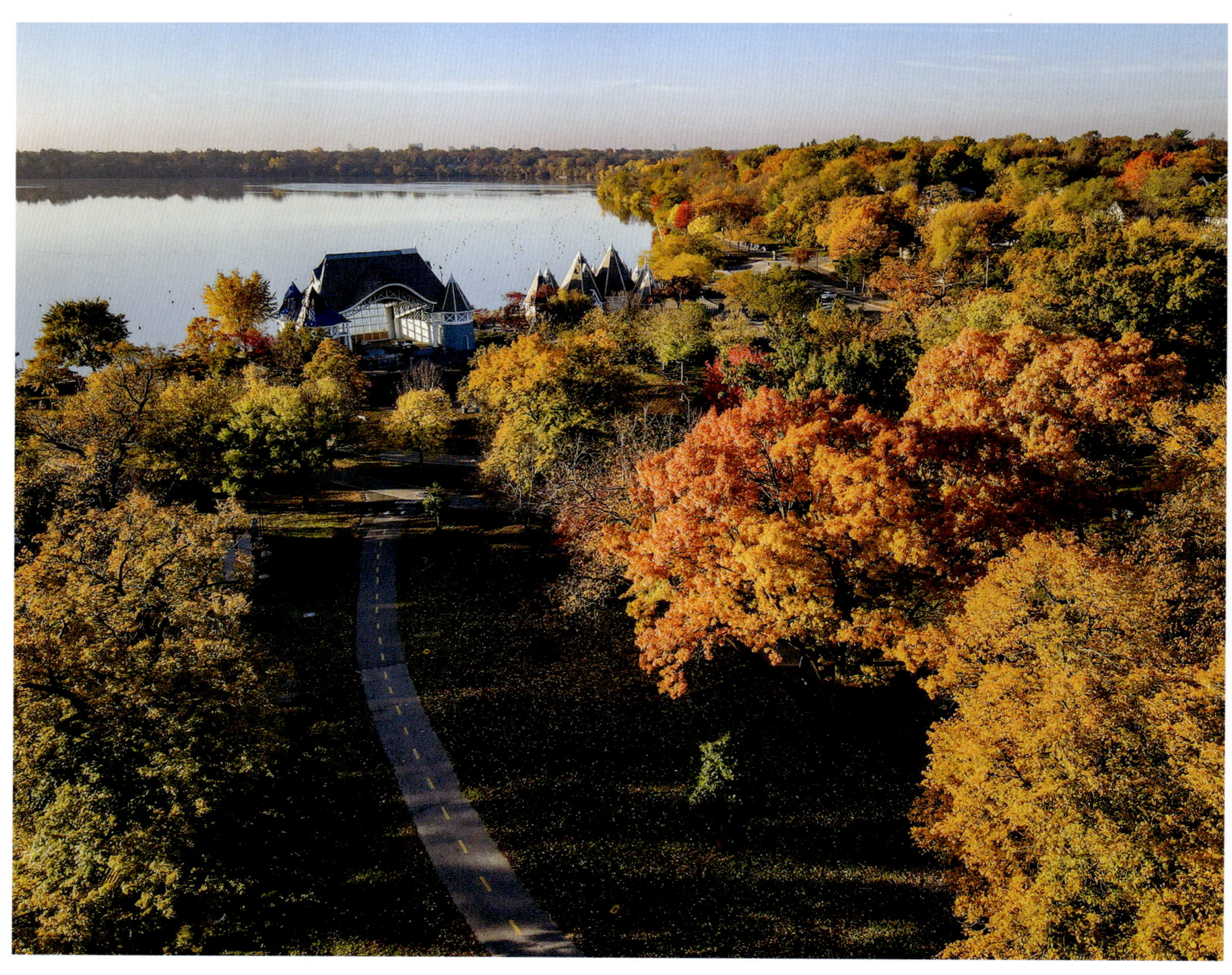

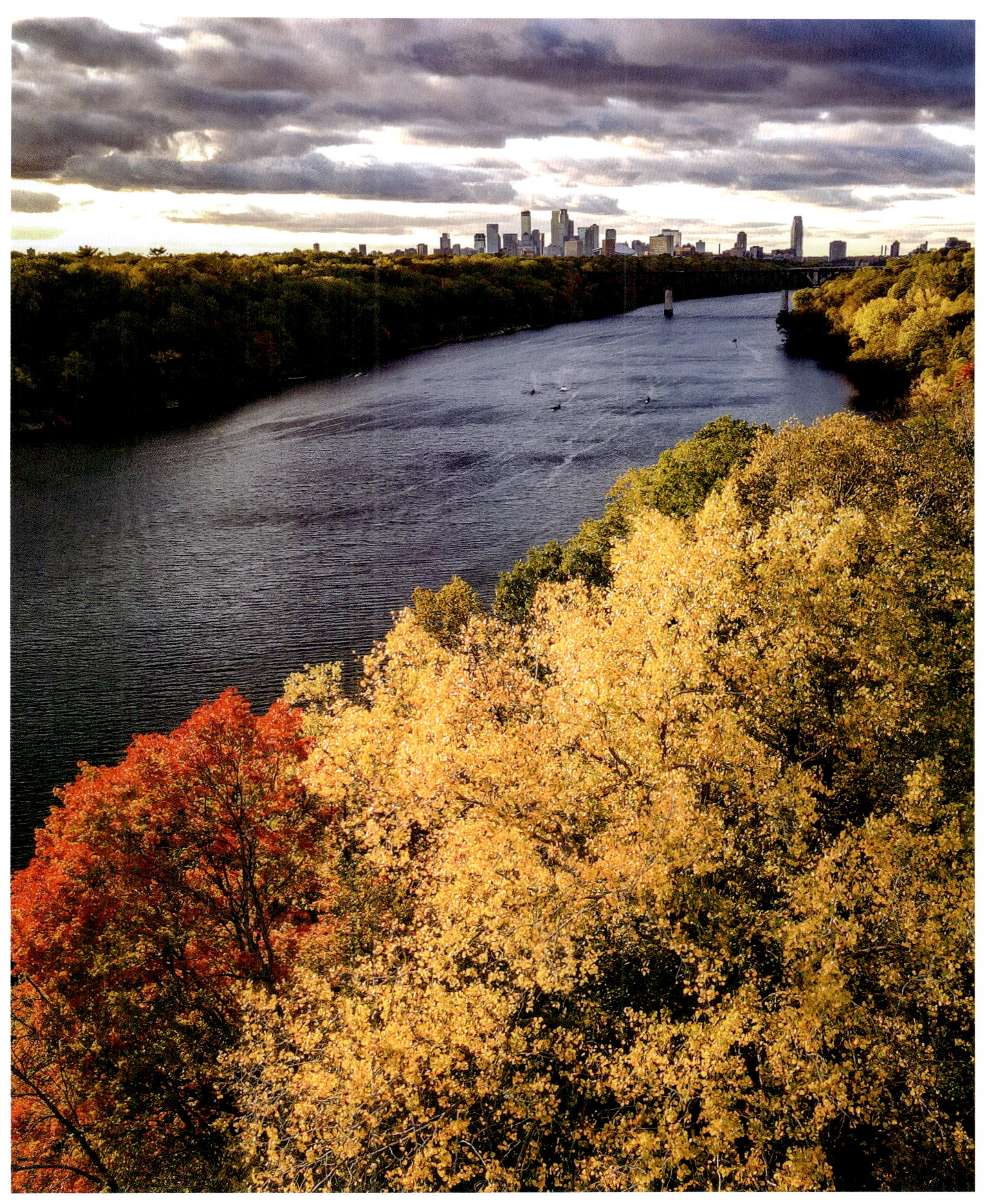

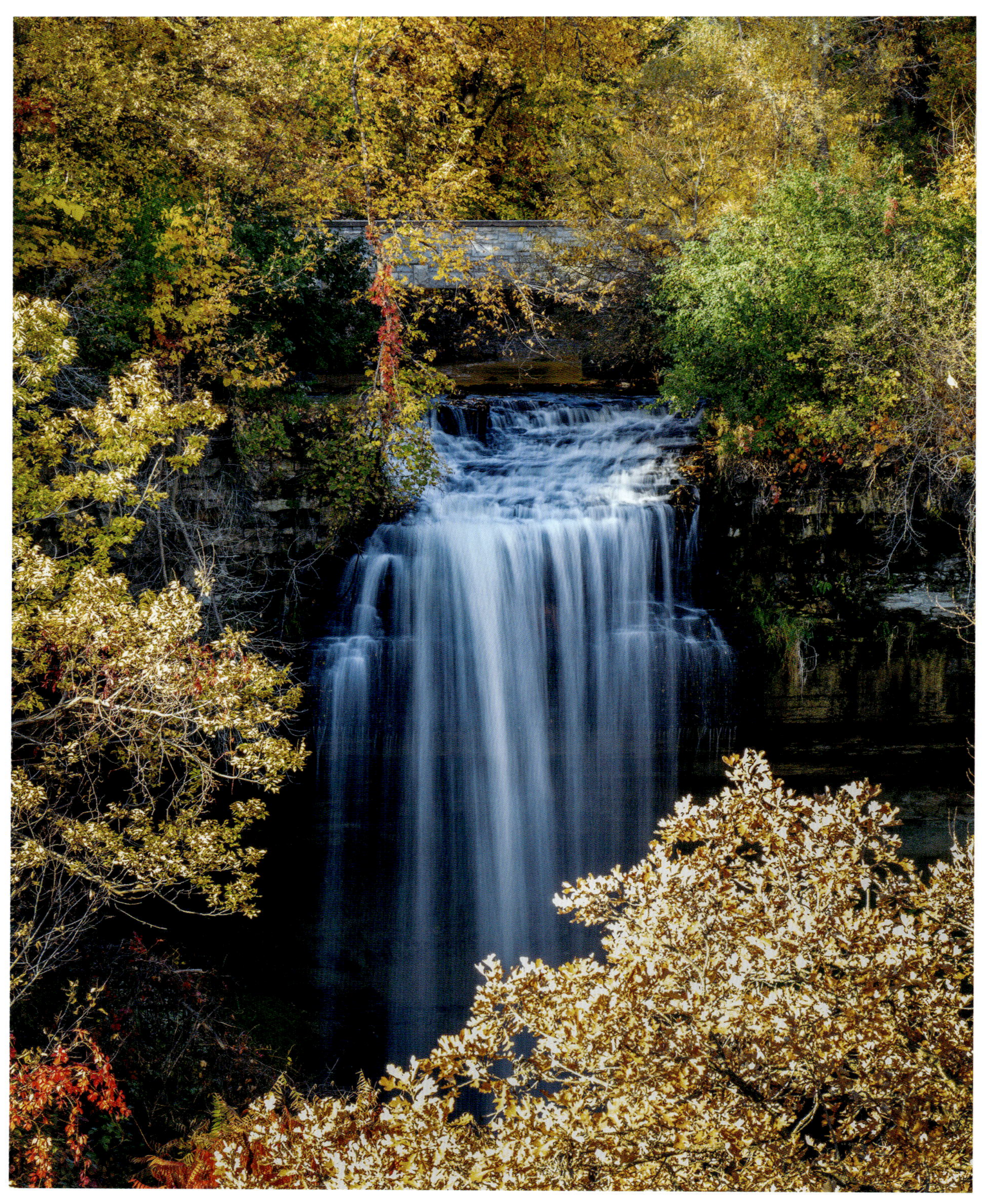

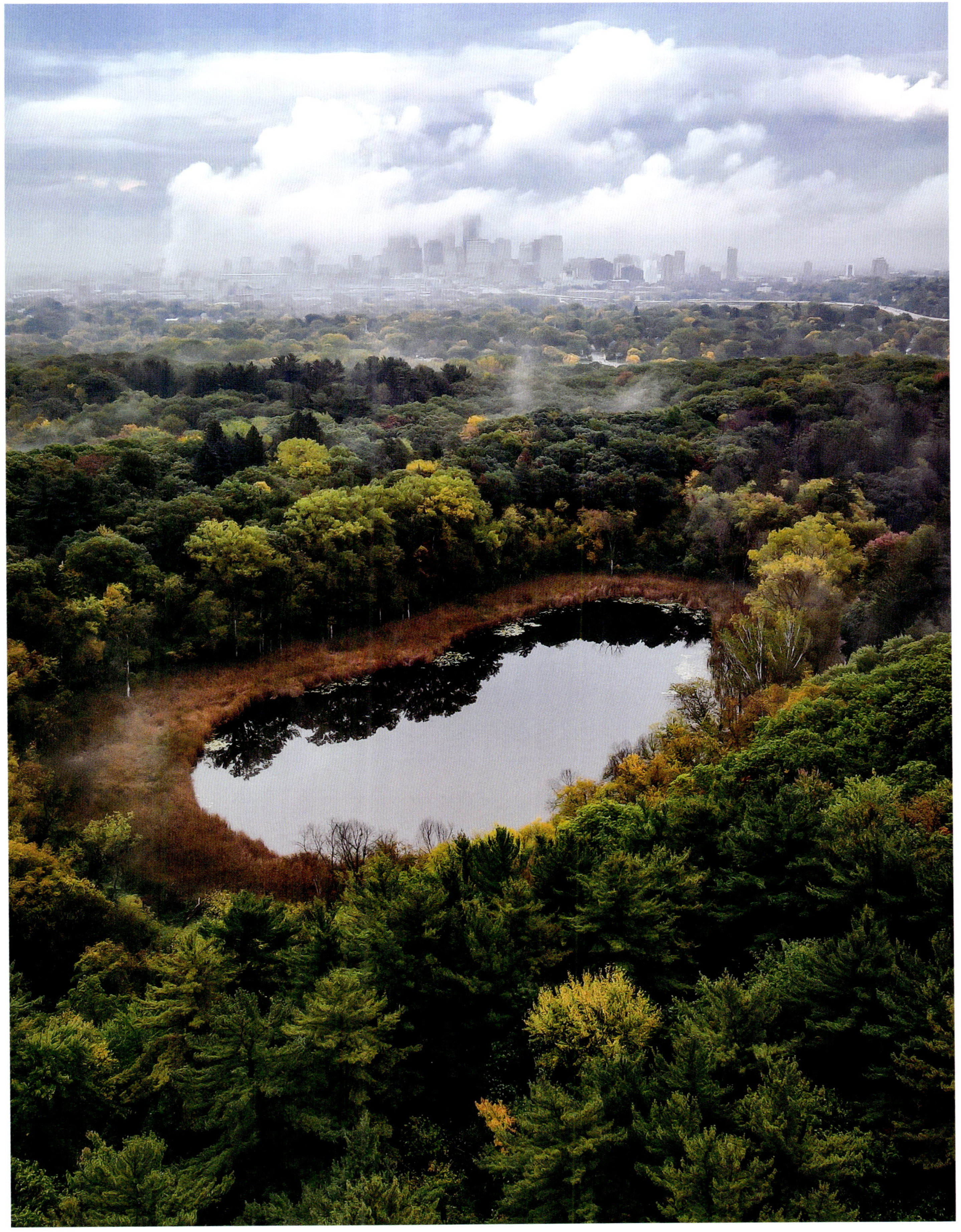

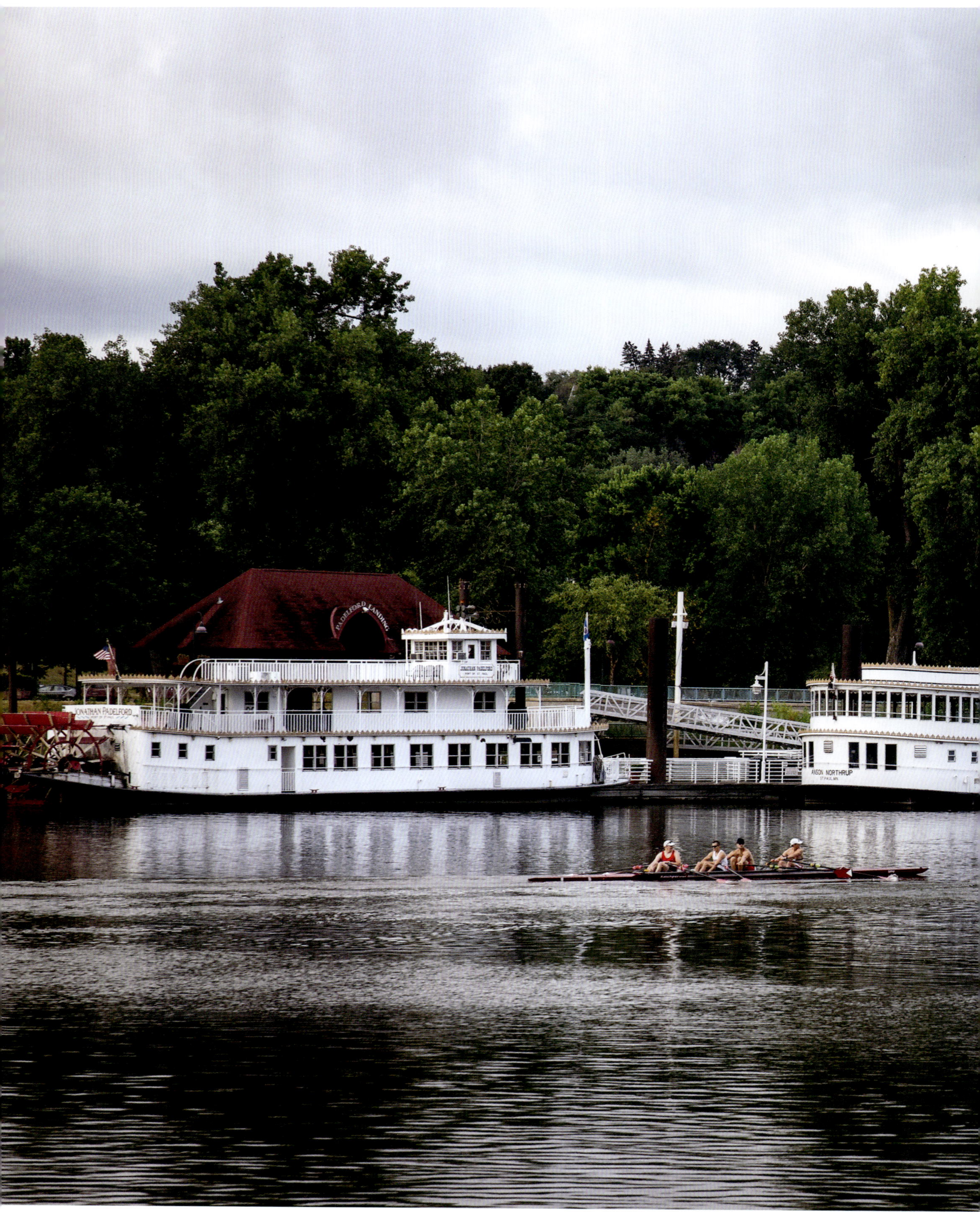

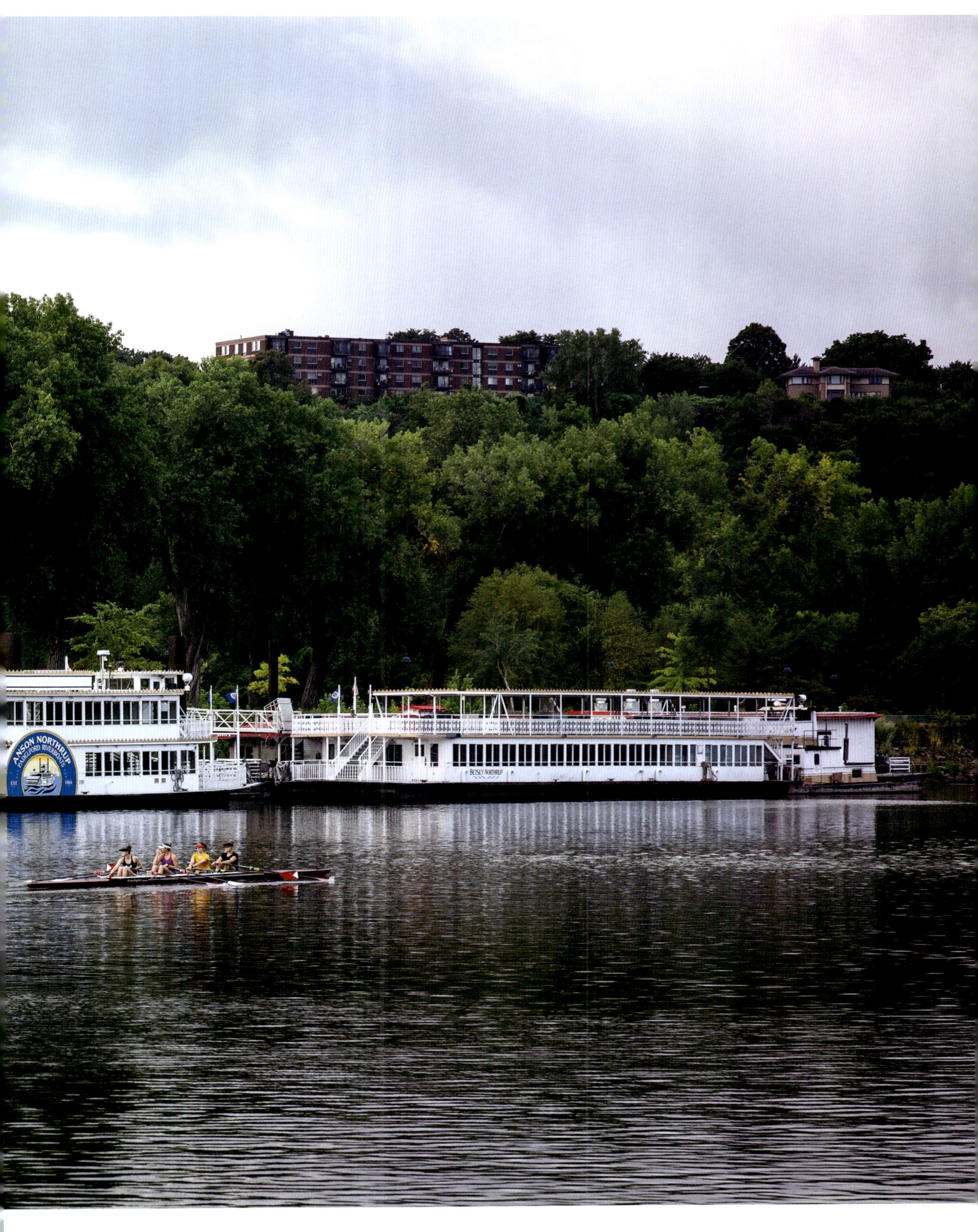

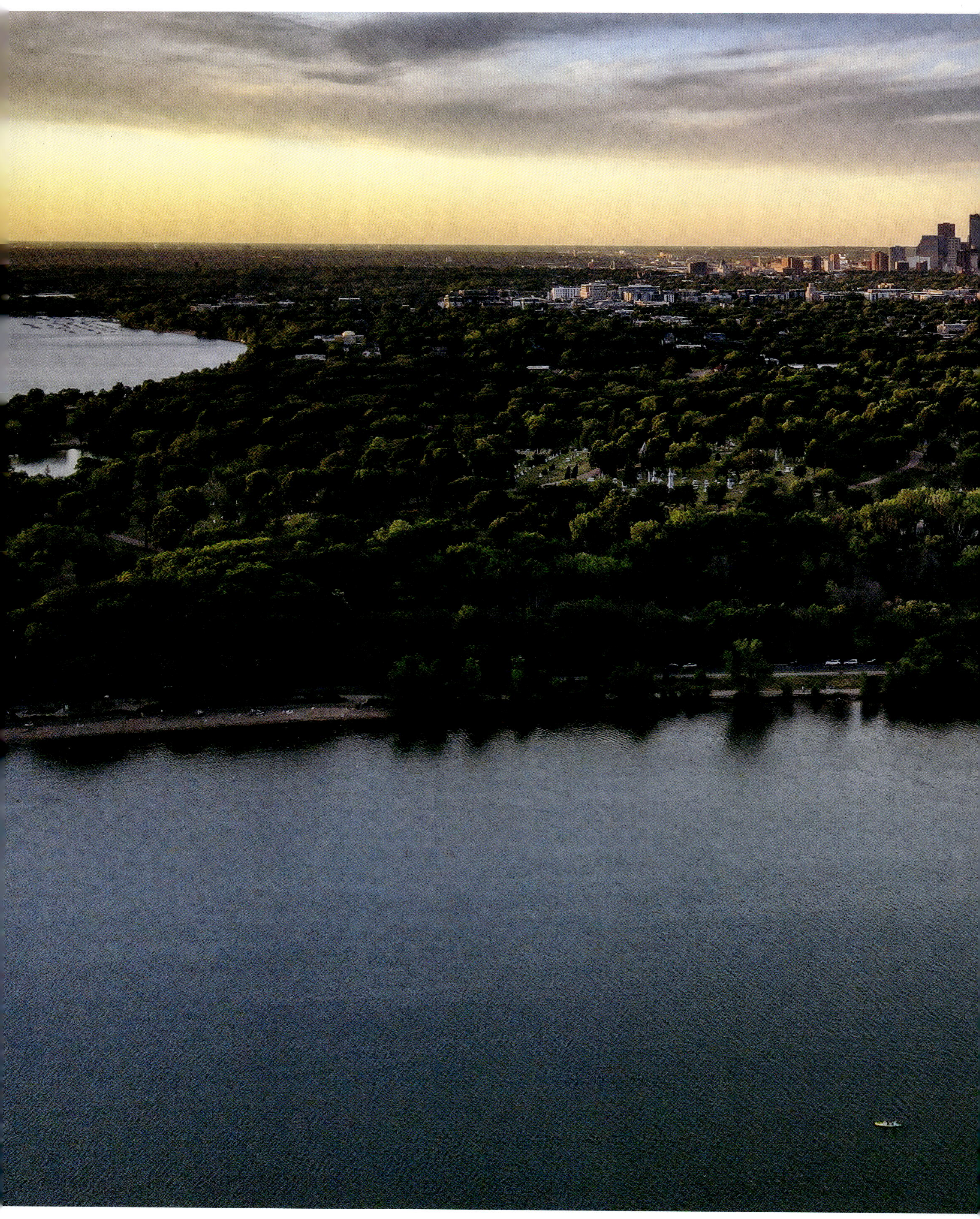

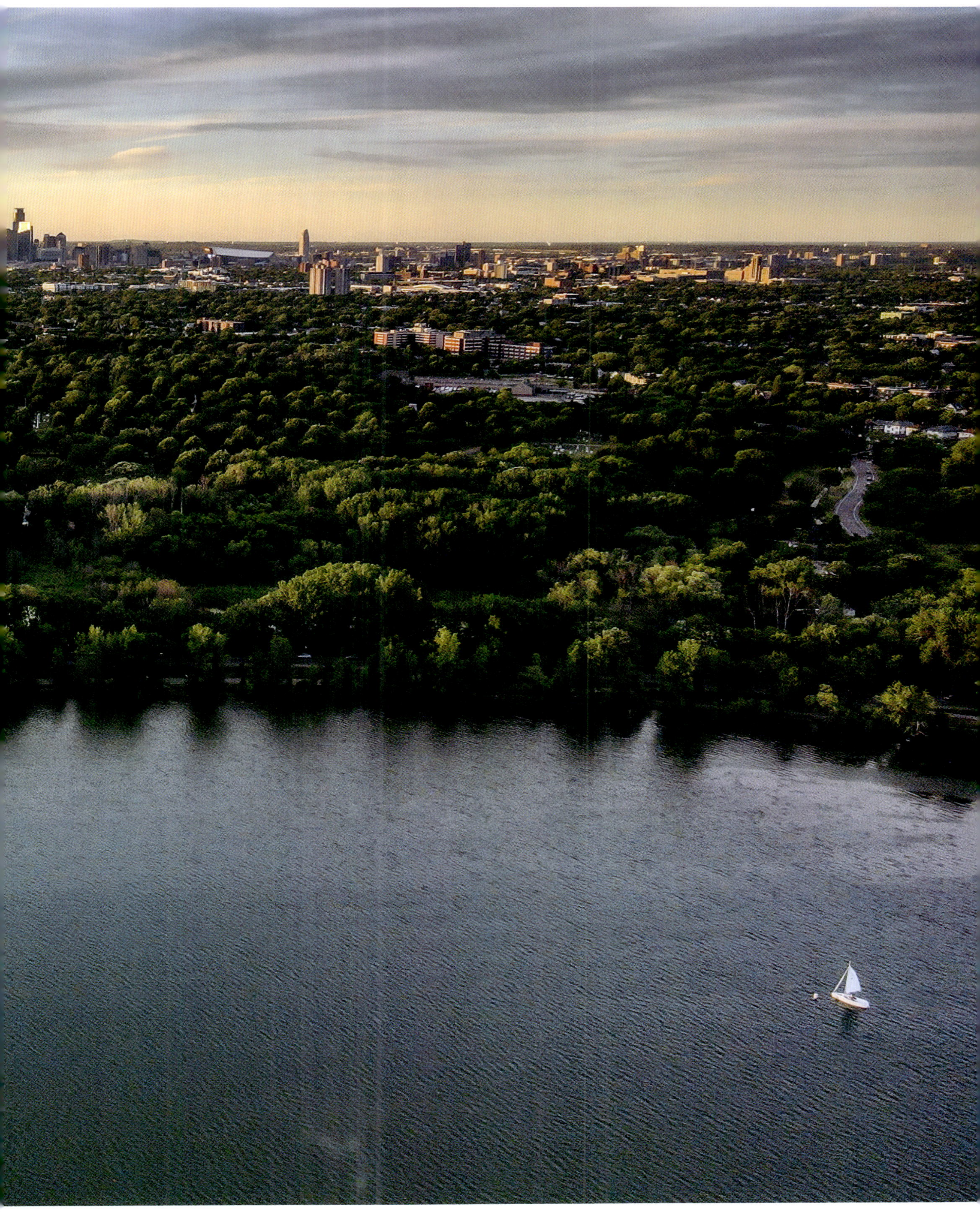

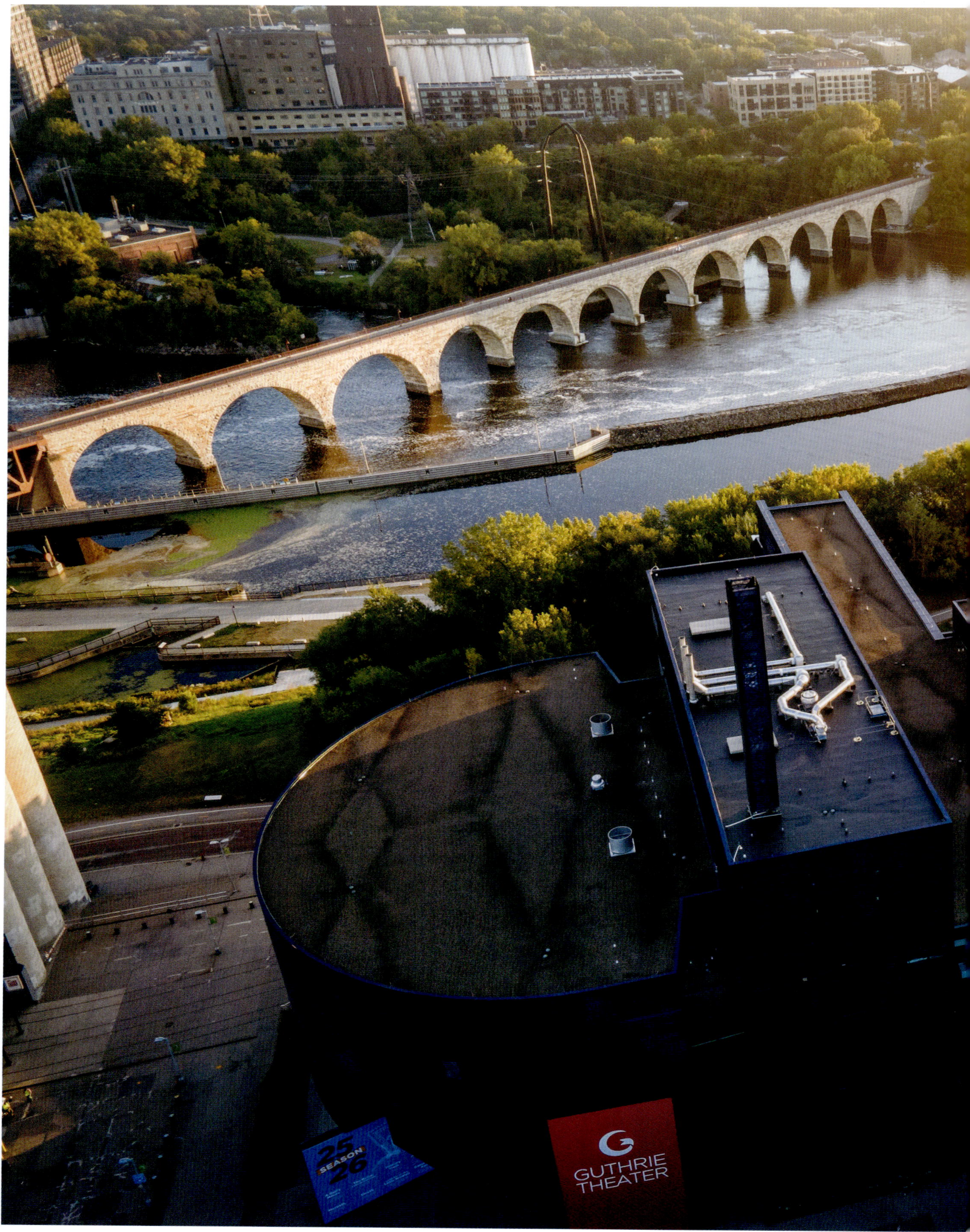
SEASON
25
26
GUTHRIE
THEATER

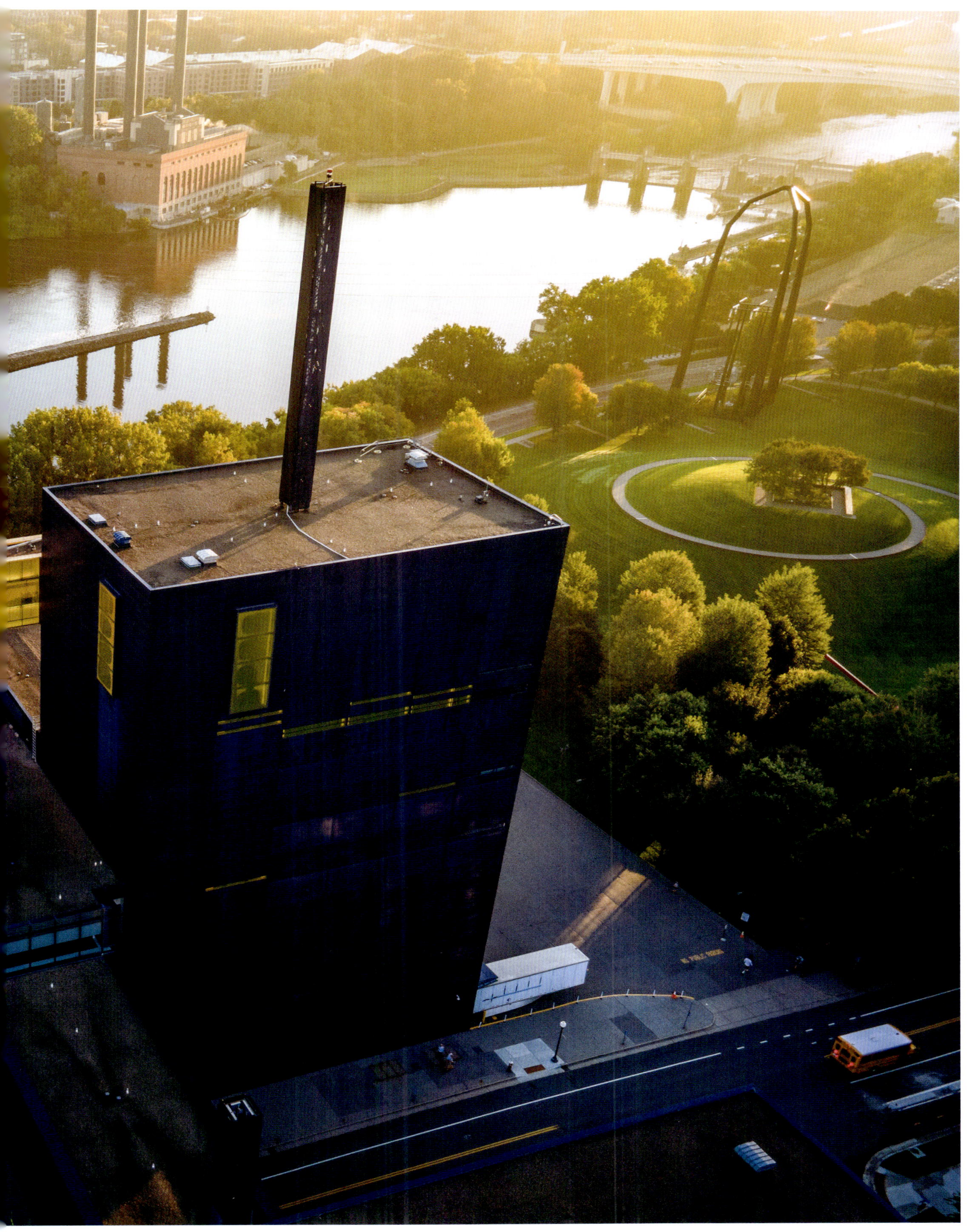

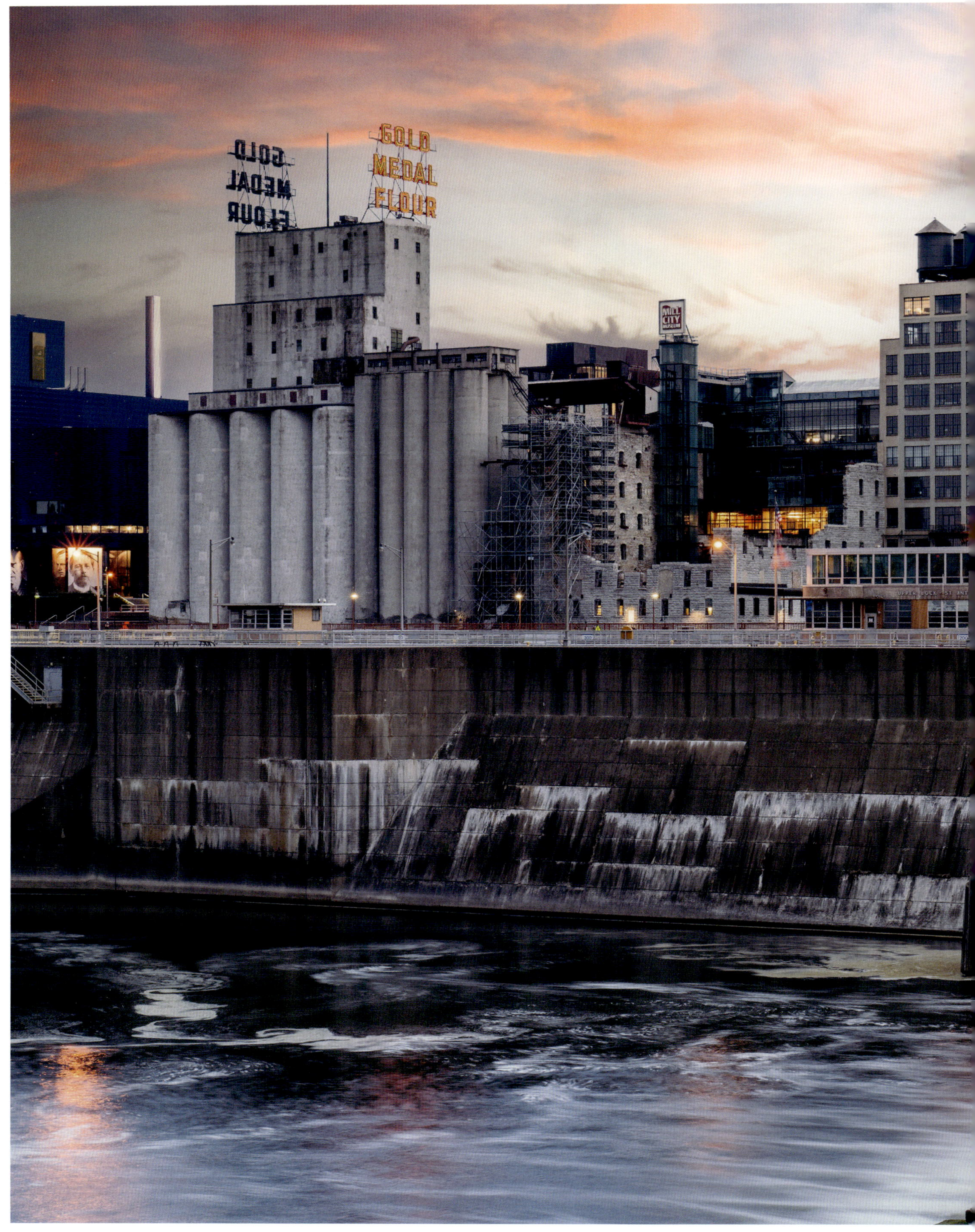
GOLD
MEDAL
FLOUR
GOLD
MEDAL
FLOUR
MILL CITY
MUSEUM

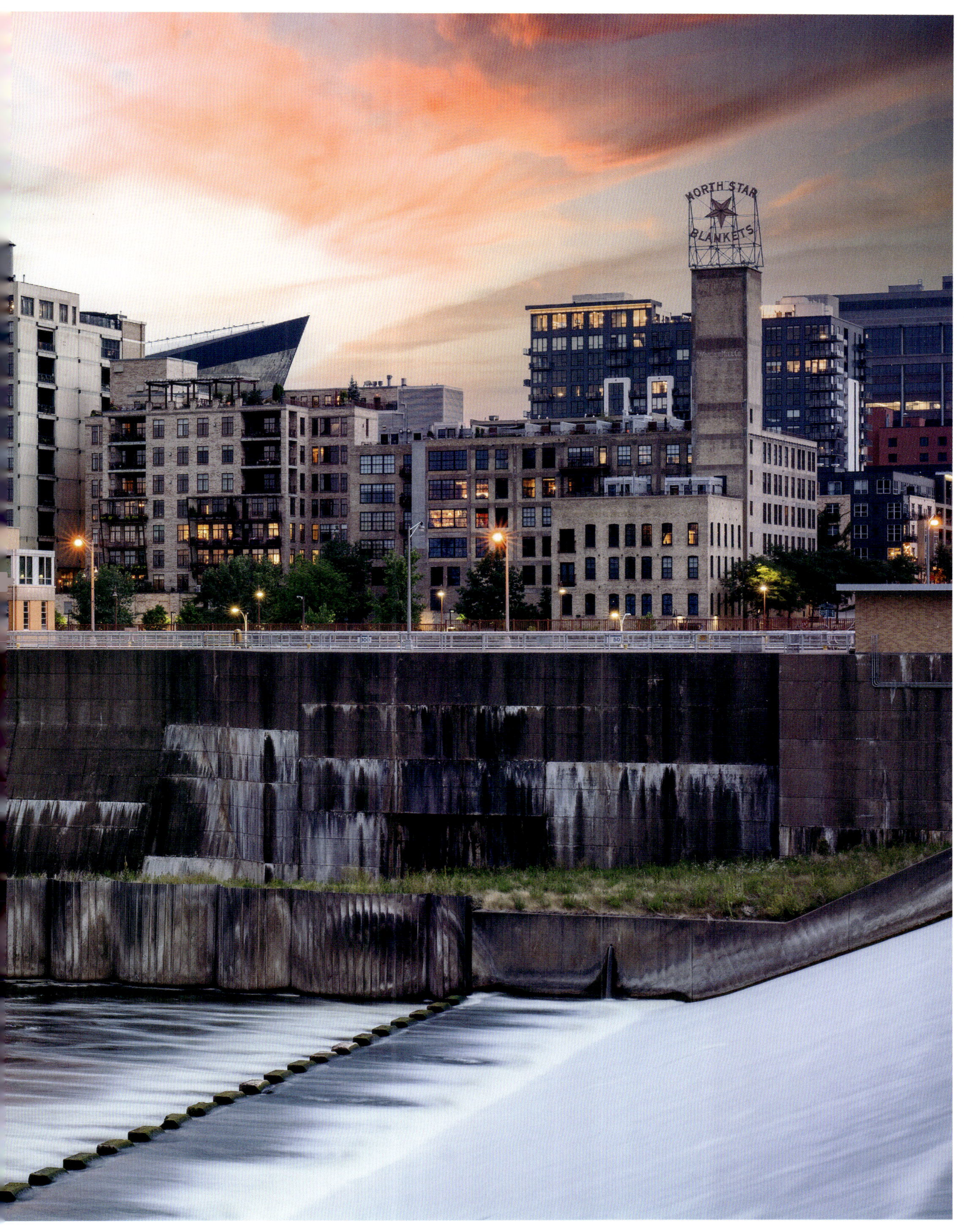
NORTH STAR
BLANKETS

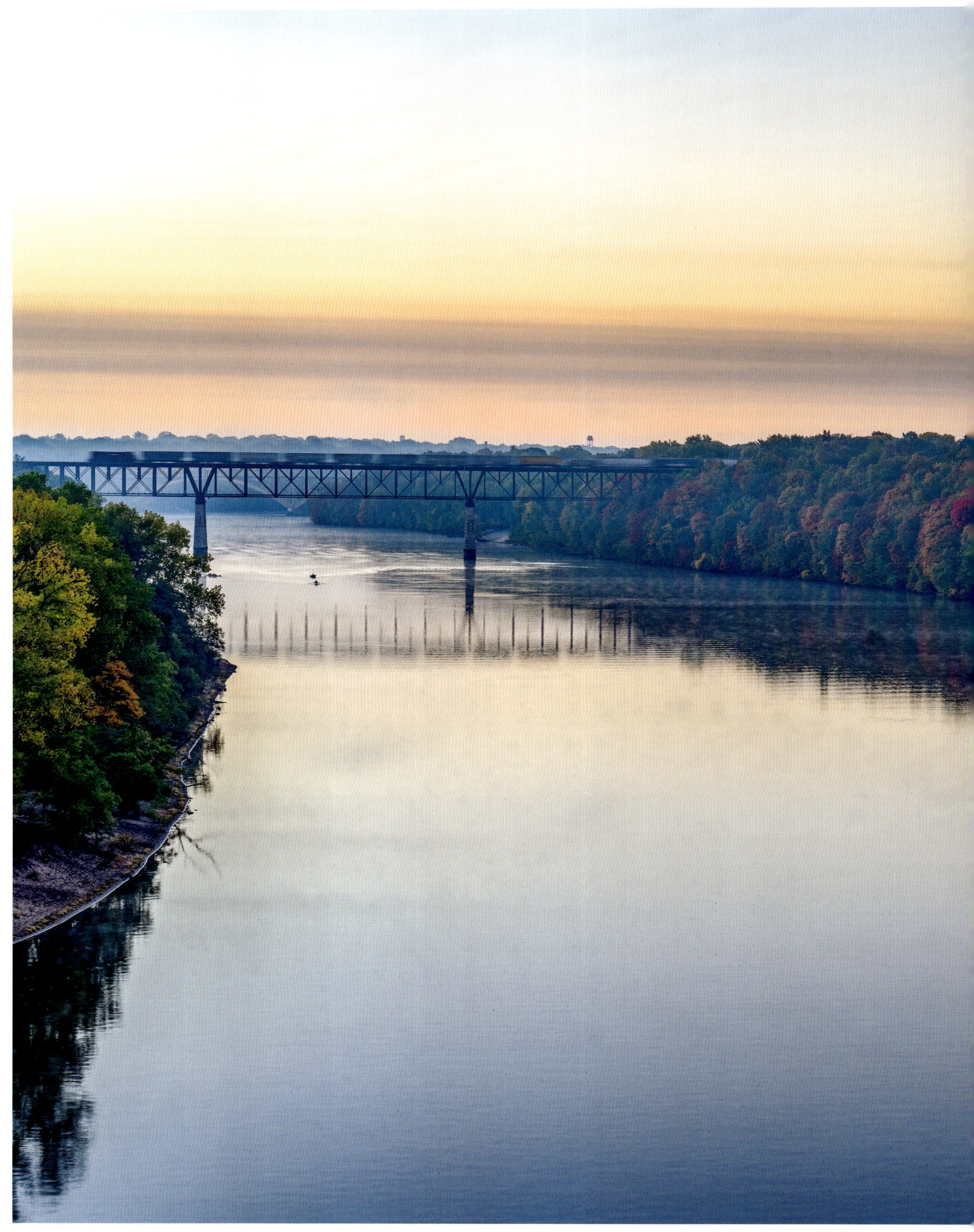

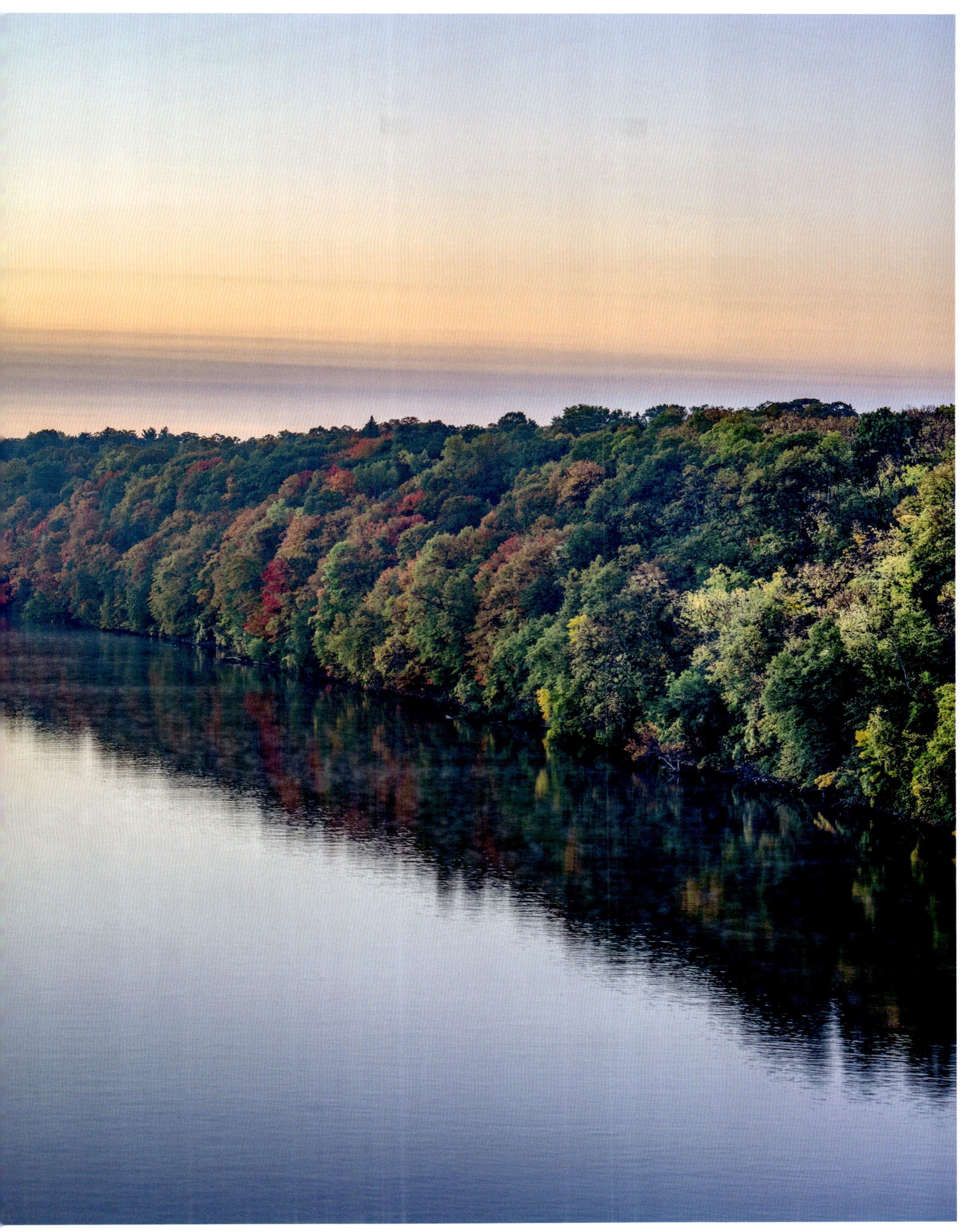

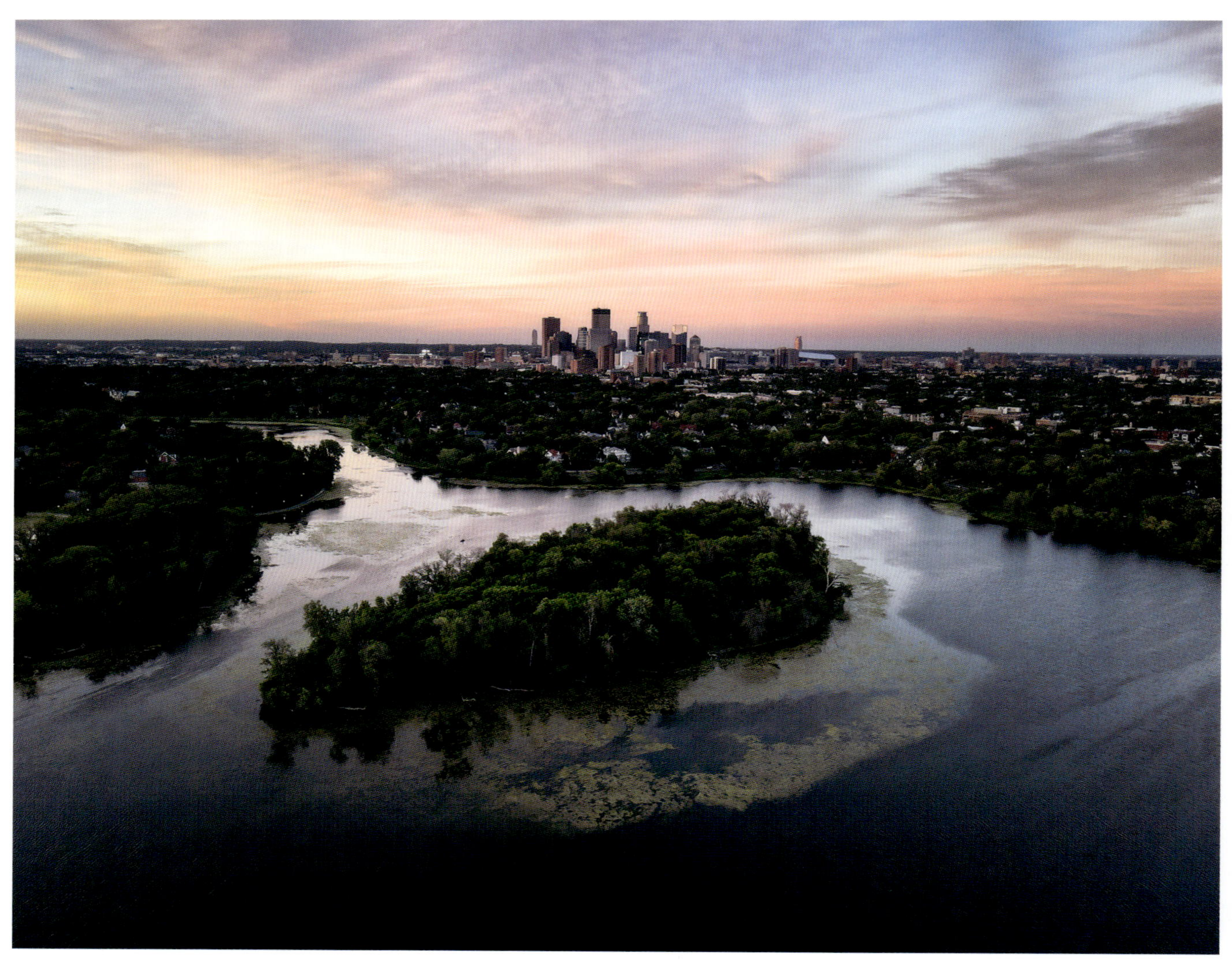

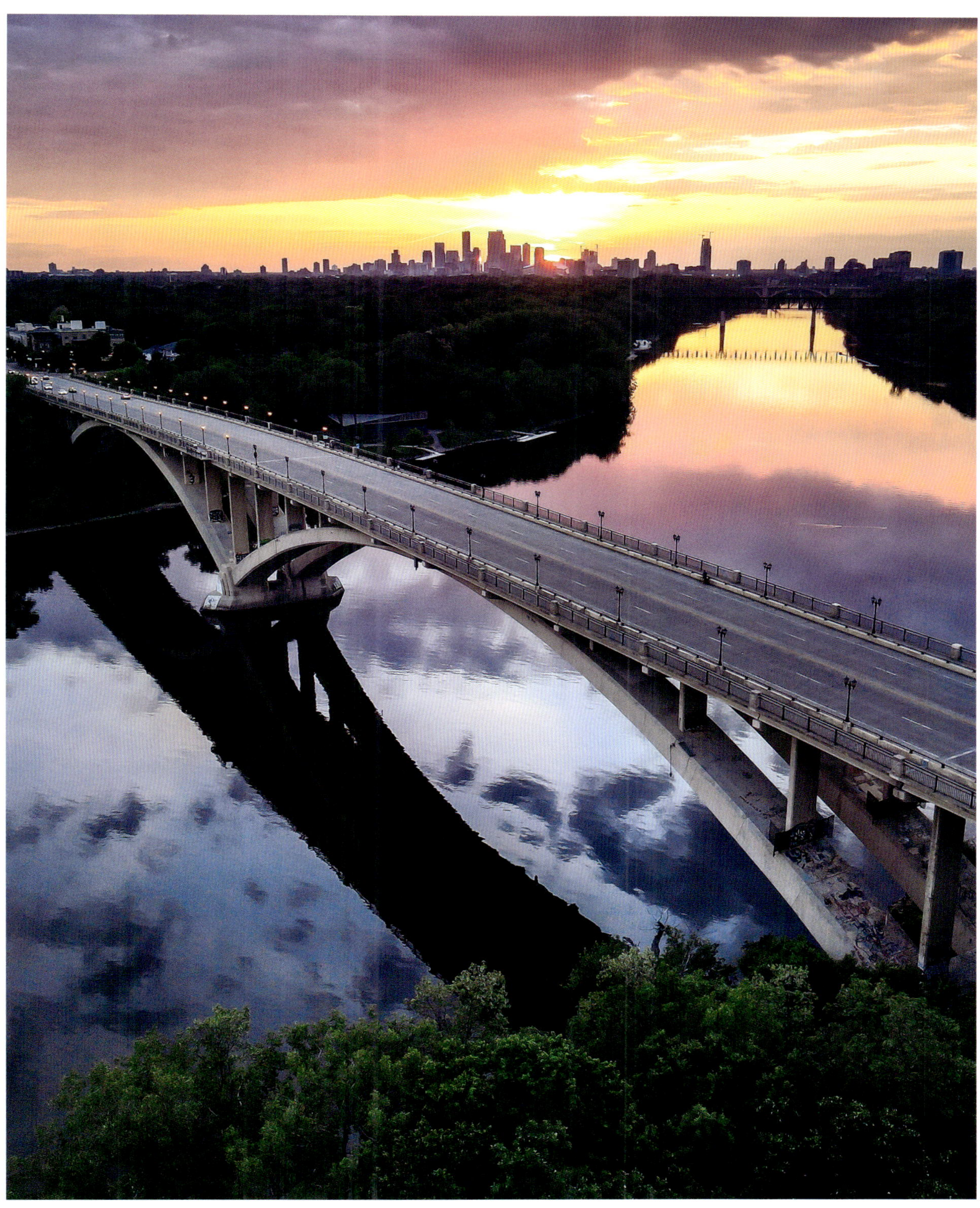

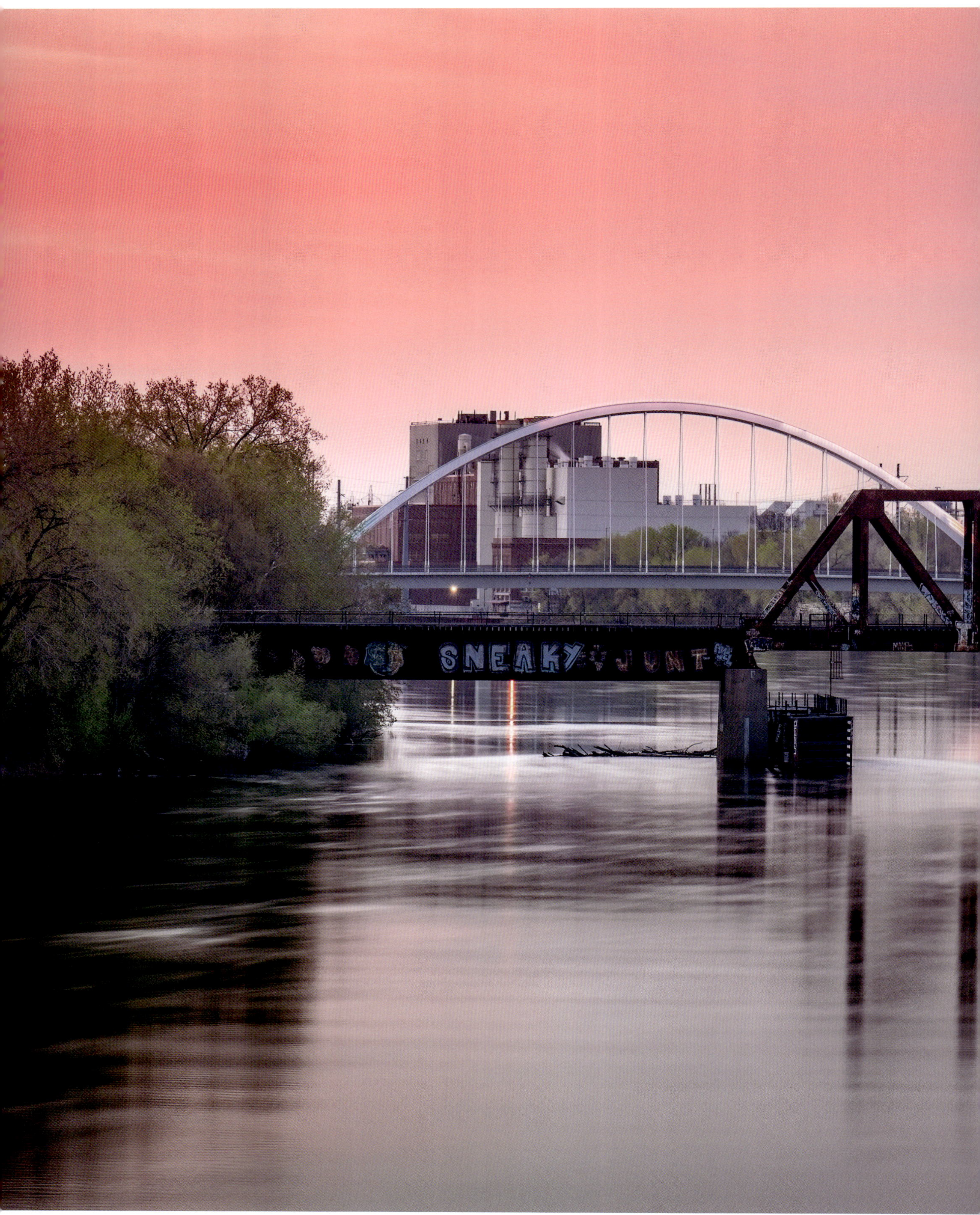
SNEAKY

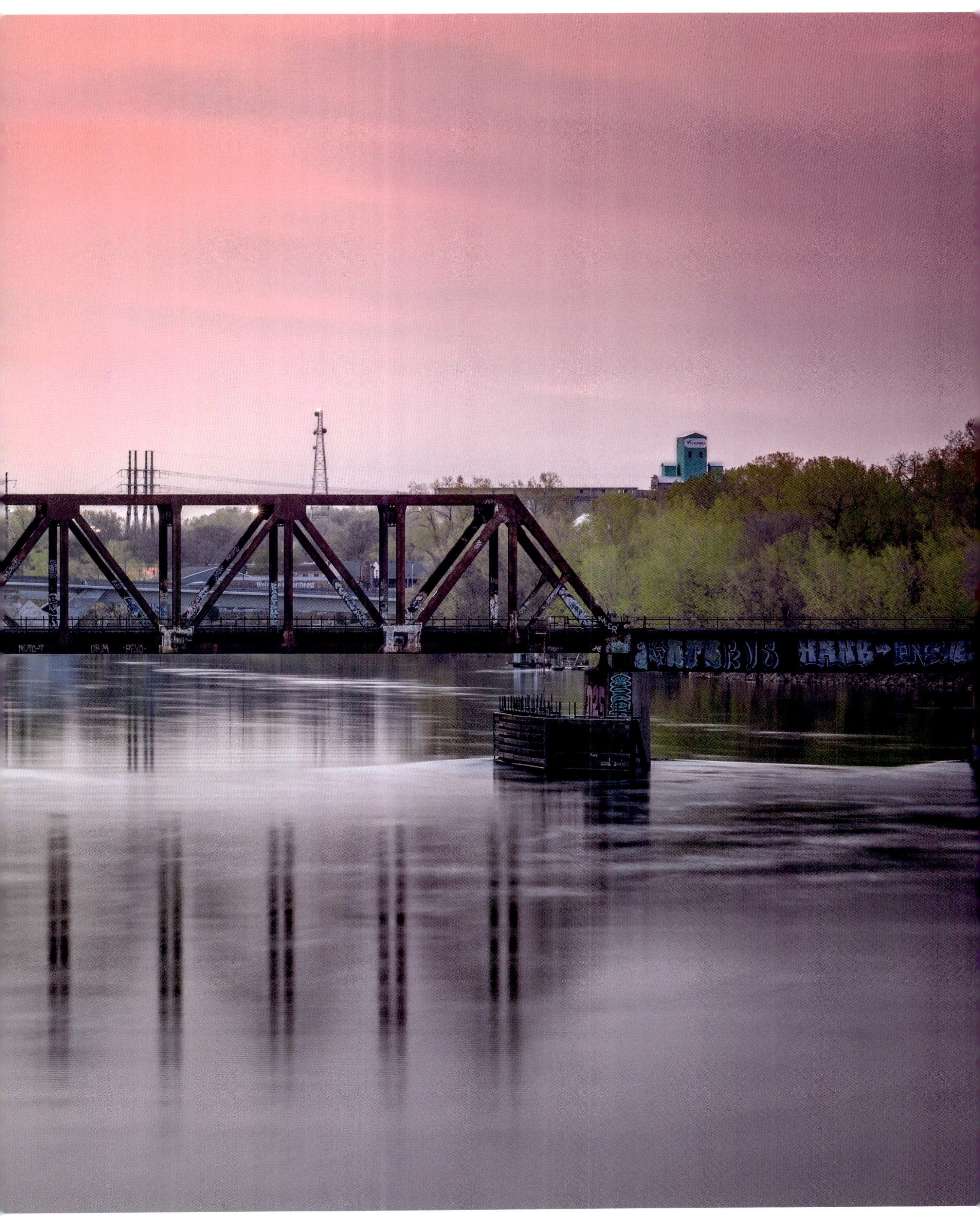

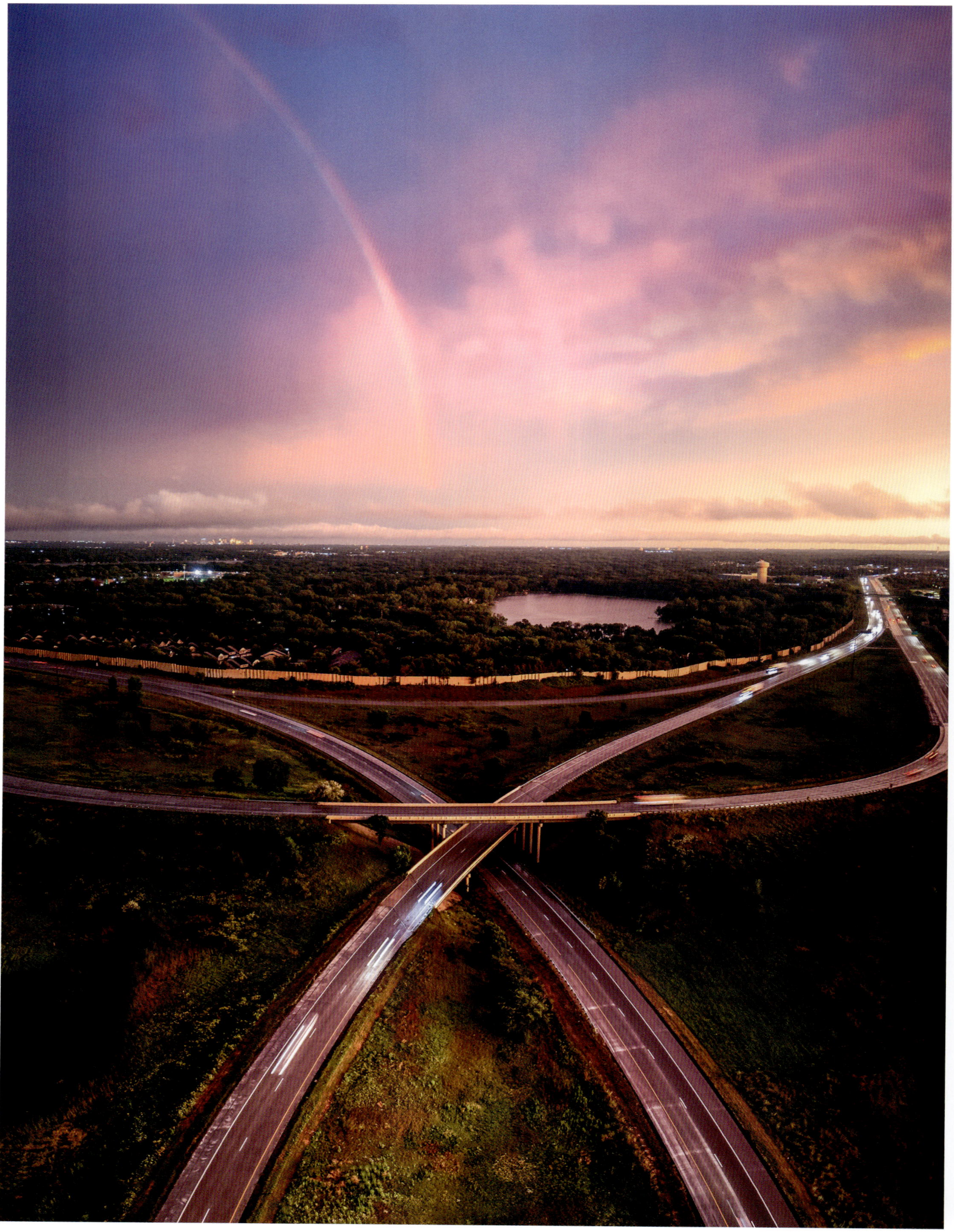

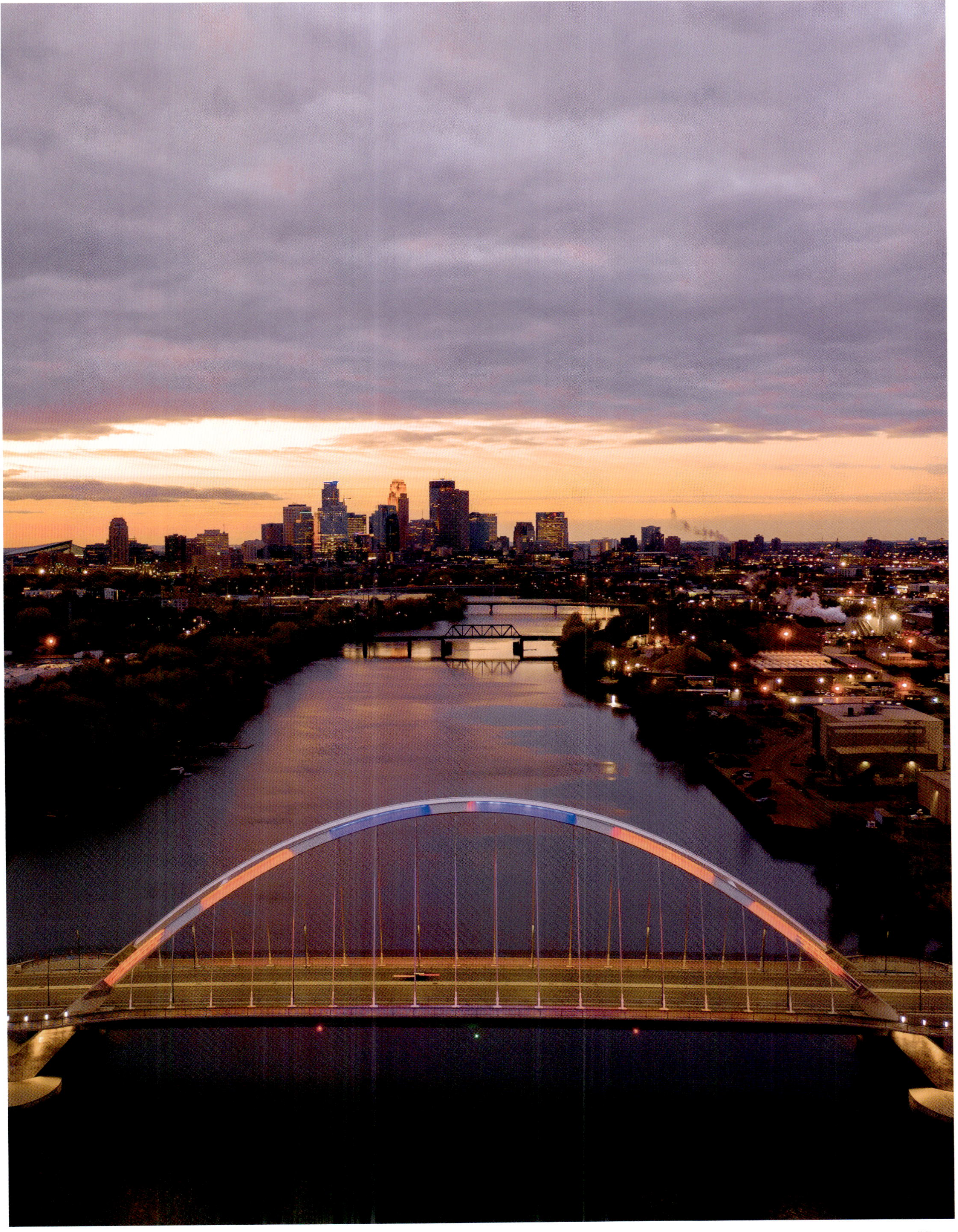

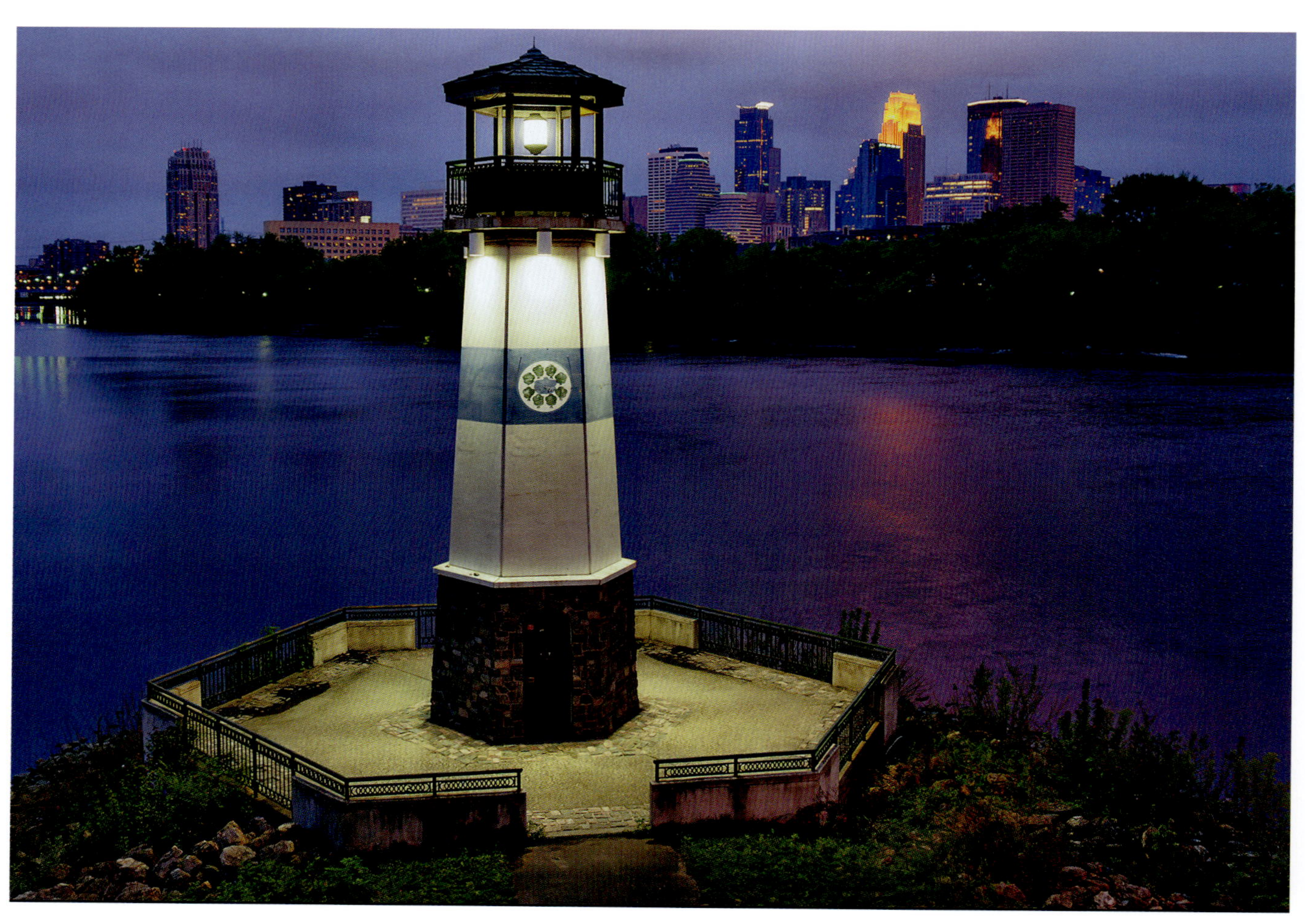

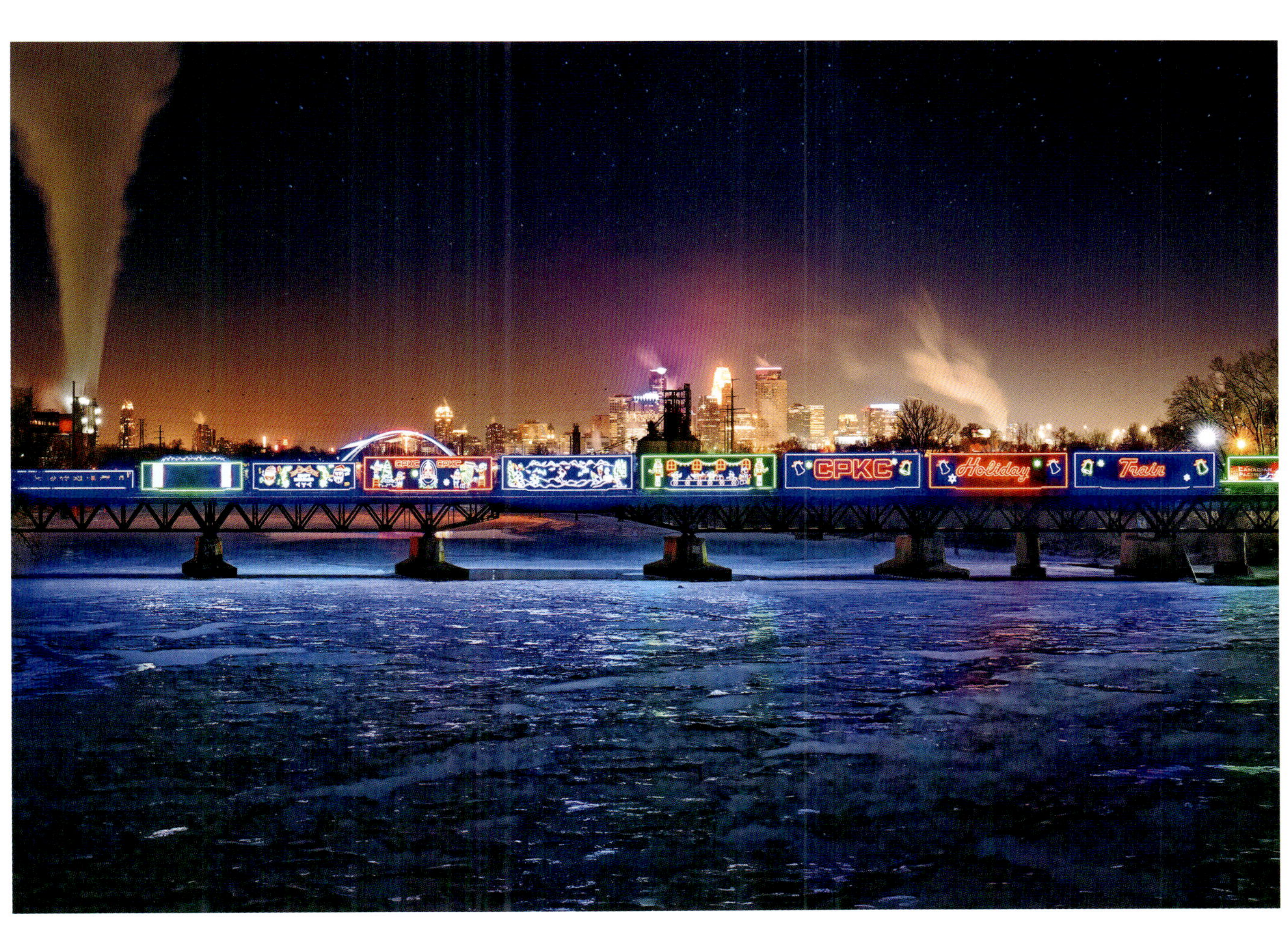
CPKC
Holiday
Train
CANADIAN PACIFIC

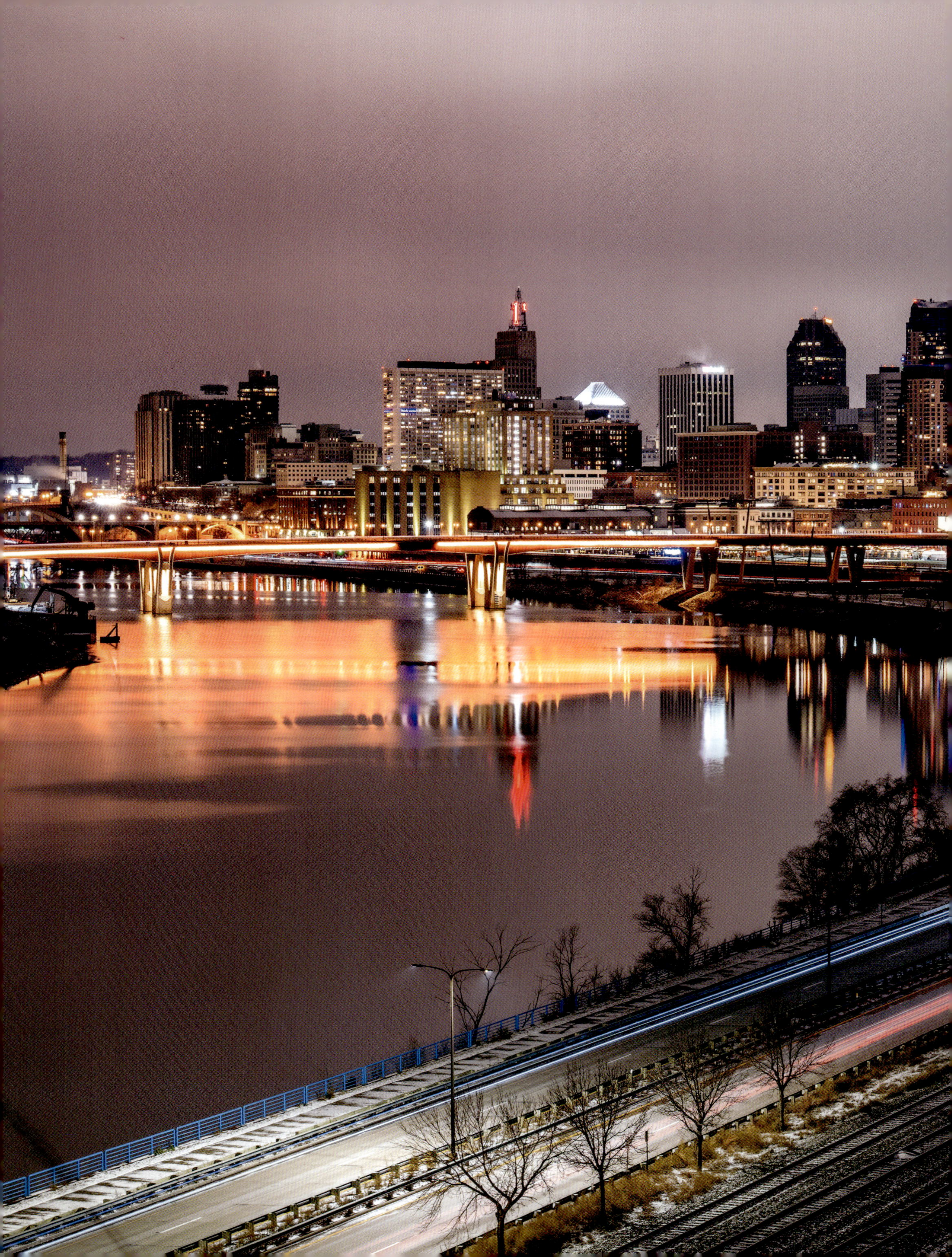

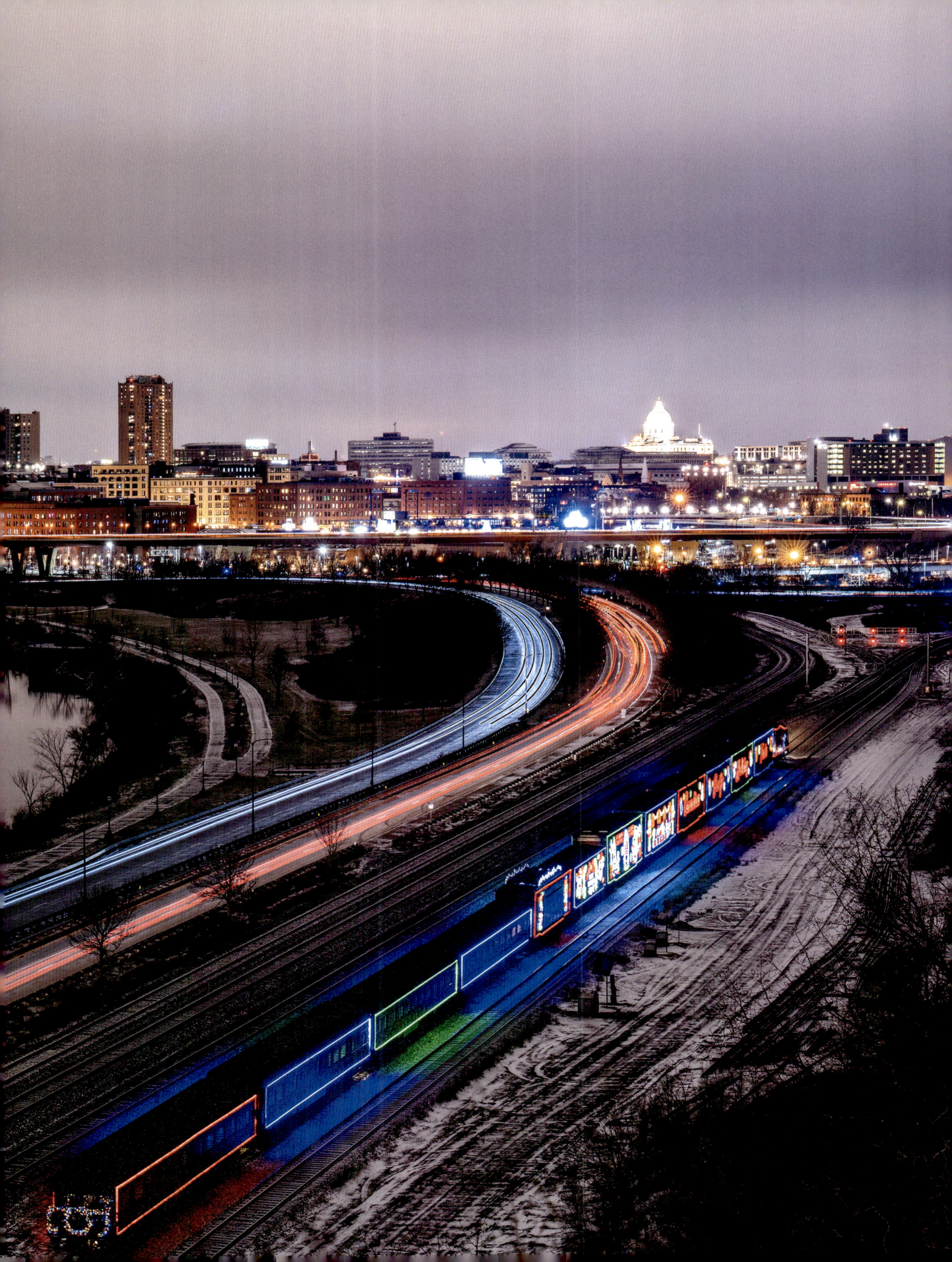

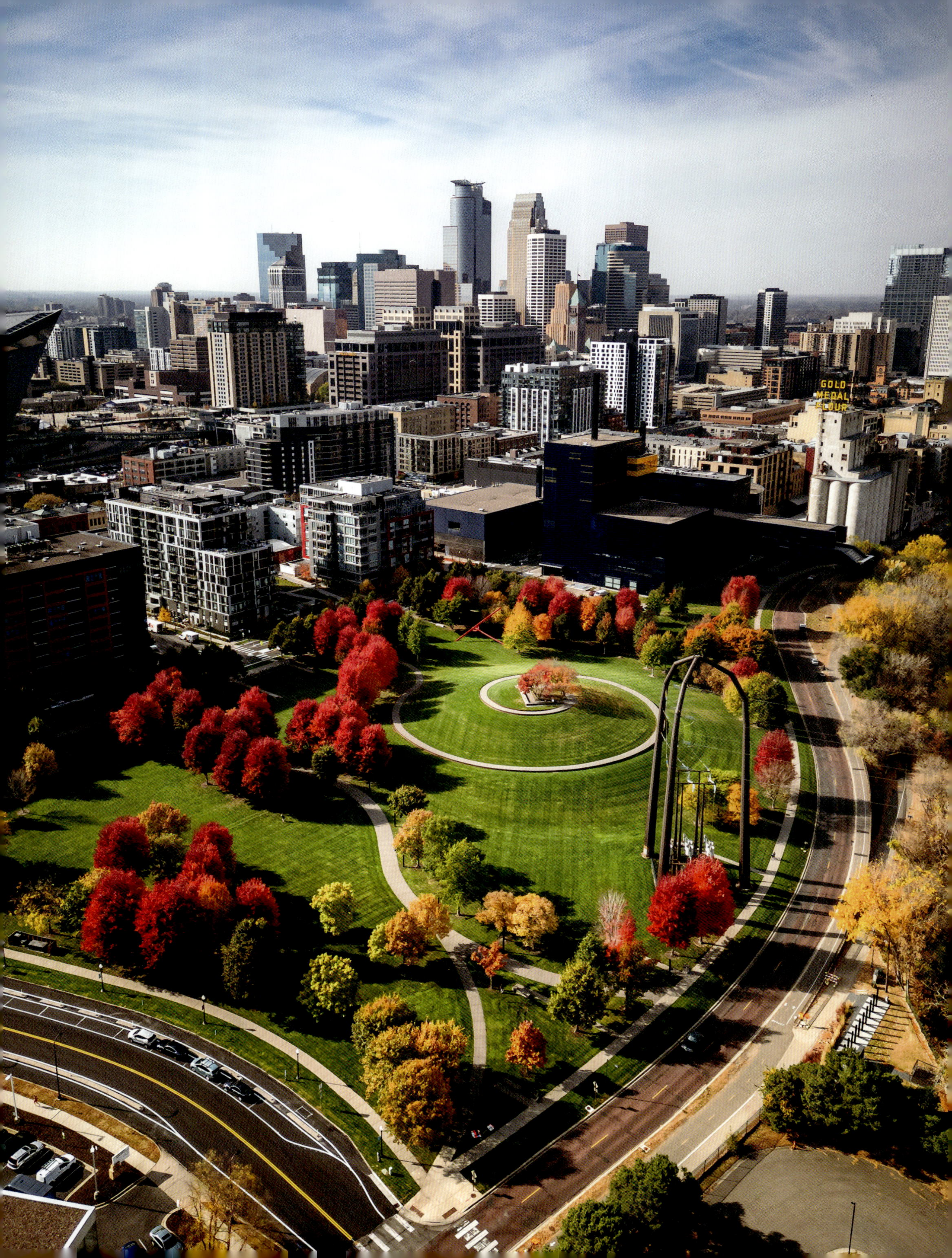

GOLD
MEDAL
FLOUR

Minneapolis ◆ The larger of the Twin Cities, Minneapolis began to grow rapidly in the mid-19th century, driven by the lumber and flour milling industries. Standing on the banks of the Mississippi River, the city's location made it an ideal spot for transportation and trade. The Mississippi River's power drove massive mills for Pillsbury and Washburn-Crosby (which became General Mills), making Minneapolis the flour milling capital of the world by the late 19th century. Grain from across the Midwest was shipped to Minneapolis, milled, and then sent around the world, helping to fuel the city's rapid growth. ◆ This industry helped propel the city's architecture, as well. The powerful barons of the late 1860s, including Charles Pillsbury, James J. Hill, and Thomas Lowry, wanted architects to create a city that rivaled the Brahmin-built edifices of the East Coast. ◆ Designed by Léon Eugène Arnal, the Foshay Tower, completed in 1929, was the first building to surpass the height of Minneapolis City Hall, completed 23 years earlier in 1906. It remained the tallest building in Minneapolis until the IDS Center surpassed it in 1972. Built by art student turned business magnate Wilbur Foshay who planned to live and work in the building, Foshay Tower was designed as an homage to the Washington Monument, with all four sides of the building sloping slightly inward and each floor slightly smaller than the one below it. Completed just weeks before the stock market crash of 1929 ignited The Great Depression, Wilbur Foshay lost his fortune and never lived in the building. But the Tower lives on, with the name "FOSHAY" appearing in 10-foot lighted letters towards the top of the building on all four sides, creating an iconic landmark in the Minneapolis skyline. ◆ Minneapolis is also known for its extensive network of enclosed pedestrian bridges known as "skyways." Developed in the 1960s and '70s as a solution to the region's hard winters, these bridges link office buildings, hotels, shops, and parking garages, helping Minnesotans move around safely and comfortably above street level, avoiding snow, ice, and subzero temperatures. The skyways are a distinctive feature of downtown Minneapolis, stretching nearly 9.5 miles in the city alone.

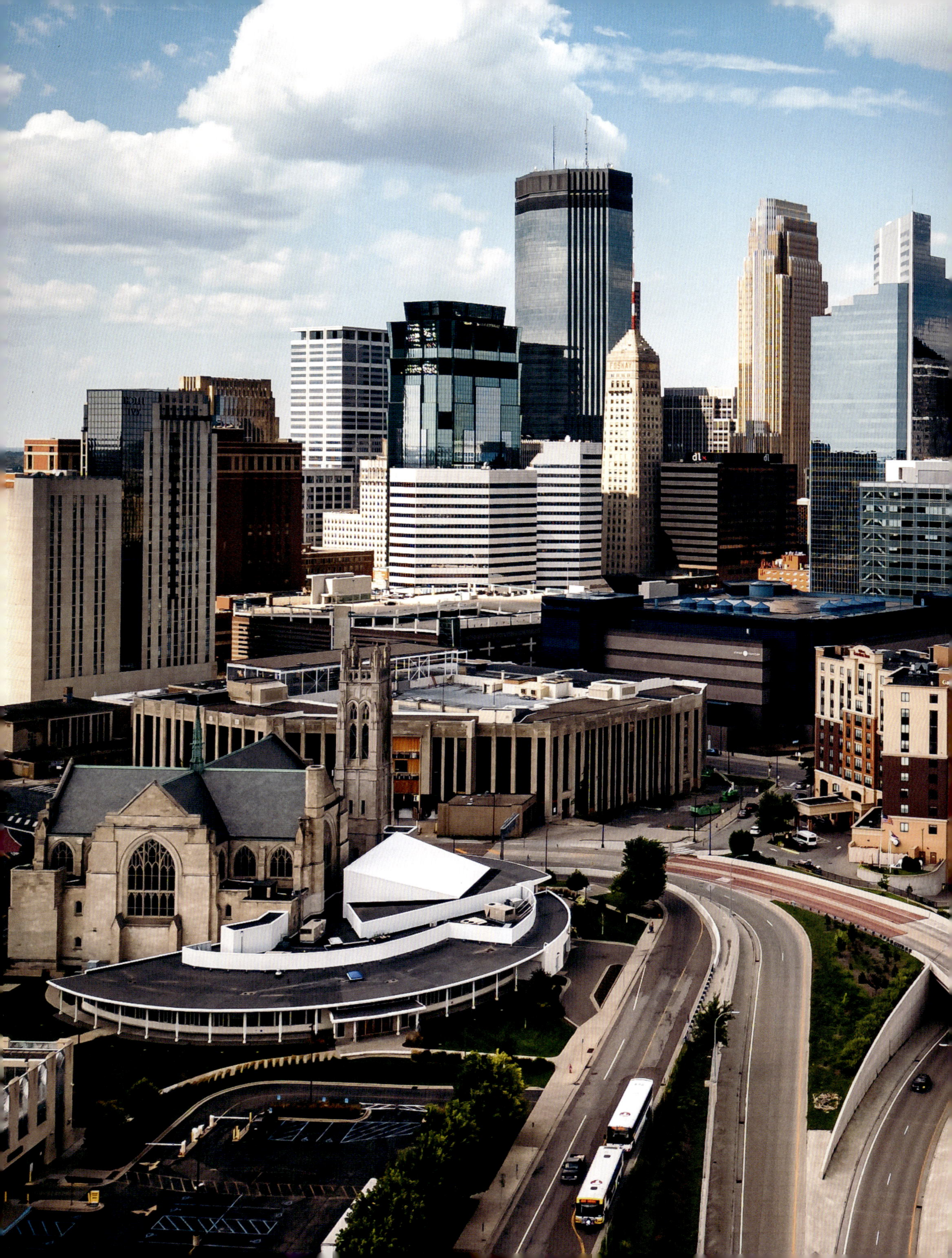

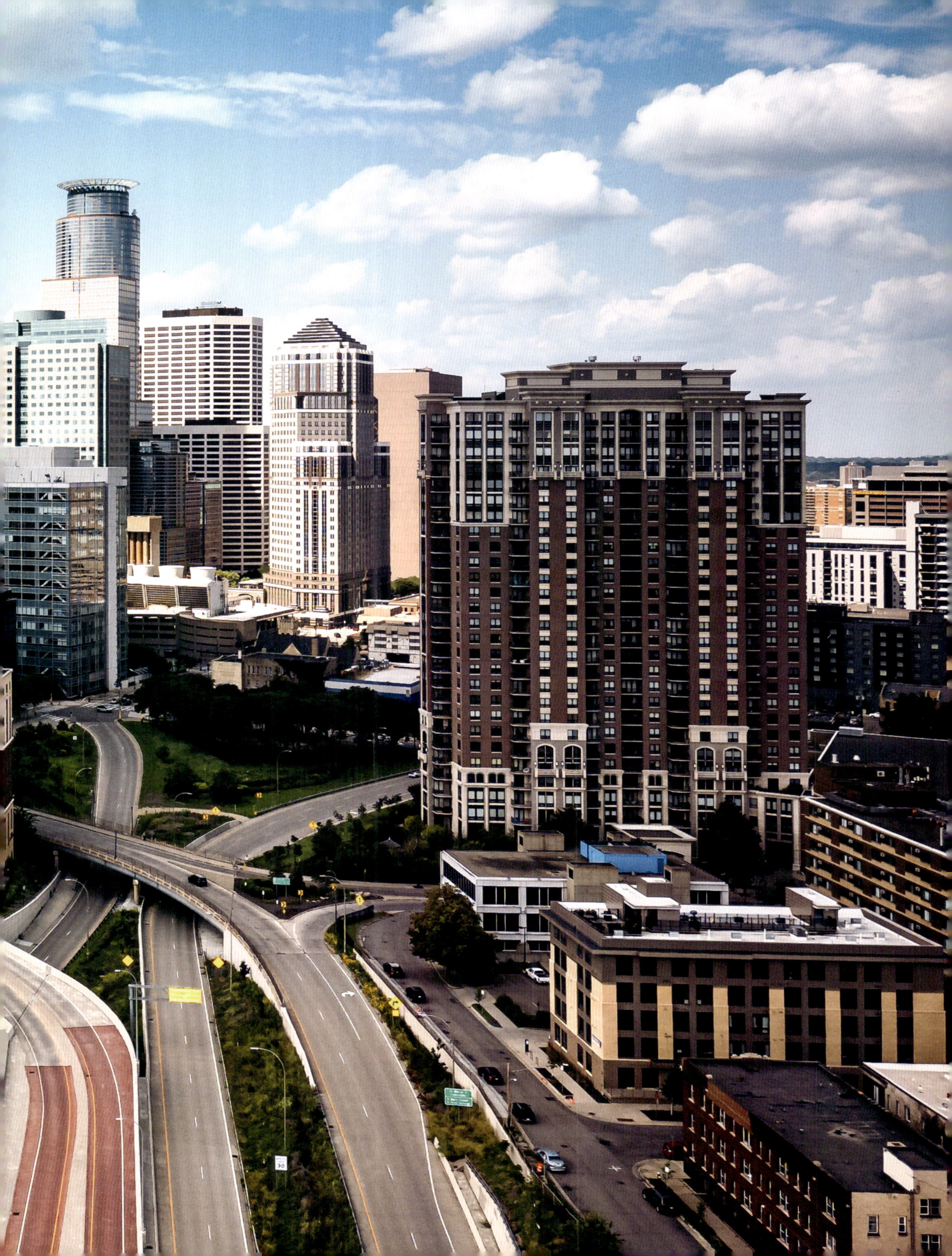

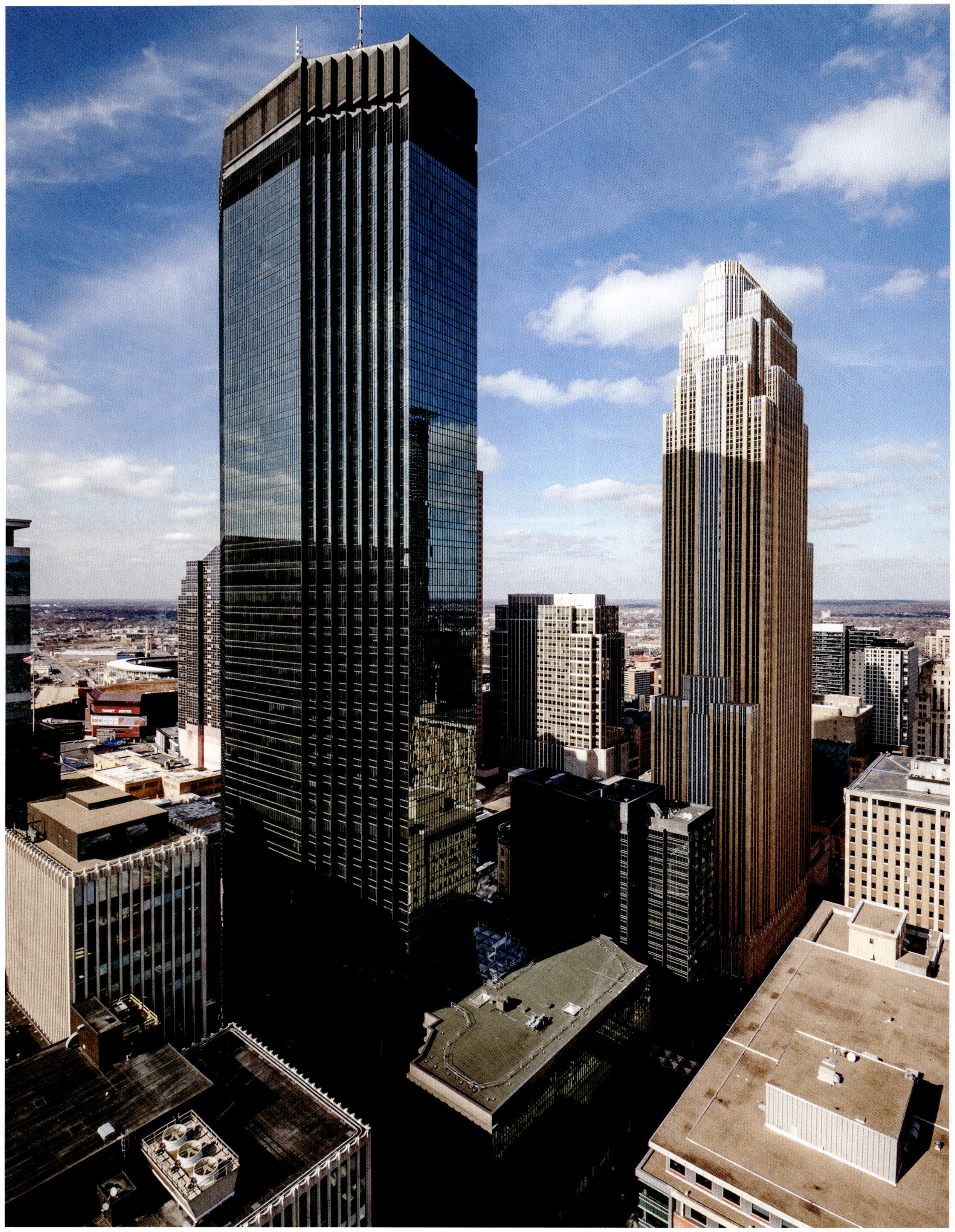

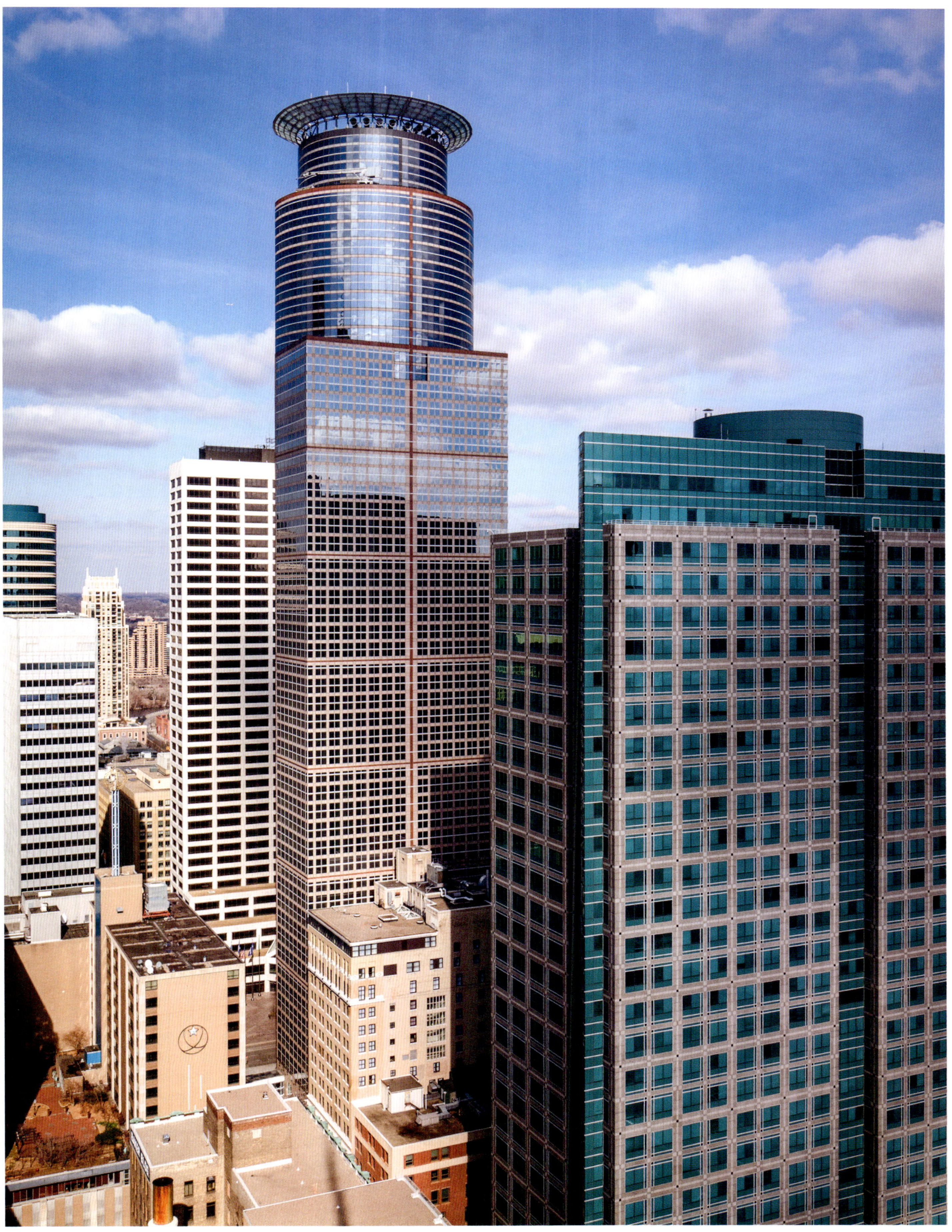

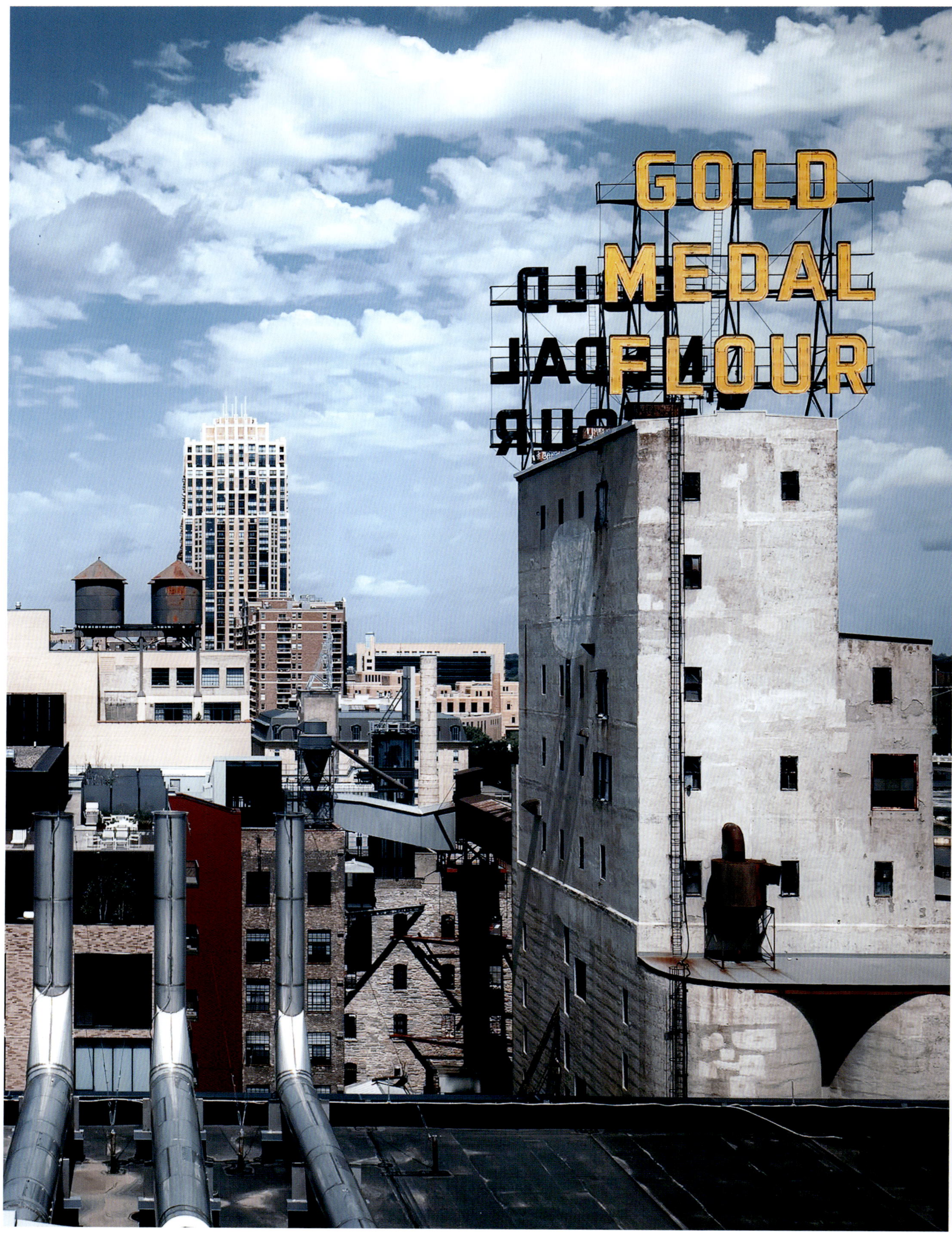

GOLD
MEDAL
FLOUR

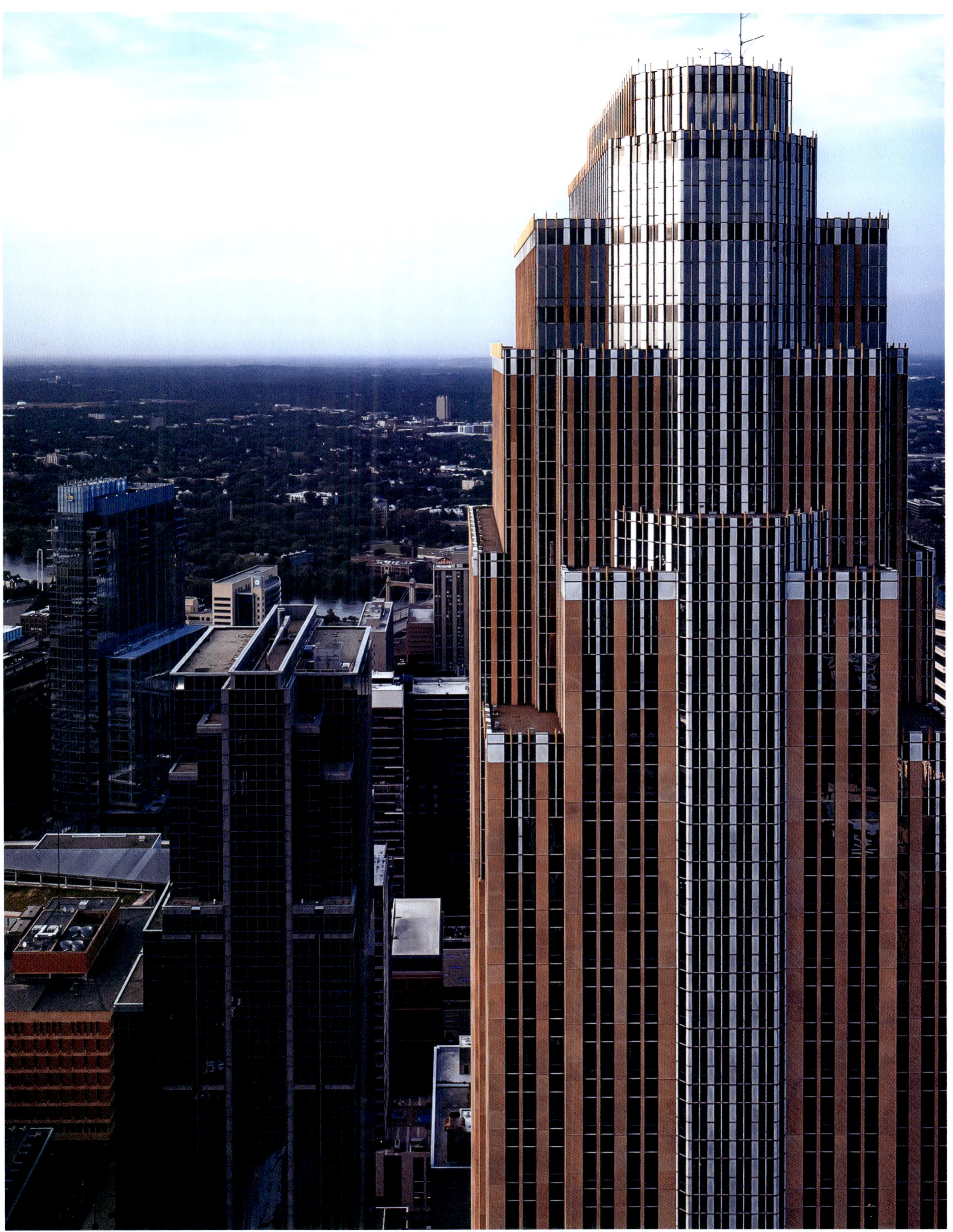

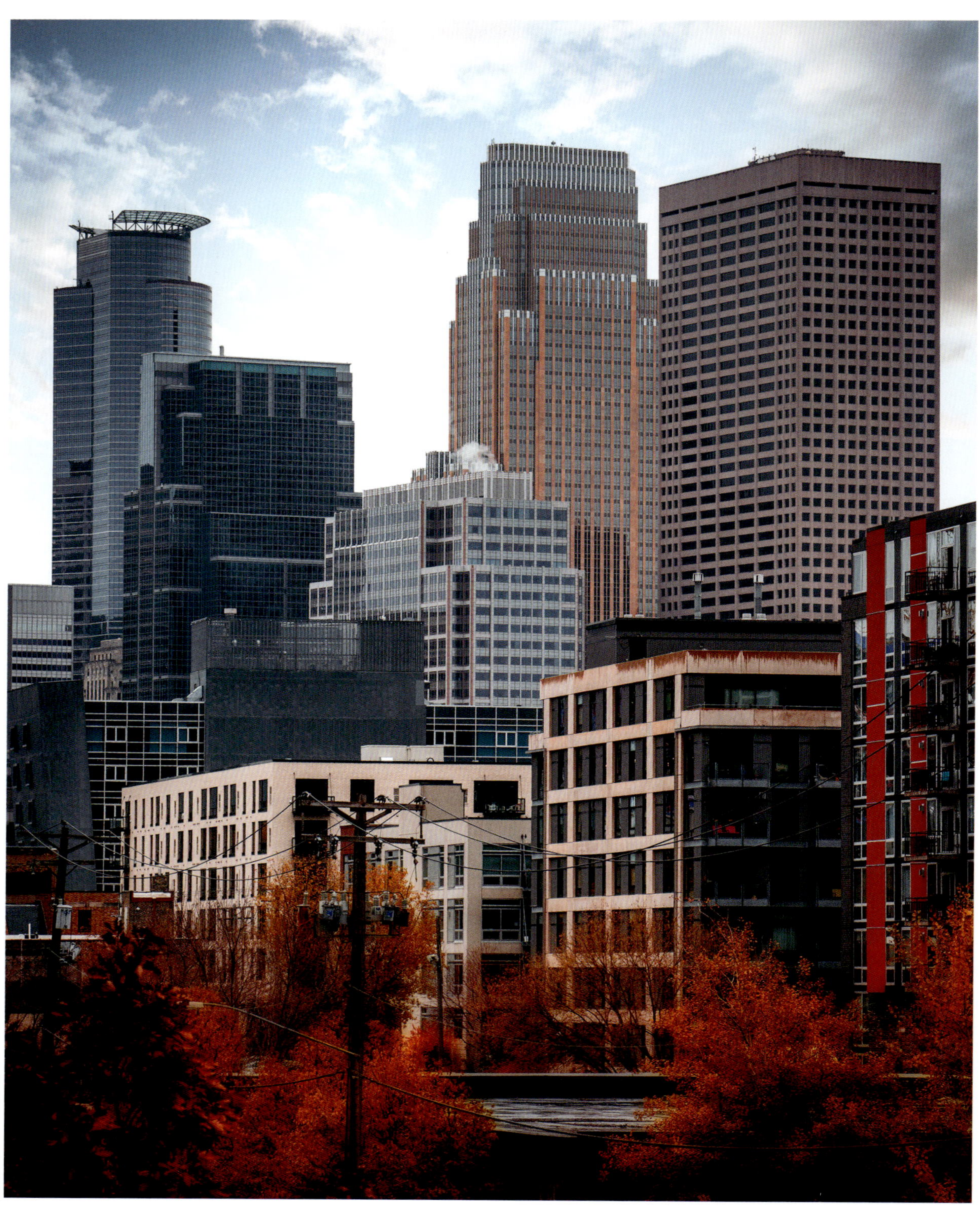

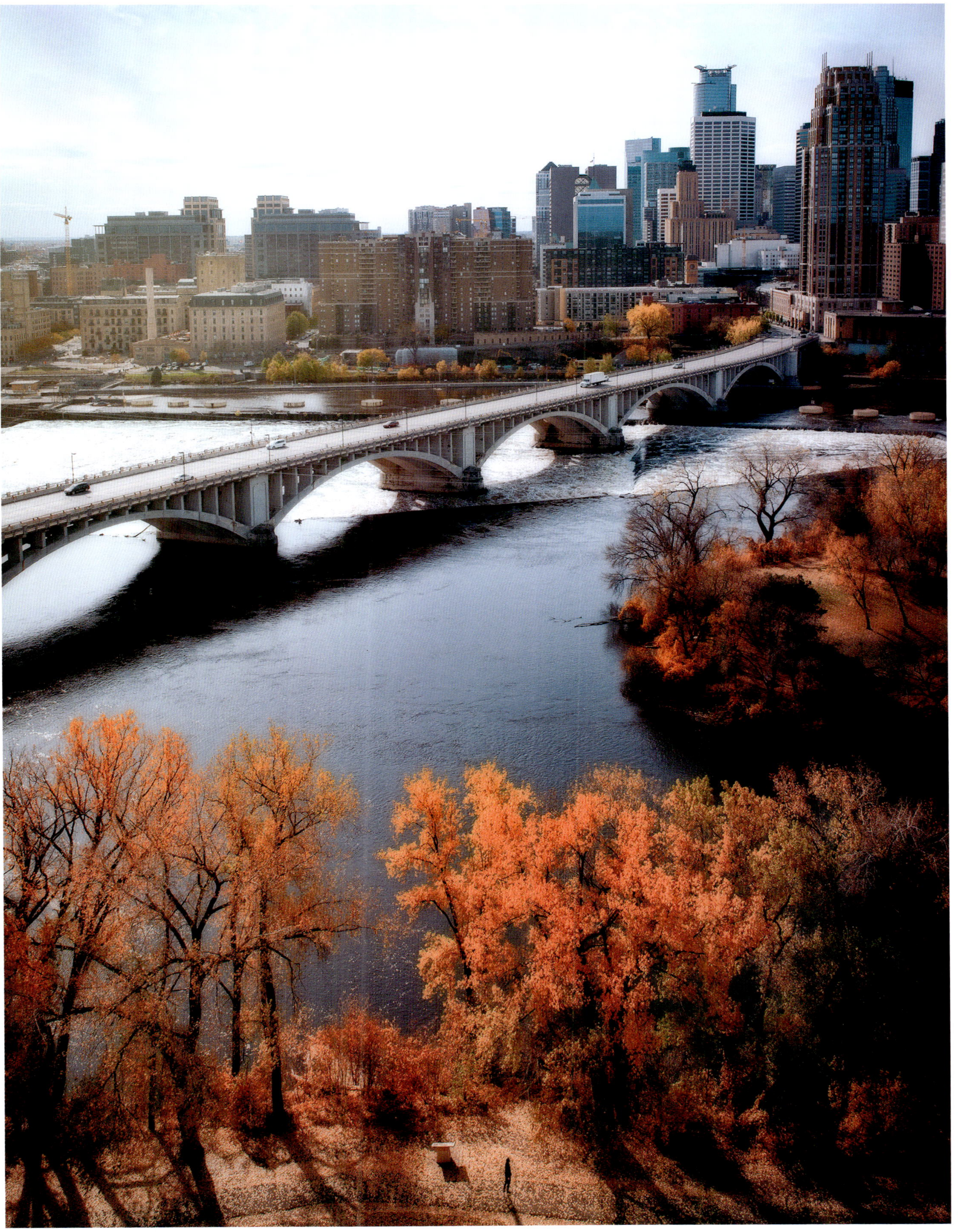

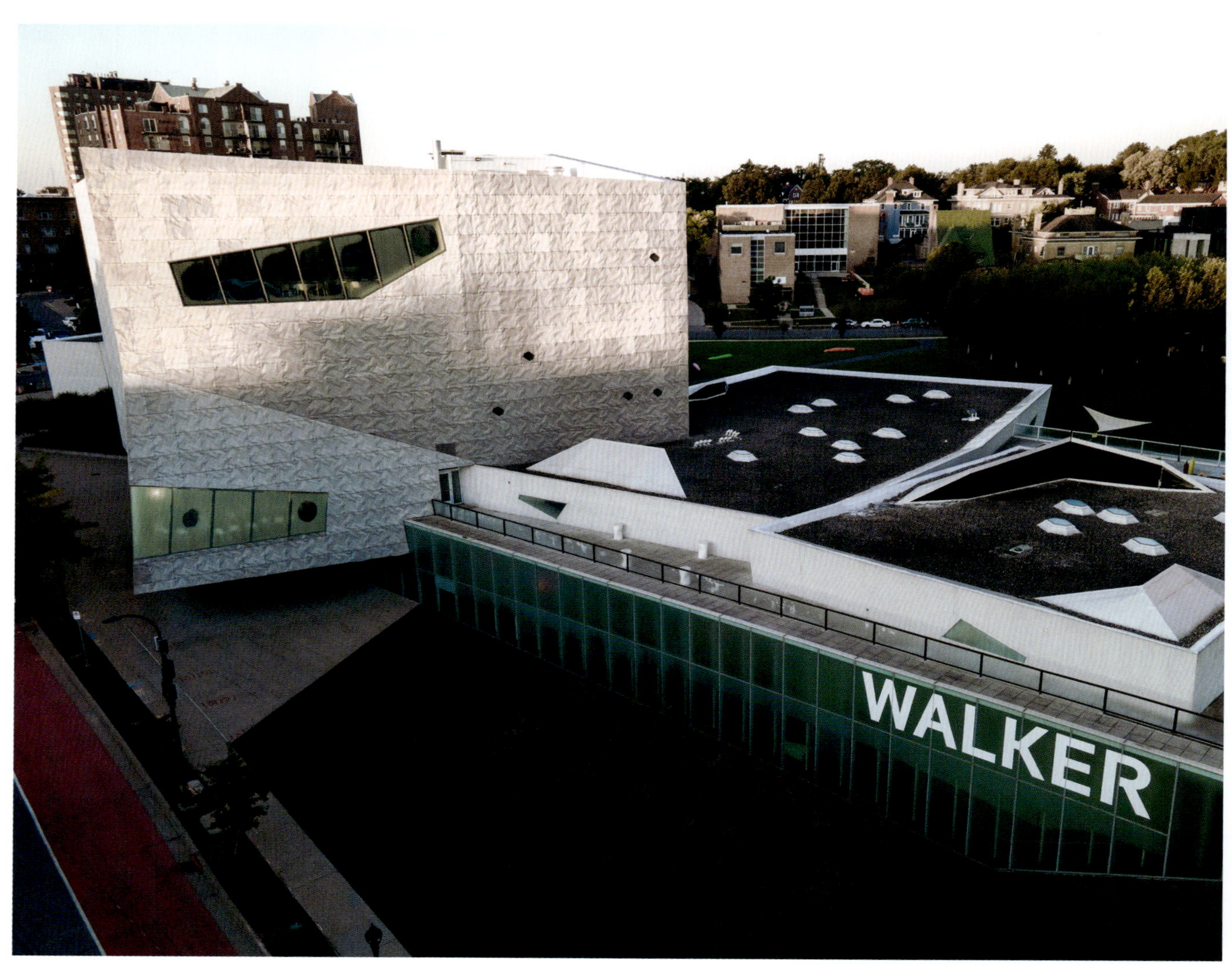

WALKER

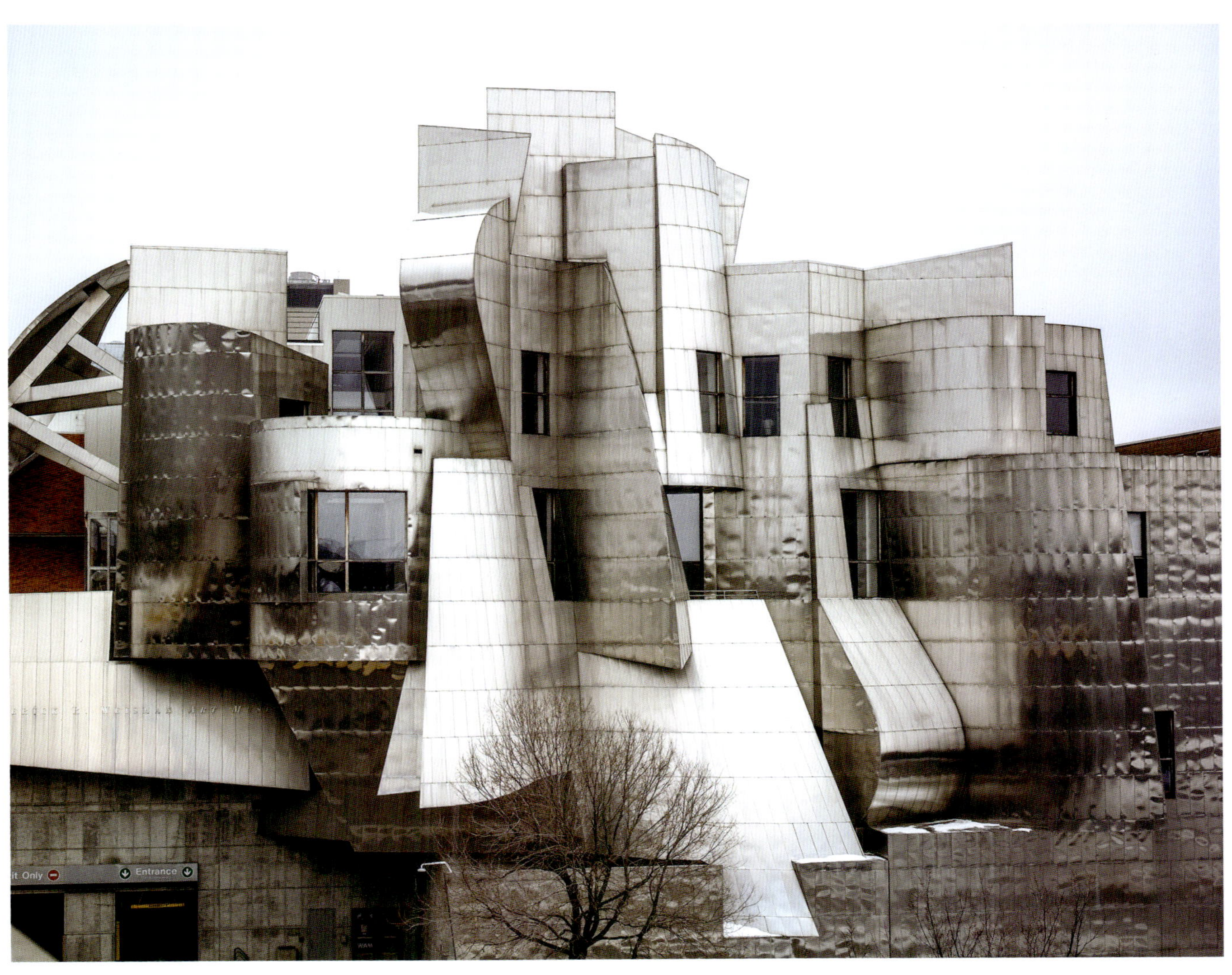

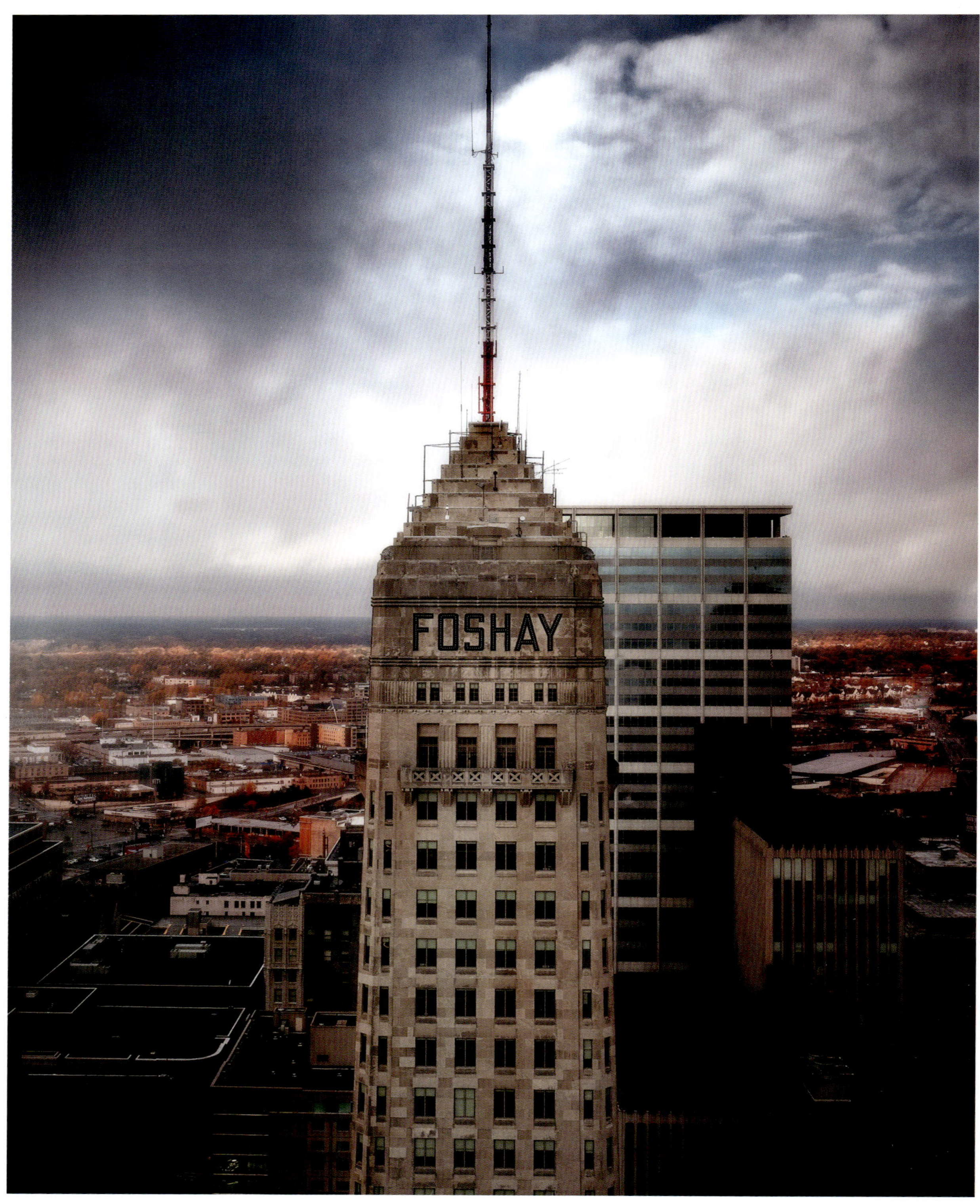
FOSHAY

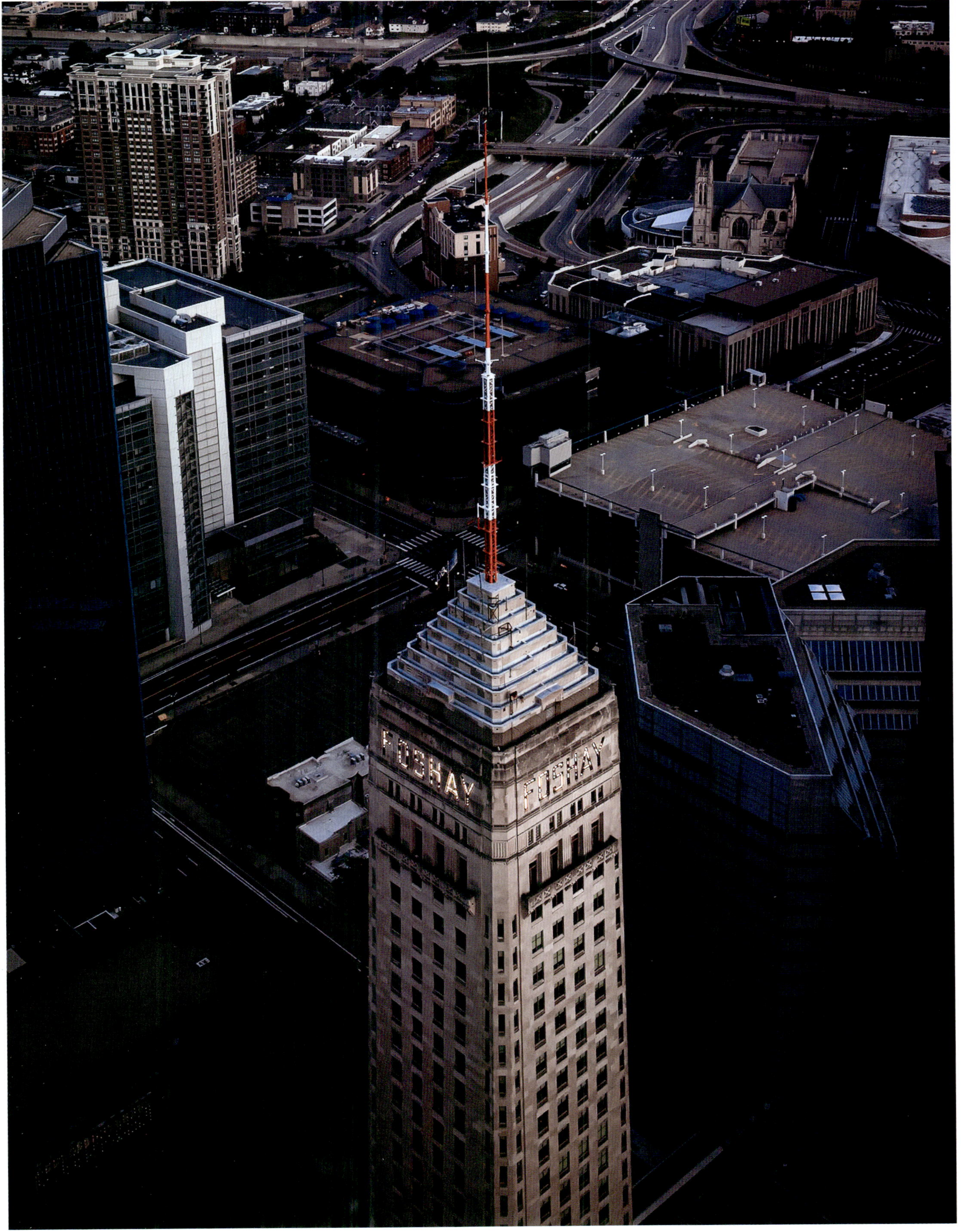
FOSHAY
FOSHAY

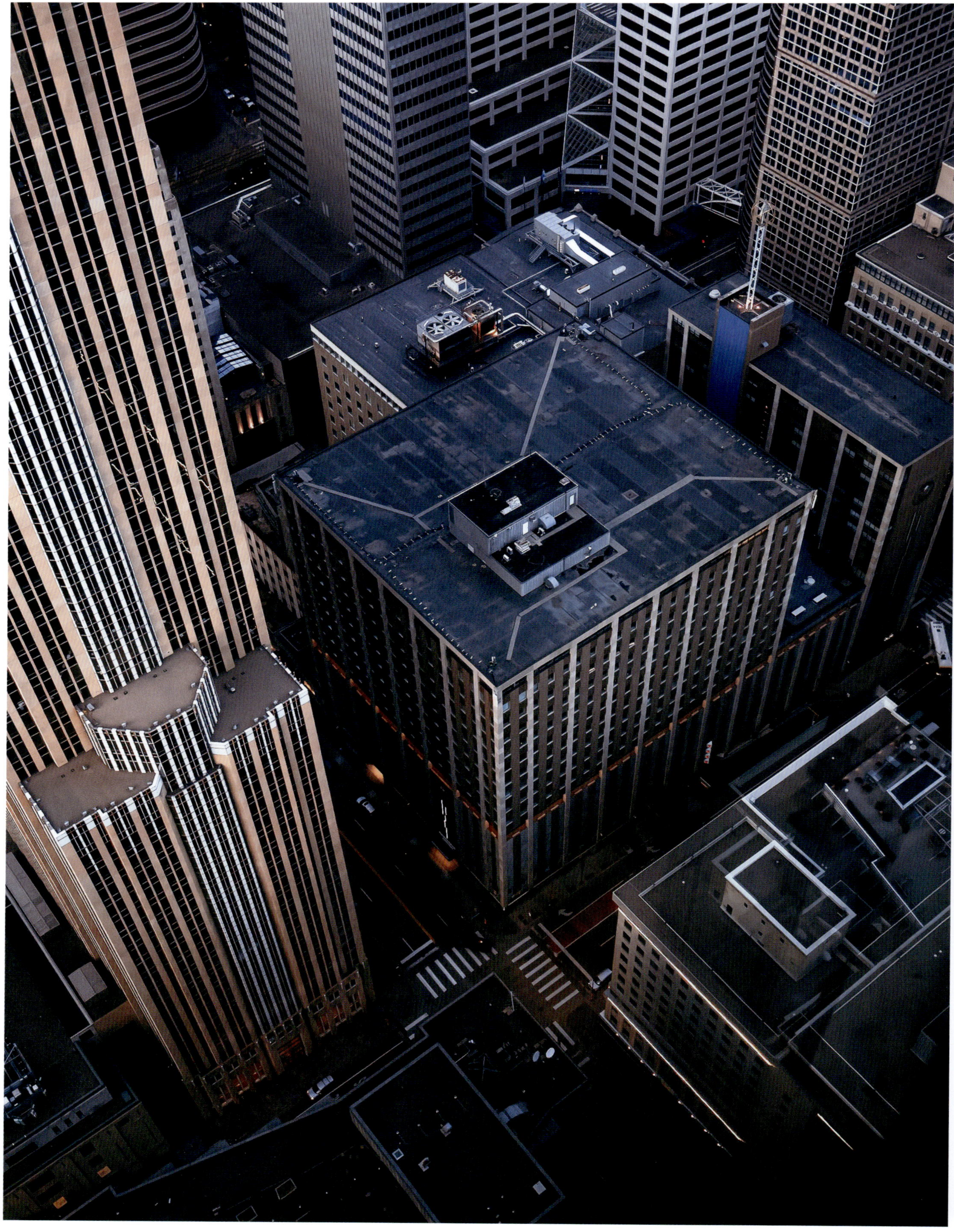

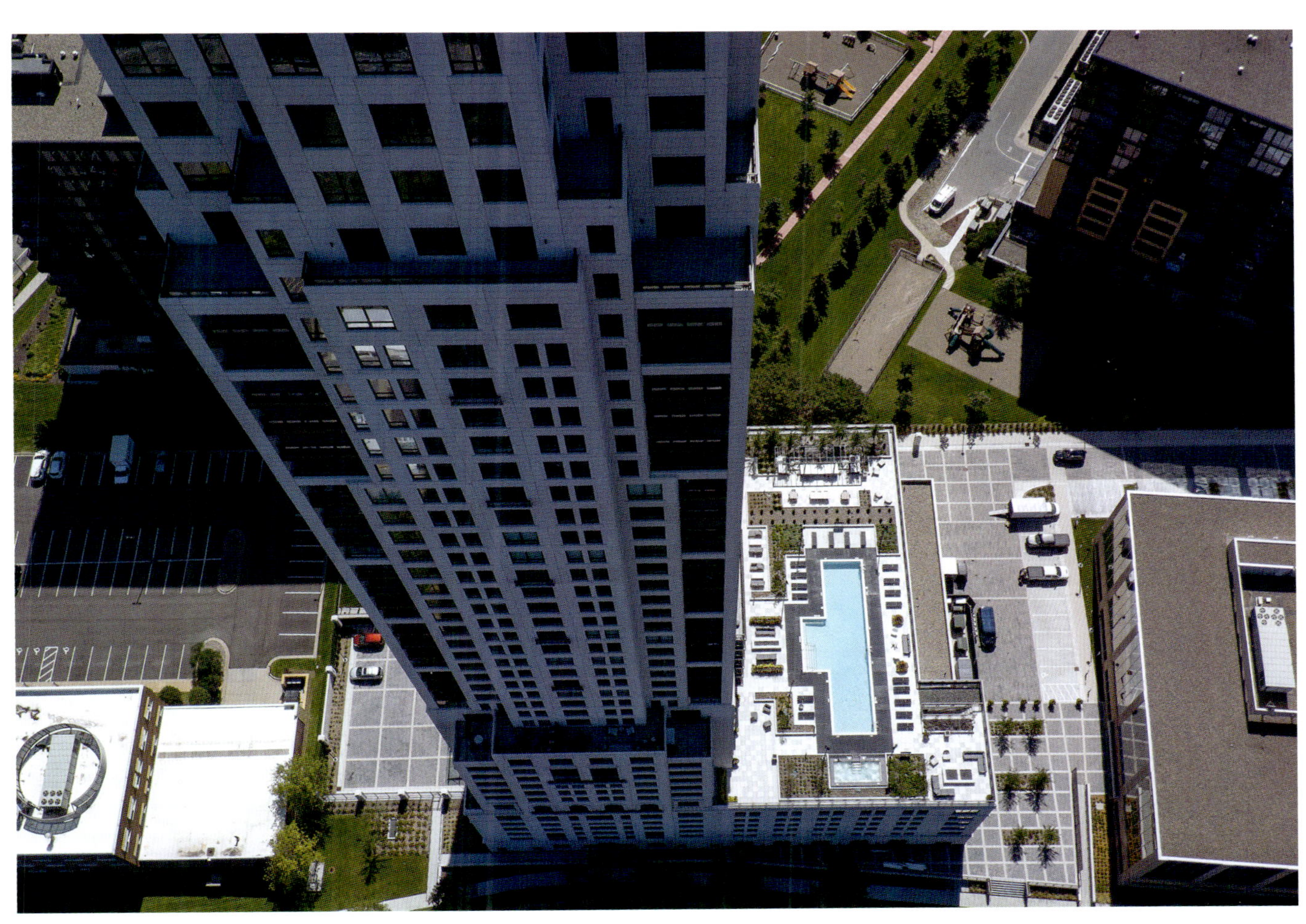

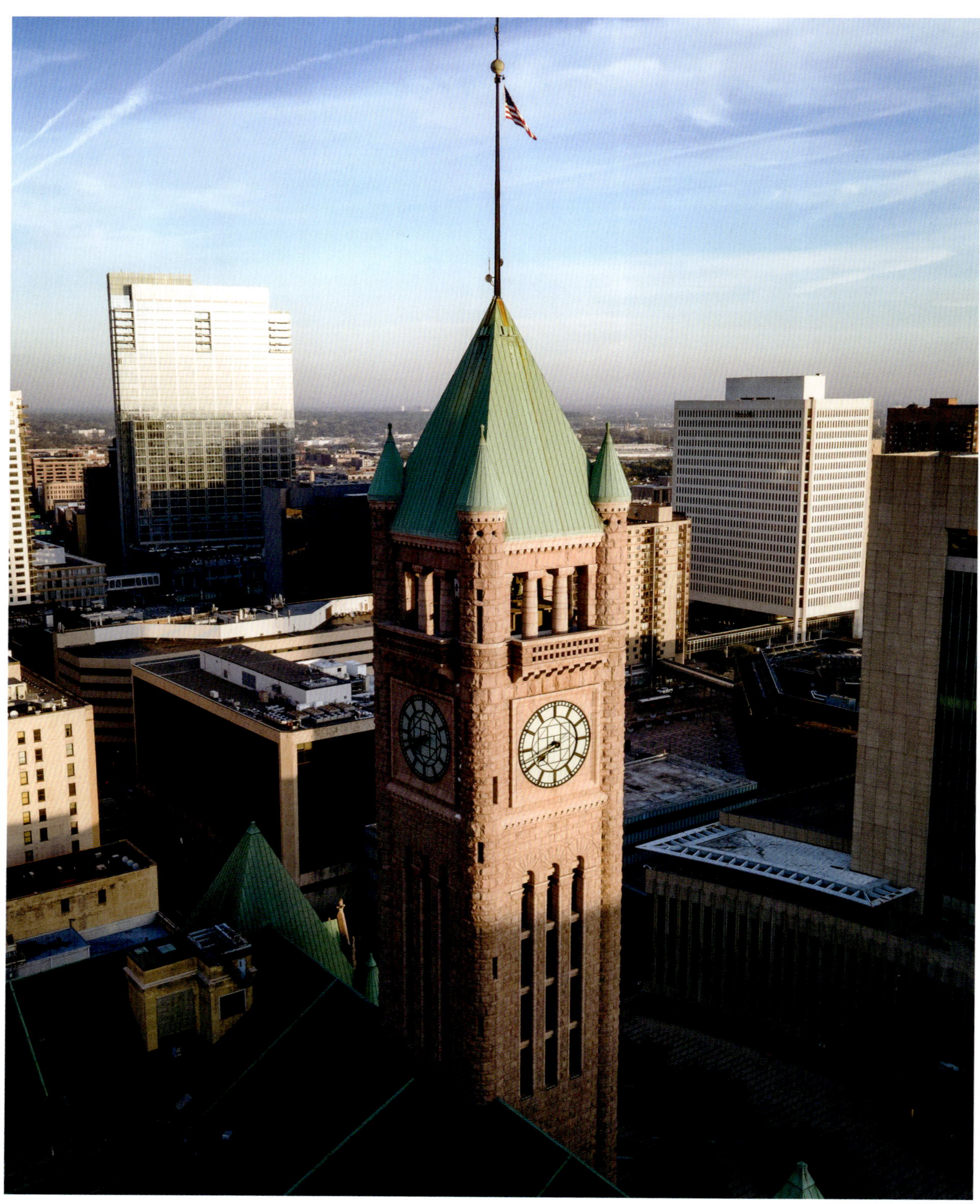

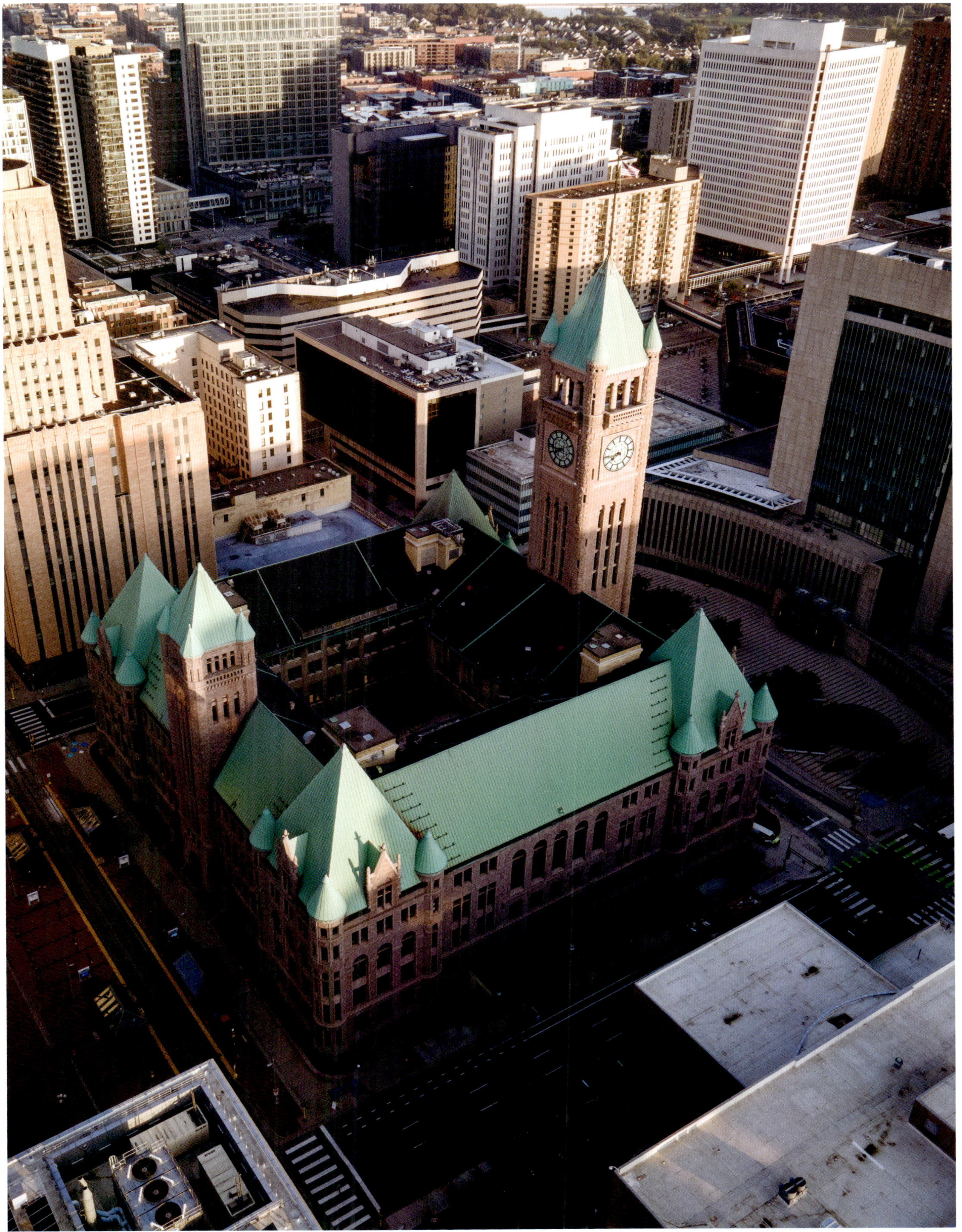

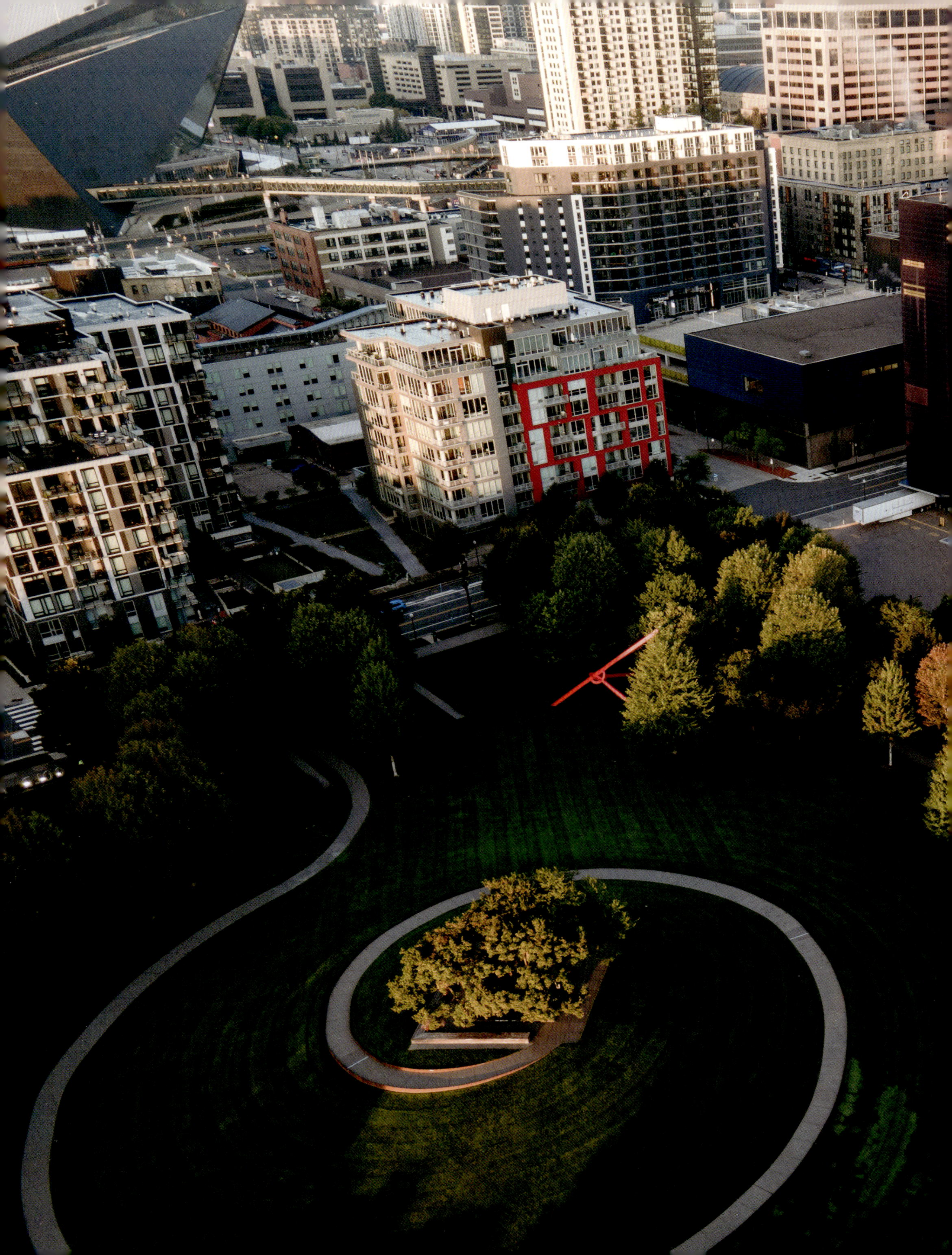

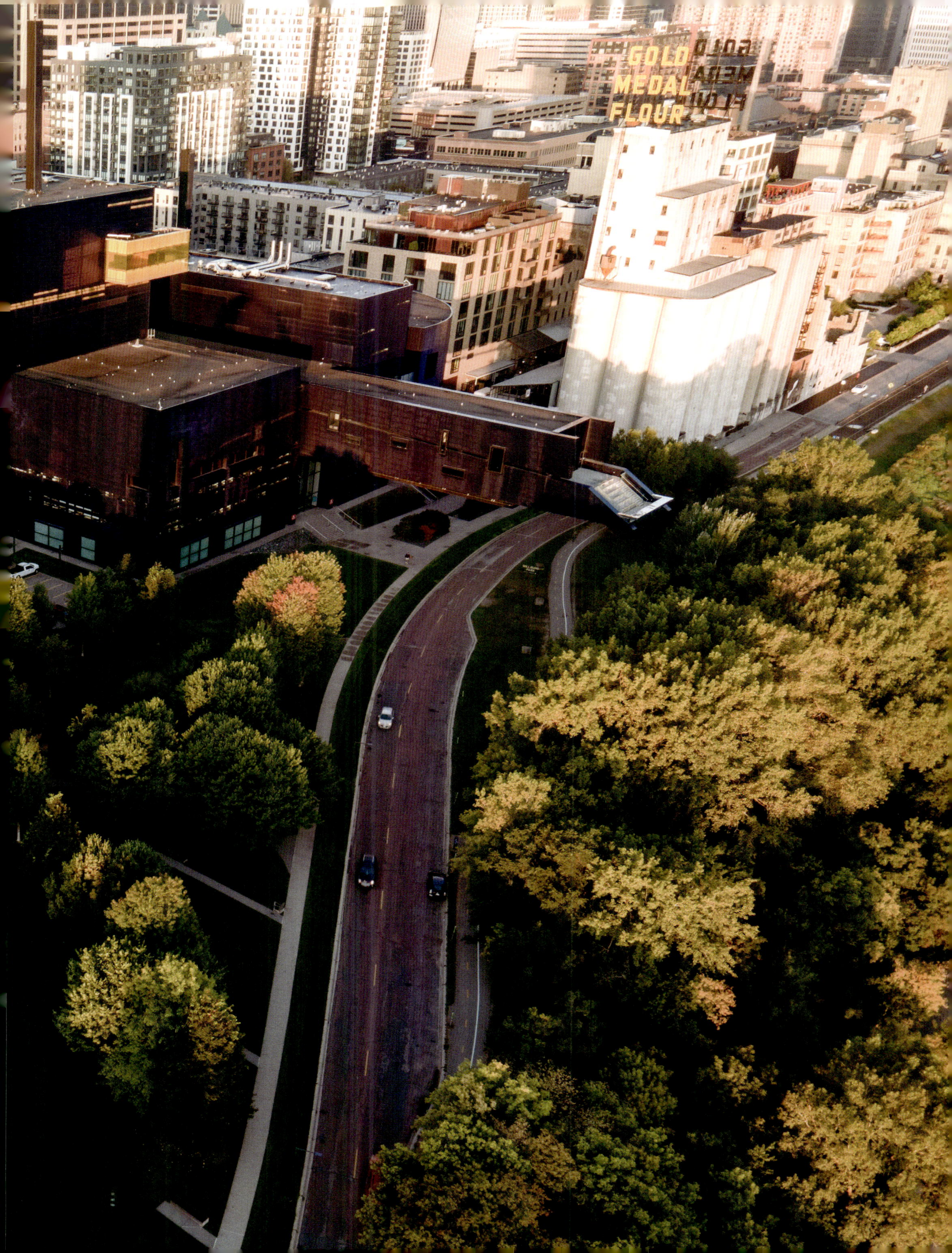

GOLD
MEDAL
FLOUR

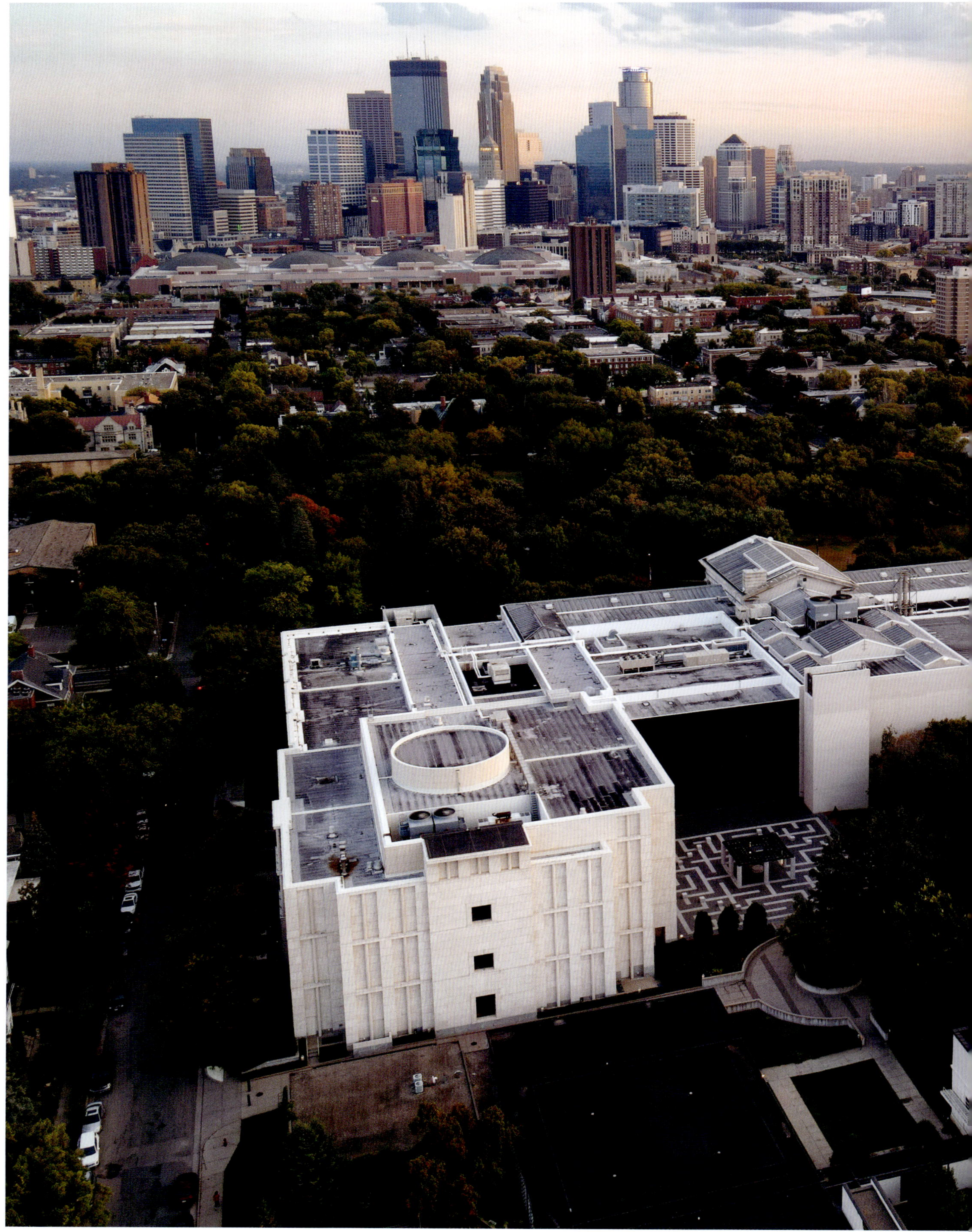

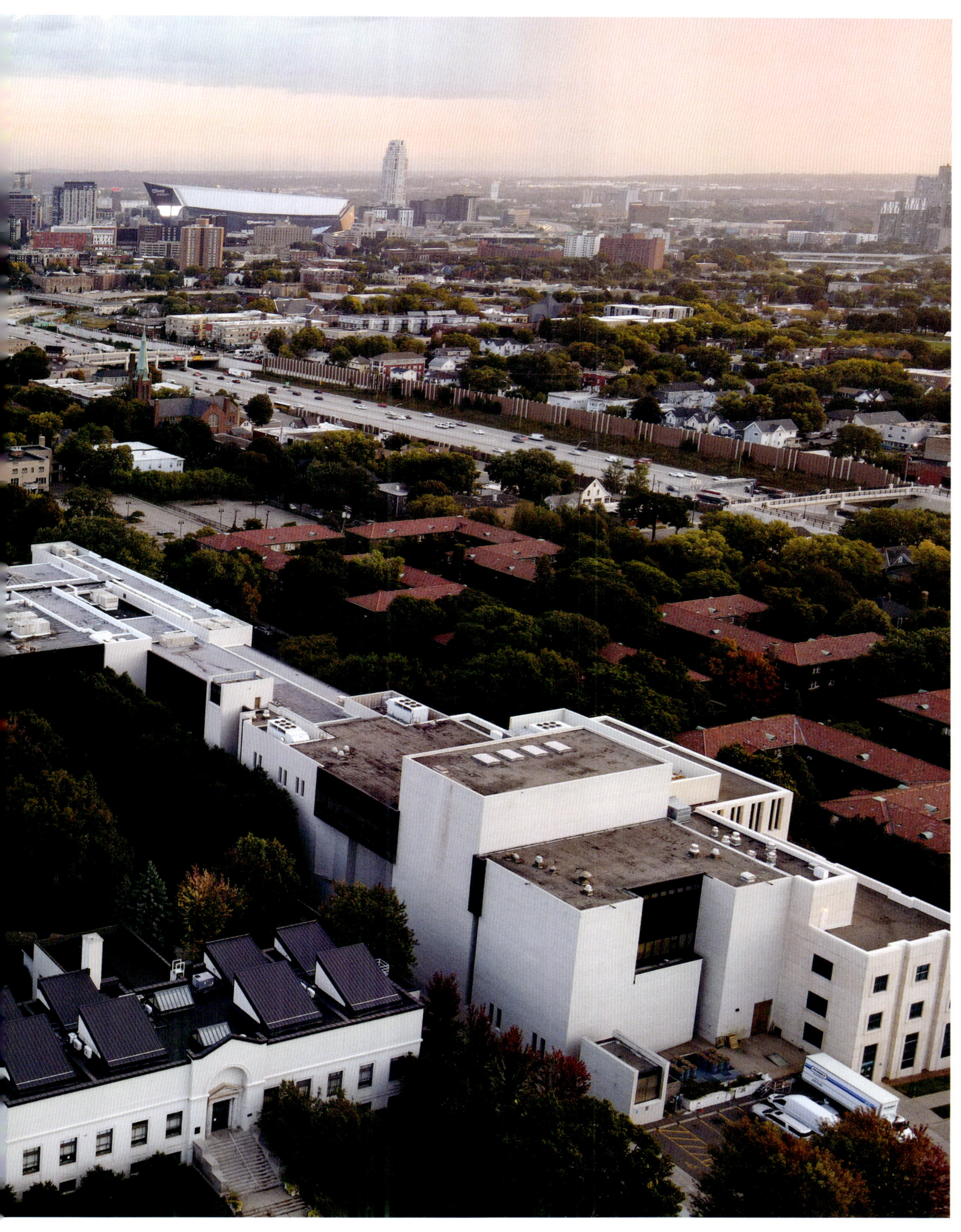

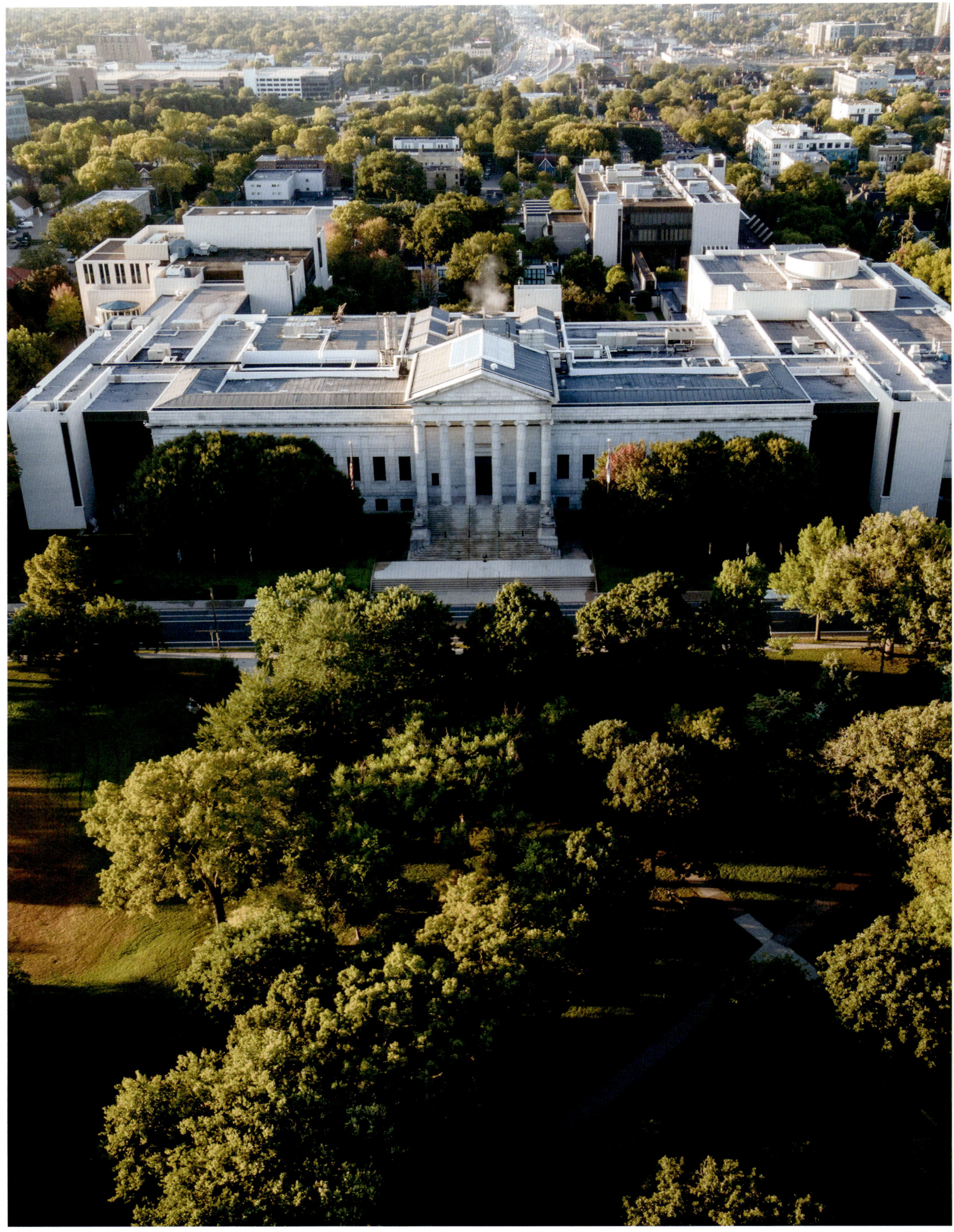

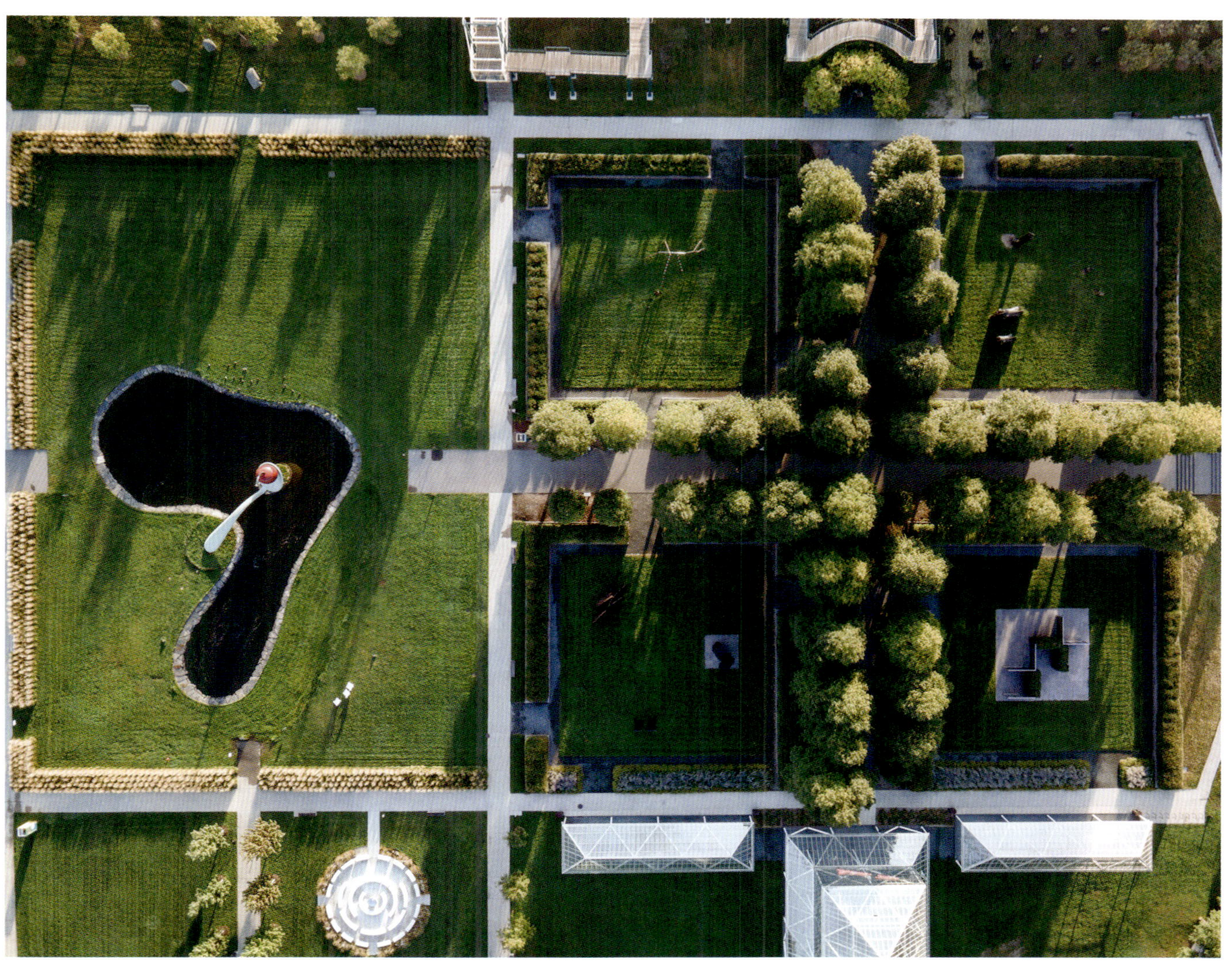

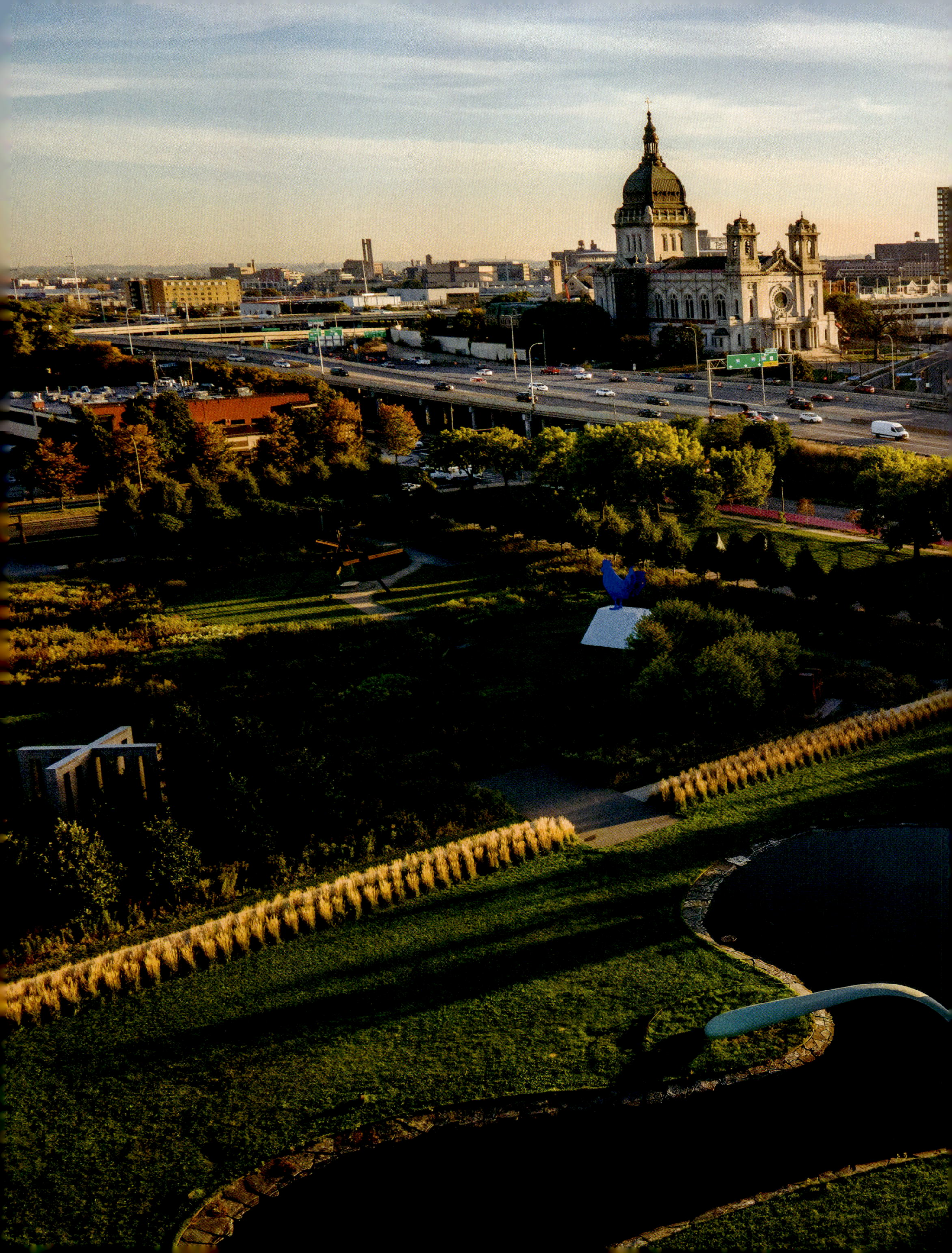

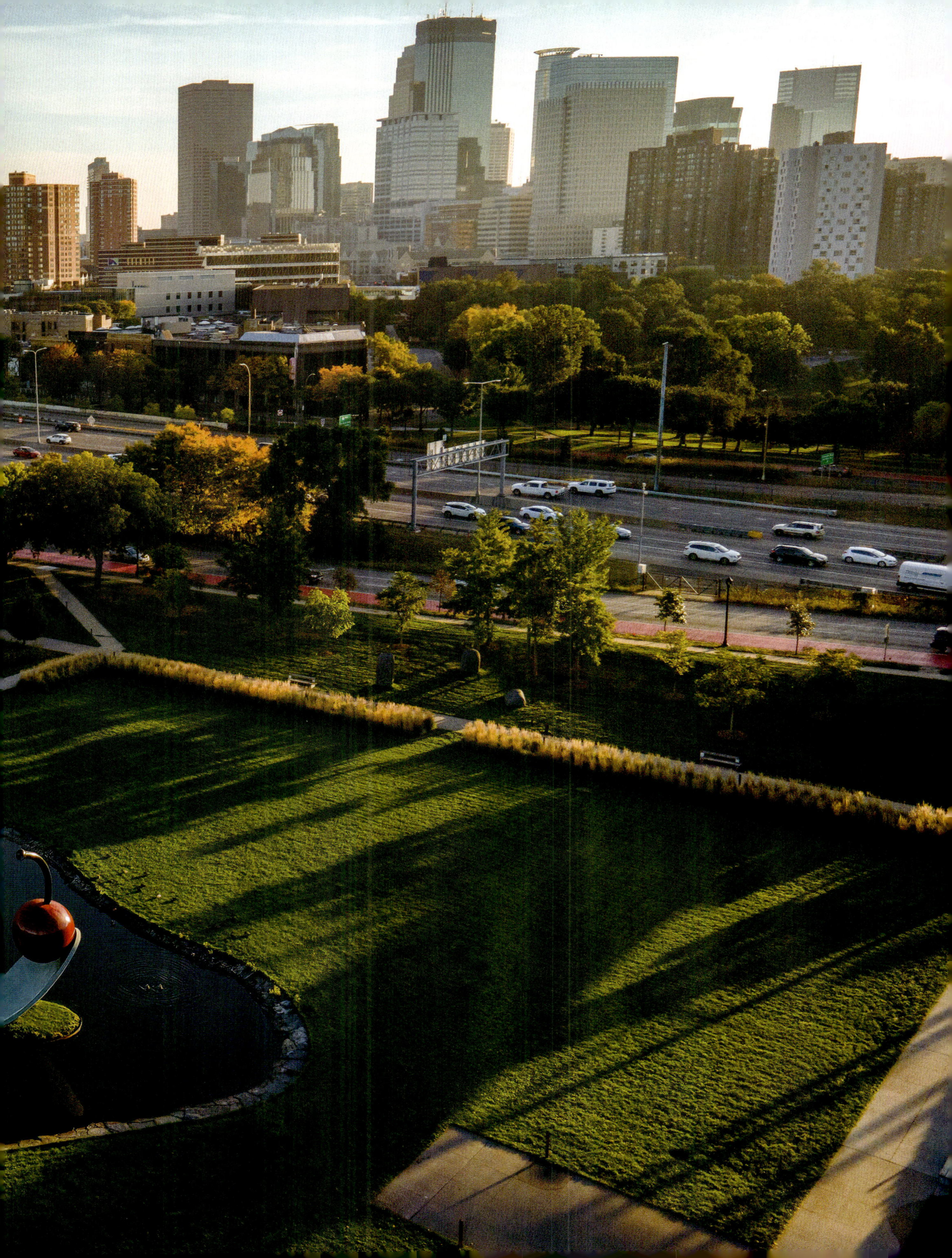

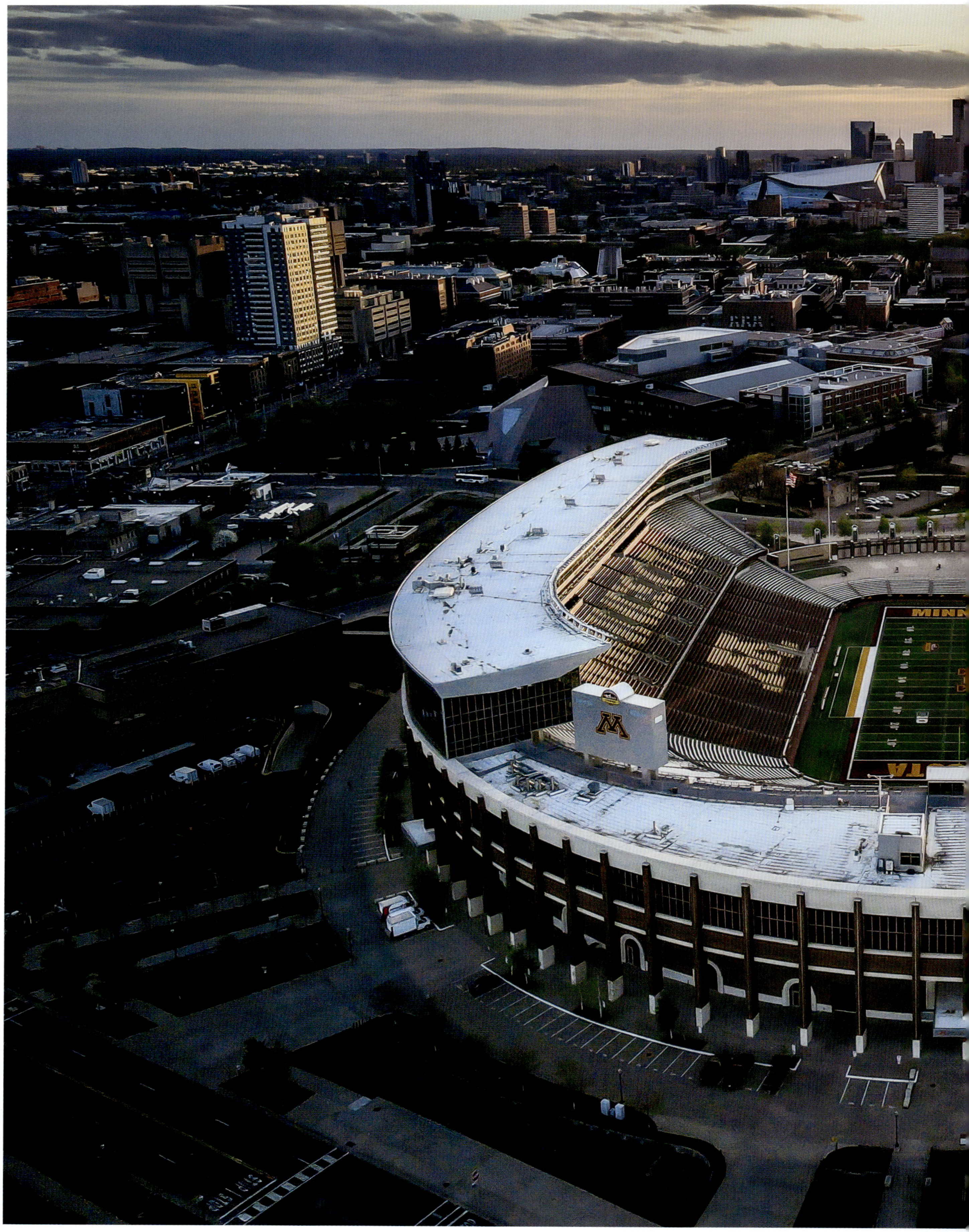

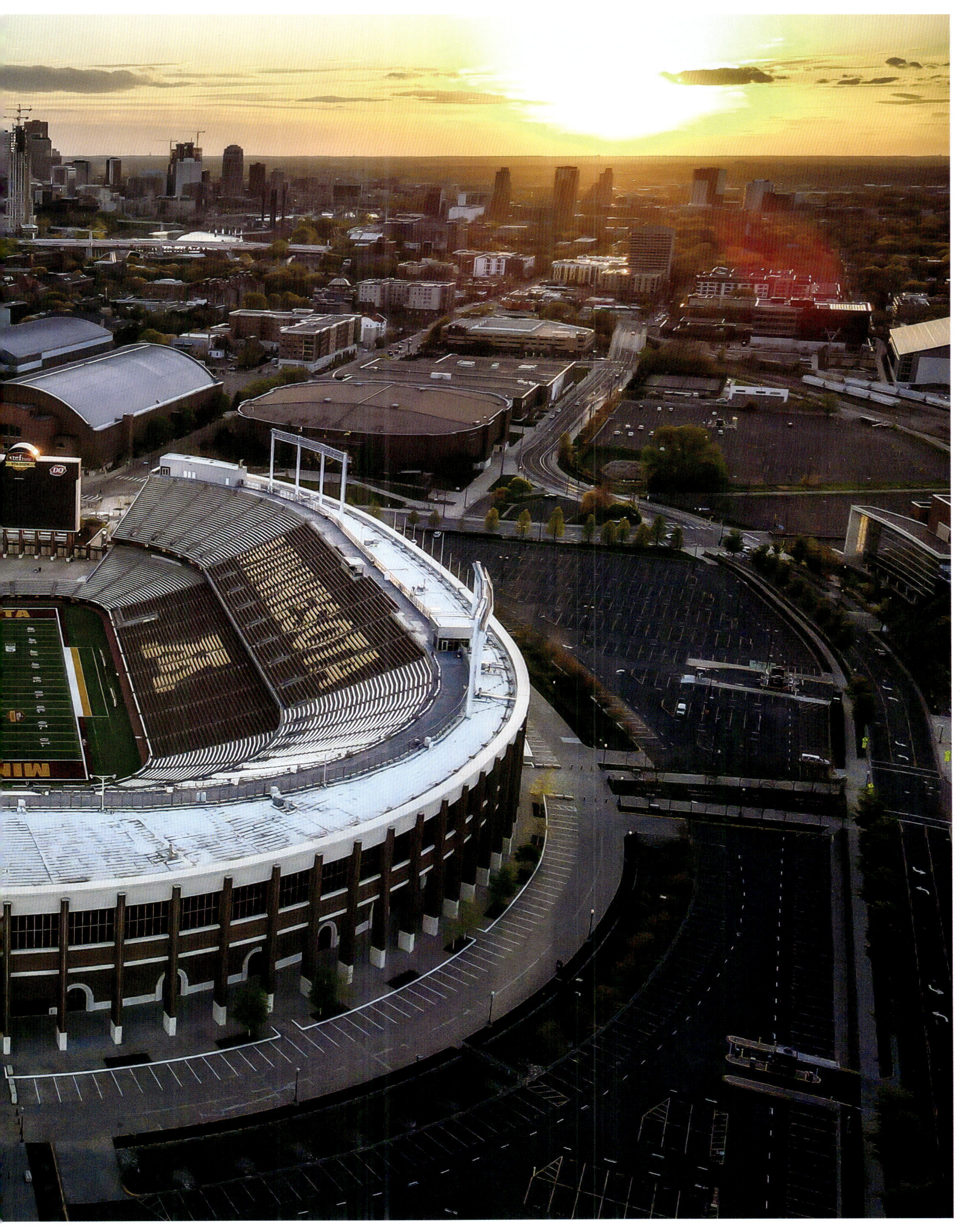

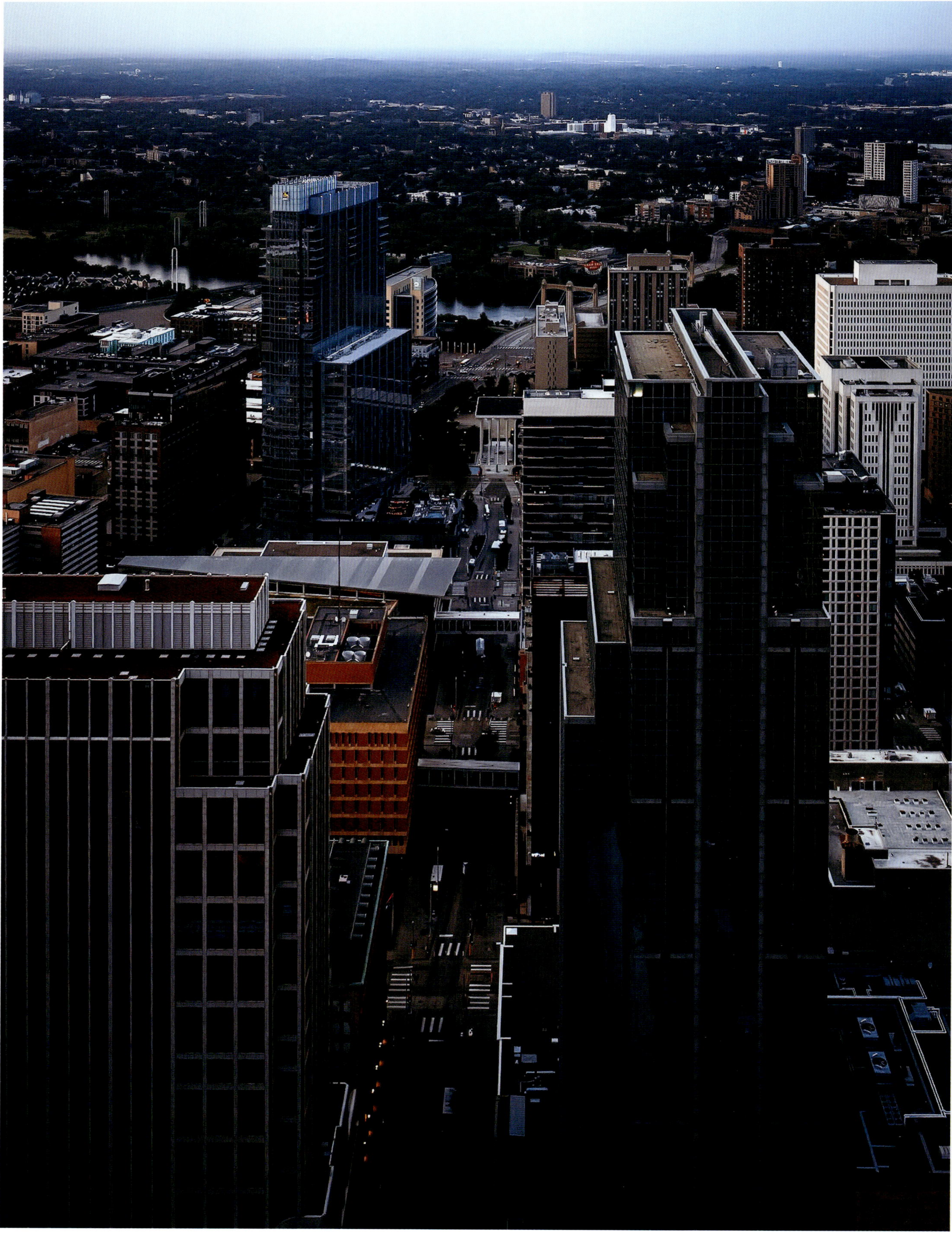

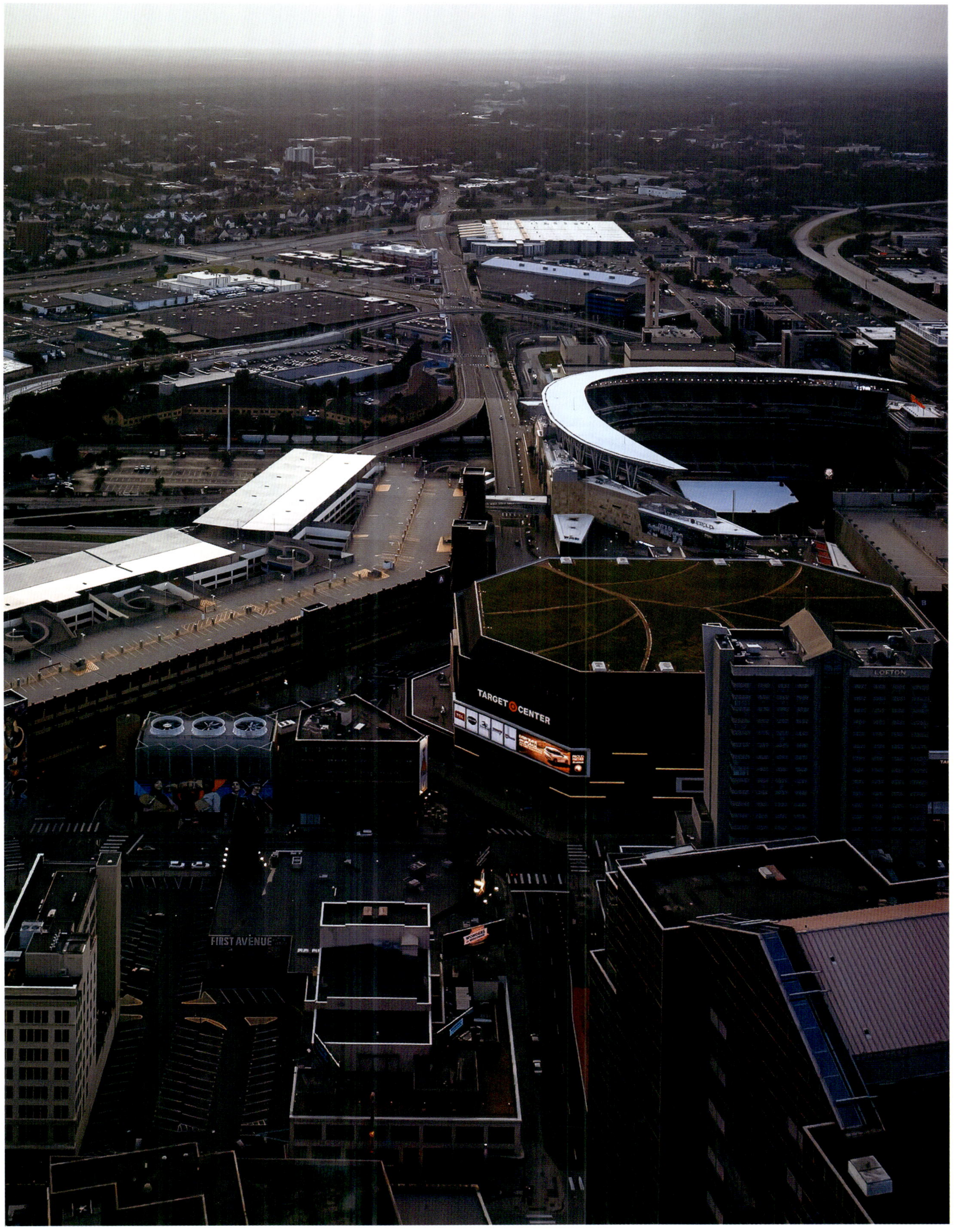

TARGET CENTER
FIRST AVENUE
LOFTON

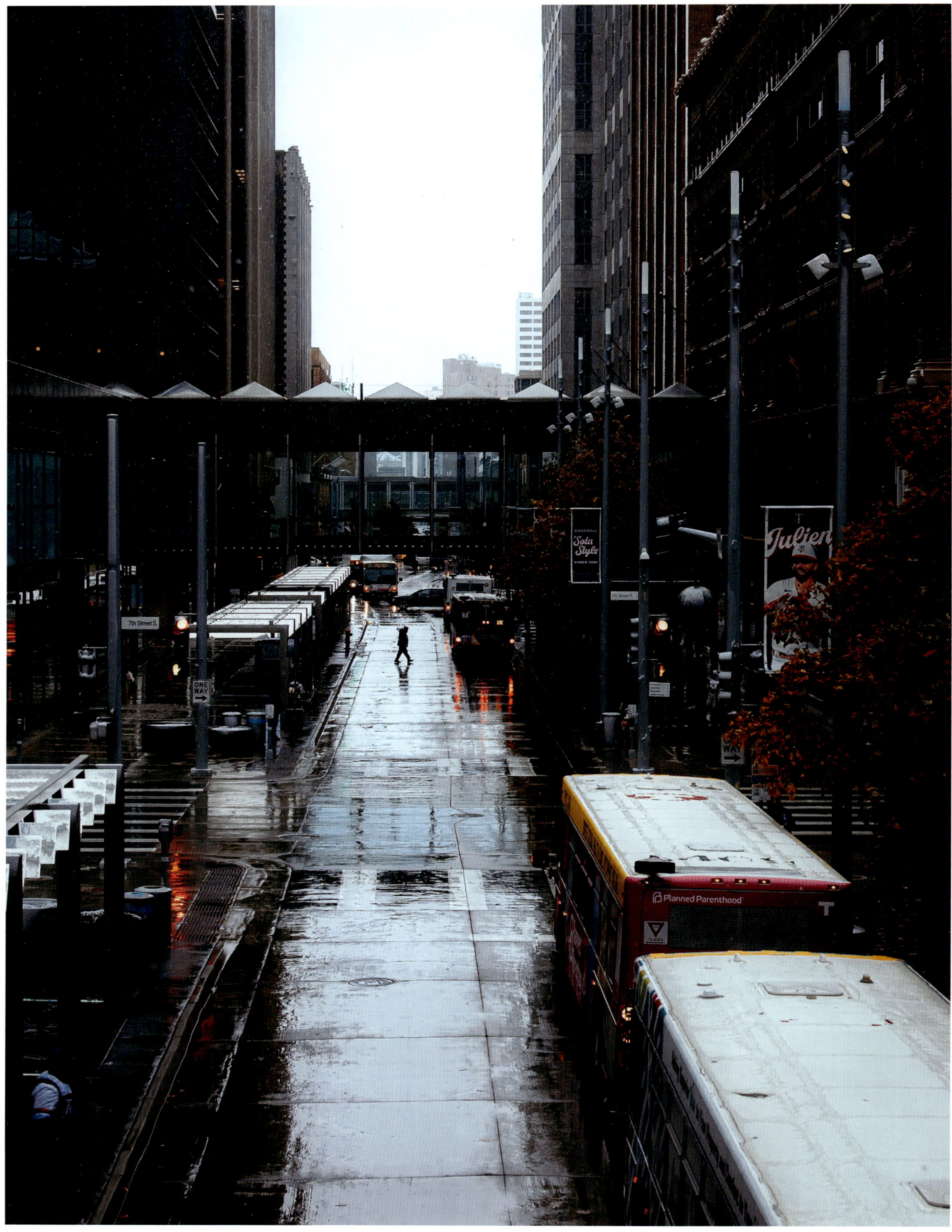

7th Street S.
7th Street S.
ONE WAY
Sota Style
Julien
Planned Parenthood
T

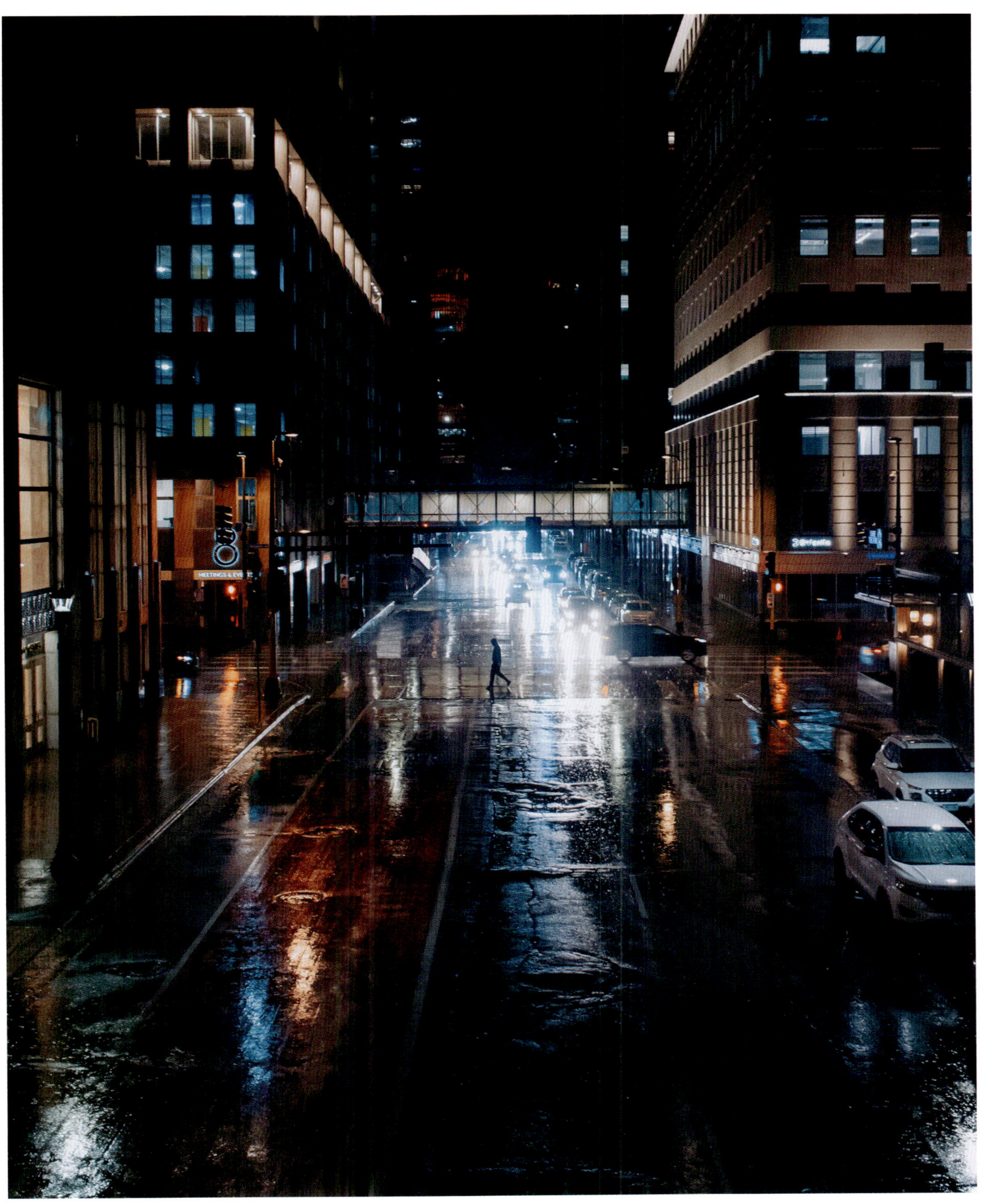

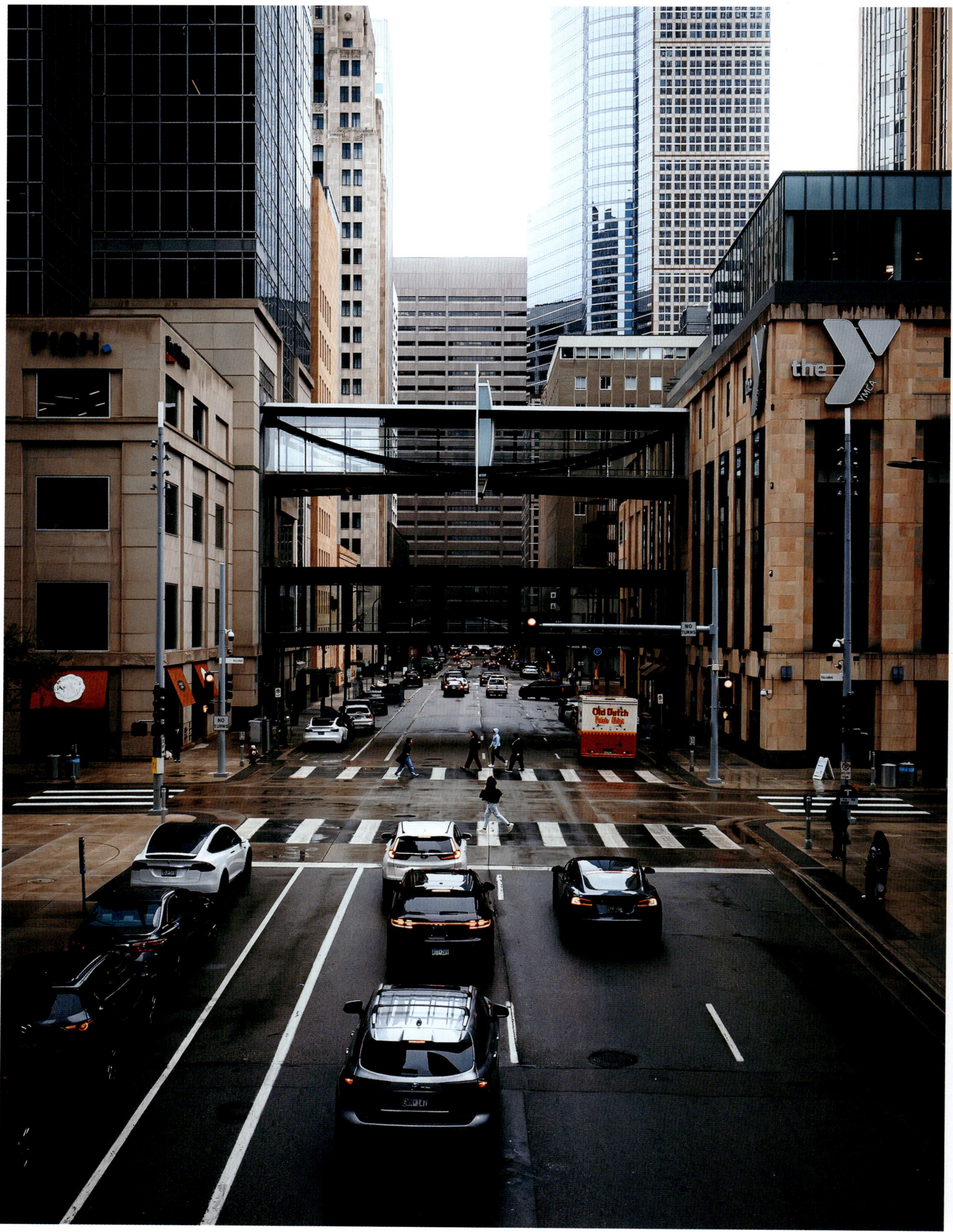

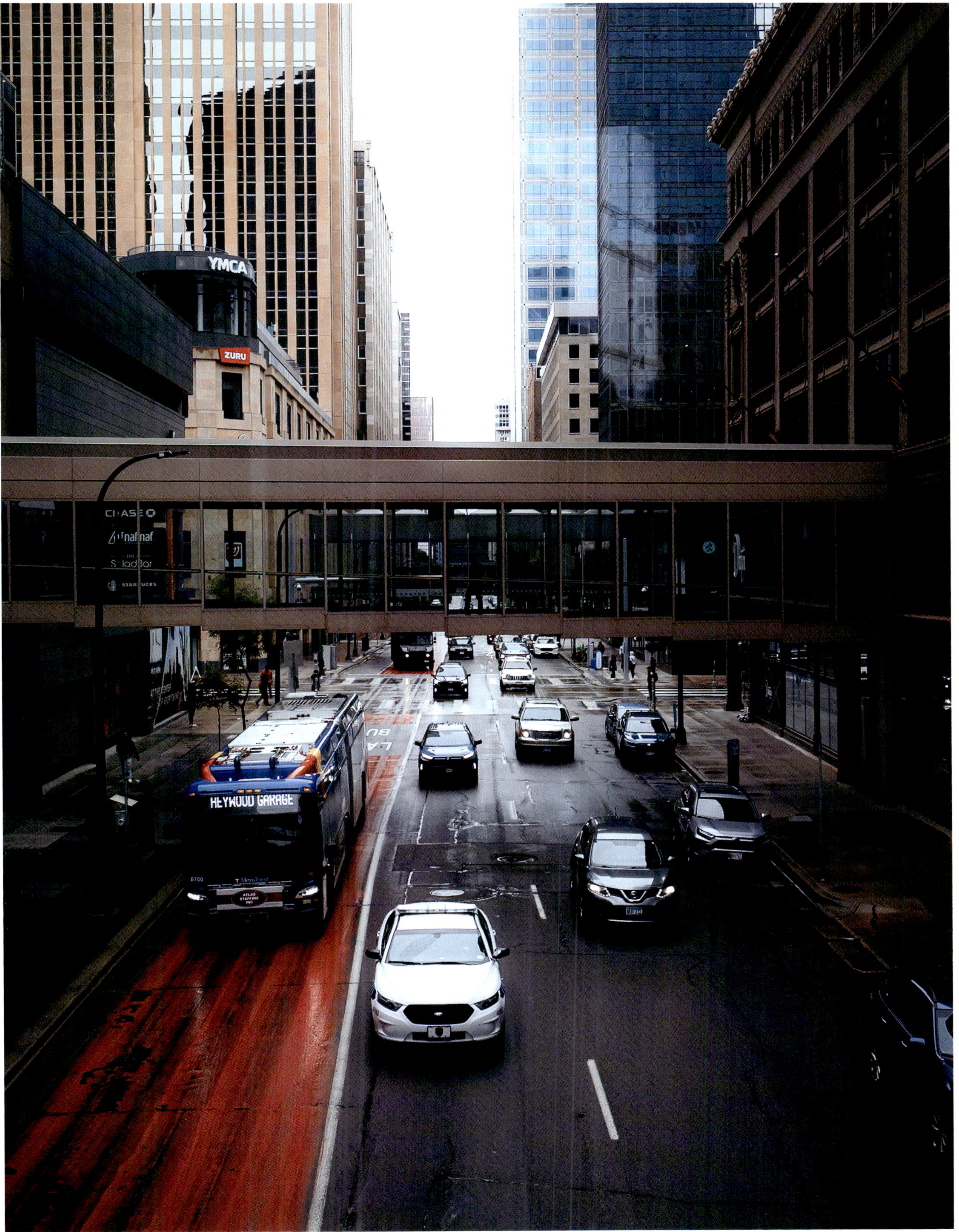

YMCA
ZURU
CHASE
naf naf
THE SaladBar
STARBUCKS
HEYWOOD GARAGE
ATLAS STAFFING INC

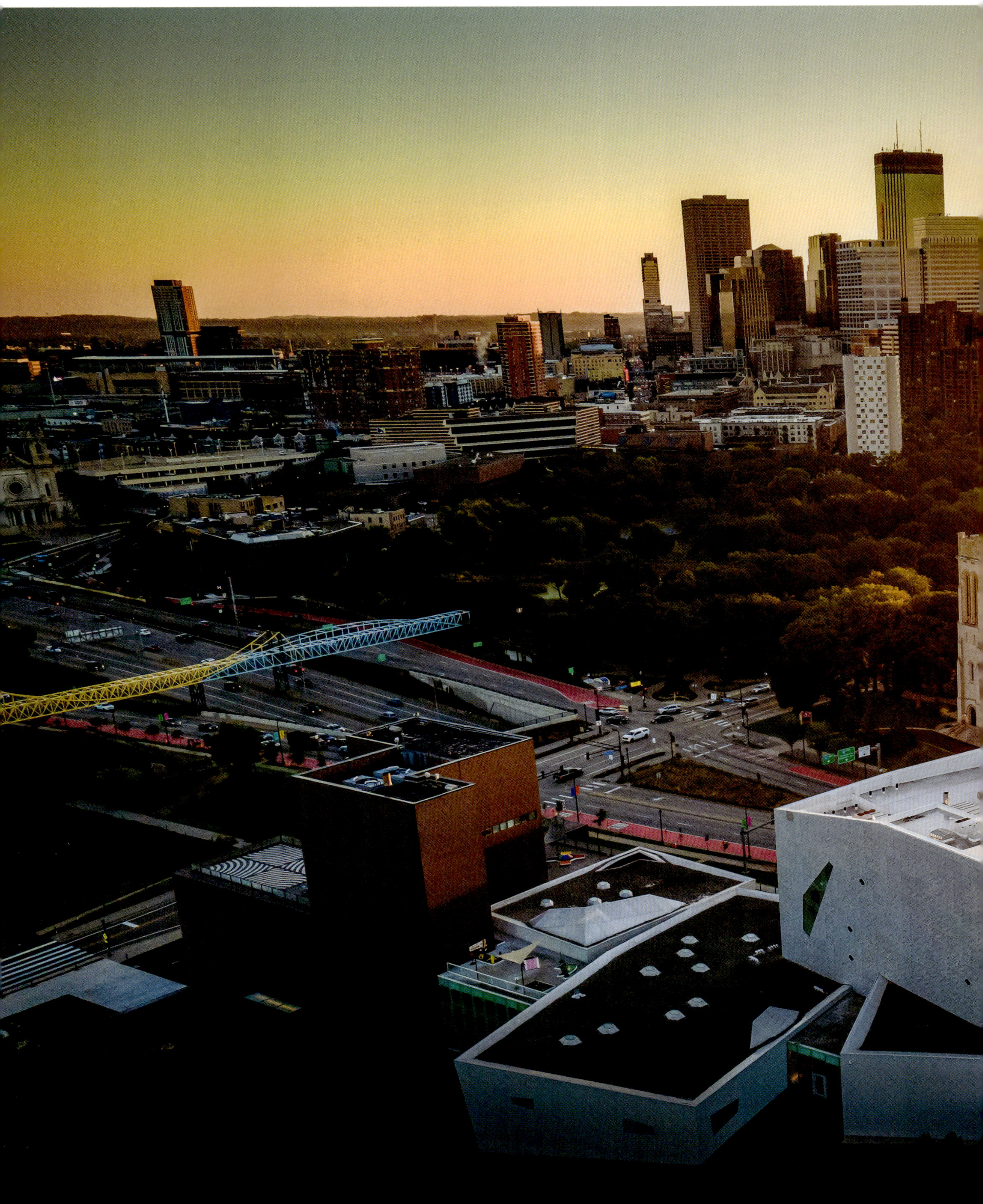

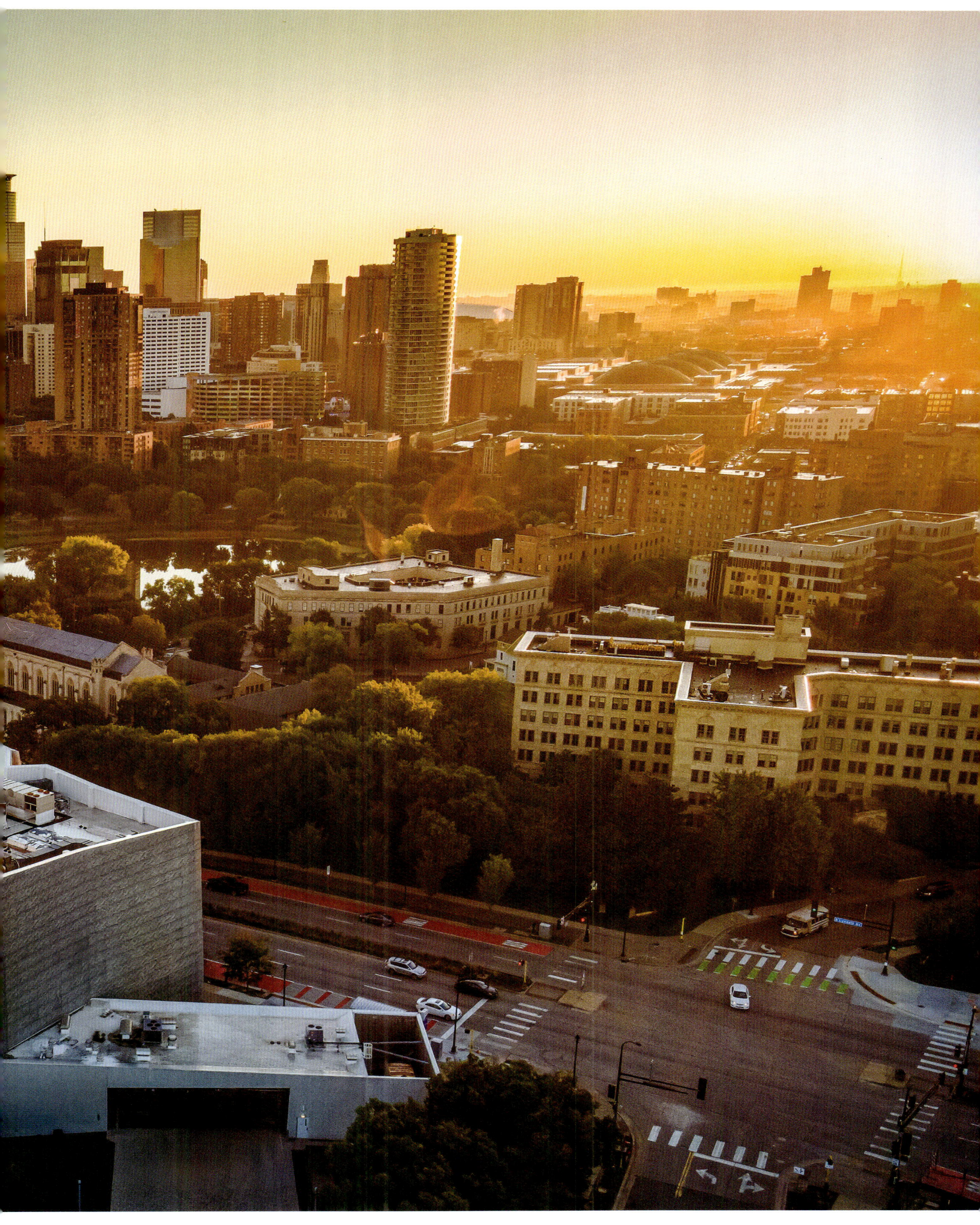

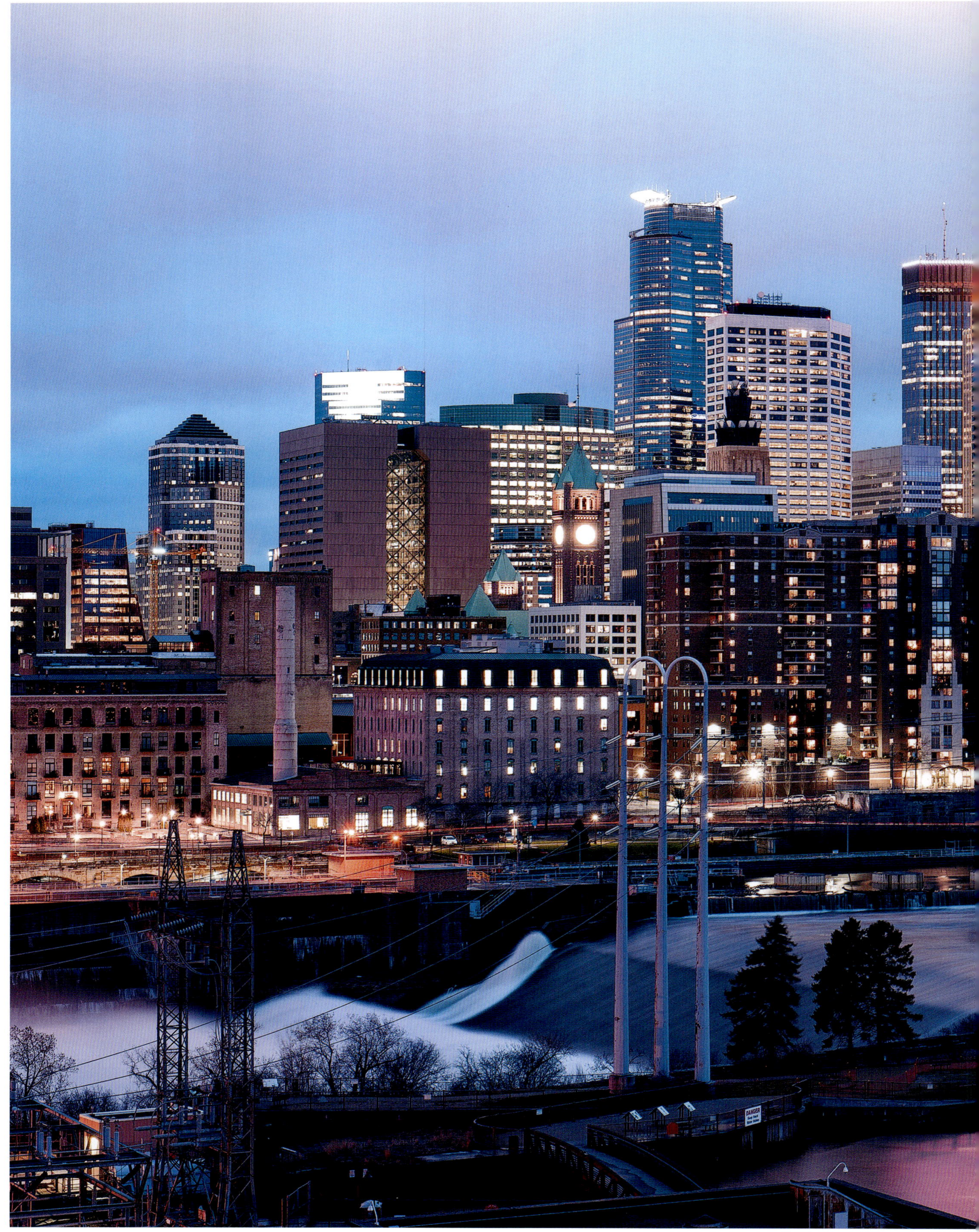

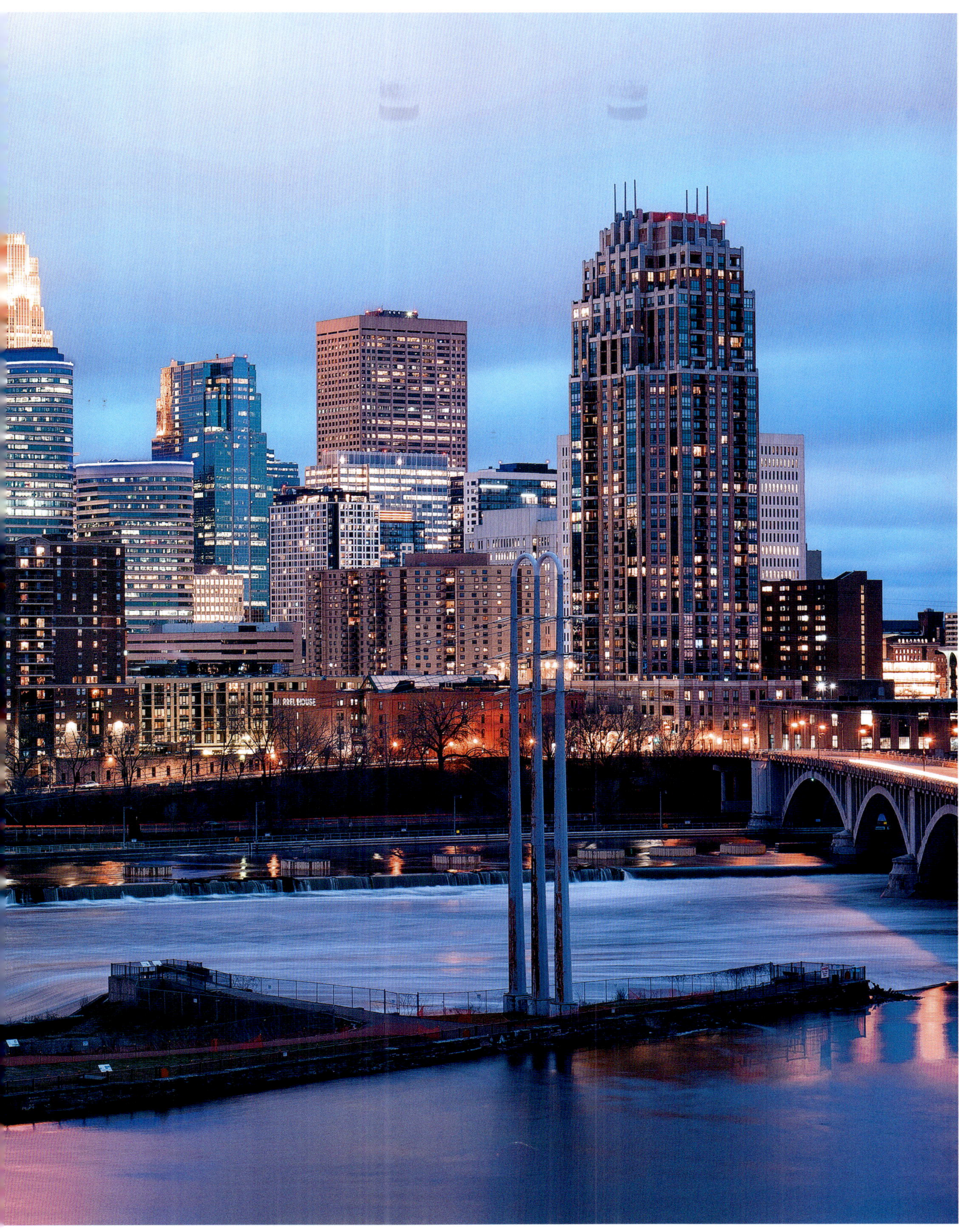

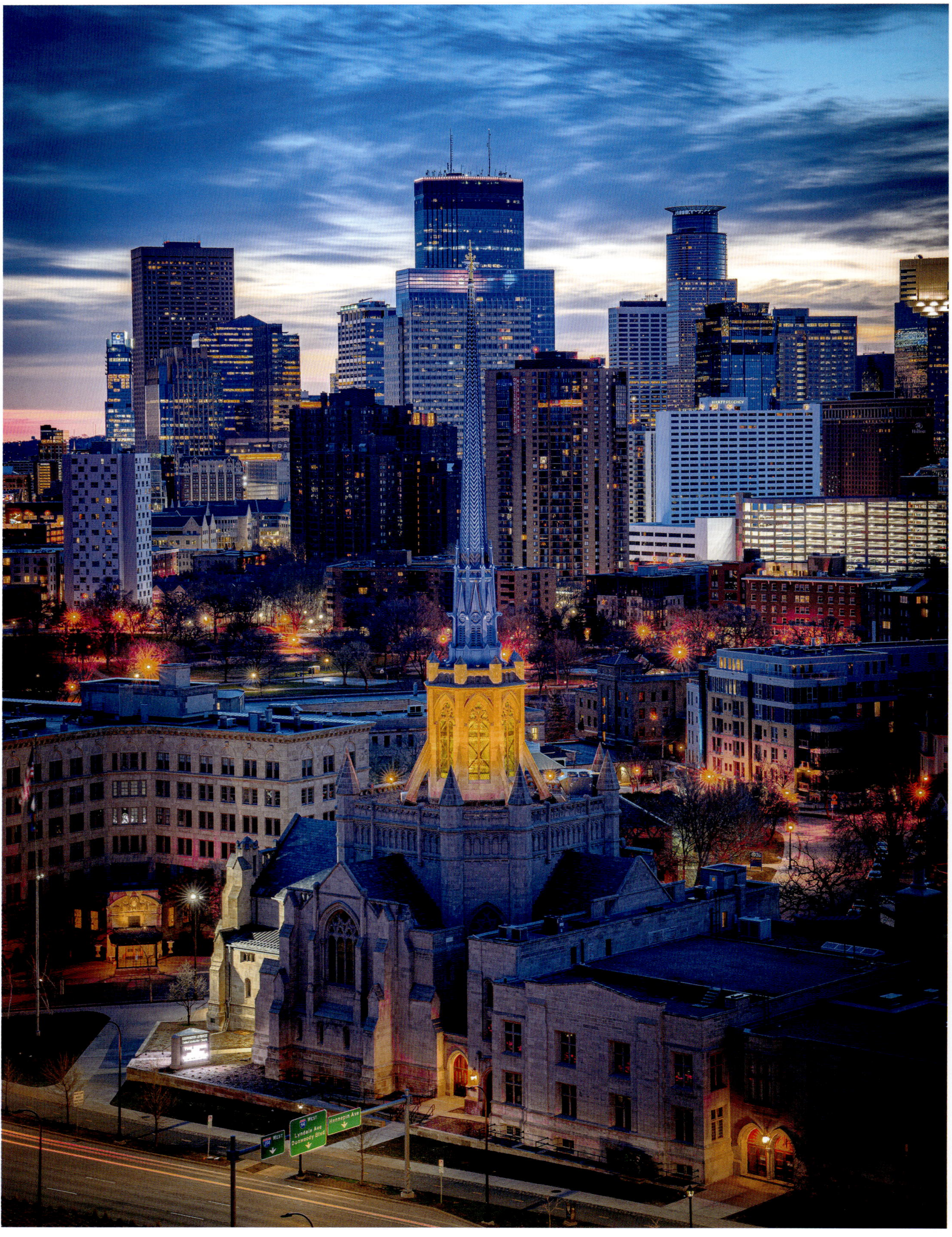

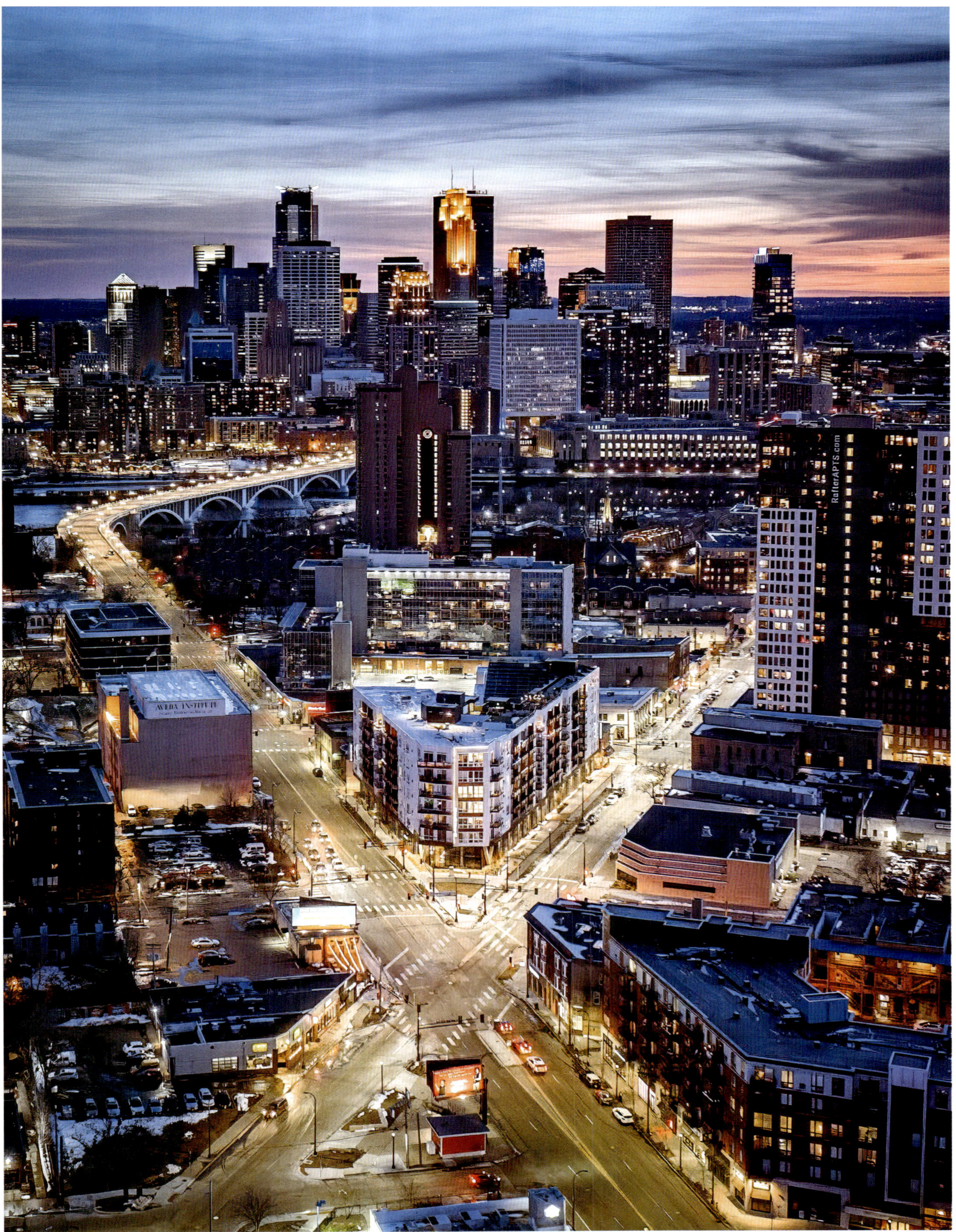

AVEDA INSTITUTE
RafterAPTS.com

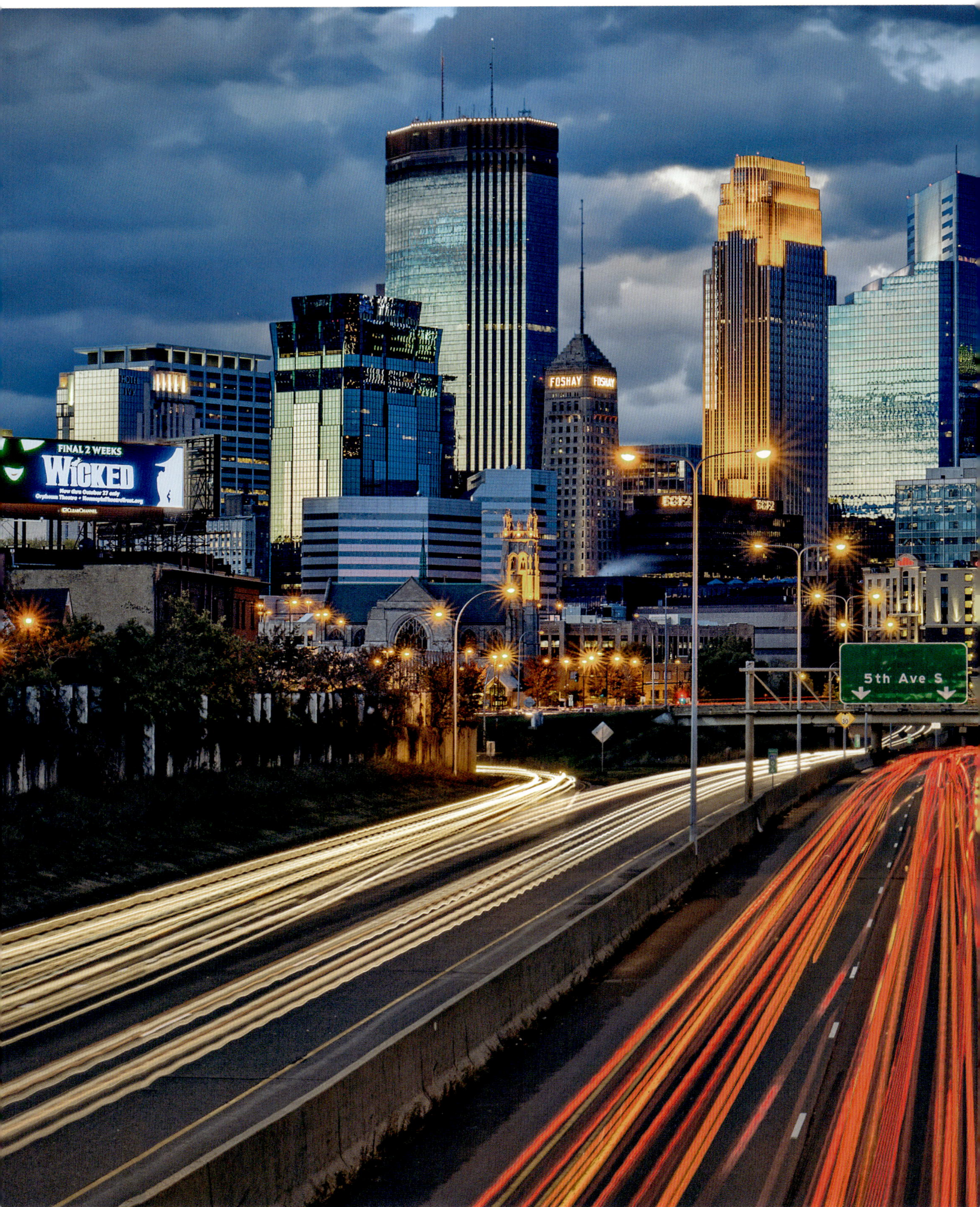
FINAL 2 WEEKS
WICKED
FOSHAY
FOSHAY
5th Ave S

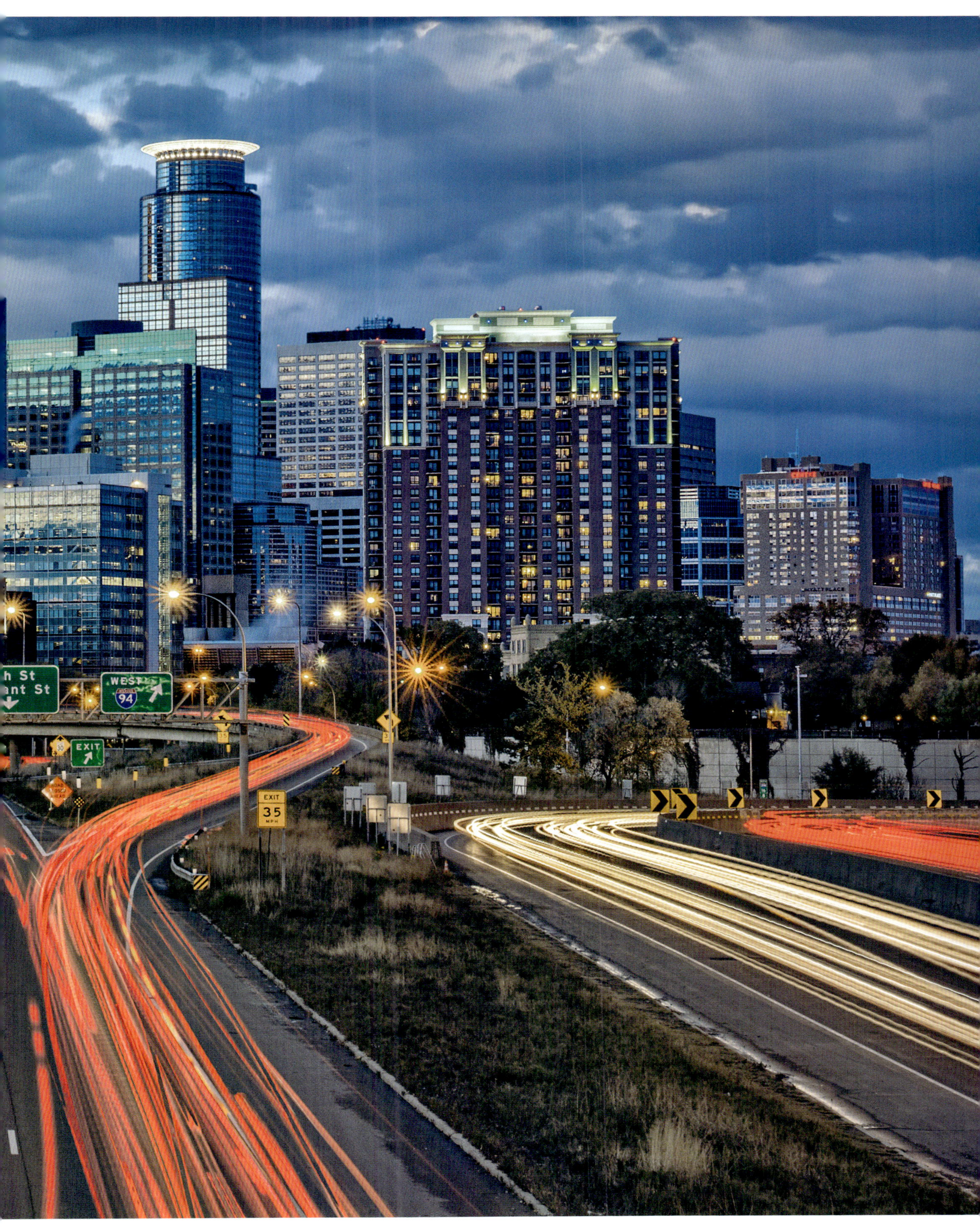
h St
ant St
WEST
94
EXIT 30
EXIT
35
MPH

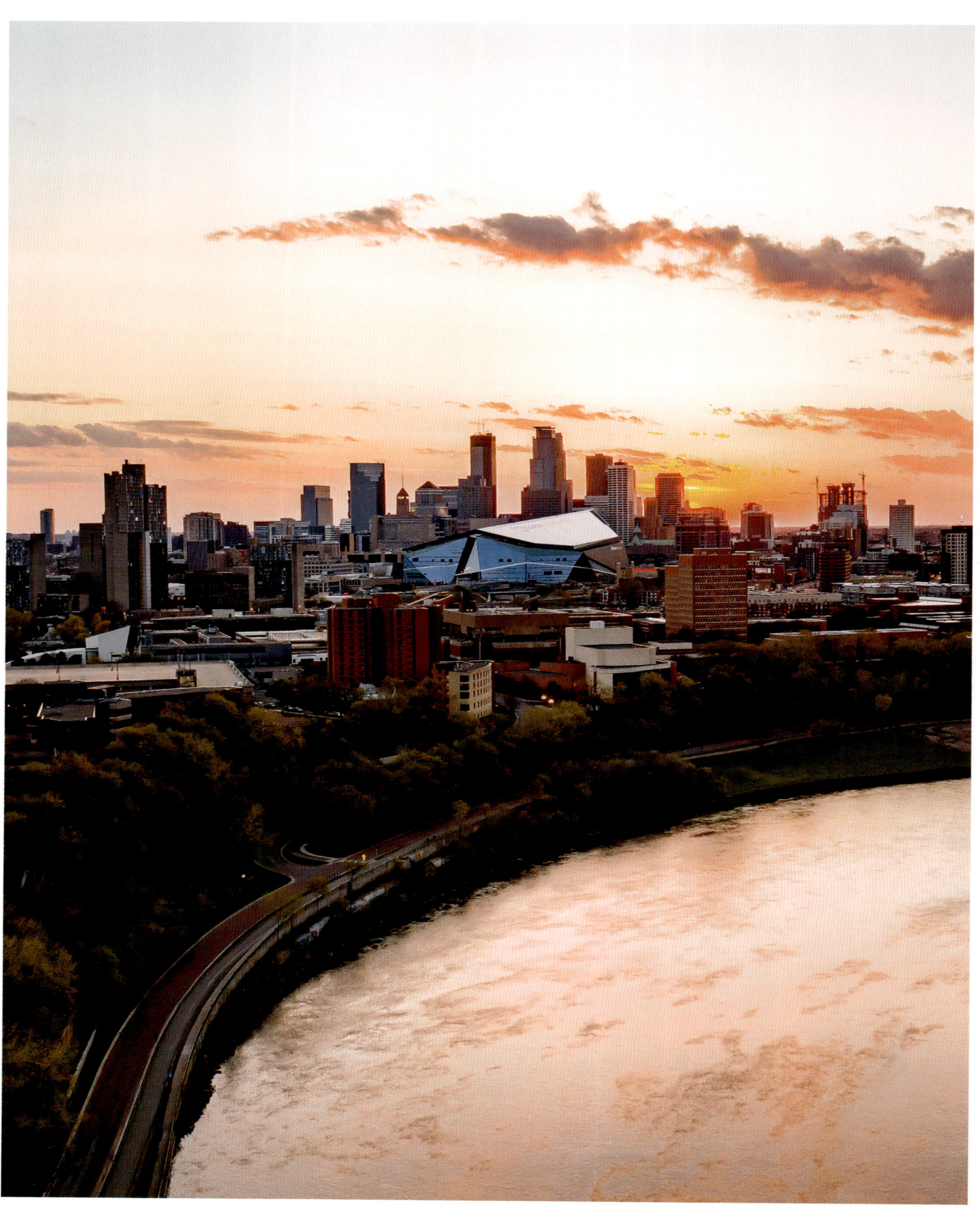

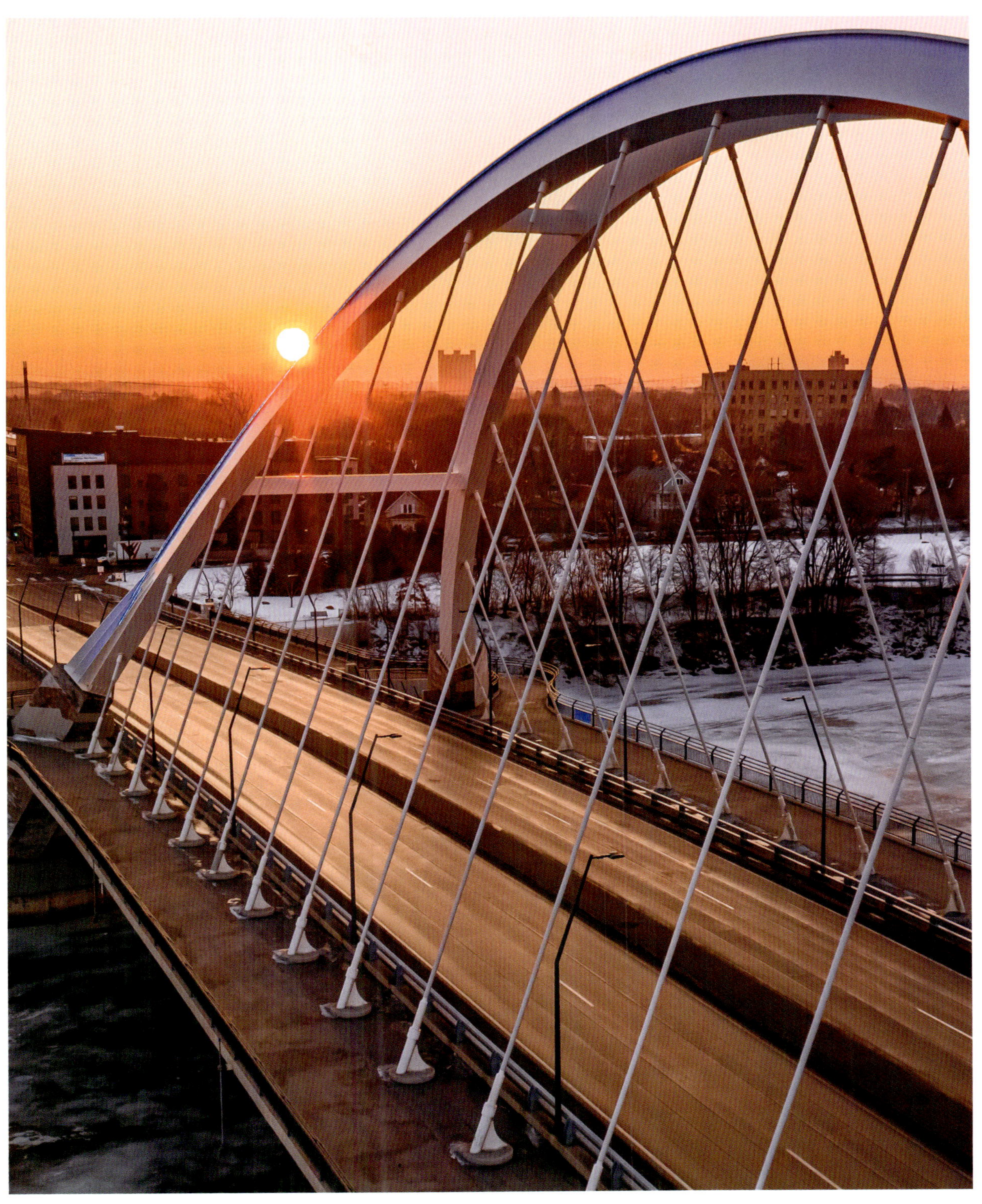

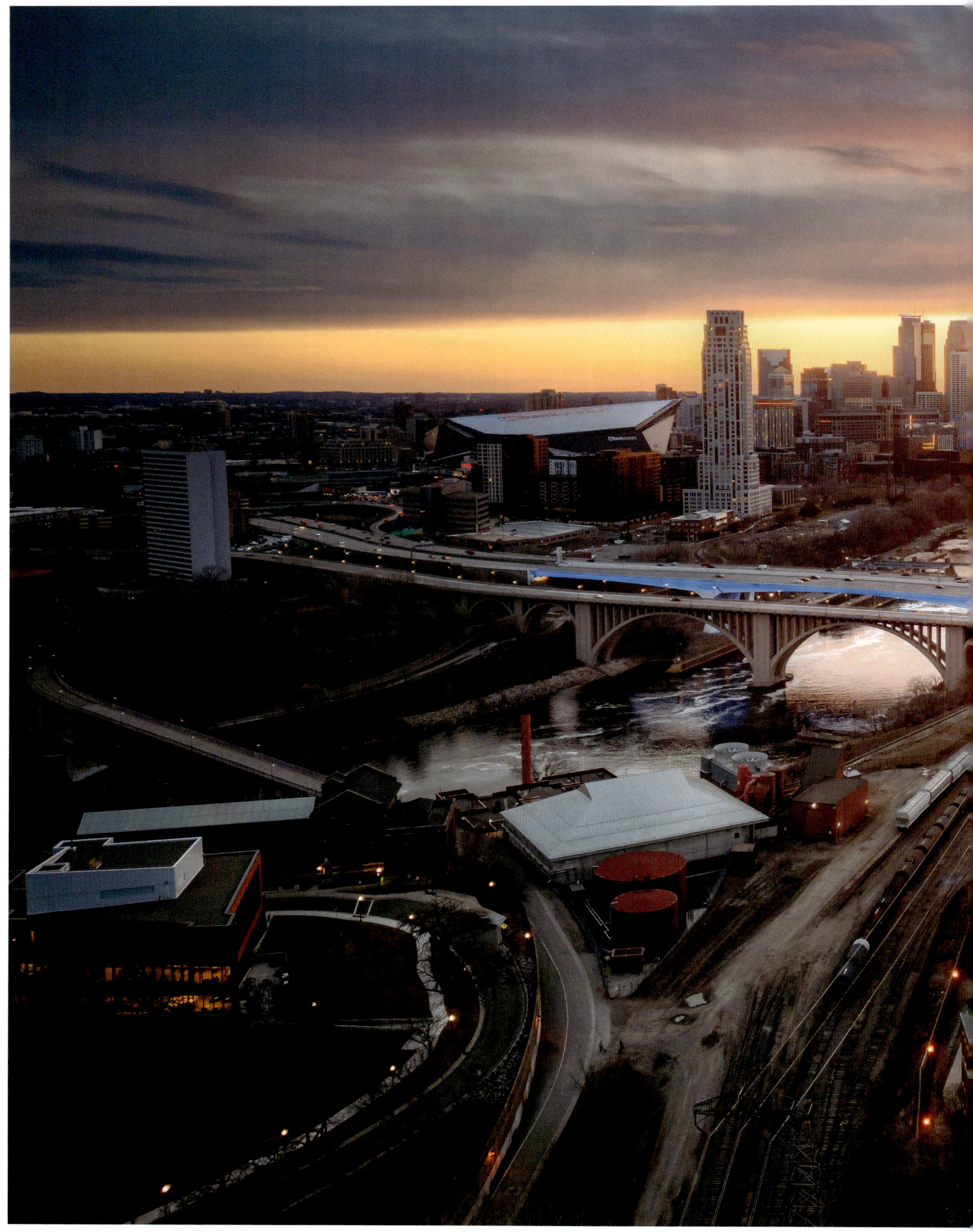

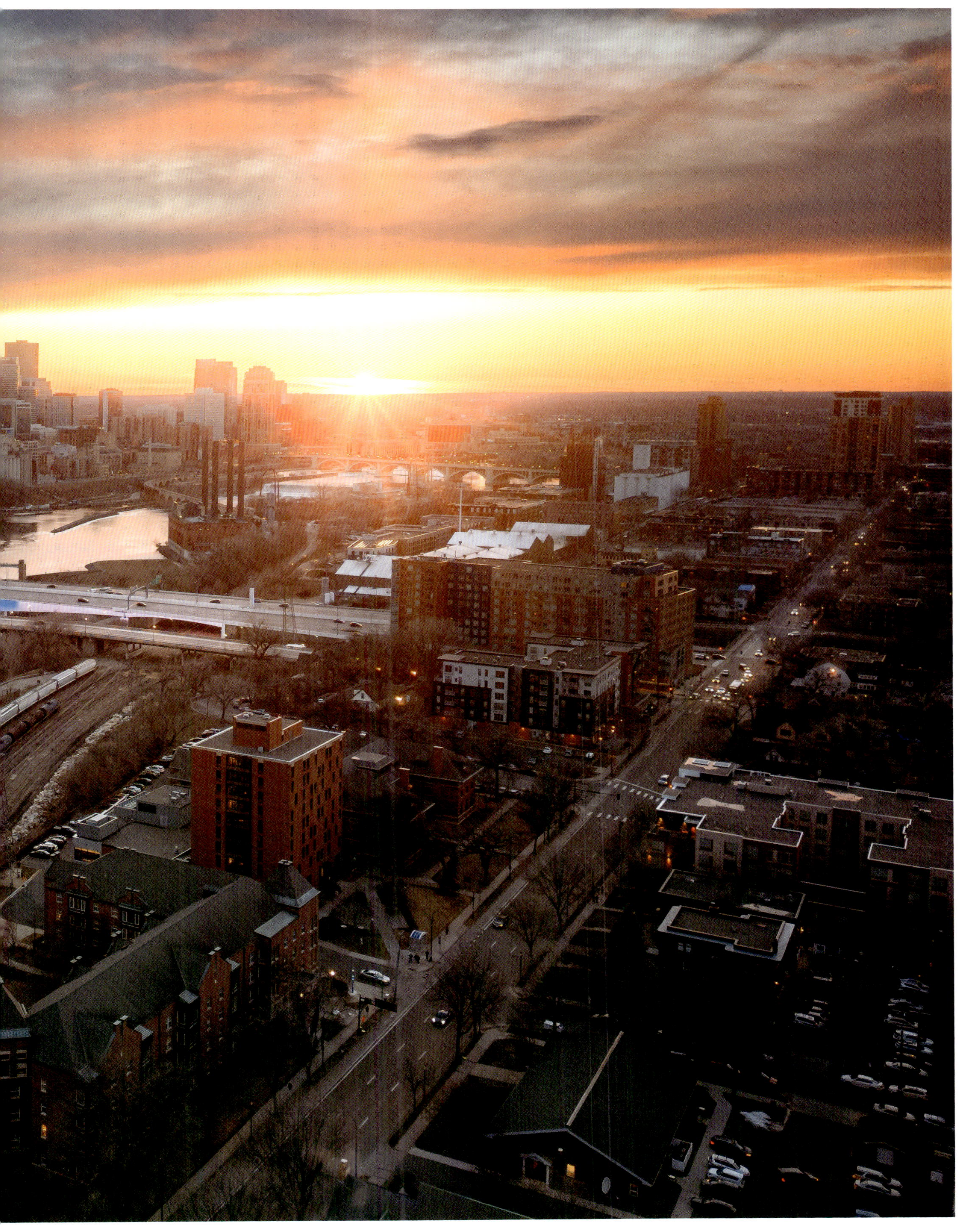

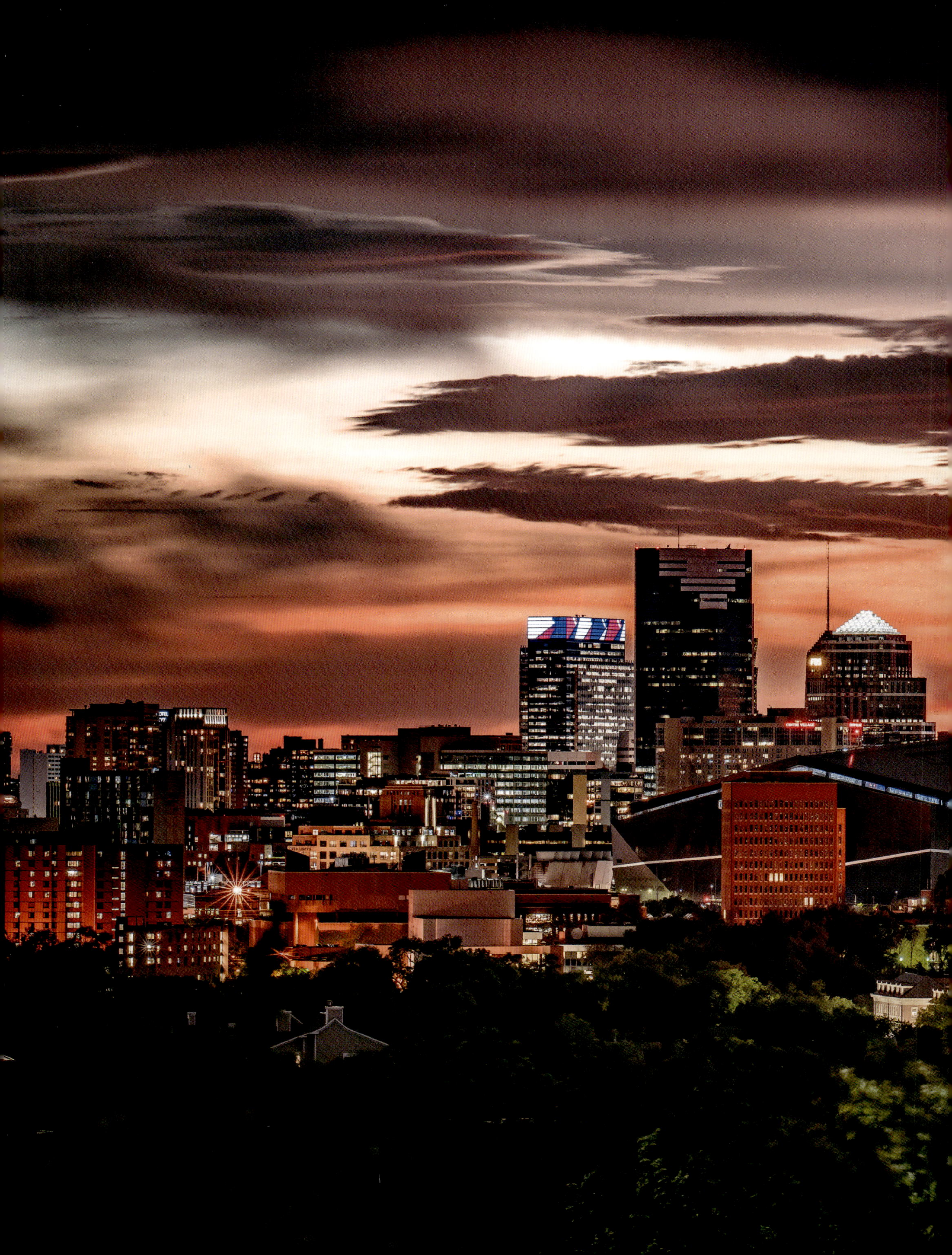

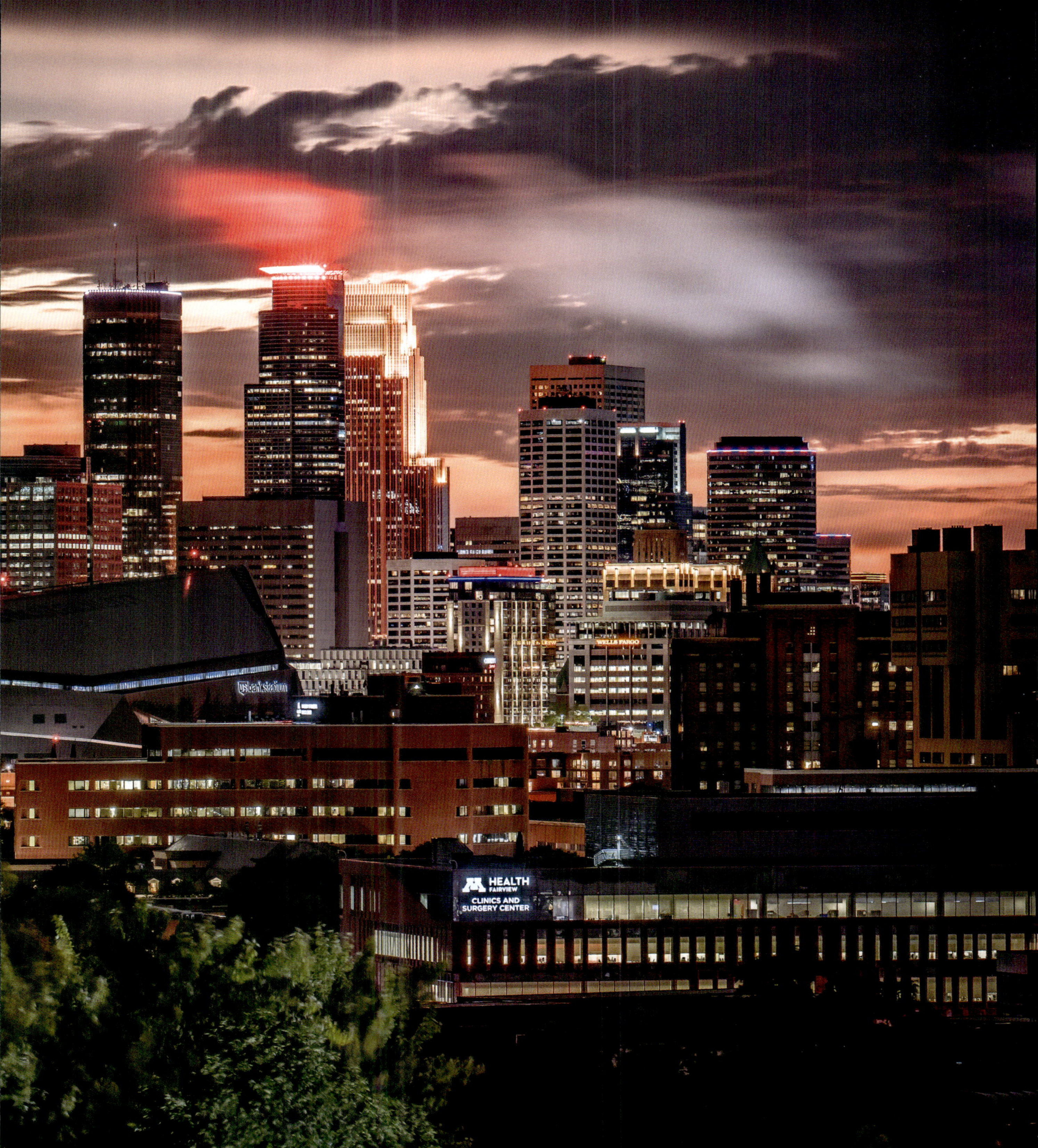
usbank stadium
WELLS FARGO
HEALTH
FAIRVIEW
CLINICS AND
SURGERY CENTER

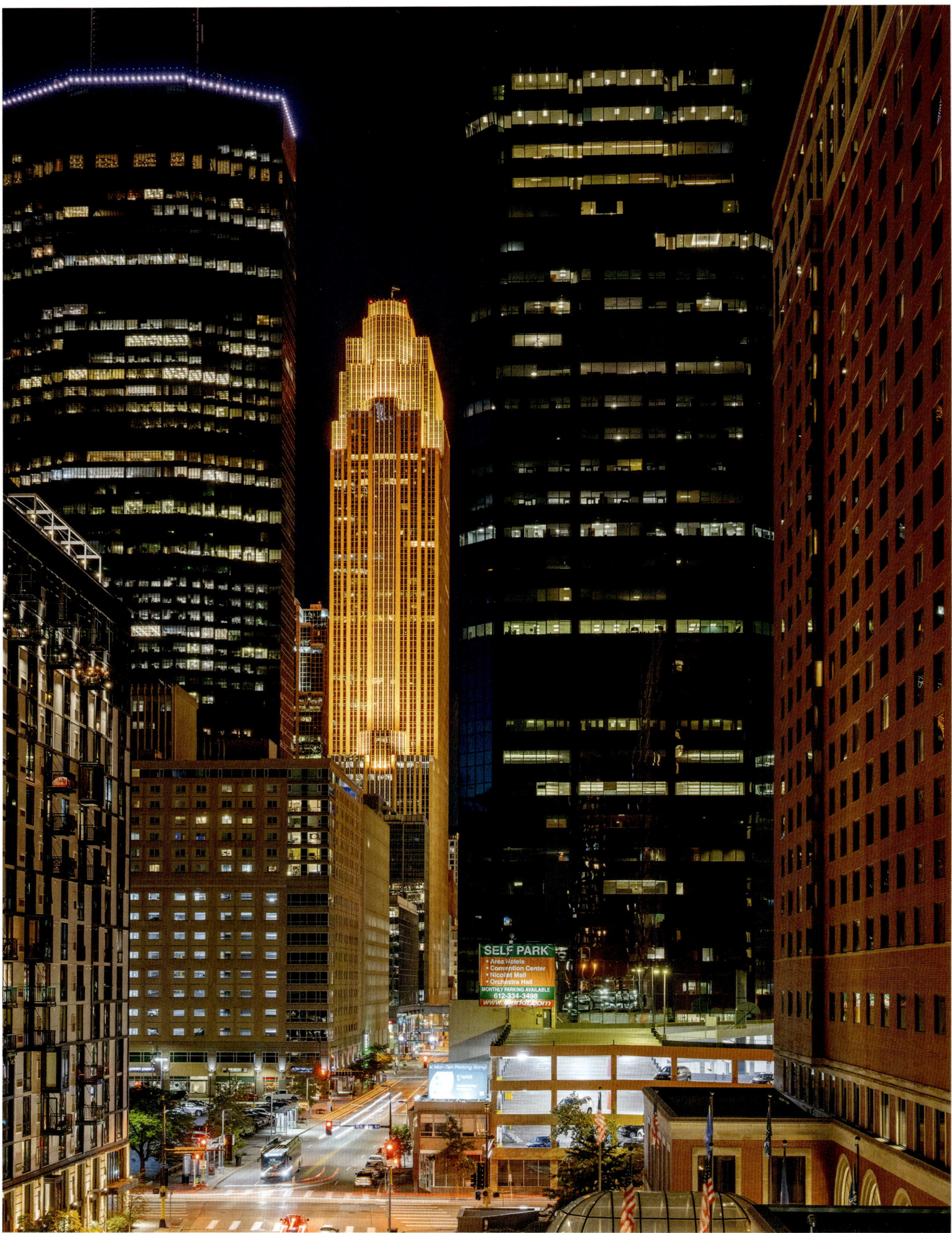

SELF PARK
Area Hotels
Convention Center
Nicollet Mall
Orchestra Hall
MONTHLY PARKING AVAILABLE
612-334-3498
www.iparkit.com

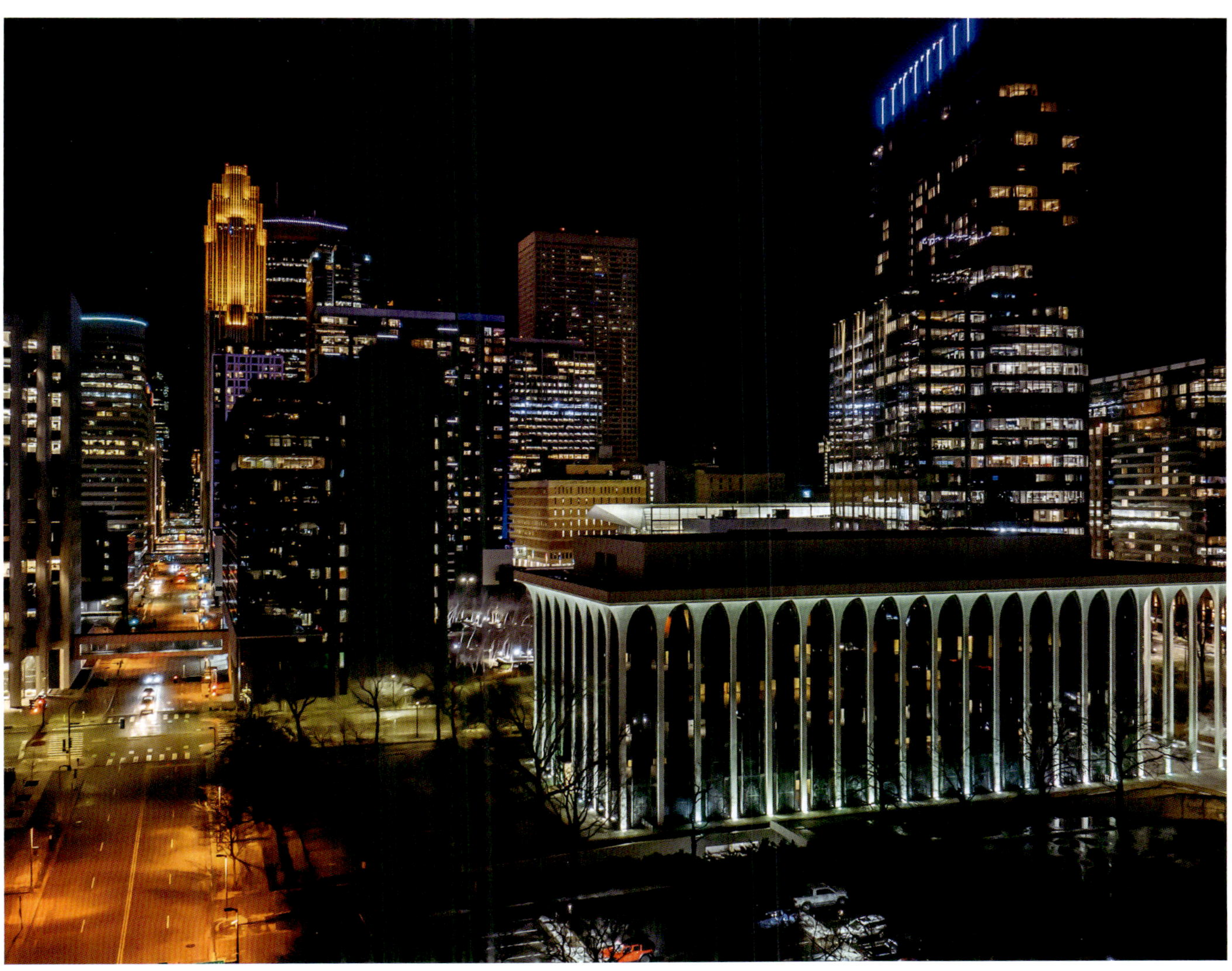

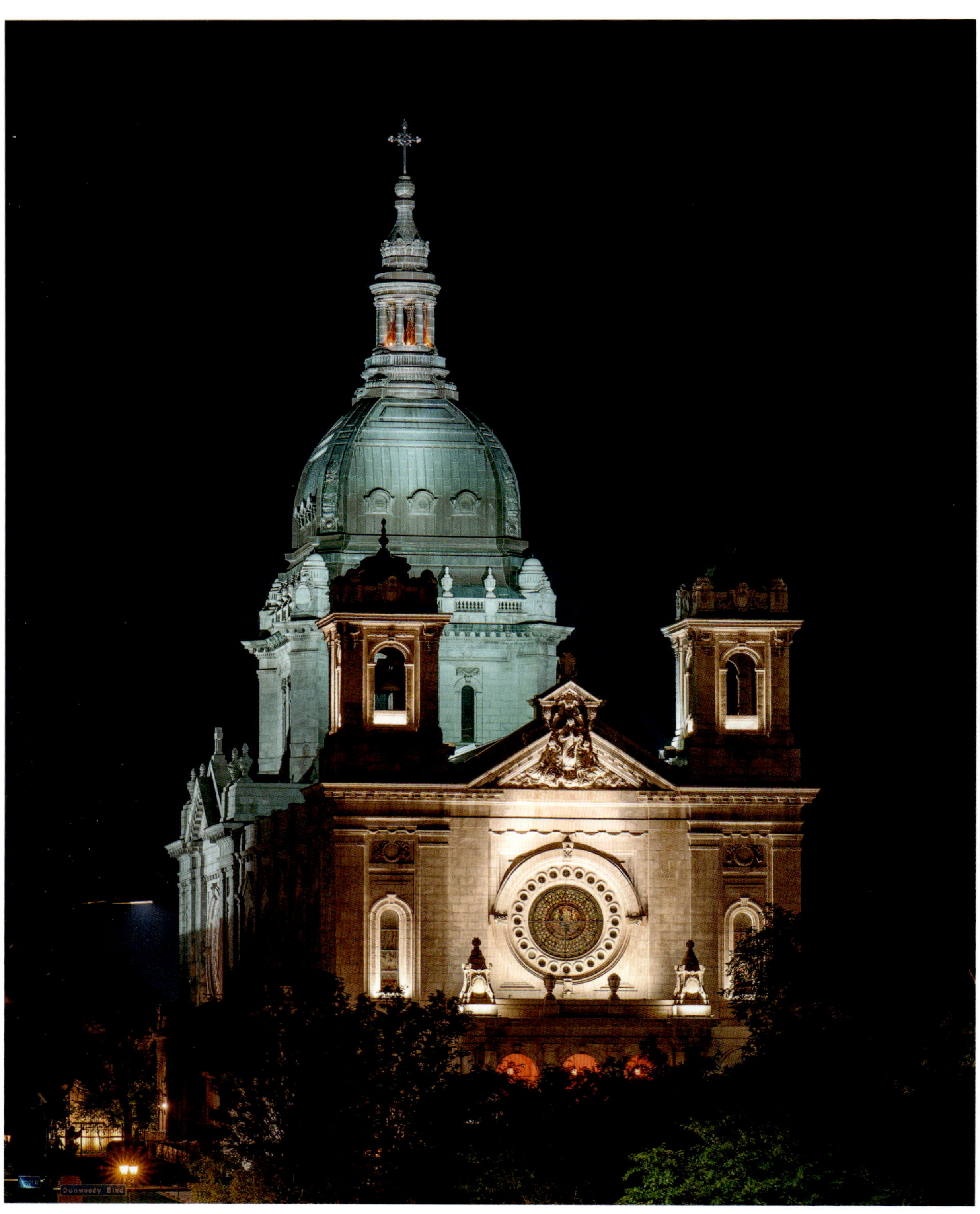

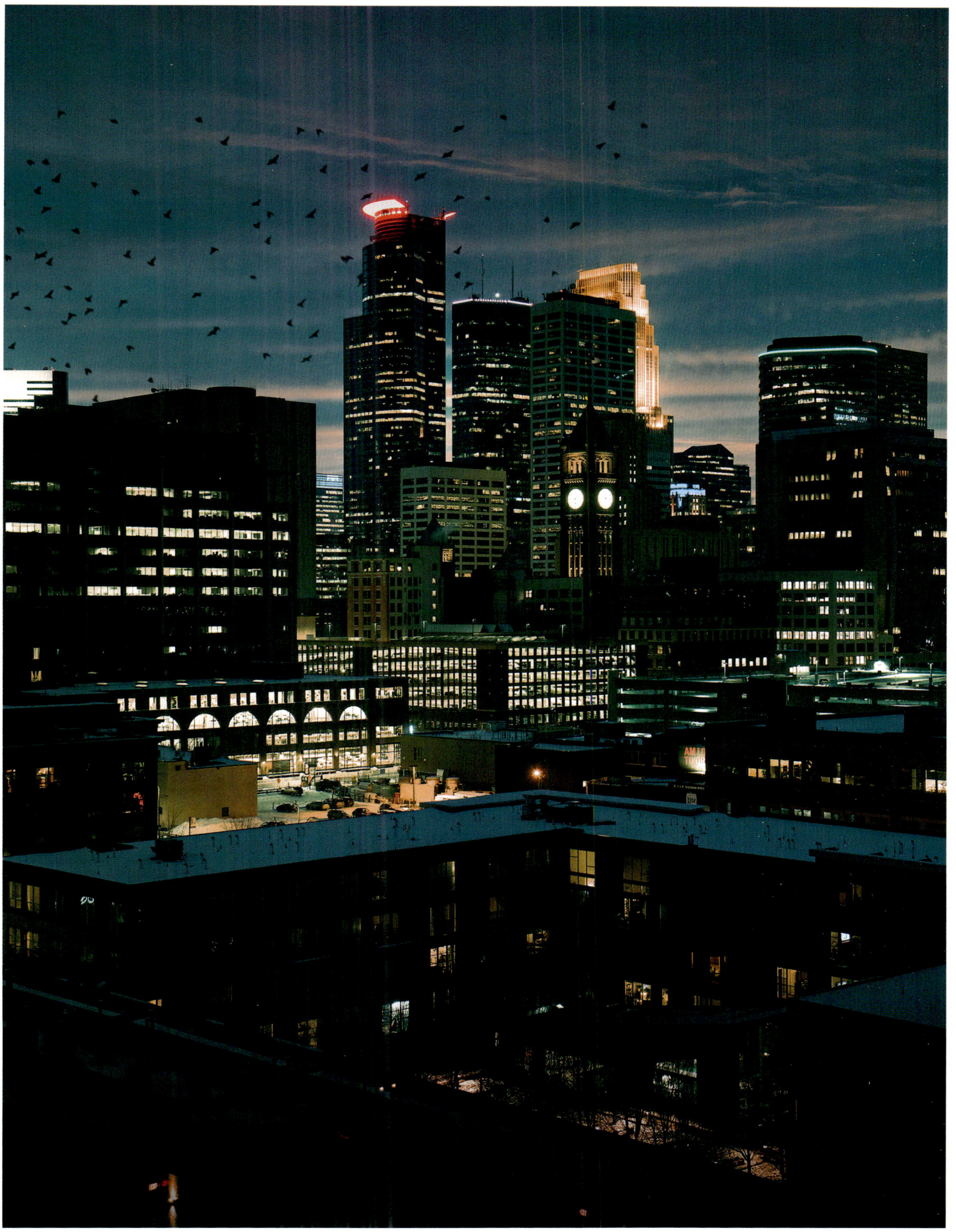

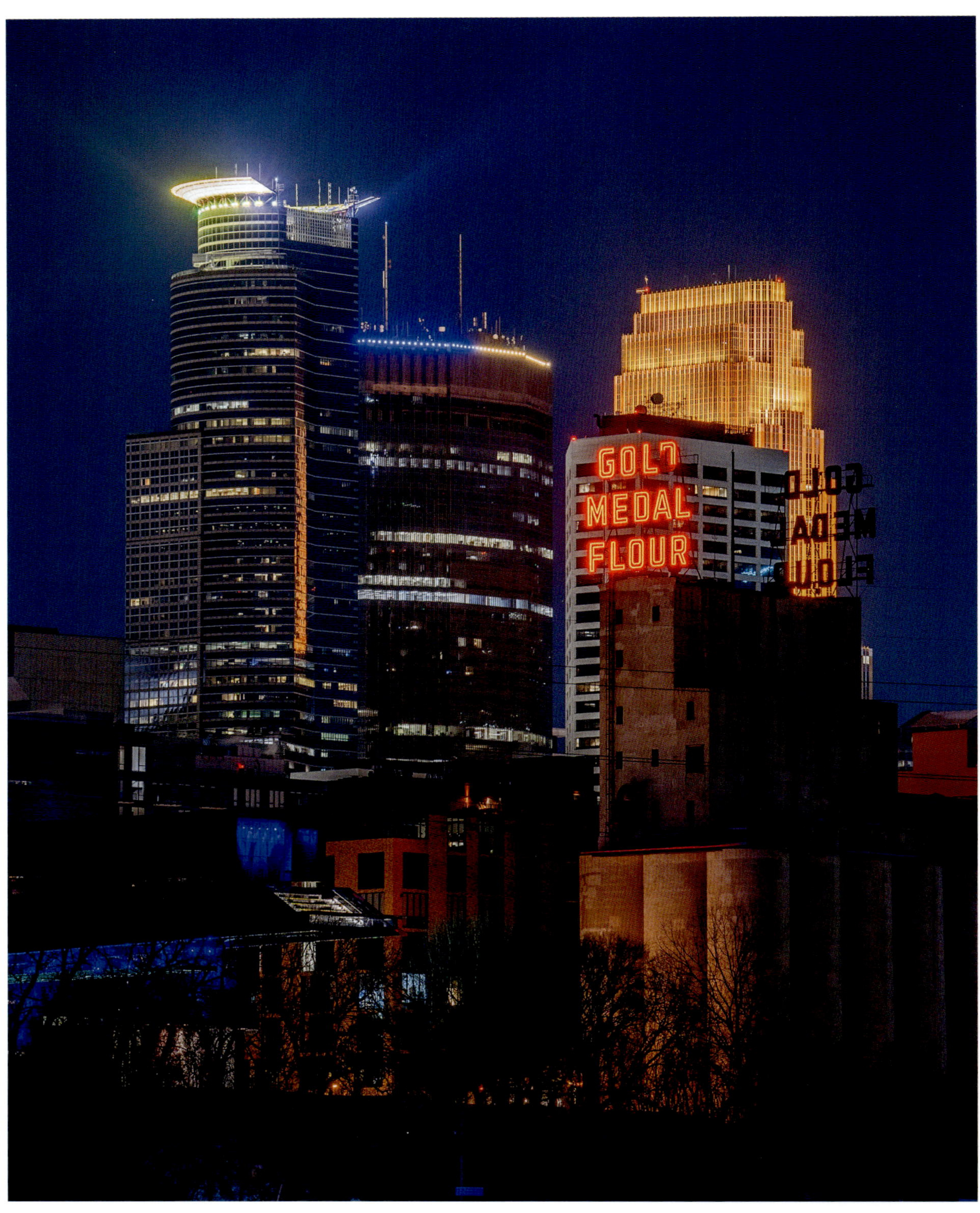

GOLD
MEDAL
FLOUR

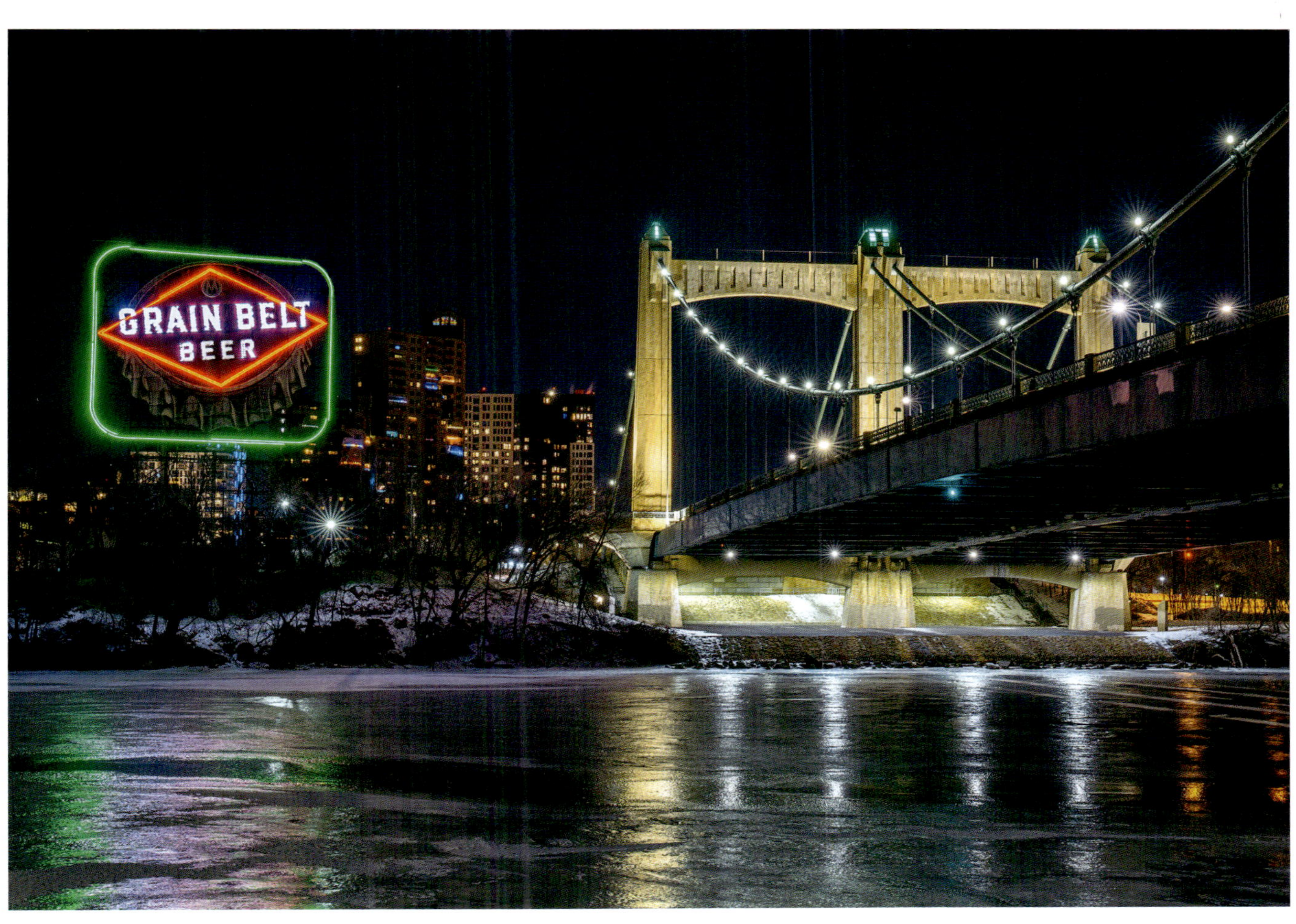

GRAIN BELT
BEER

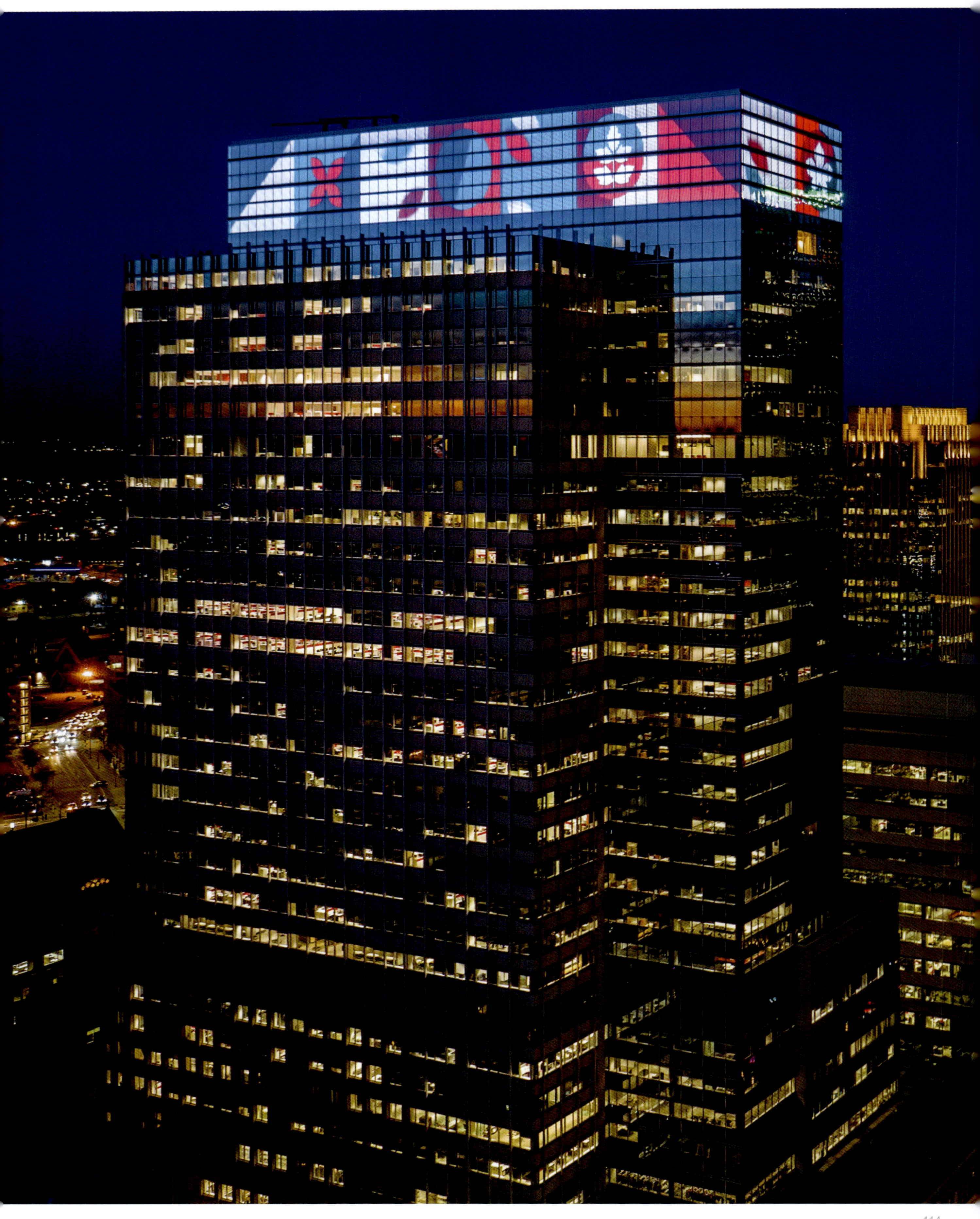

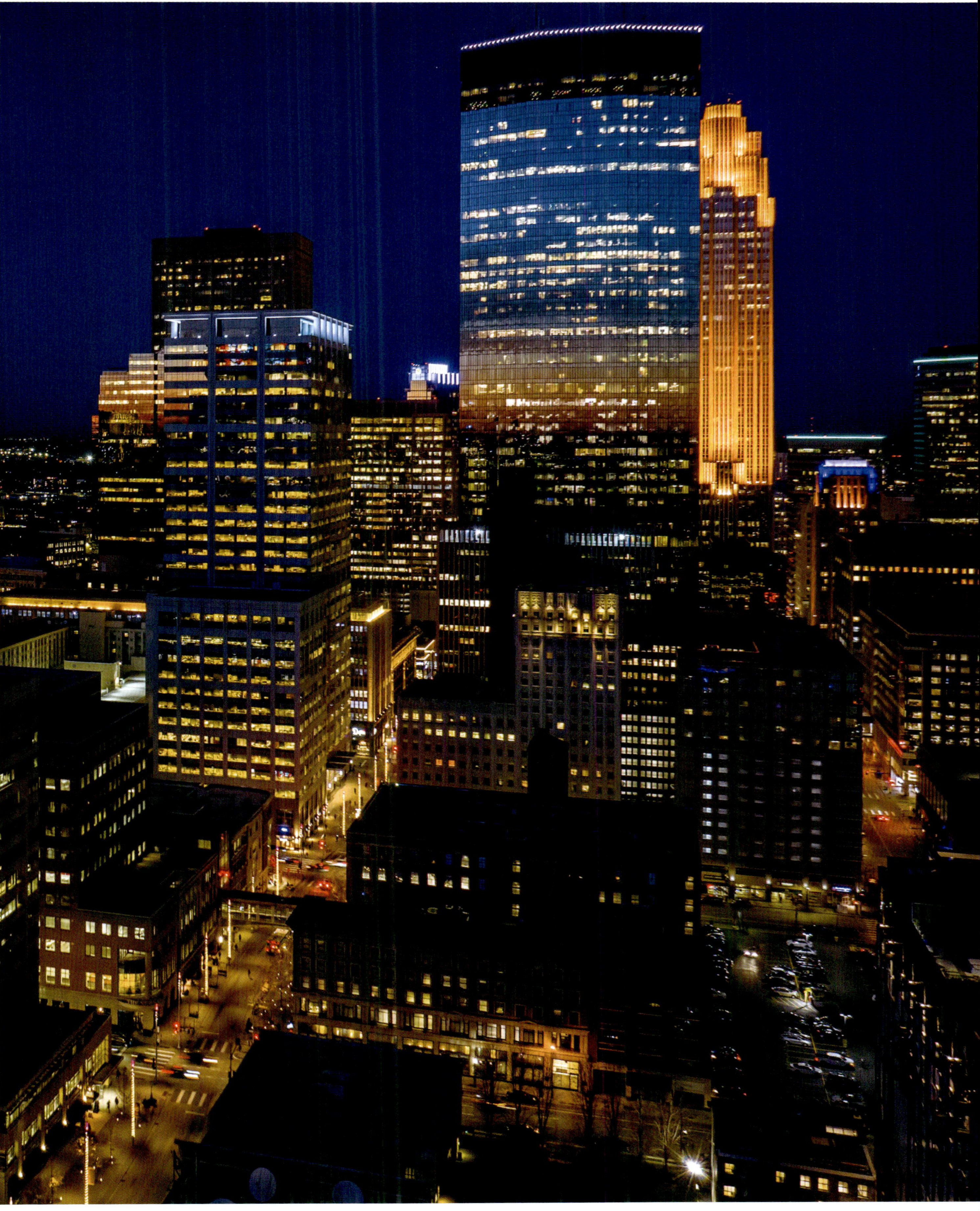

Winter Weather ♦ Winters in the Twin Cities are famously long, cold, and snowy. Temperatures frequently dip below freezing, but locals are prepared. And once the first real cold front settles and the lakes start their long freeze, Minneapolis and St. Paul transform into a paradise of ice and snow, with Minnesotans embracing winter activities like ice skating, skiing, and ice fishing. ♦ Snow is abundant in the Twin Cities, with the first snowflakes of the season typically arriving in late October, and measurable snowfall of an inch or more in early to mid-November. The Twin Cities sit far enough north to be regularly influenced by Arctic and Canadian air masses. When these cold, dry systems sweep down during winter, they create the perfect conditions for snow anytime moisture becomes available. But rather than retreat inside during periods of snow, locals bundle in layers including parkas, wool hats, shearling-lined boots, and insulated gloves, and embrace their cities becoming winter wonderlands. ♦ The Minneapolis Chain of Lakes, Theodore Wirth Park, and Fort Snelling State Park all offer miles of groomed trails for cross-country skiing. And the winter weather doesn't close the paths to walking and winter running. Snow is plowed and maintained regularly for brisk winter walks or cold-weather jogs. ♦ The region's lakes are also hubs of winter activities. Once the ice is thick enough, residents come out to take advantage of these outdoor playgrounds. While ice skating is a given, with many lakes maintaining skating rinks with warming houses, lights, and music, this isn't where the action stops. Pick-up games of ice hockey are a winter staple, as well as broomball, a quirky, beloved Twin Cities sport played with brooms and a ball instead of the typical stick and puck used in hockey. On windy days, adventurous souls harness the gusts and glide across the ice with snow kites. It's dramatic, fast, and surprisingly graceful. And on Lake Harriet, Bde Maka Ska, and Lake Nokomis, you'll often find heated, portable ice fishing shelters dotting the frozen lakes as ice fishermen take part in that most classic Minnesota activity.

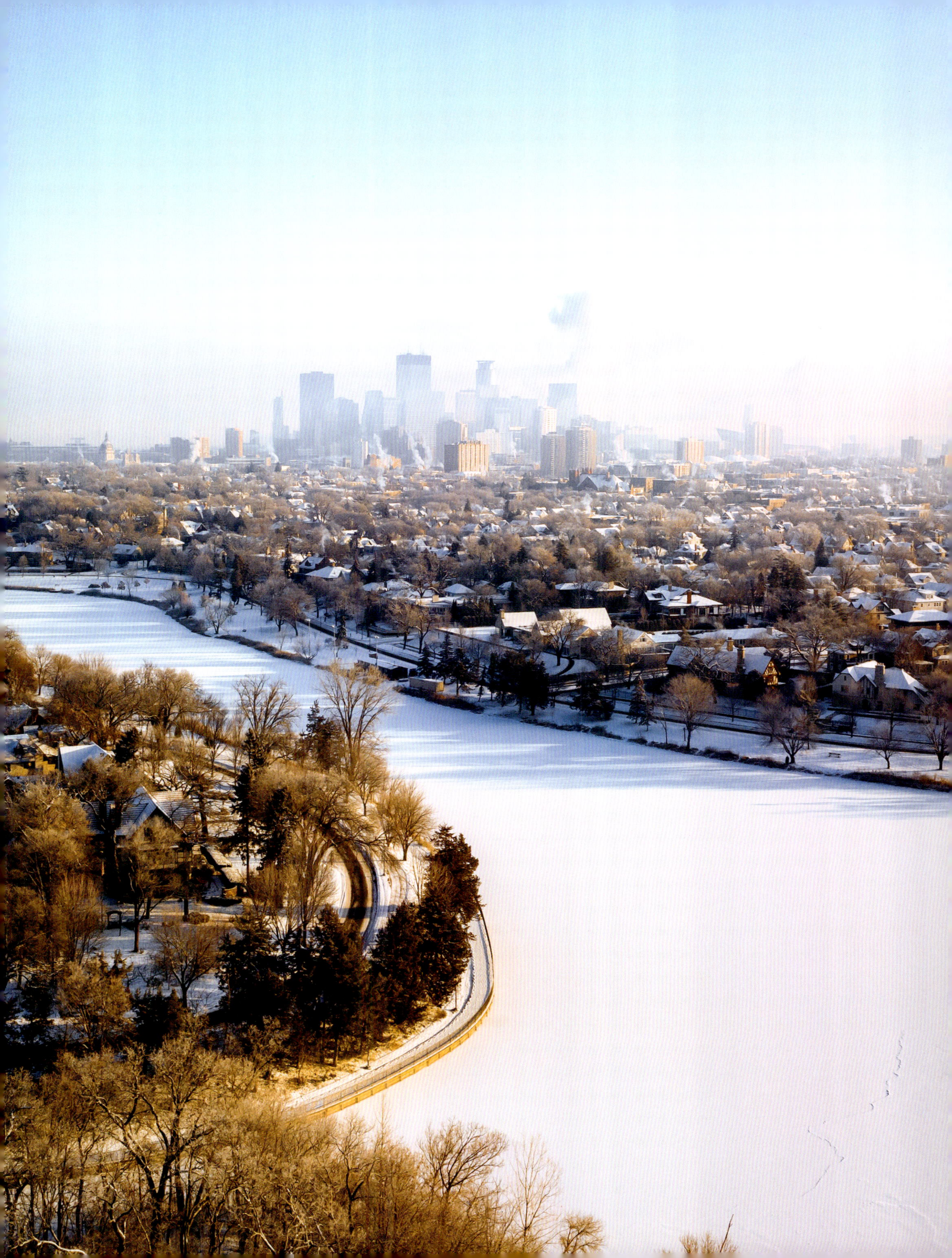

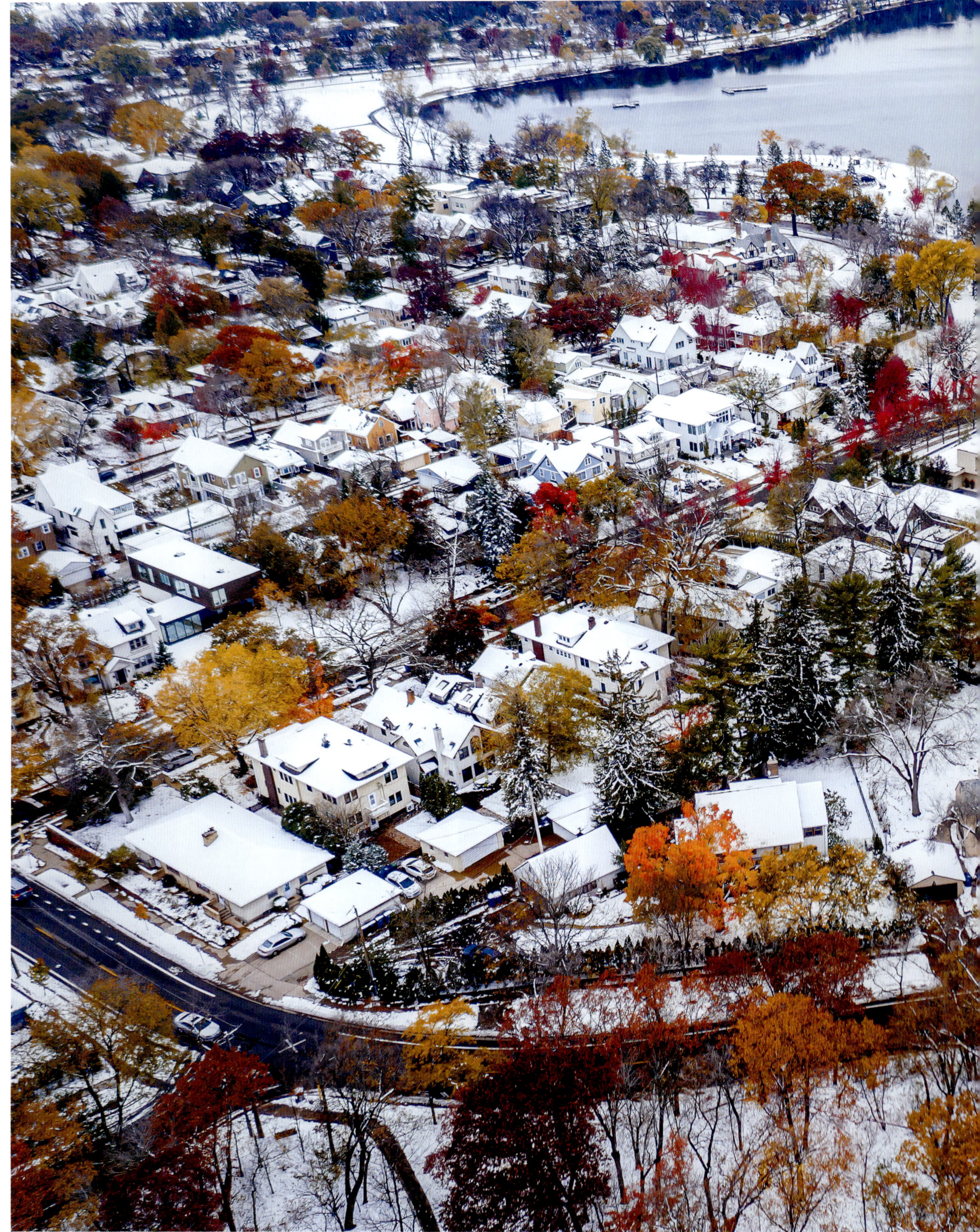

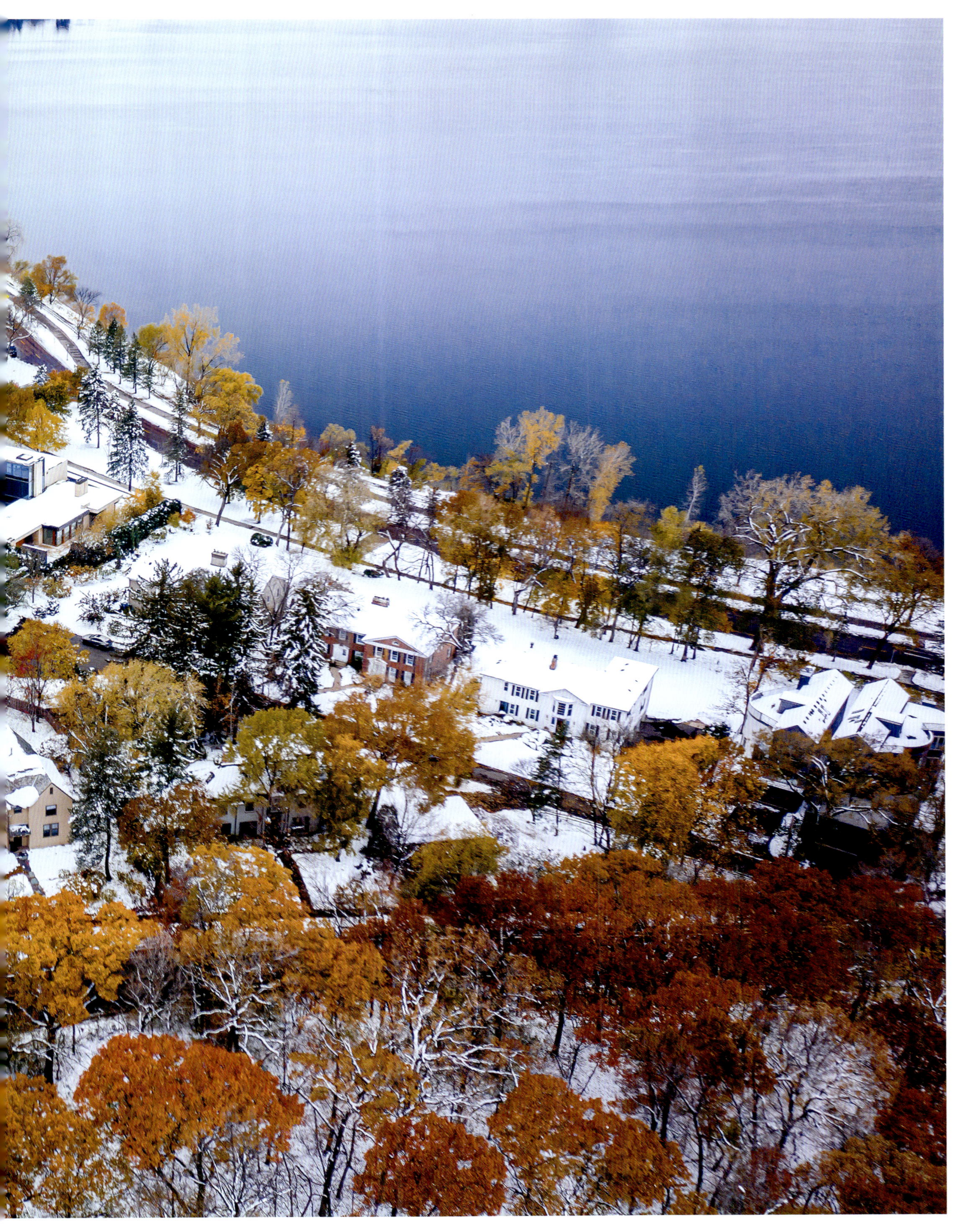

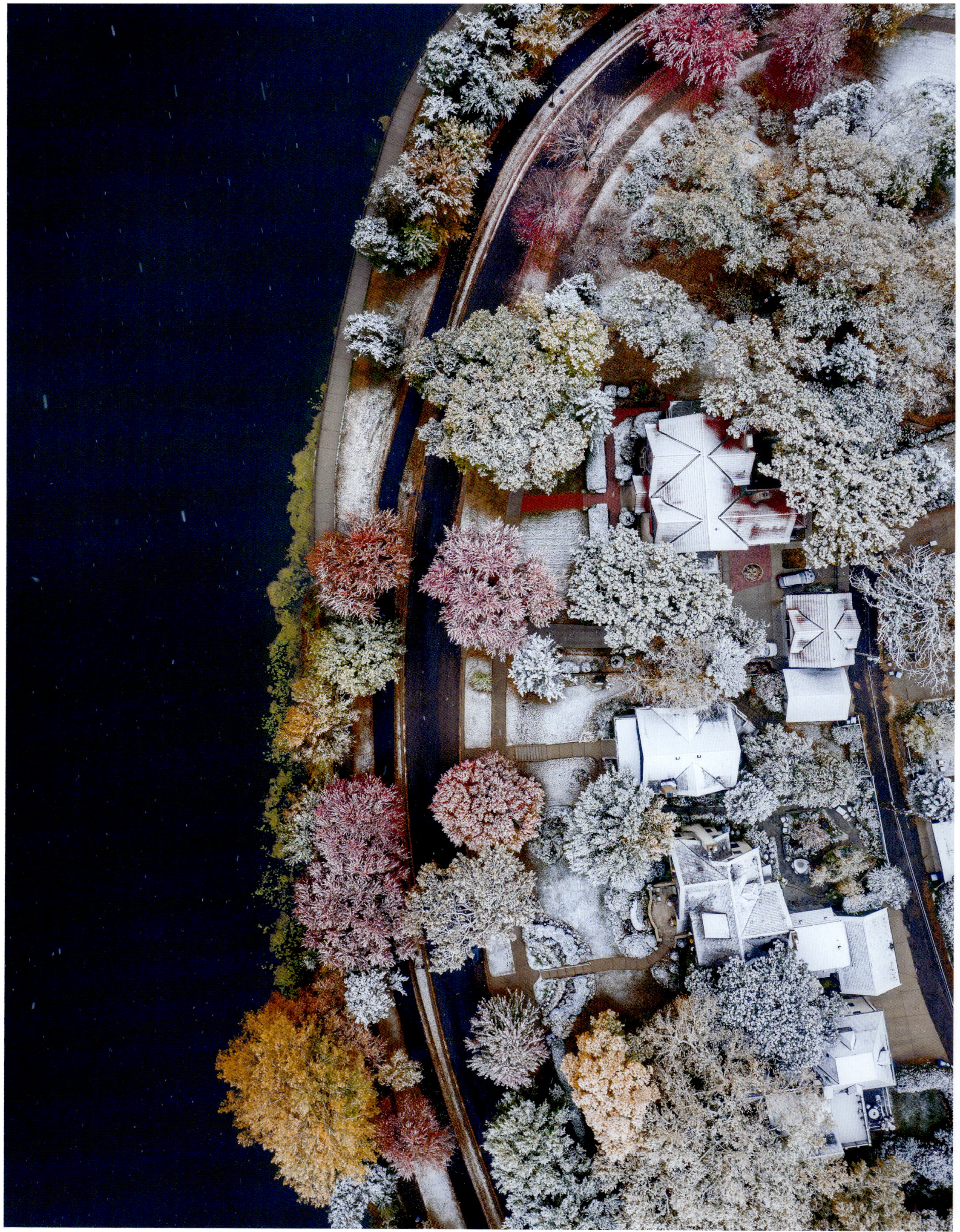

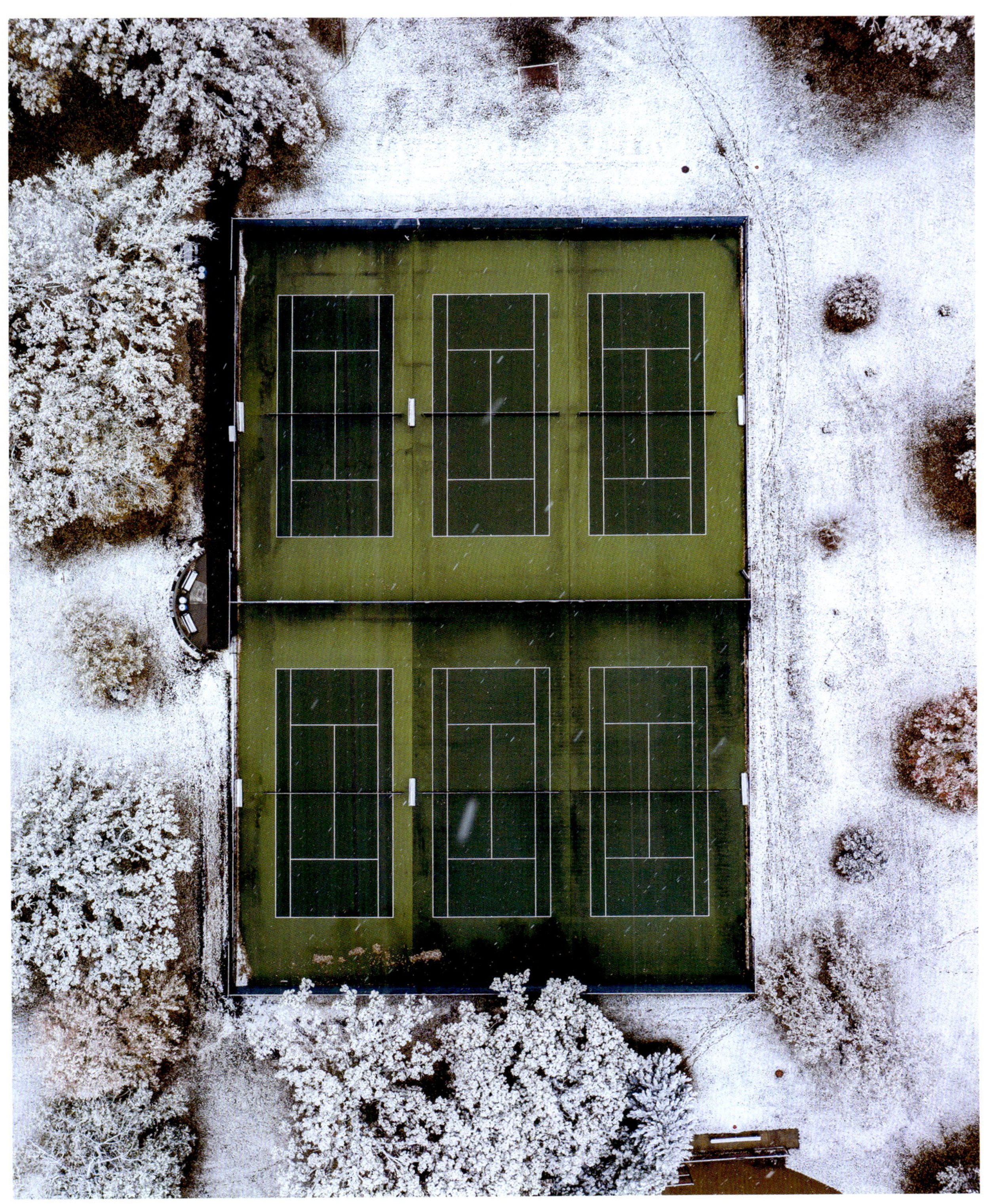

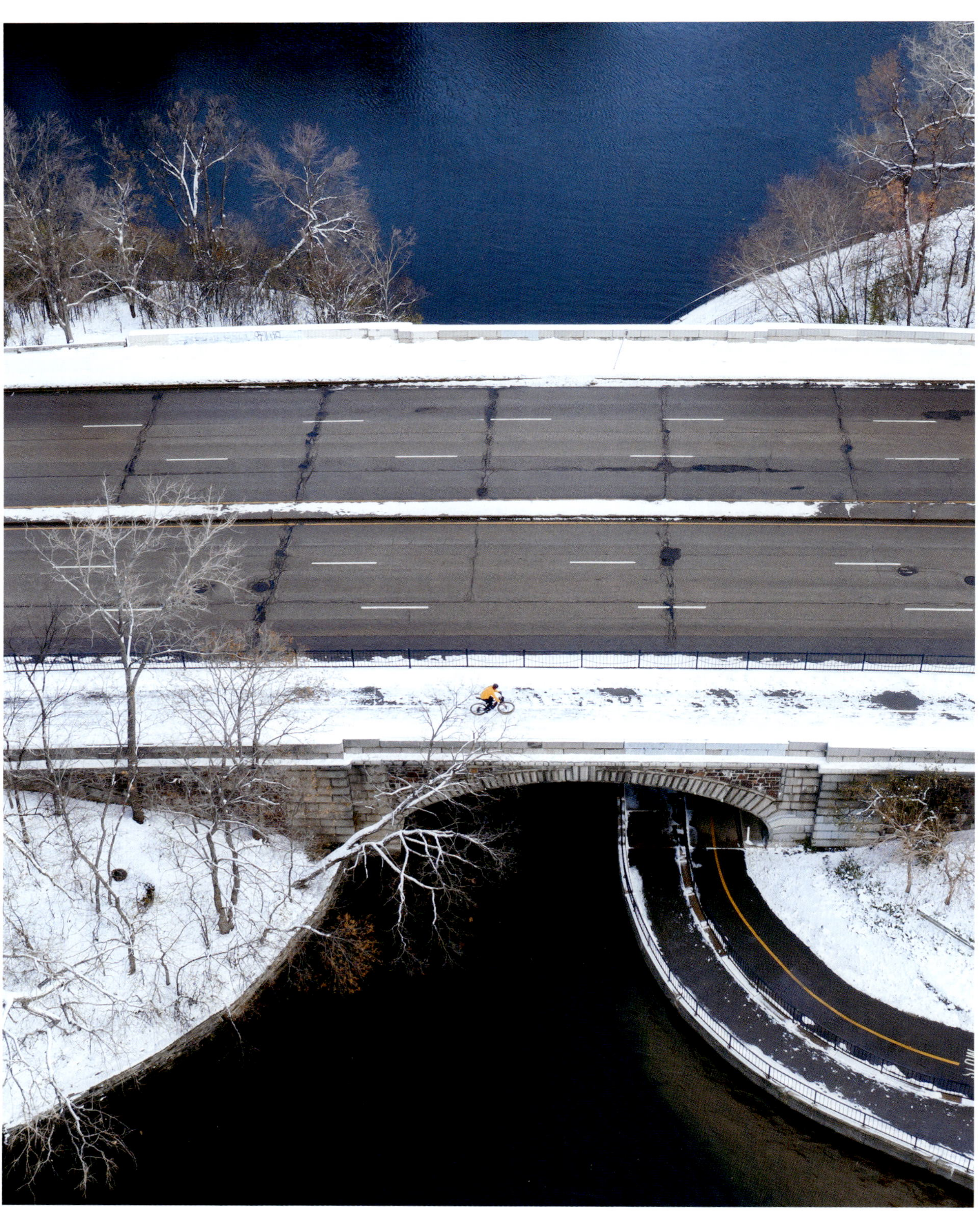

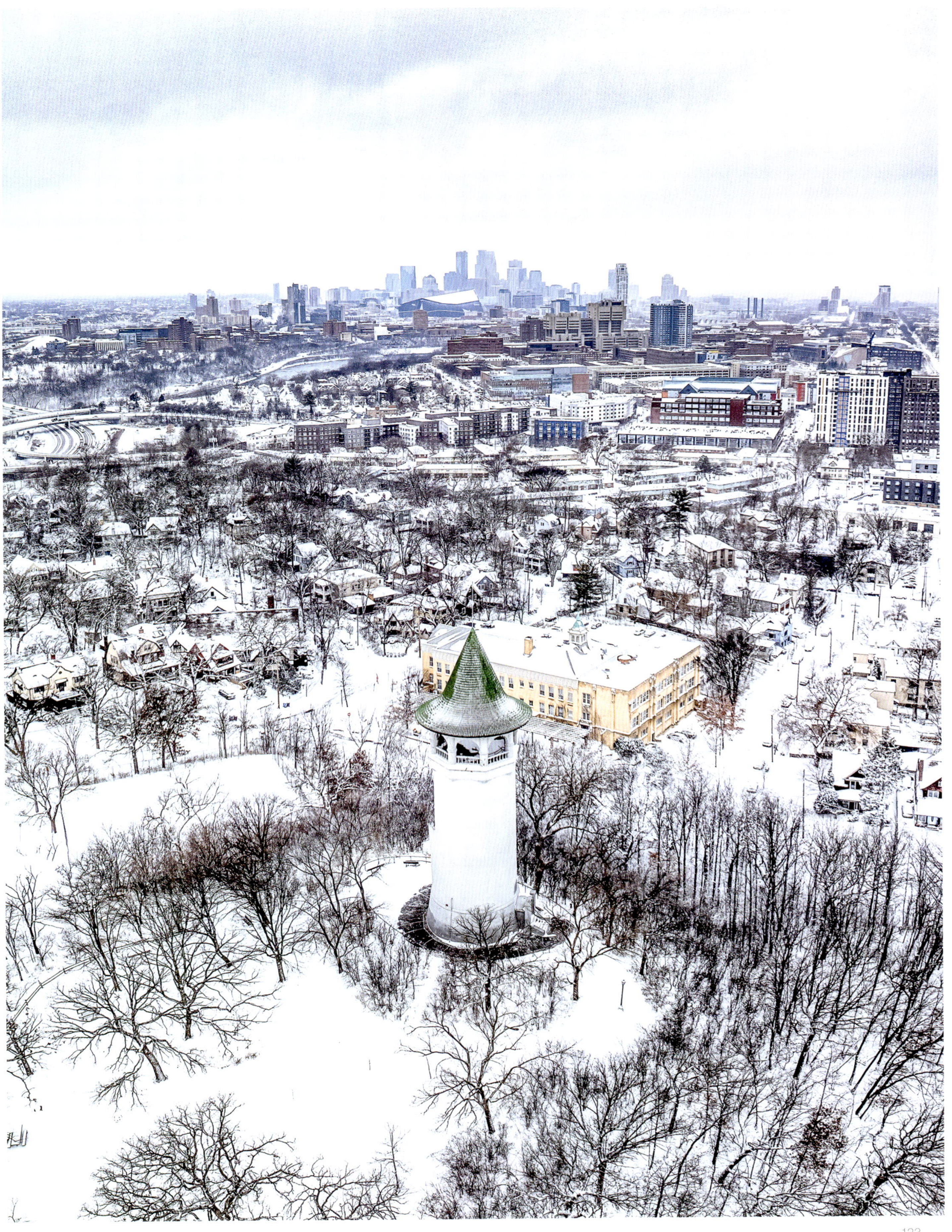

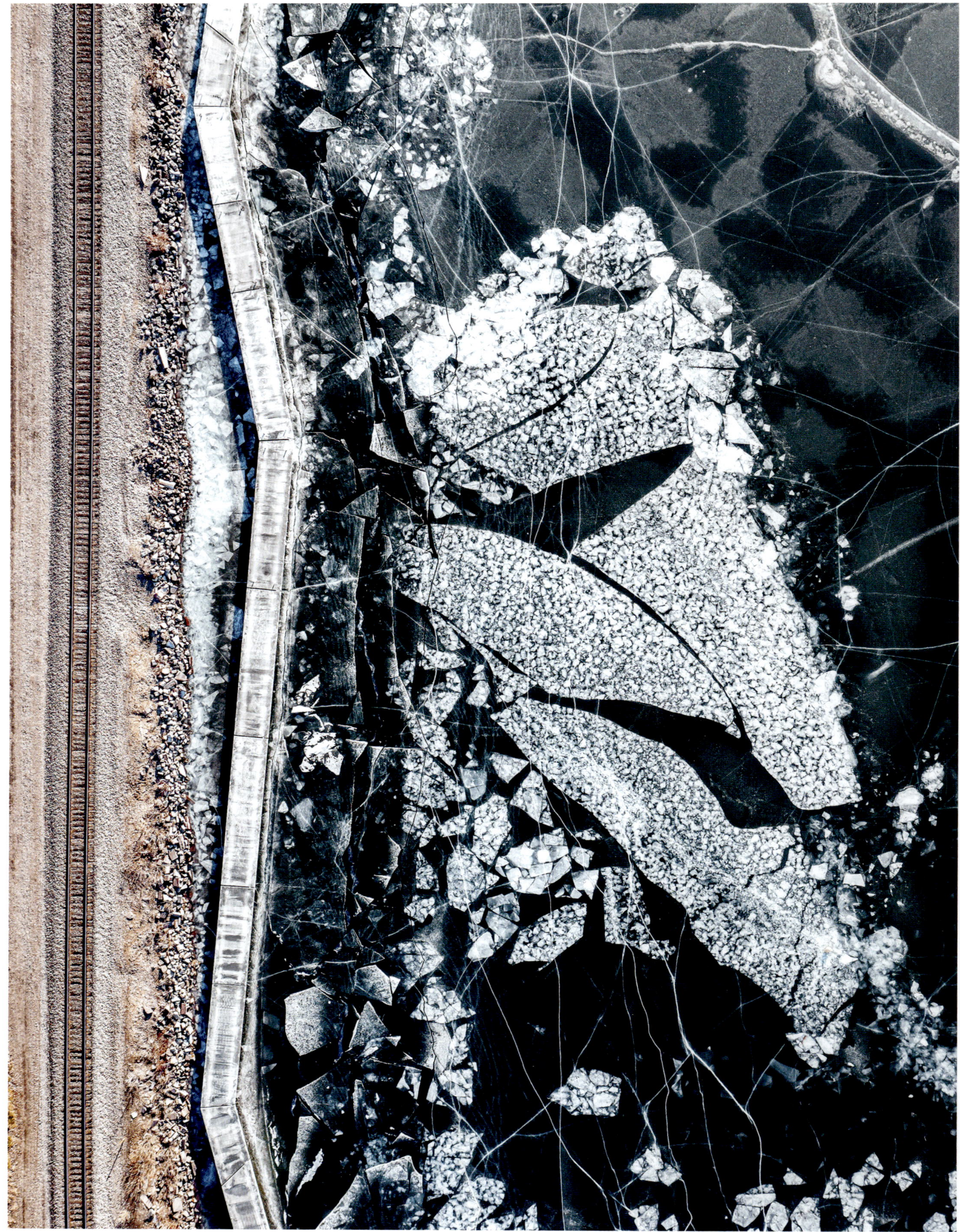

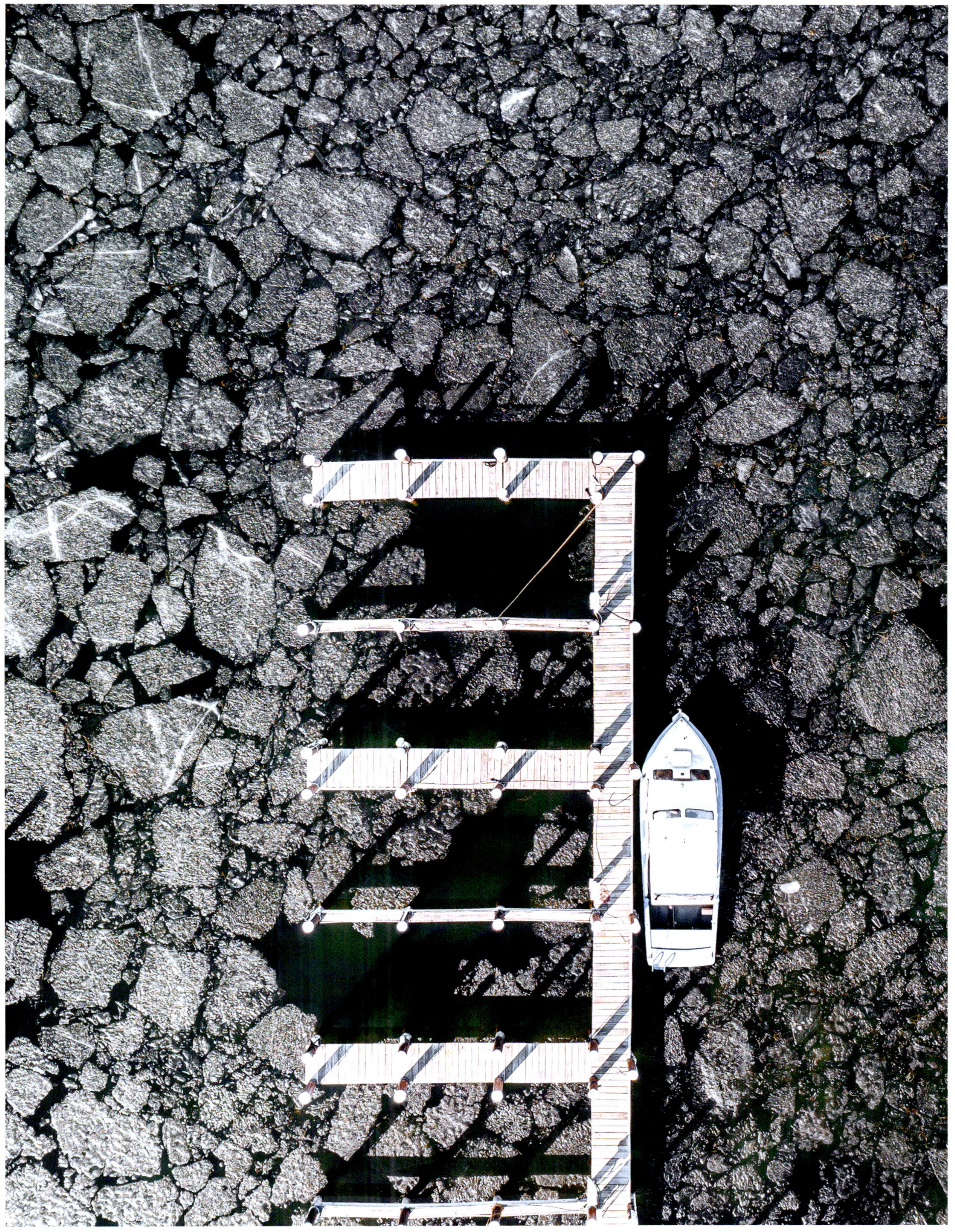

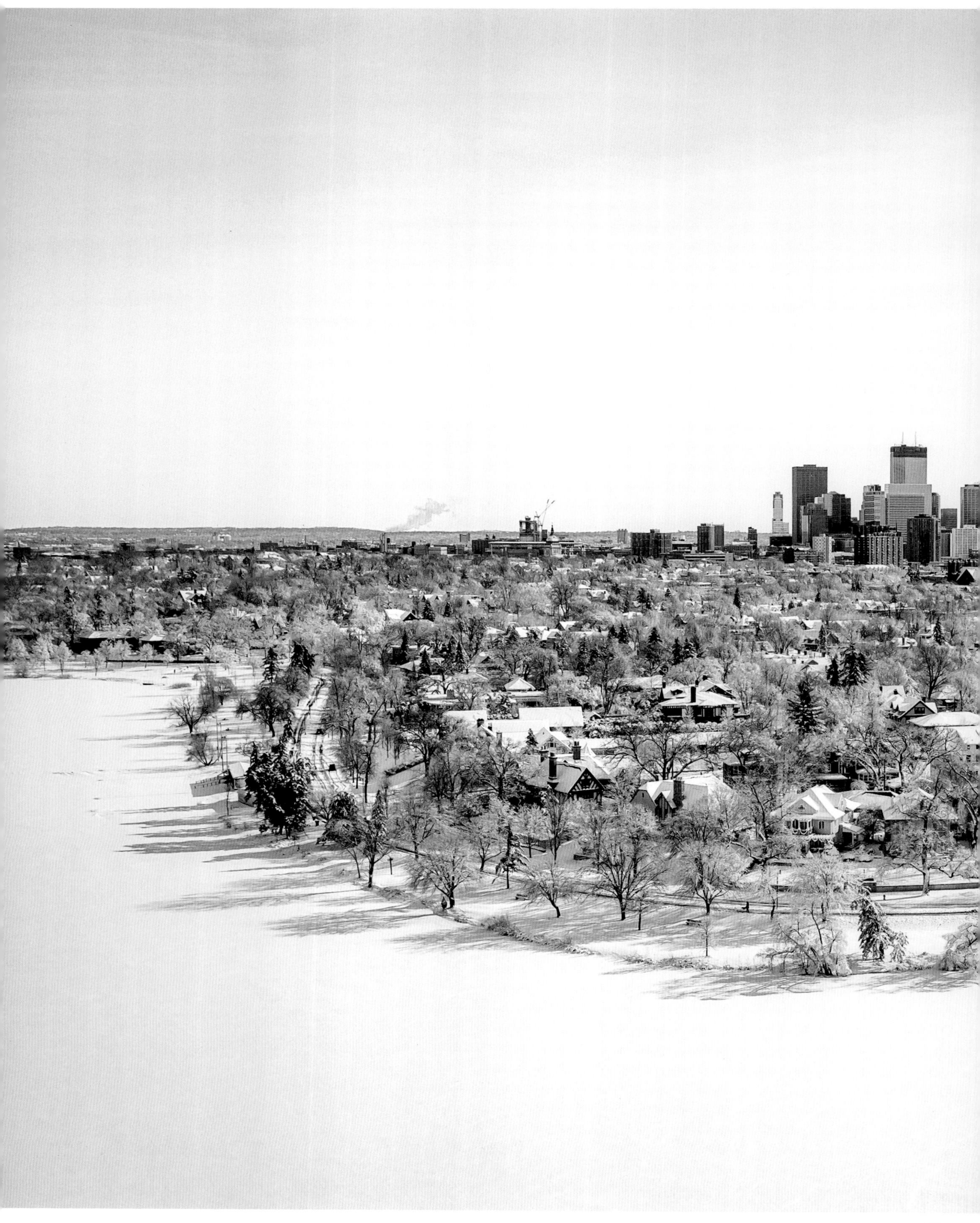

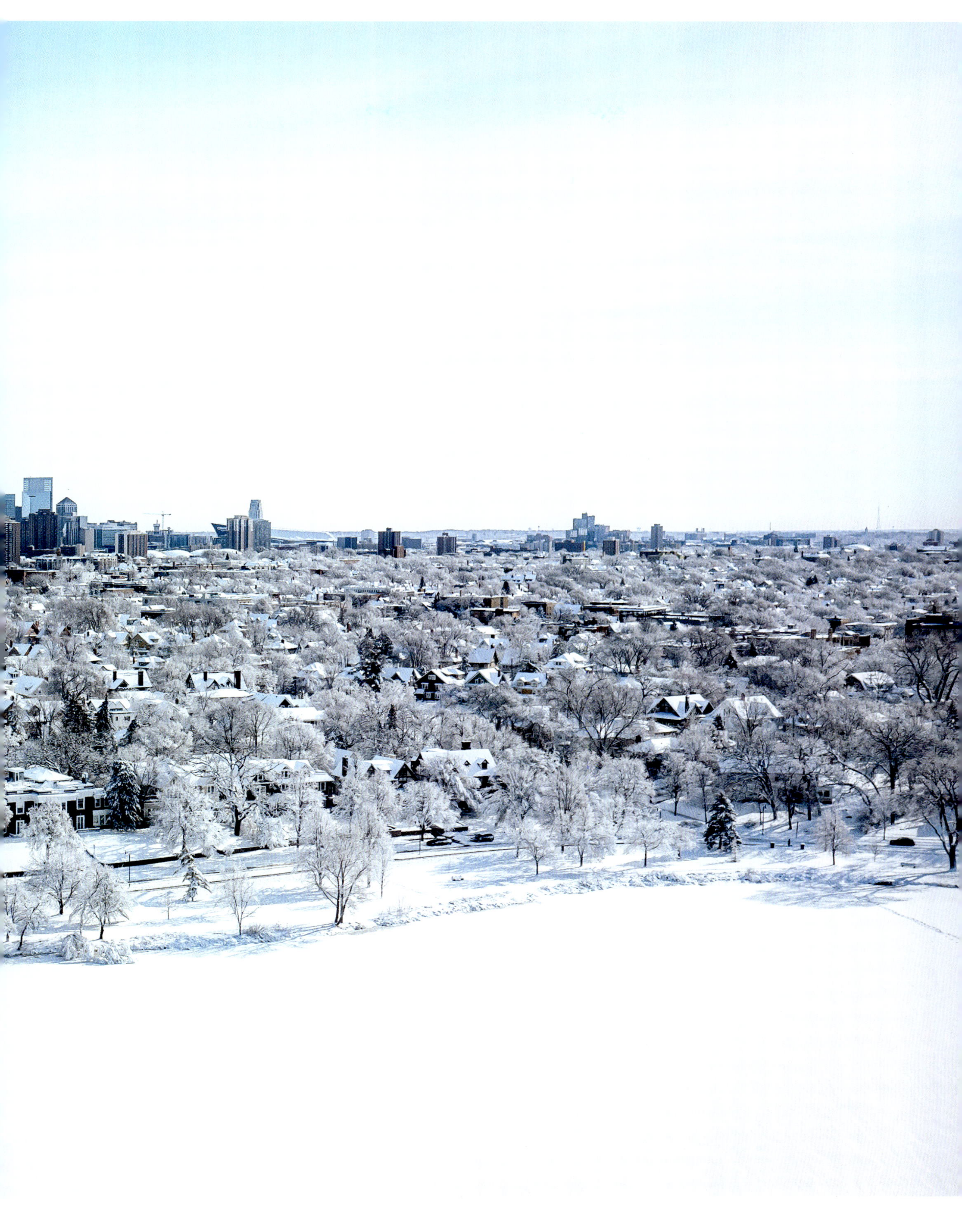

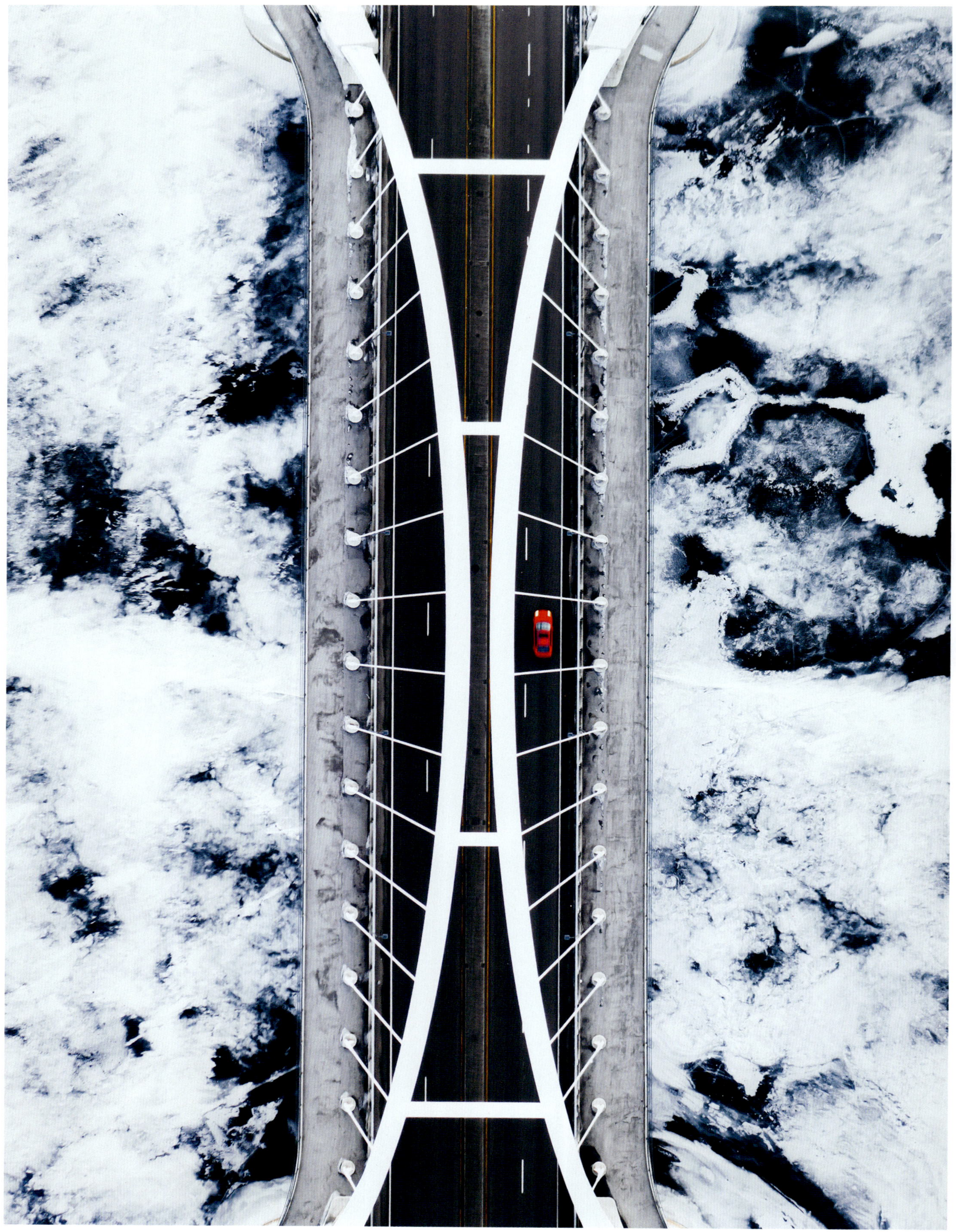

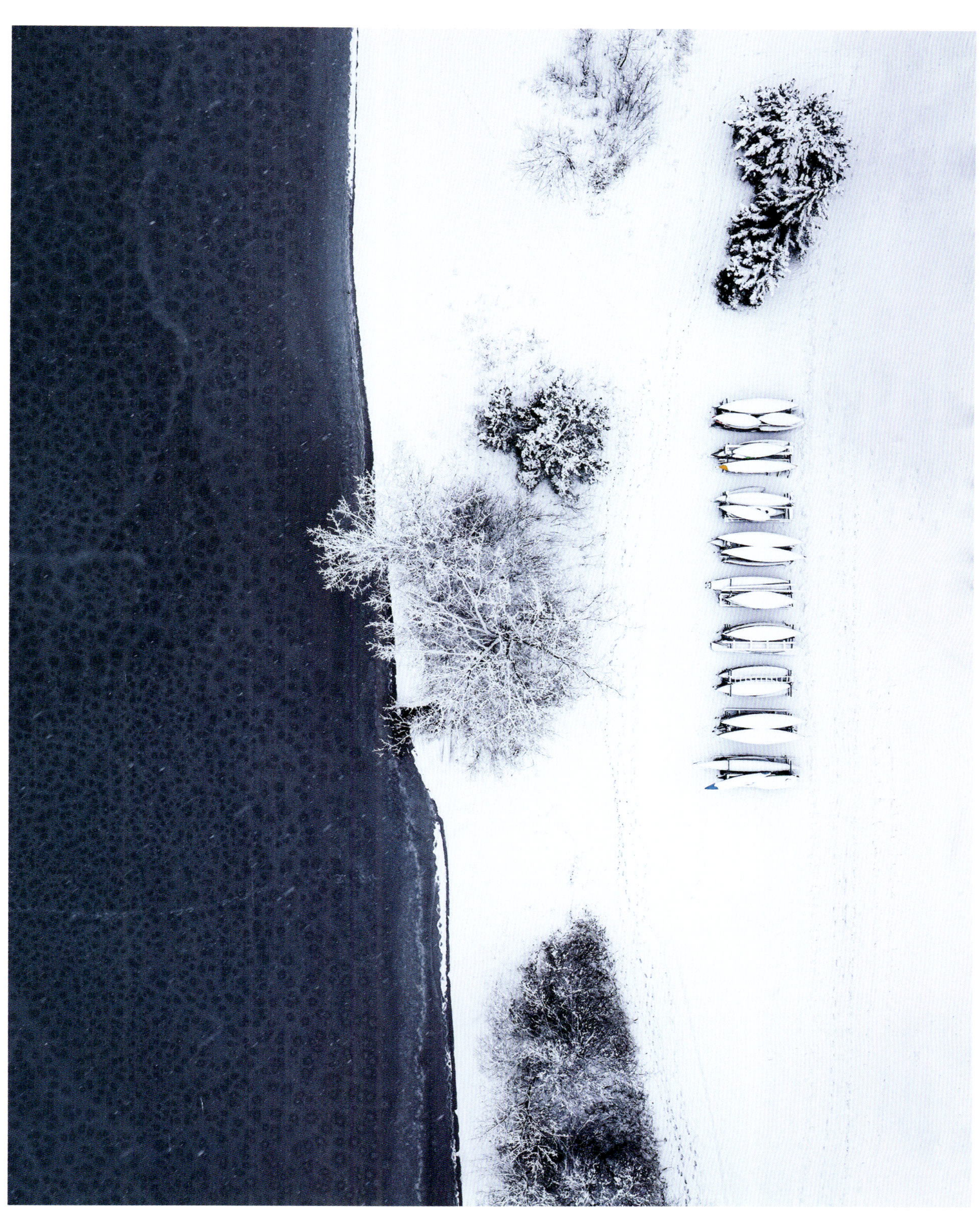

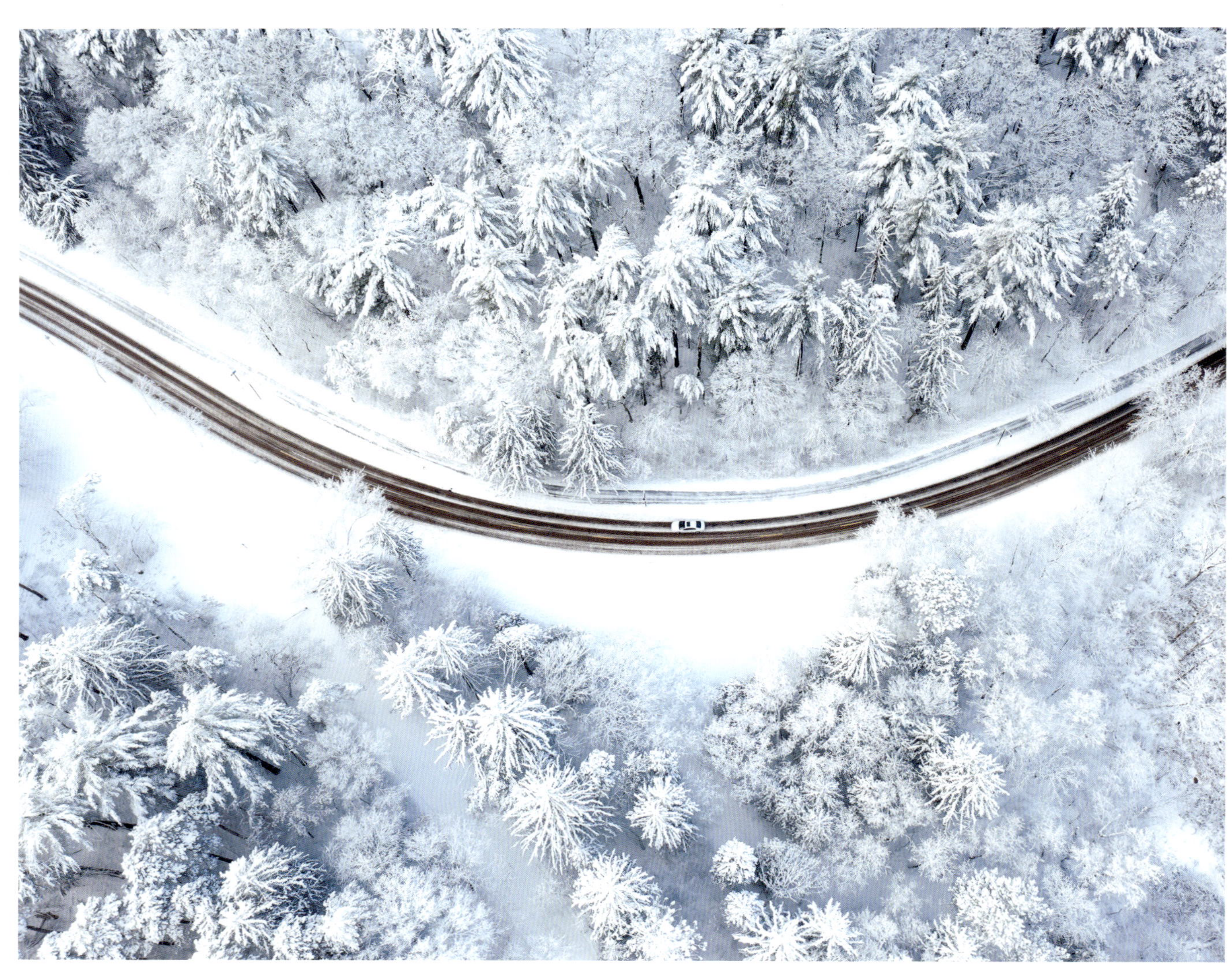

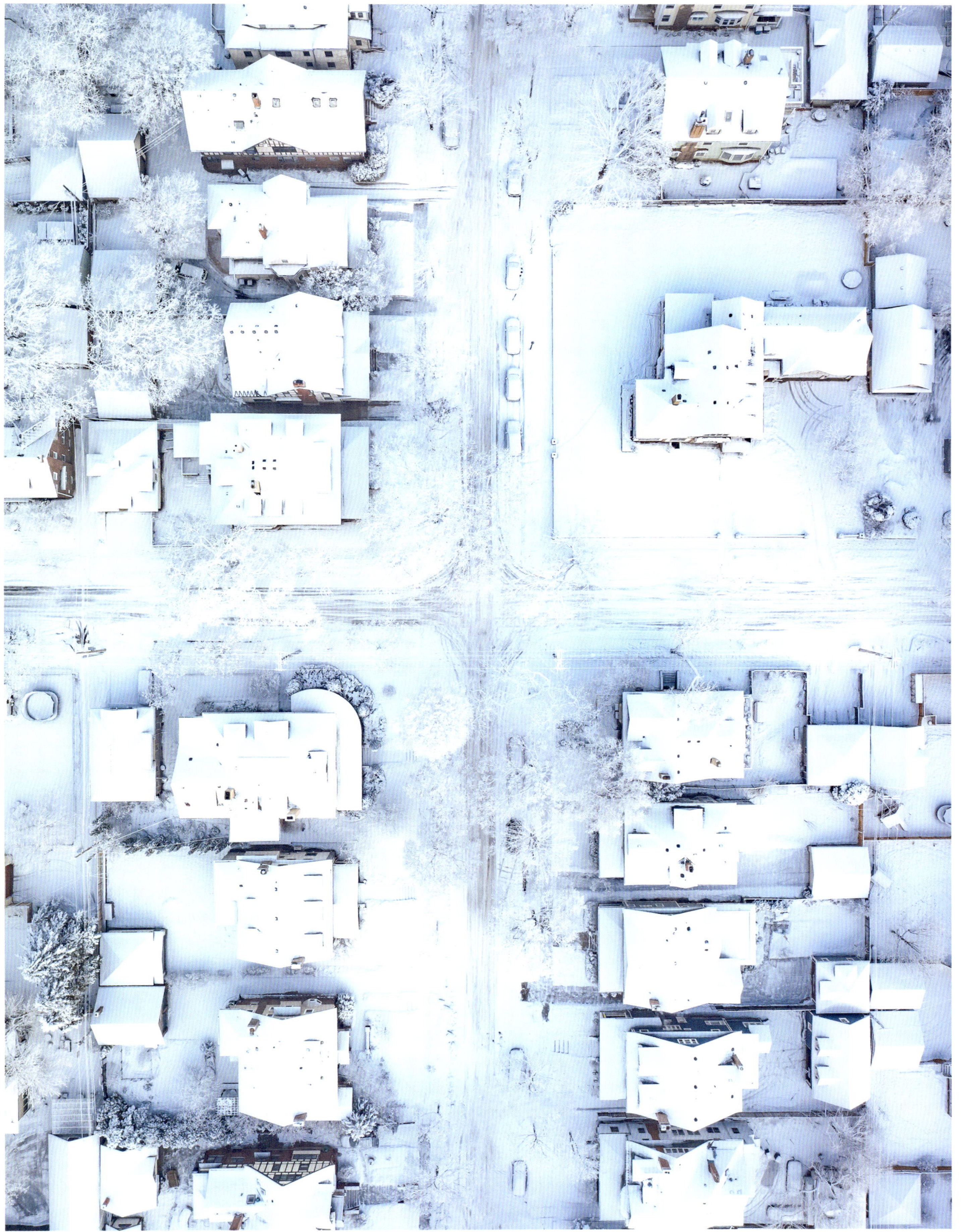

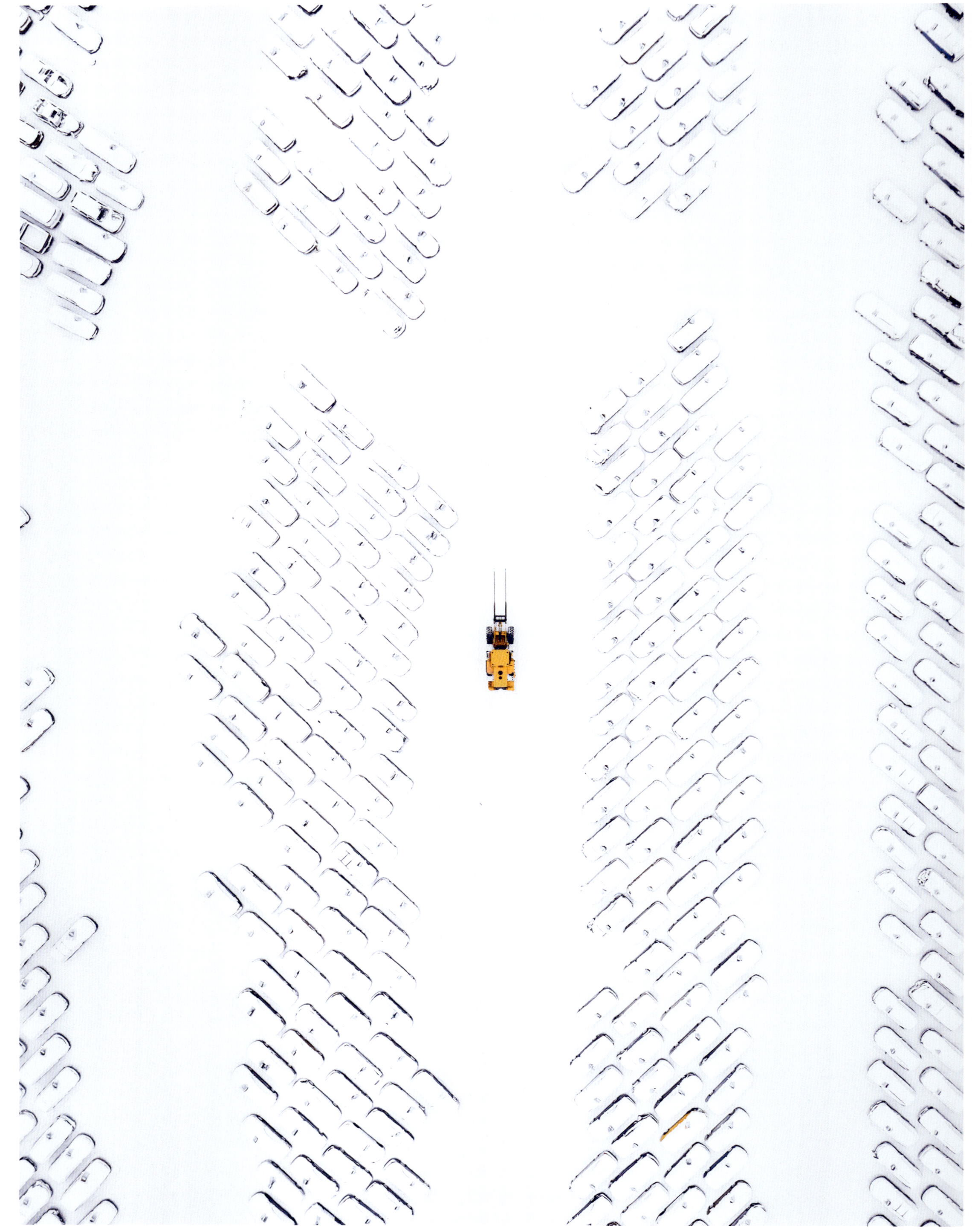

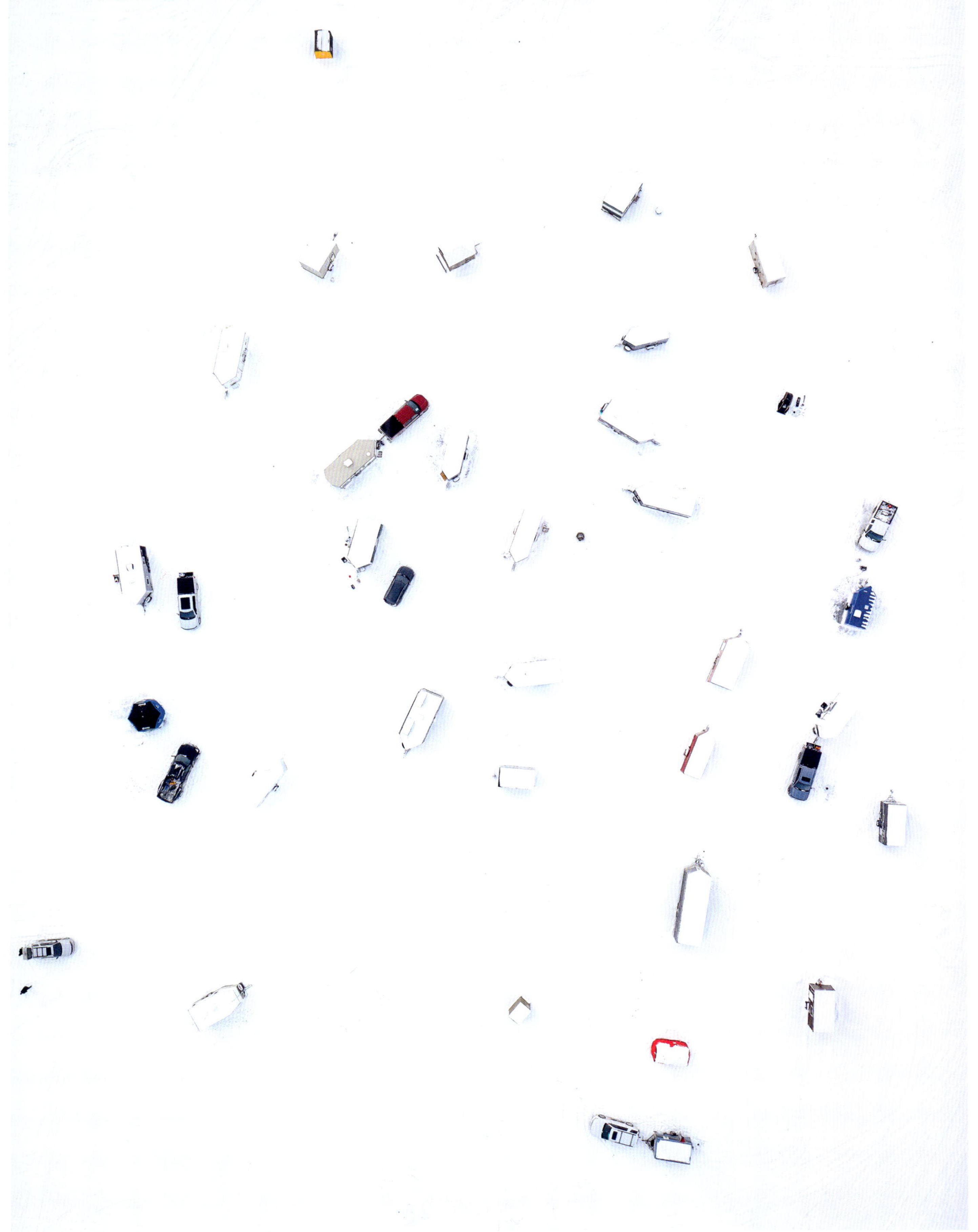

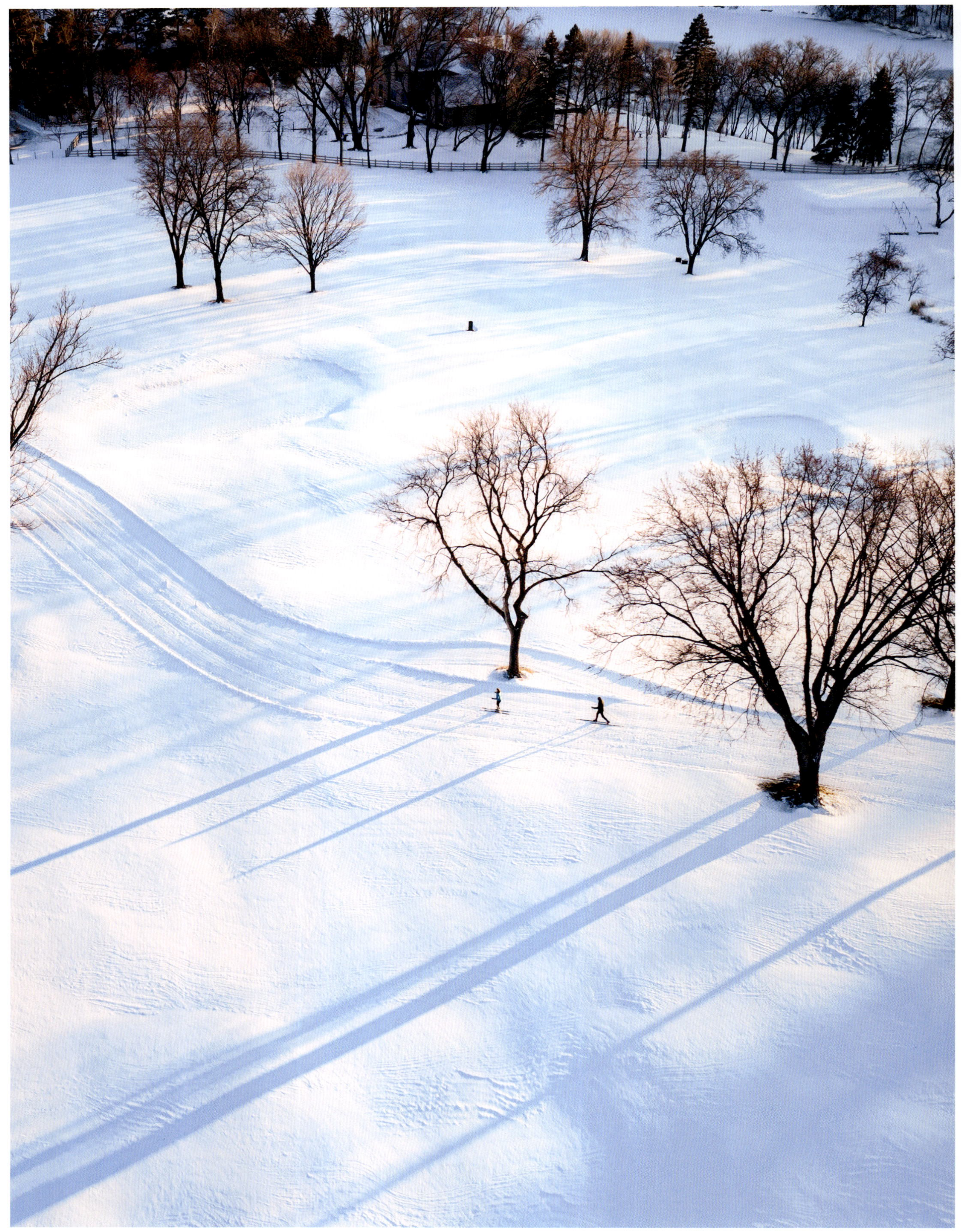

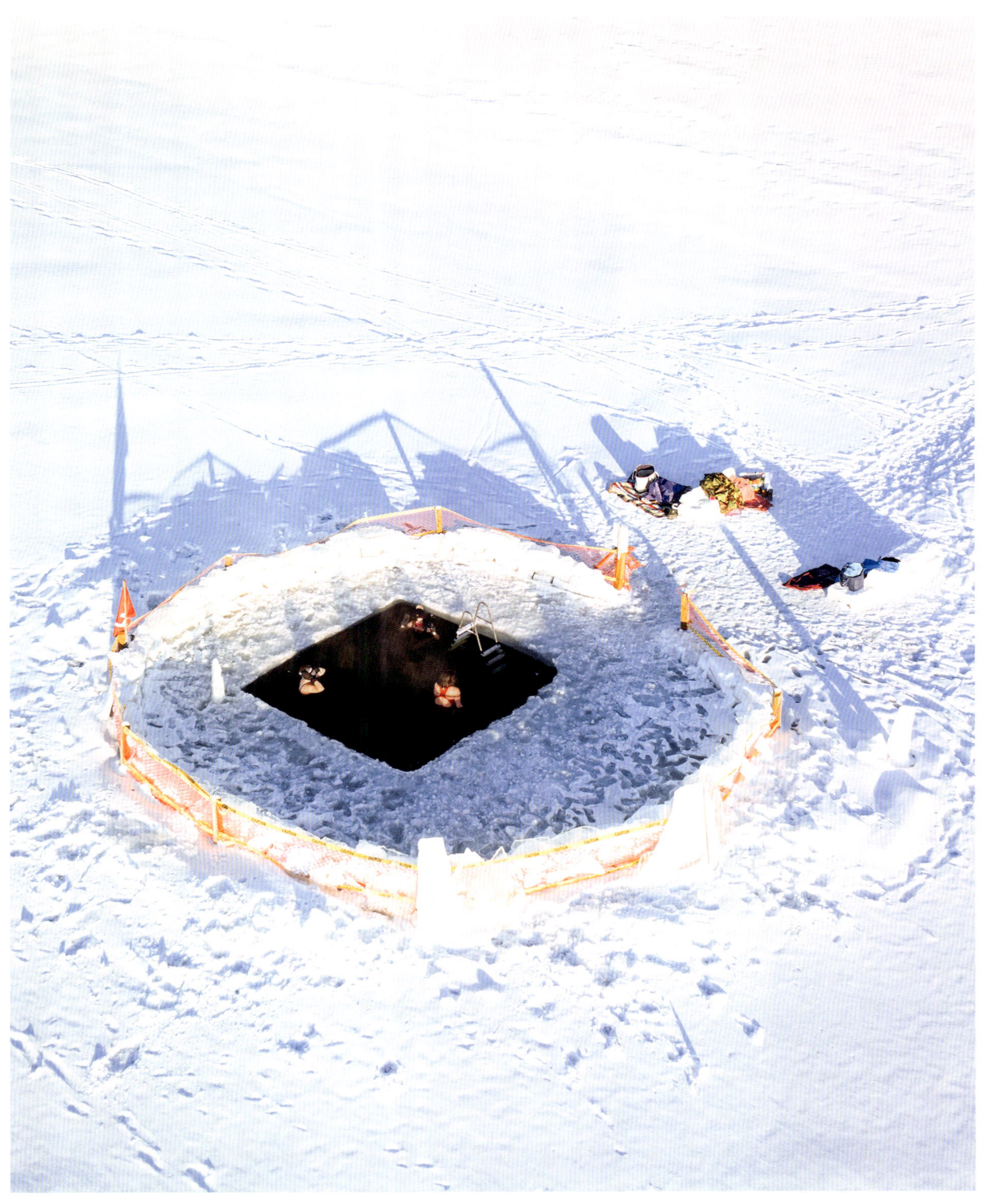

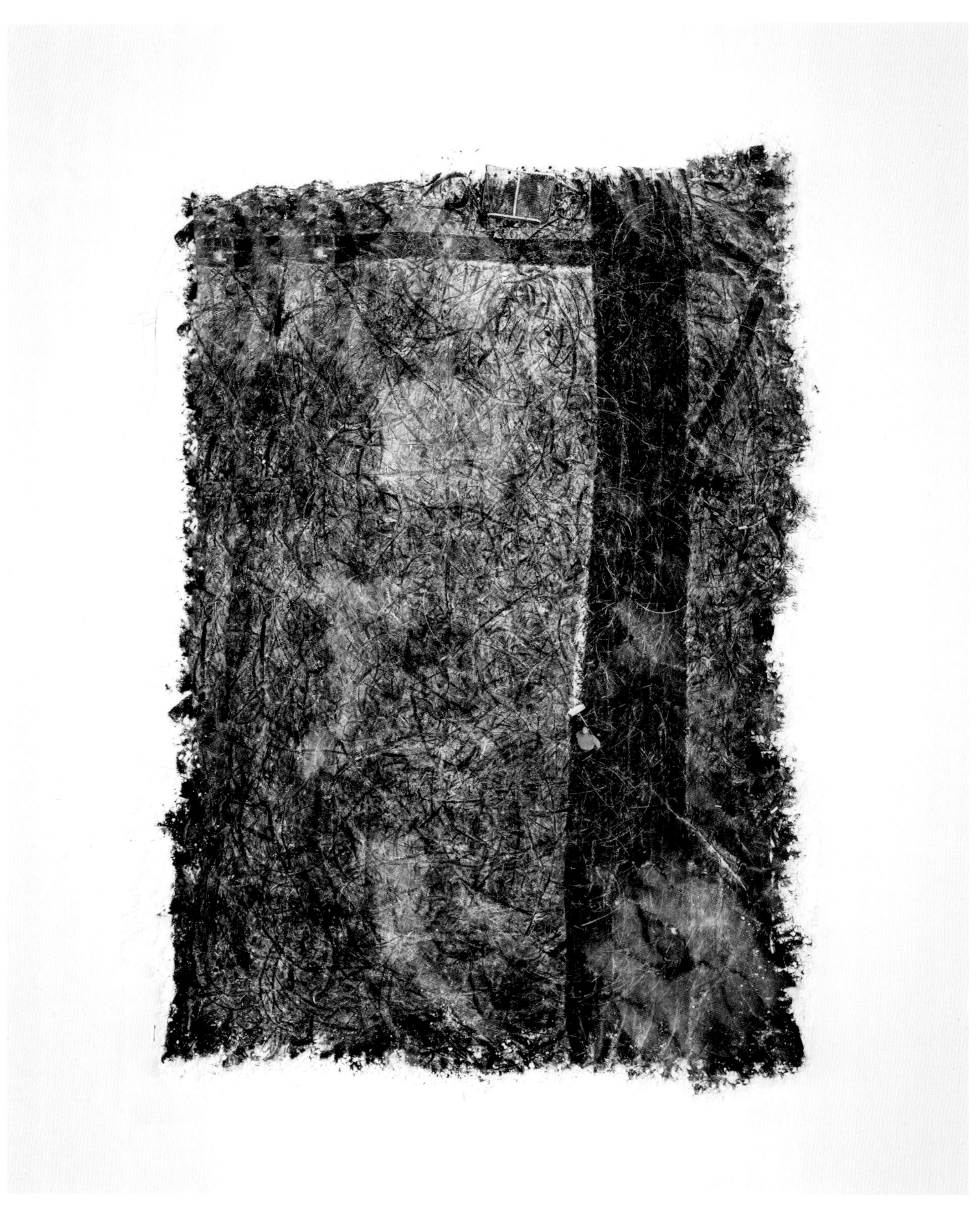

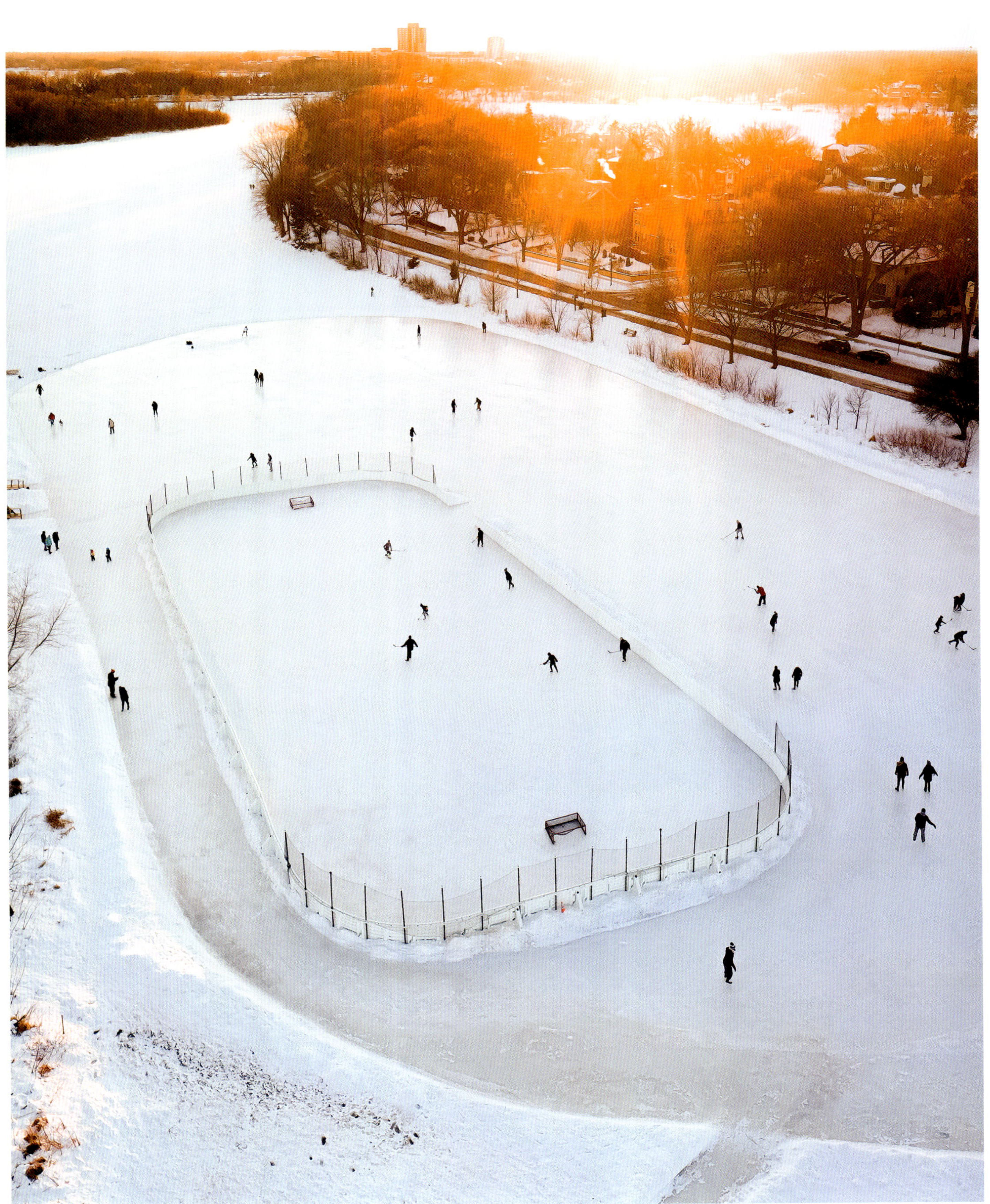

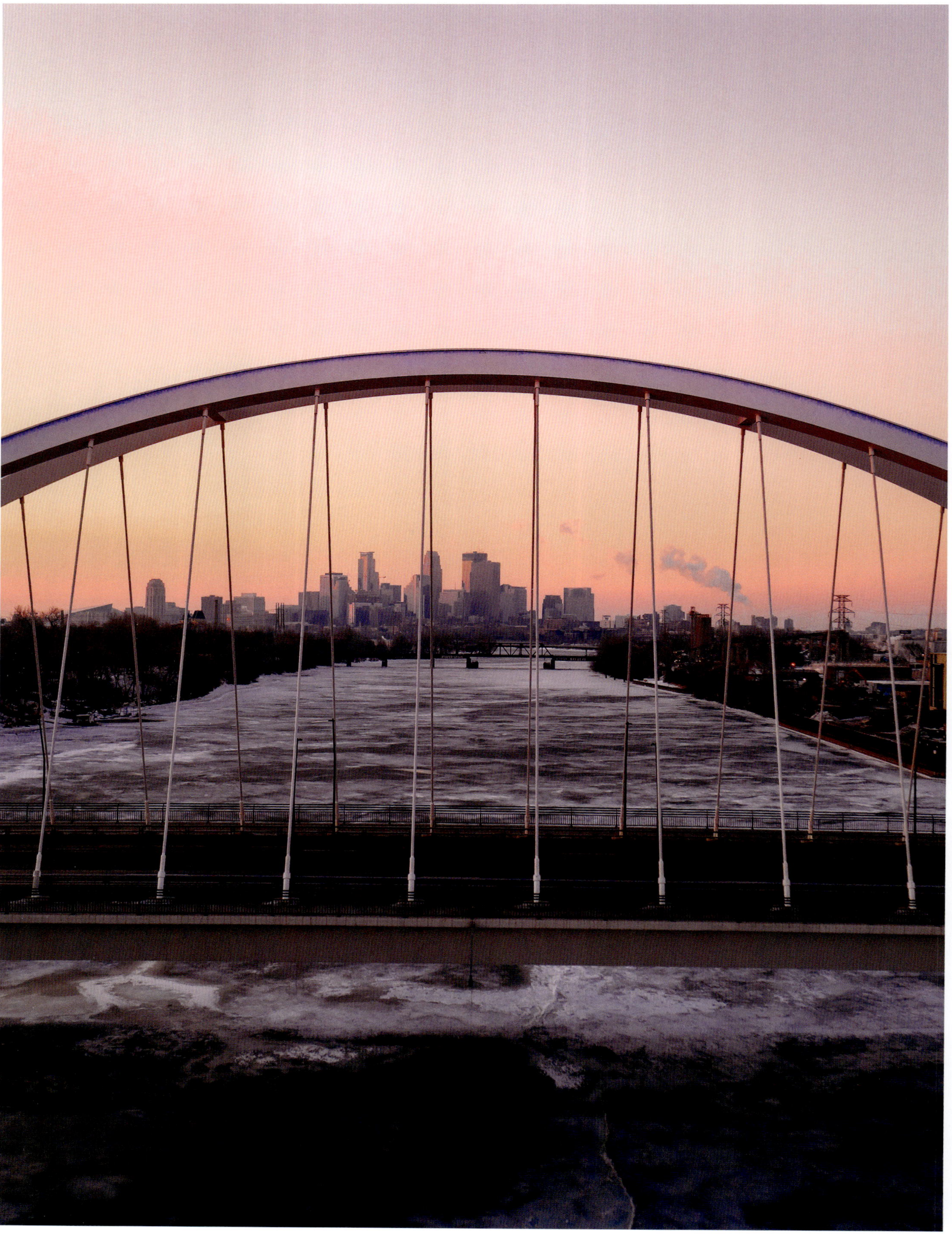

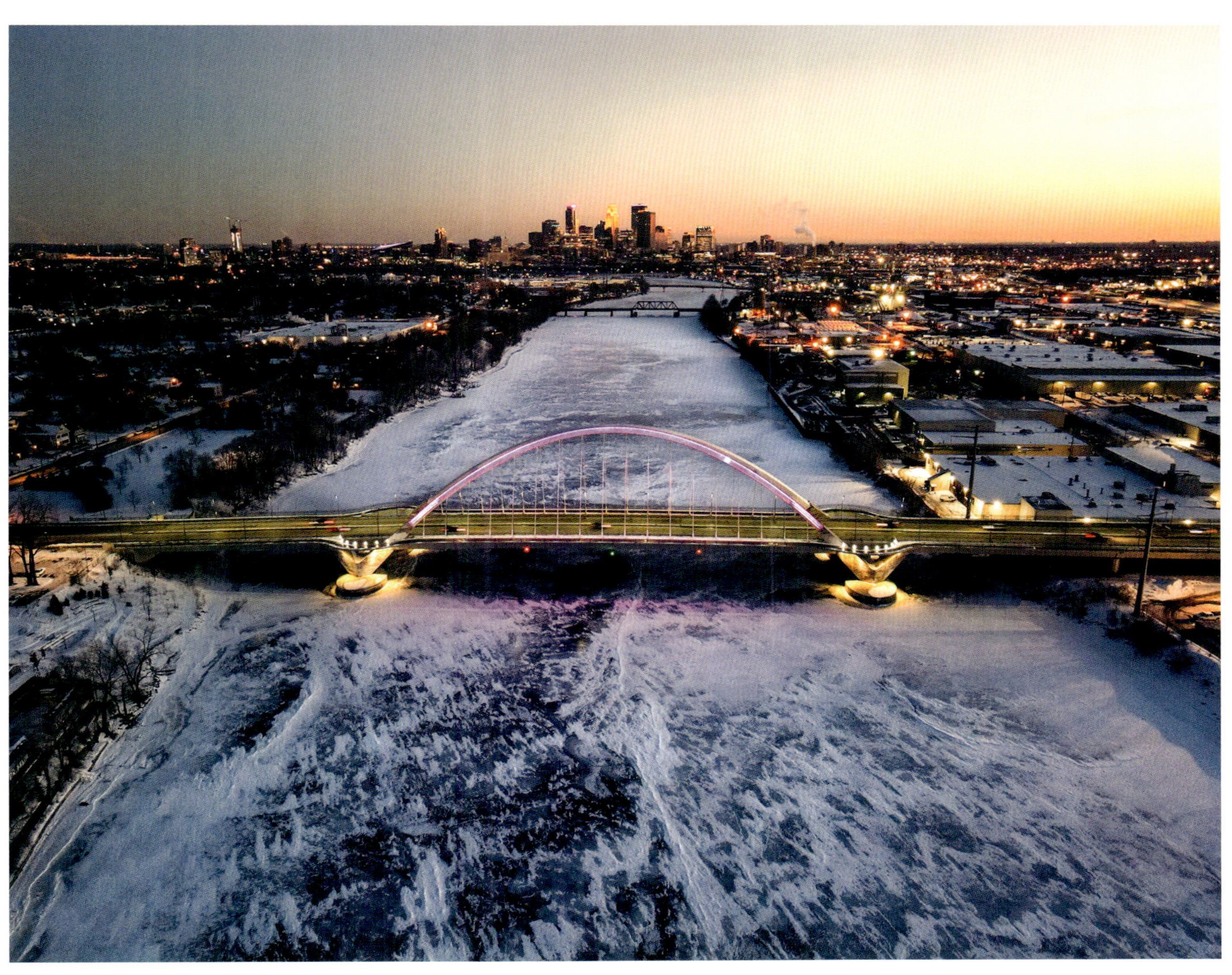

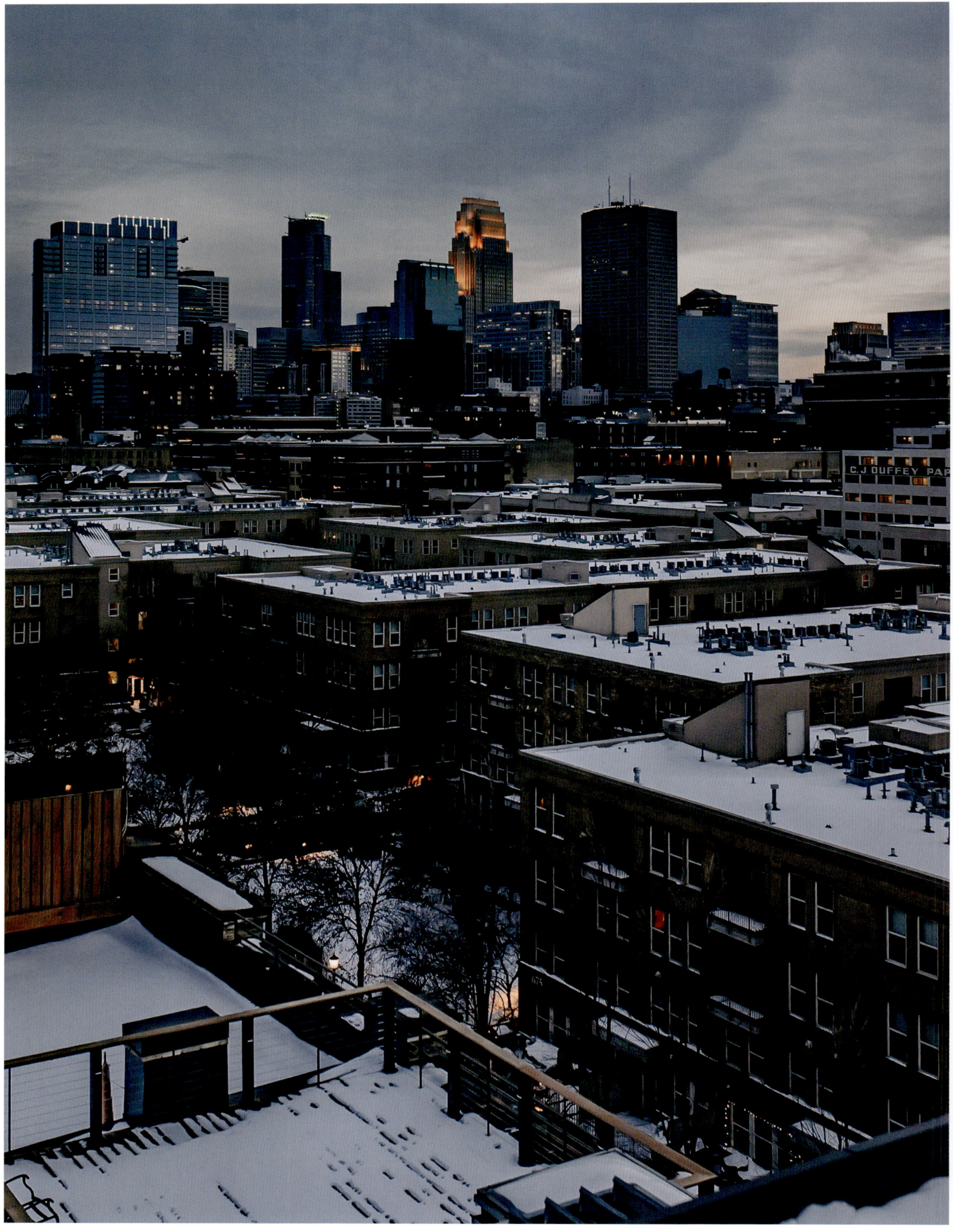

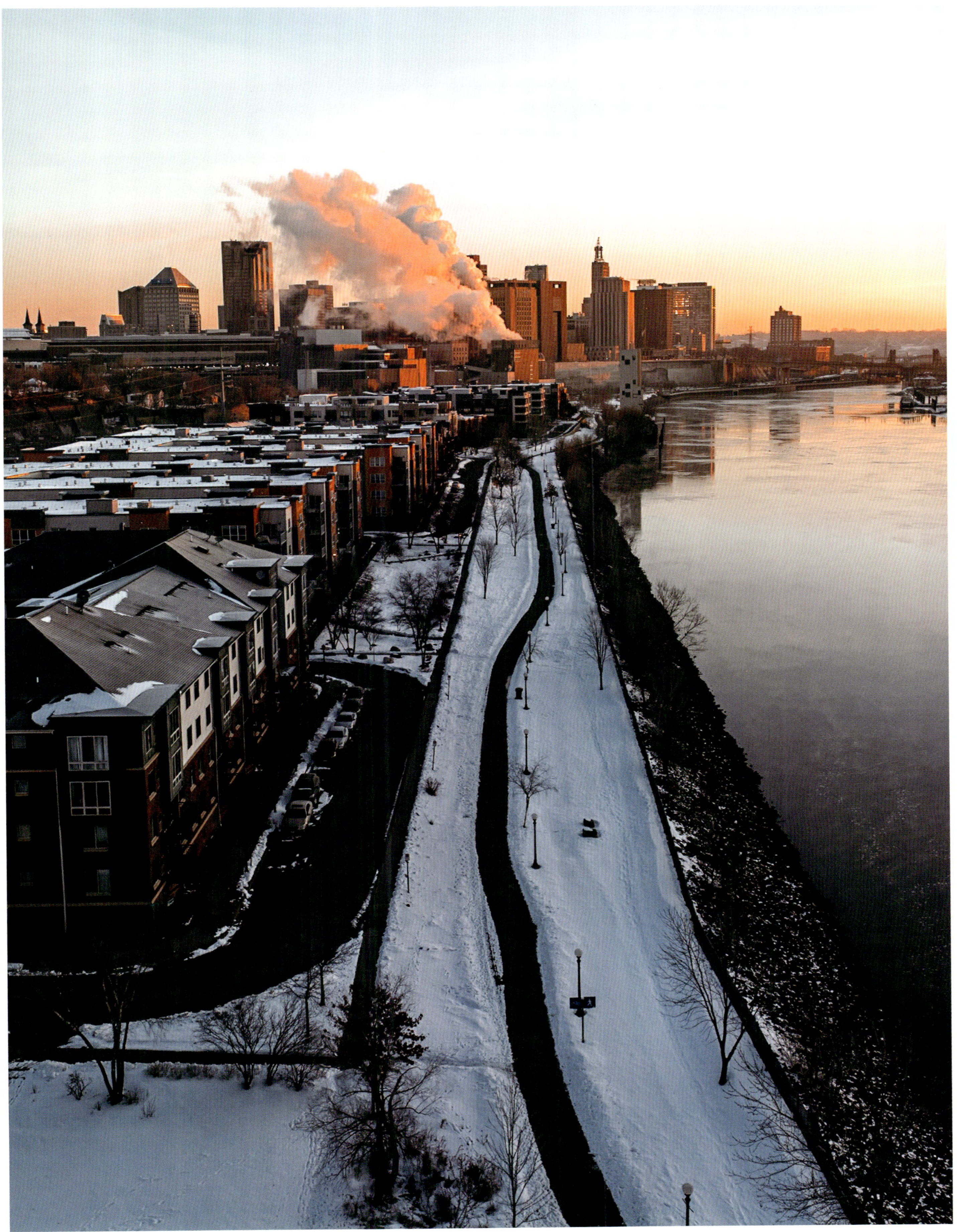

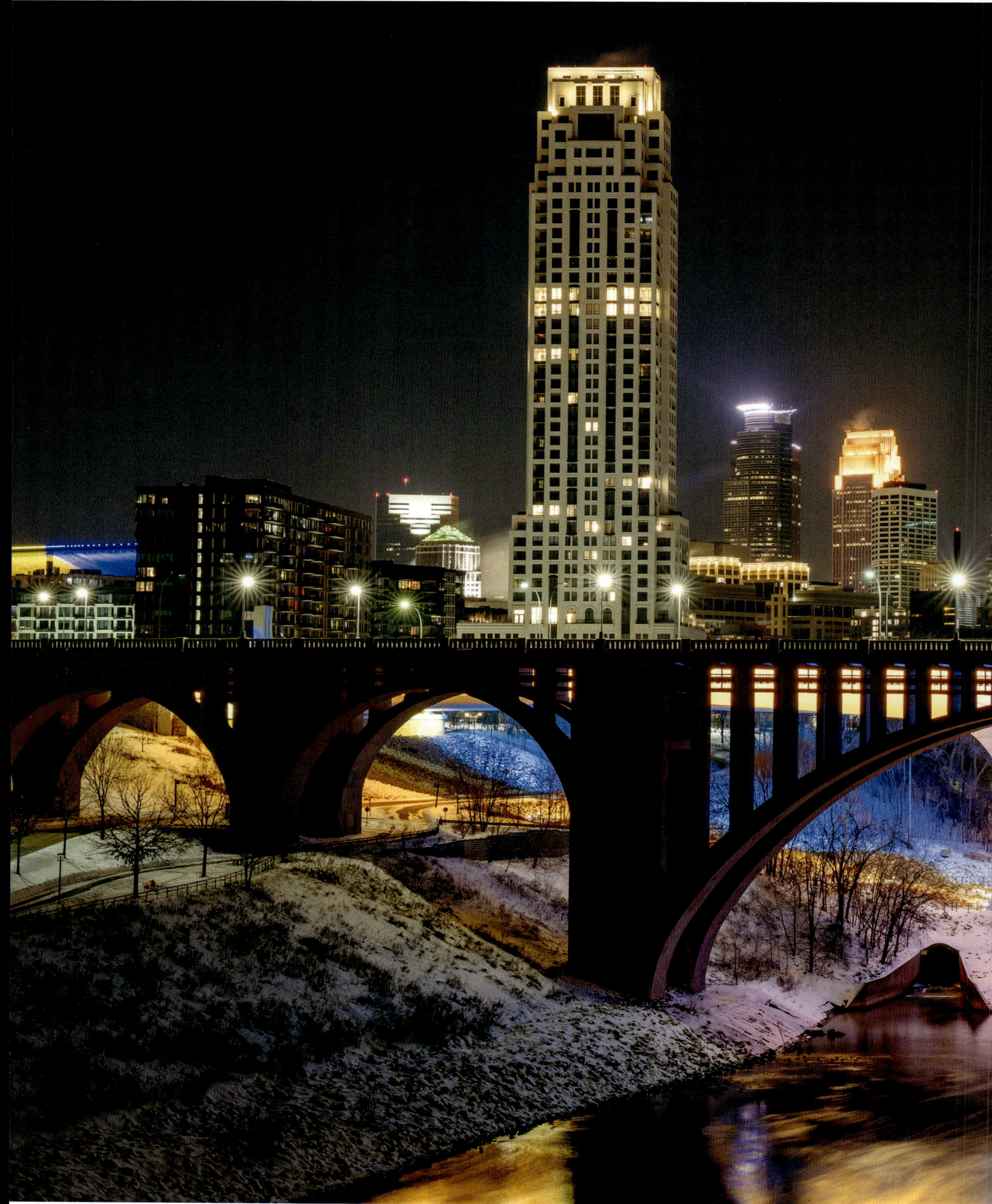

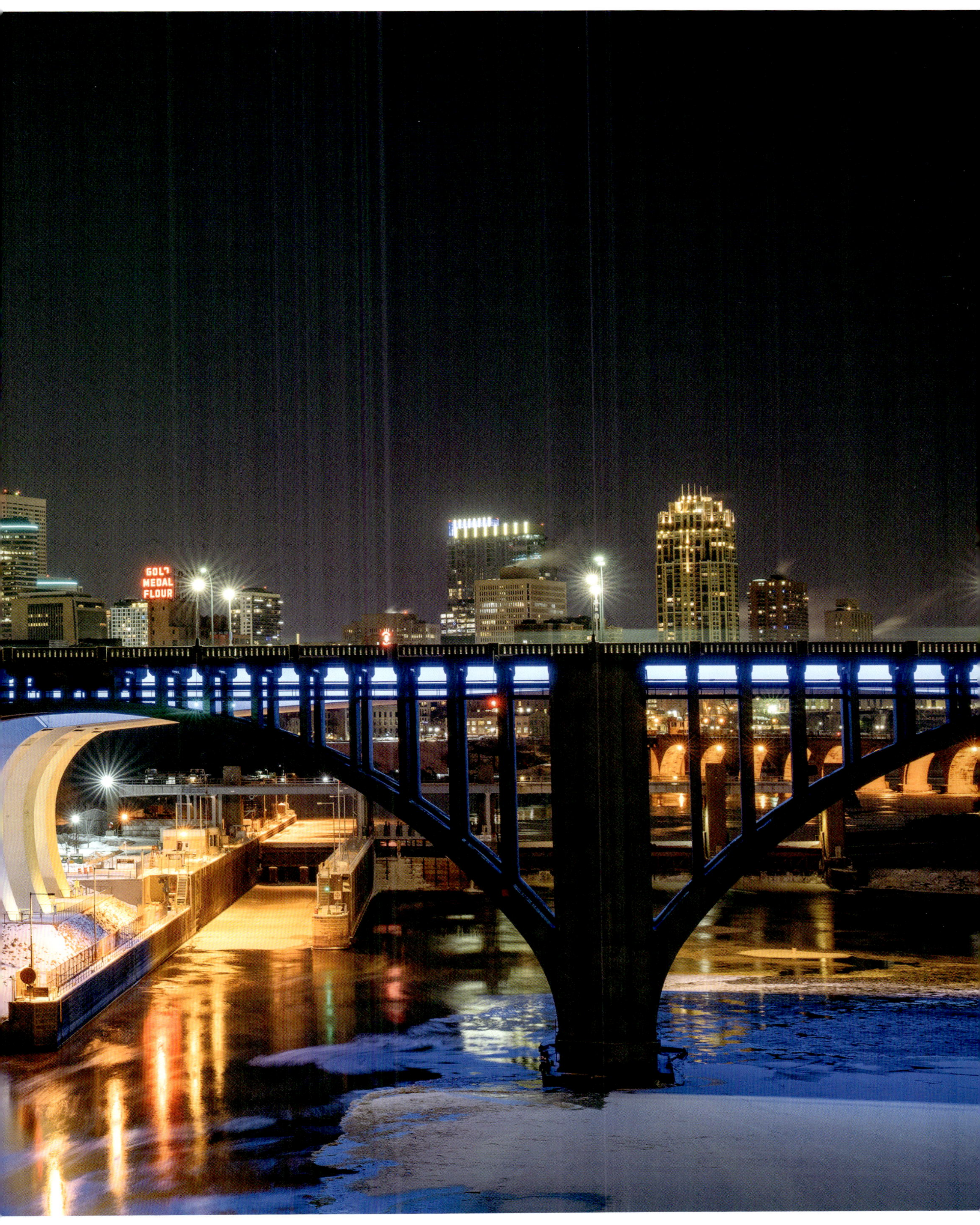

GOLD
MEDAL
FLOUR

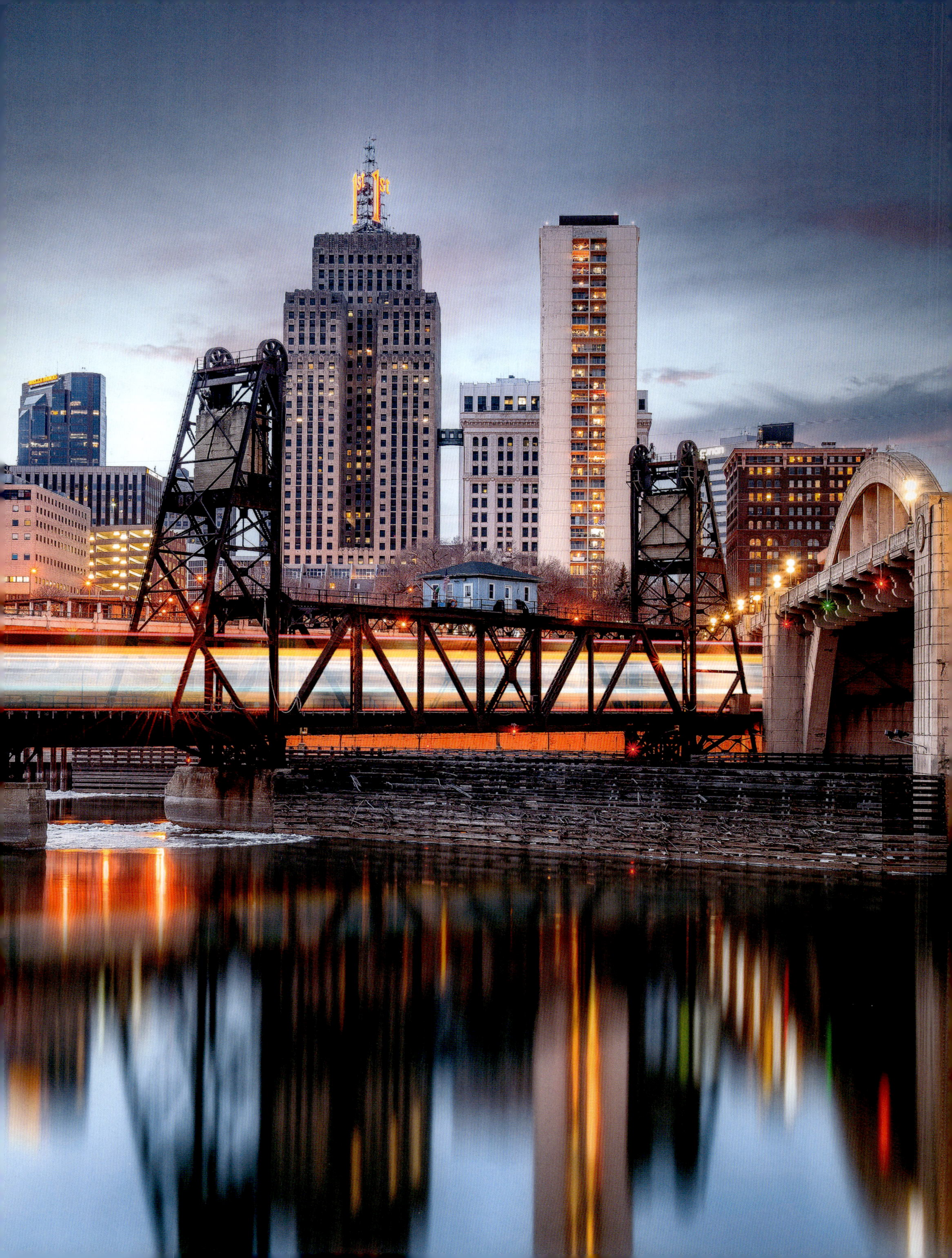

St. Paul ♦ St. Paul, the state capital and the smaller half of the Twin Cities, has a rich history that reflects its early role as a transportation hub, a political center, and a cultural crossroads. Its story begins long before European settlement, when the Dakota people inhabited the area along the Mississippi River, utilizing its fertile banks for hunting, fishing, and trade. ♦ St. Paul's location along the Mississippi River made it a natural transportation hub. Steamboats connected St. Paul to other river towns, and by the late 19th century, the arrival of railroads solidified the city's position as a gateway to the Upper Midwest, earning it the nickname "The Last City of the East" as it was the final stop on major river and rail routes heading west. ♦ The current Minnesota State Capitol building, located on a natural rise overlooking the Mississippi River known as Capitol Hill, was completed in 1905, but is actually the third Minnesota State Capitol. The first statehouse was a modest wooden structure on Wabasha Street, built in 1853 shortly after Minnesota became a territory. It served the early government but quickly became too small for the growing state. In 1882, a second, more substantial Capitol built of stone and brick in a Victorian style was constructed nearby. However, this building proved inadequate as Minnesota's population and government functions expanded rapidly, and it suffered from functional limitations and safety concerns. ♦ A new, grand capitol was authorized by the Minnesota Legislature in 1895, and a national design competition was held. Rising New York architect Cass Gilbert won the commission with a design inspired by classical European architecture, particularly the US Capitol building in Washington, DC. His design incorporated Greek and Renaissance elements and emphasized symmetry, monumental scale, and classical detailing. Its massive central dome rises 186 feet, making it the second-largest self-supported marble dome in the world after St. Peter's Basilica in Rome. The historic landmark remains in use today, housing the offices of the governor, the state Supreme Court, and the Minnesota Senate and House of Representatives.

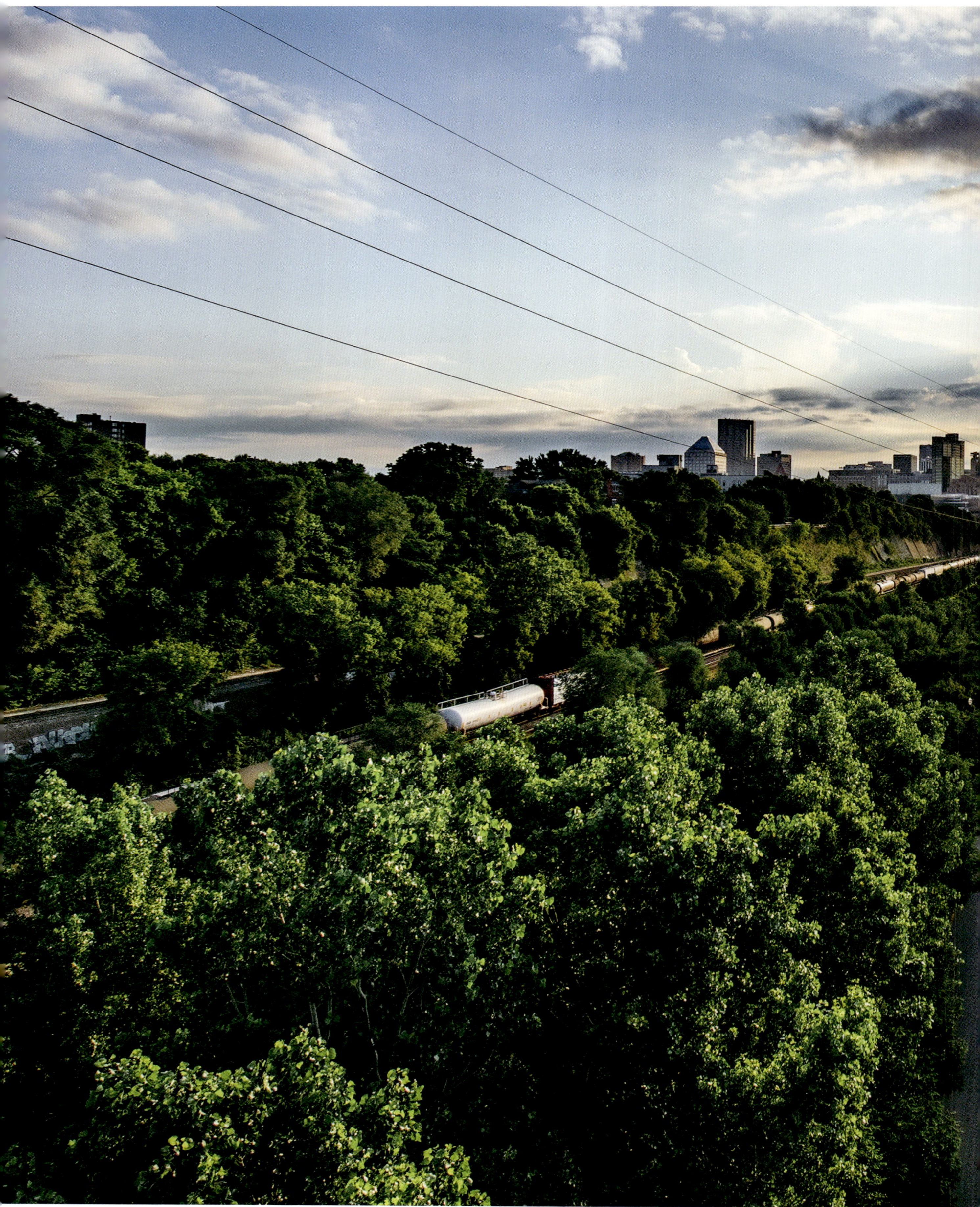

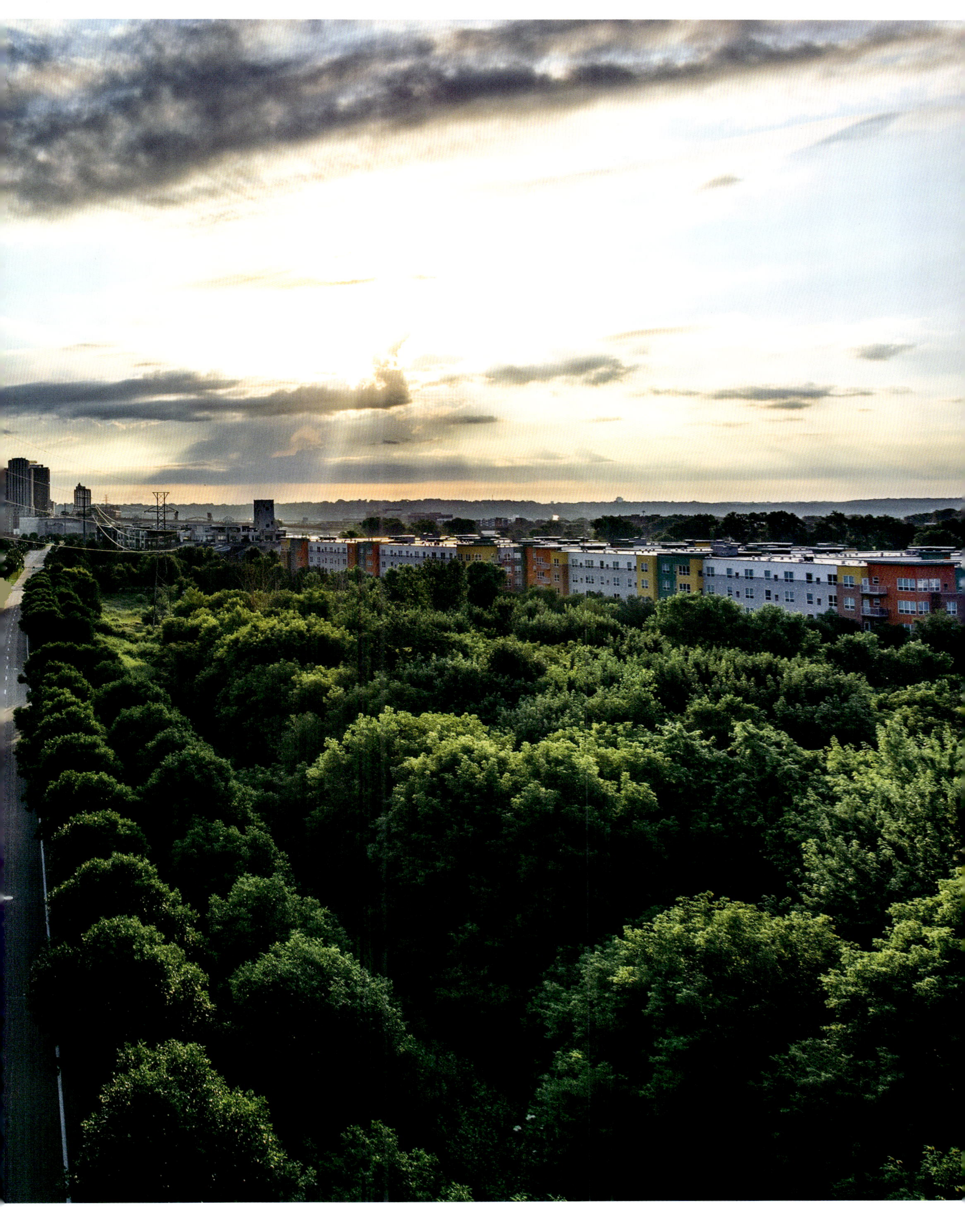

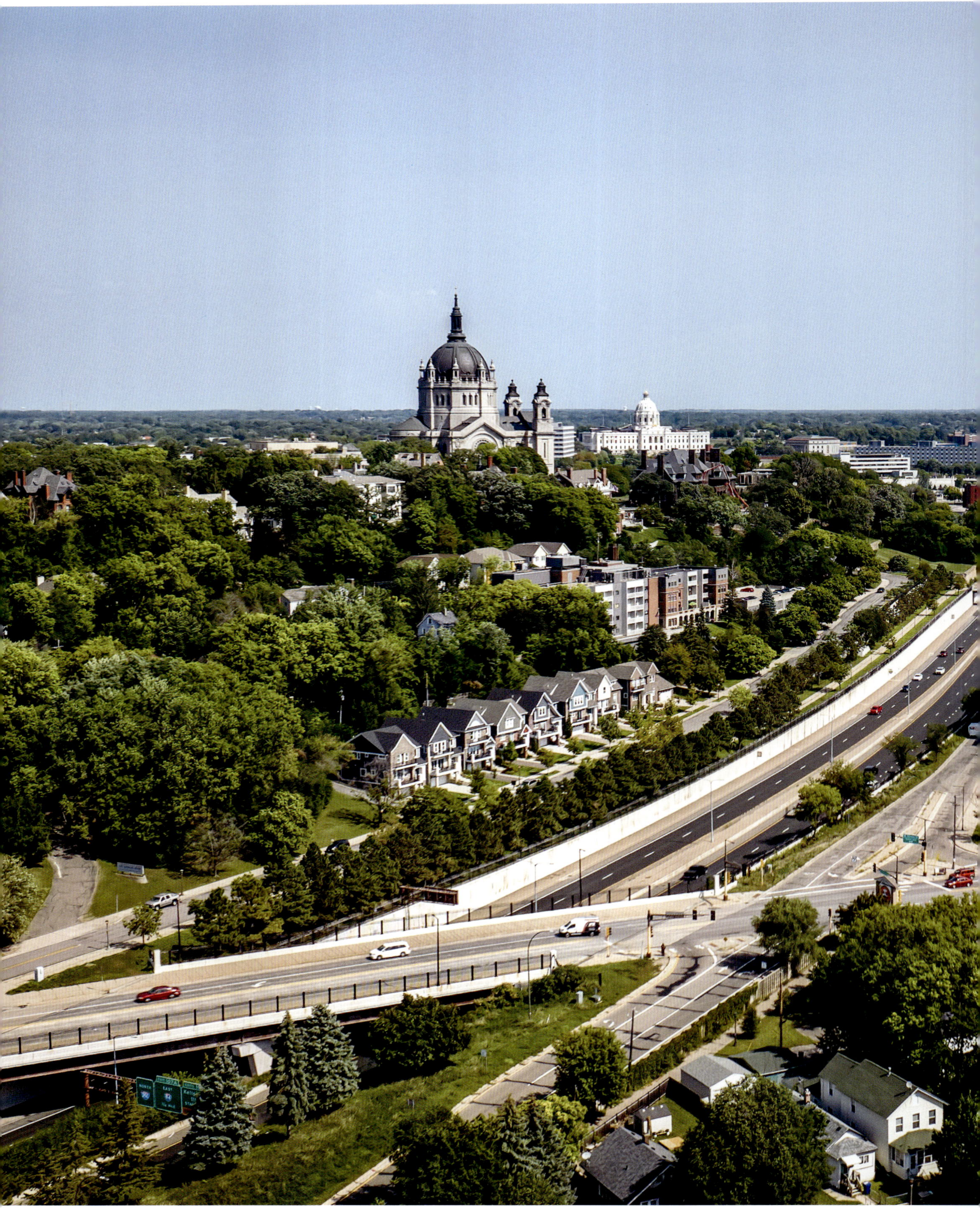

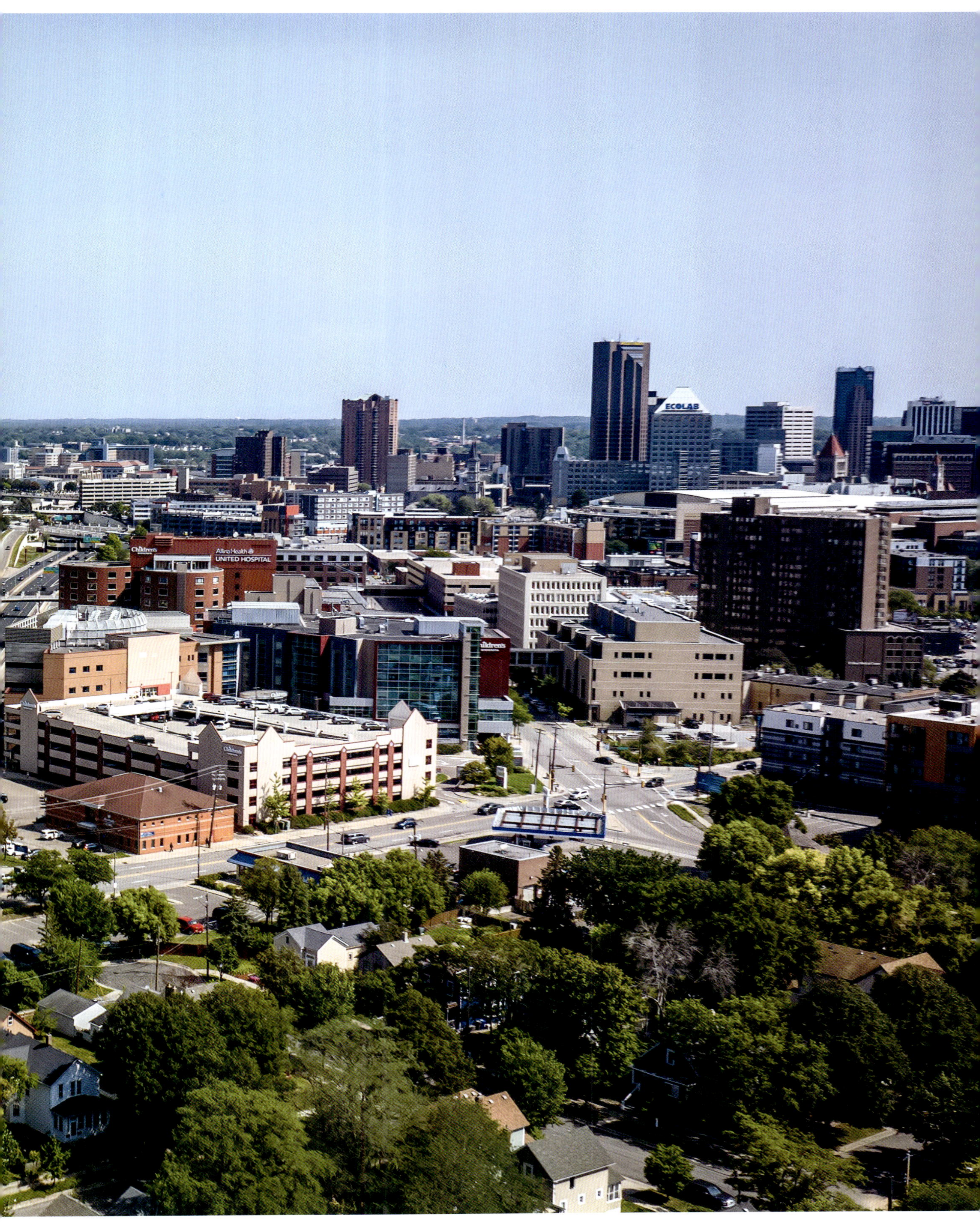

ECOLAB
Children's
Allina Health
UNITED HOSPITAL
Children's

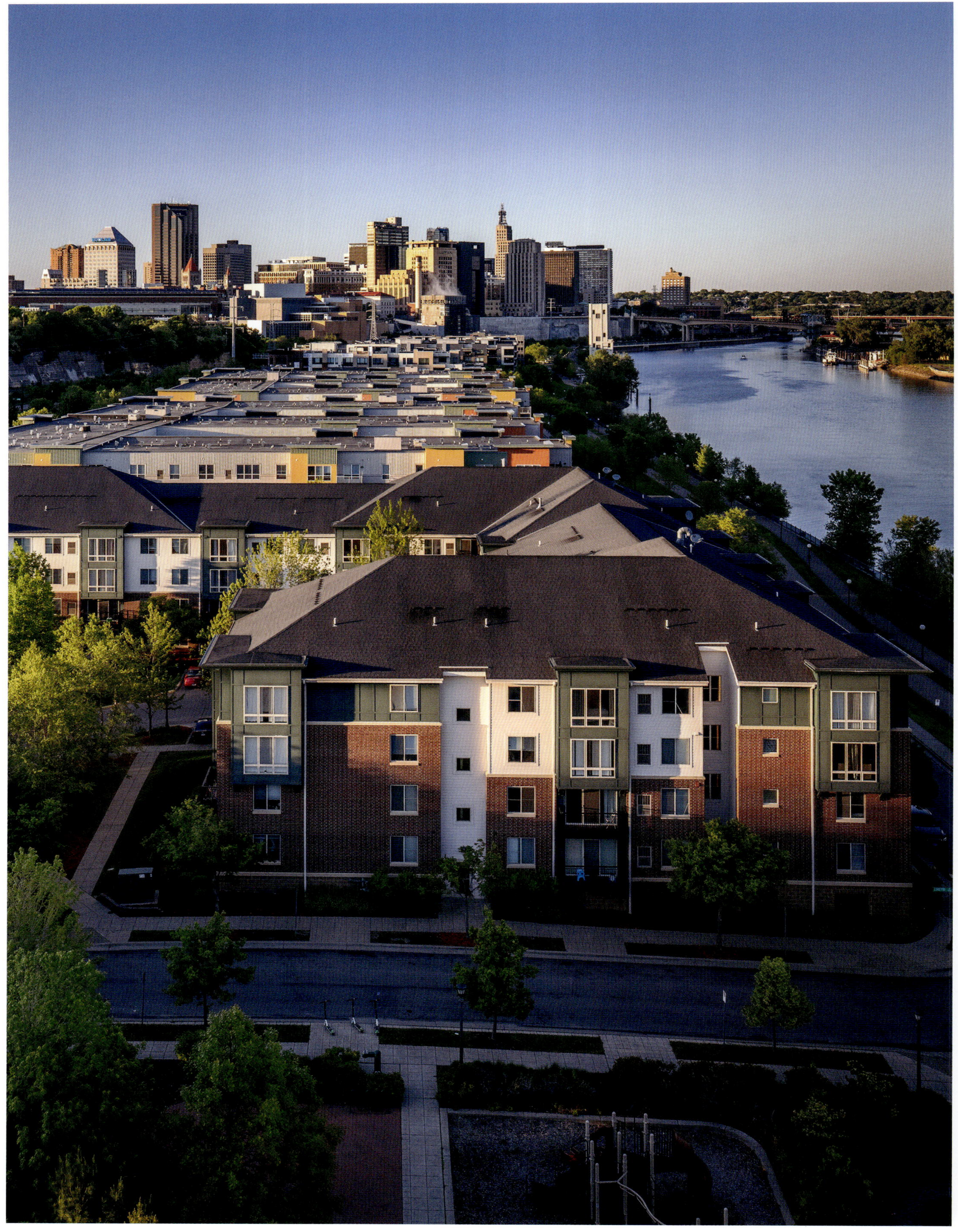

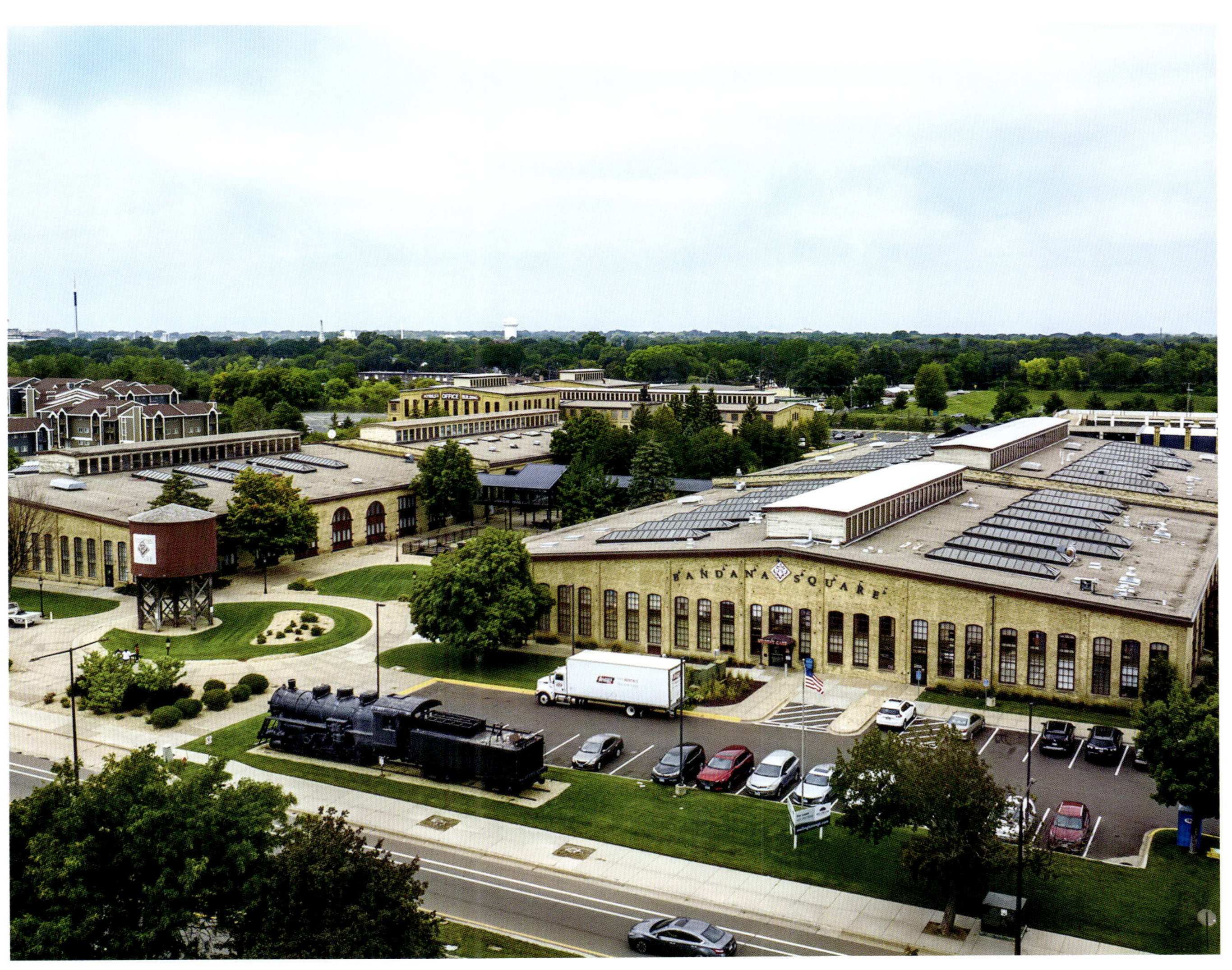
BANDANA SQUARE

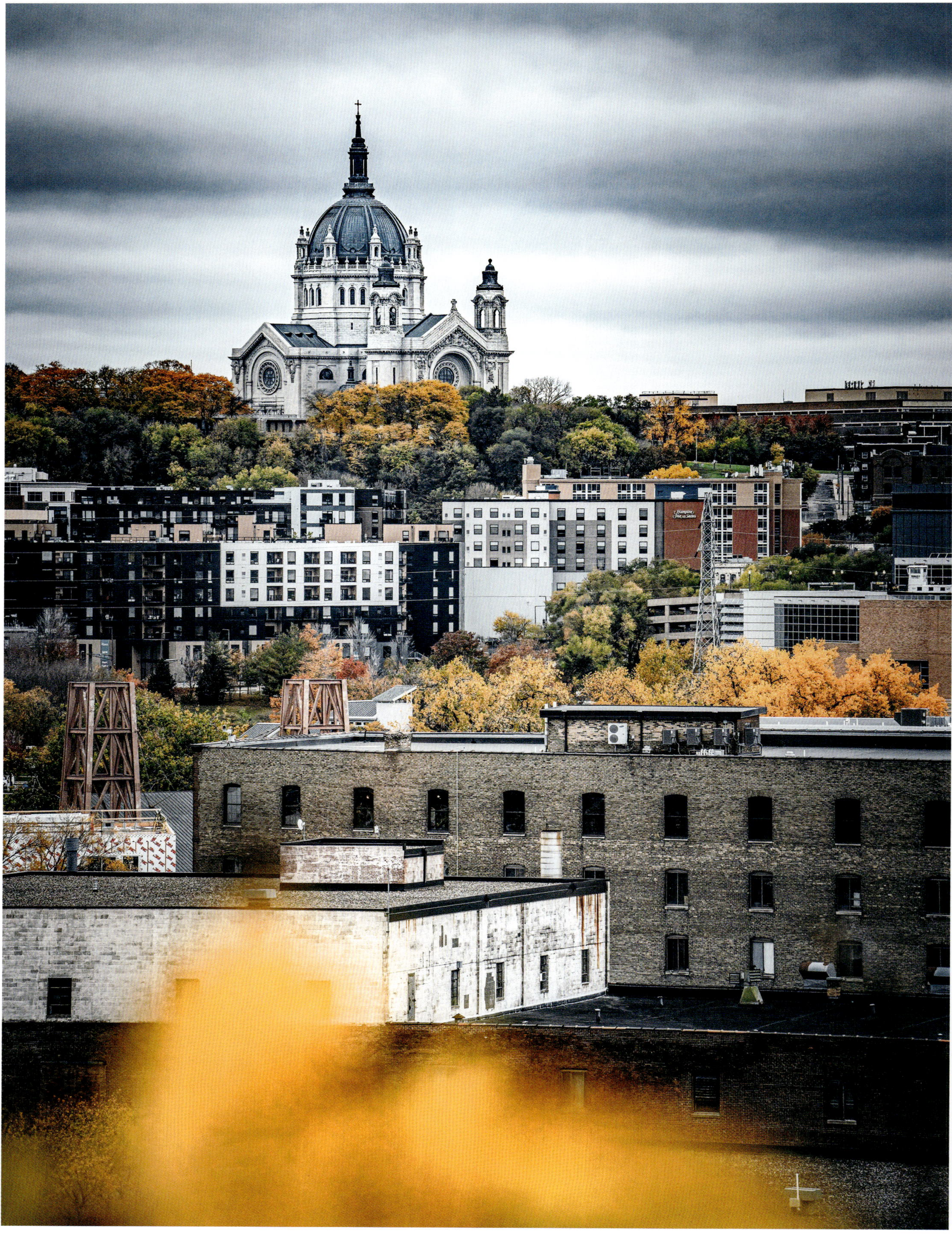

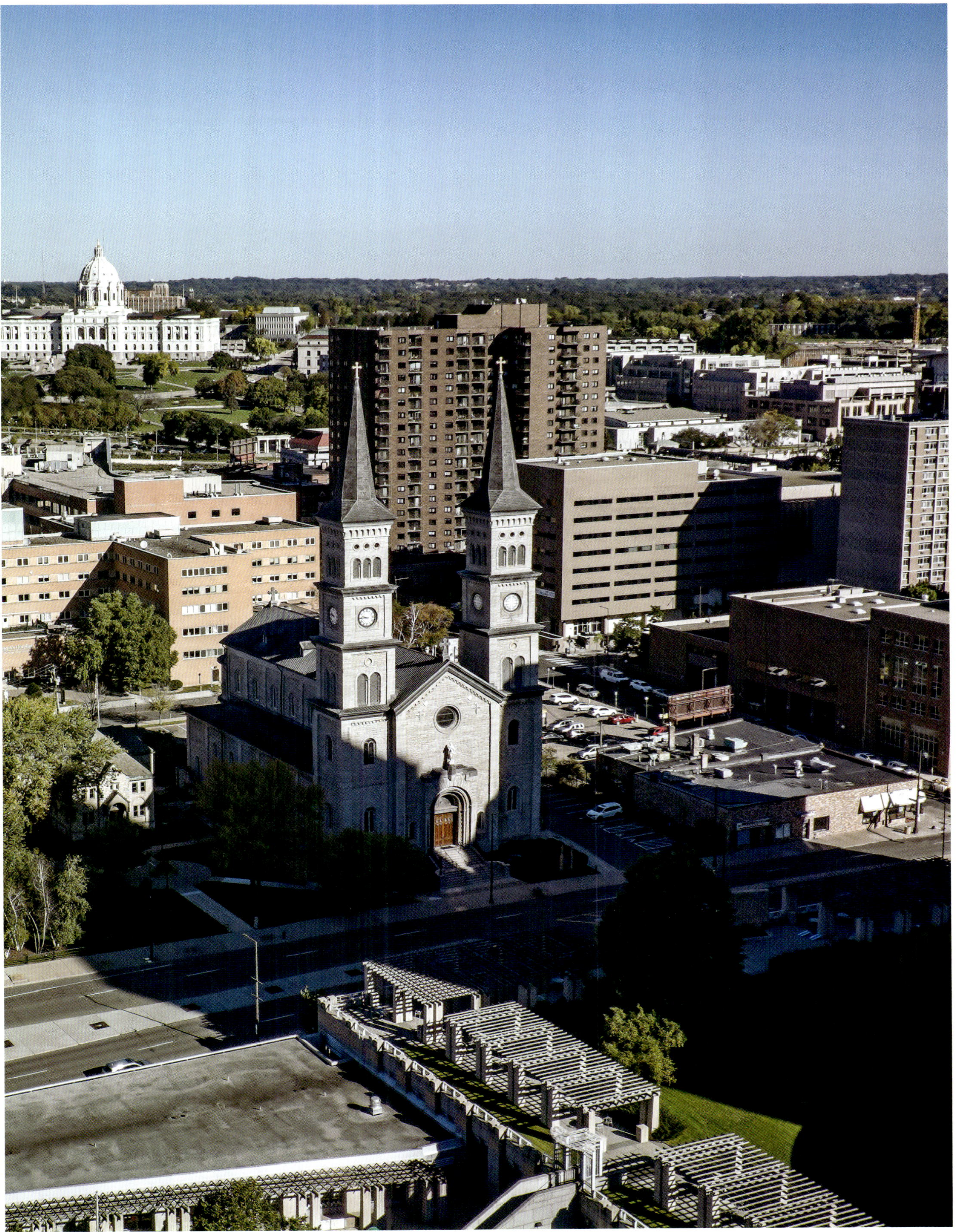

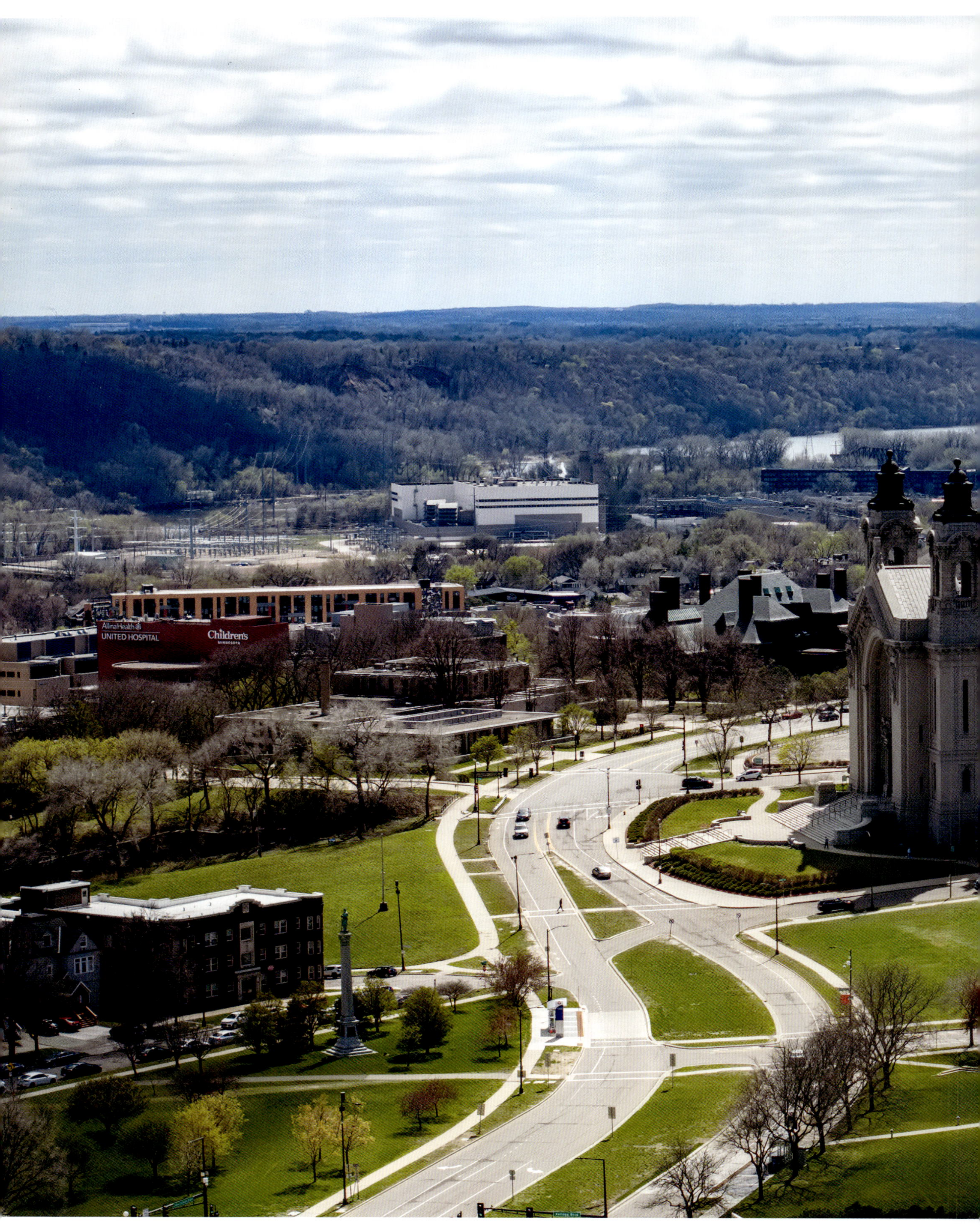
AllinaHealth
UNITED HOSPITAL
Children's
MINNESOTA

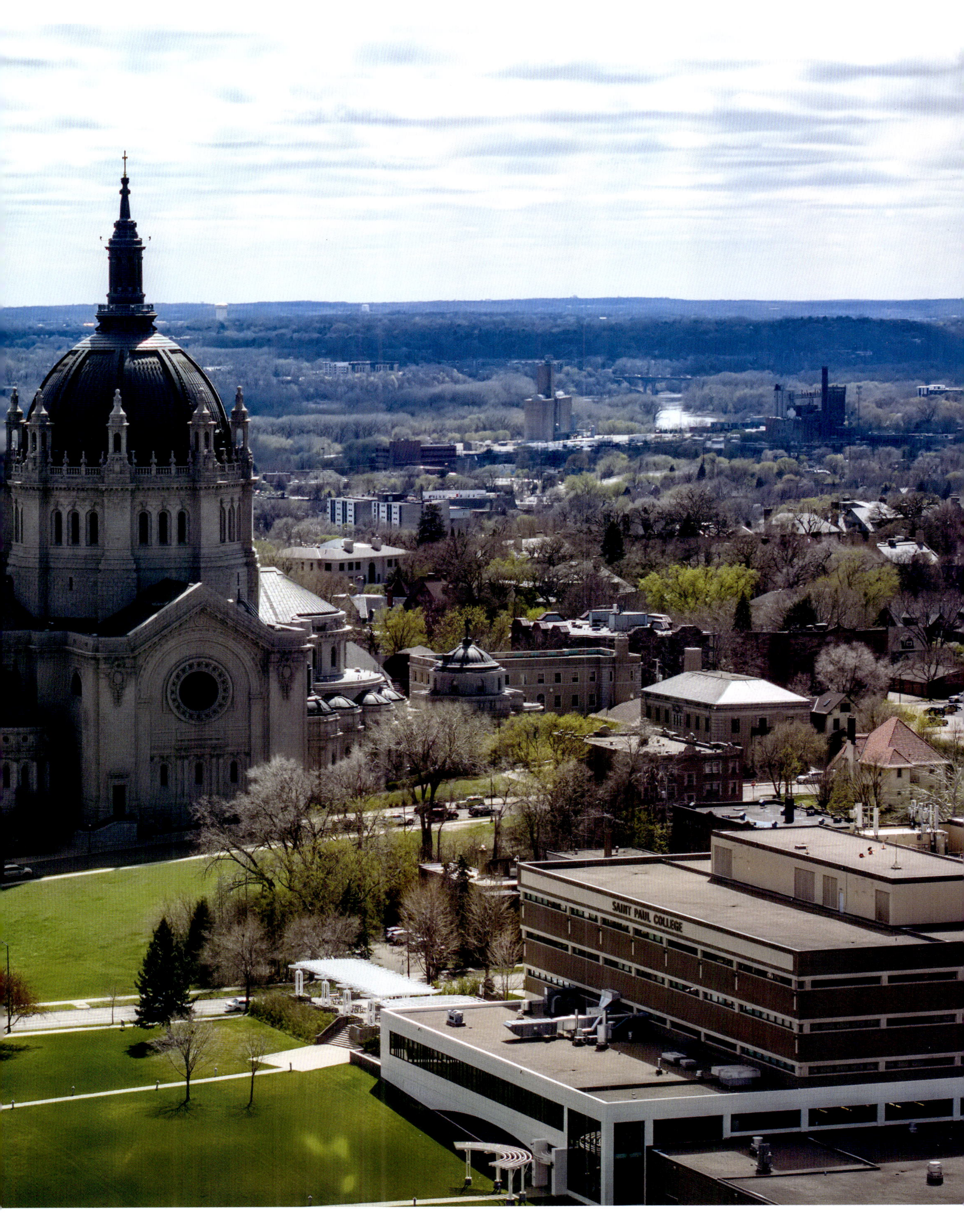
SAINT PAUL COLLEGE

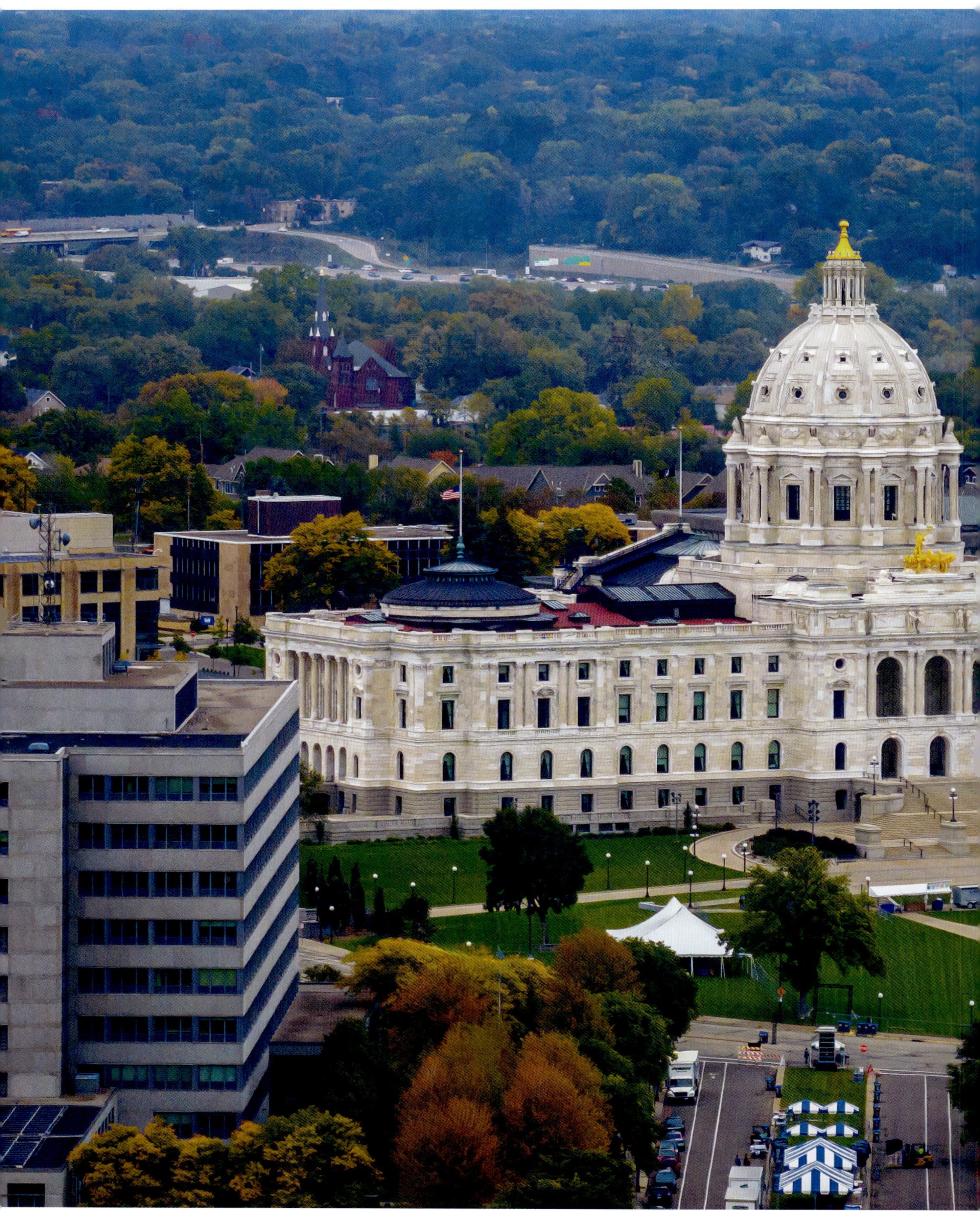

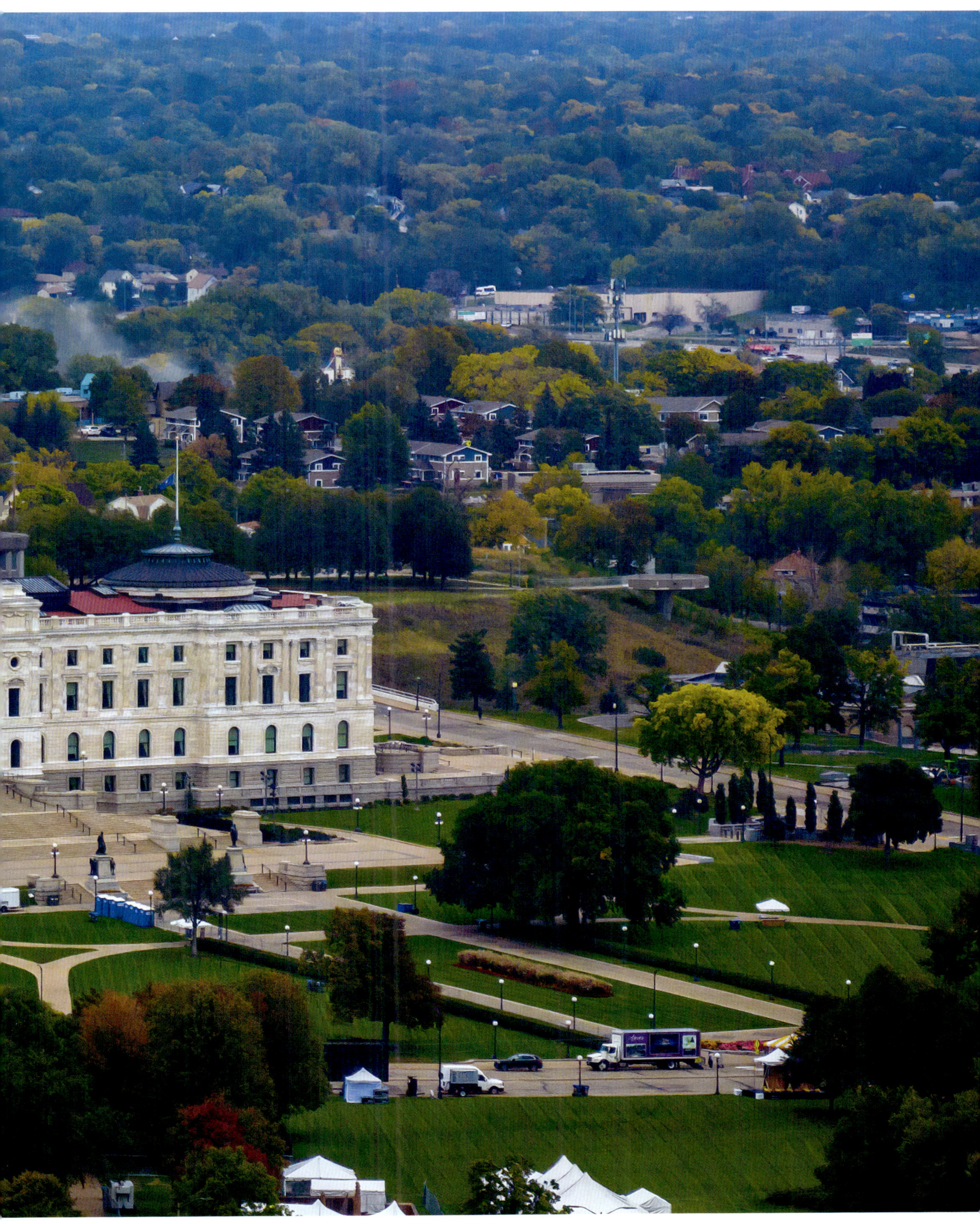

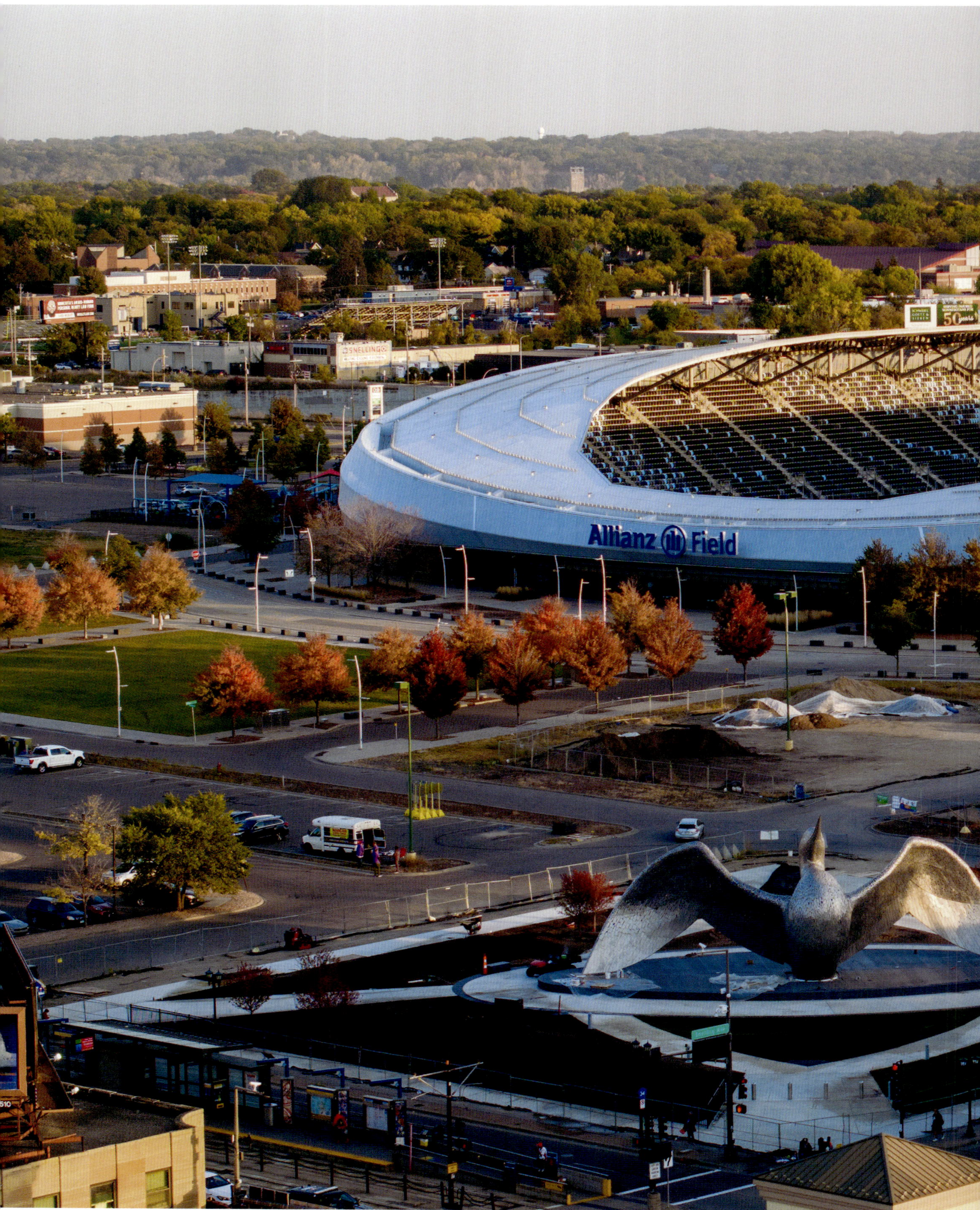

Allianz Field

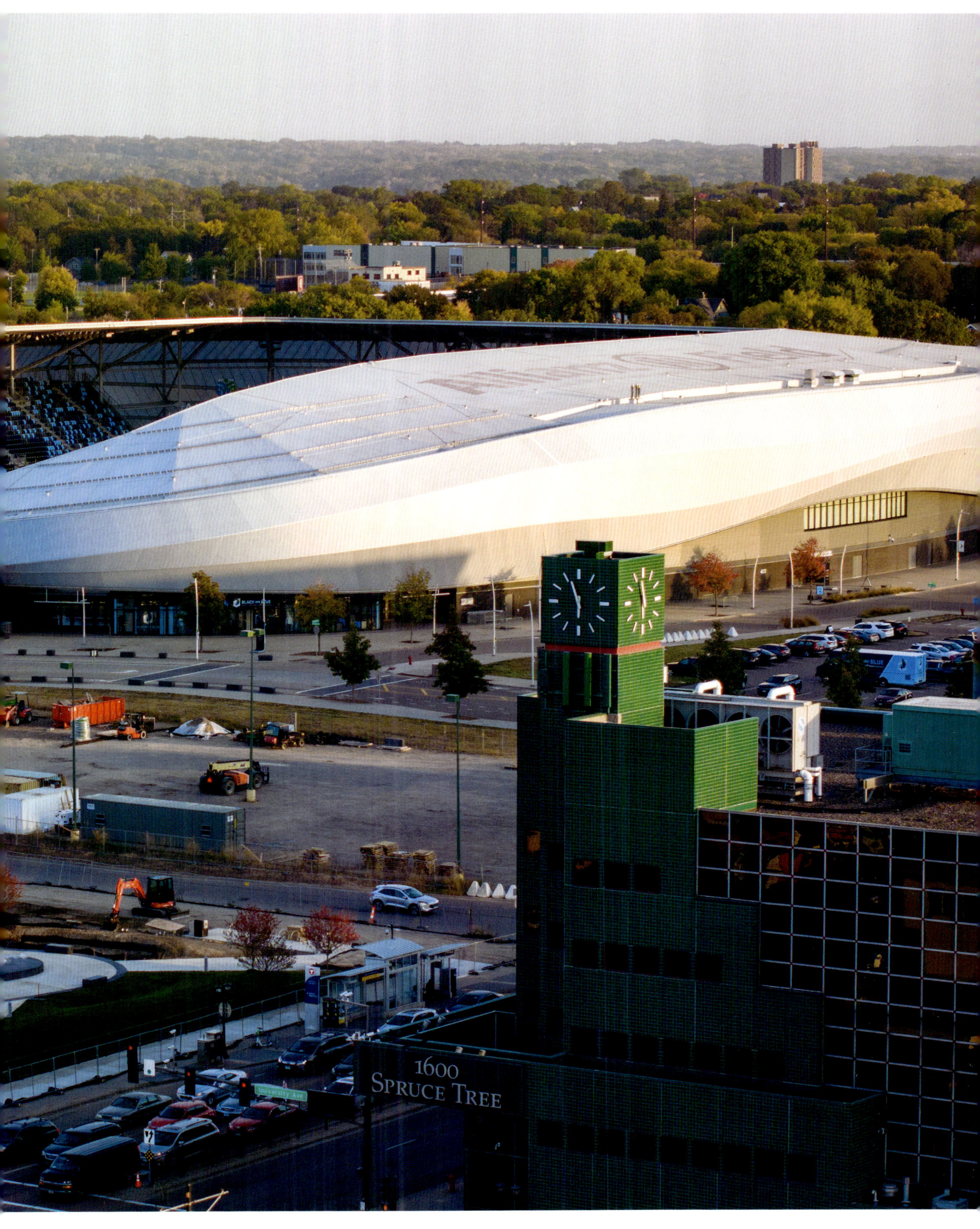
BLACK AND BLUE
1600
SPRUCE TREE

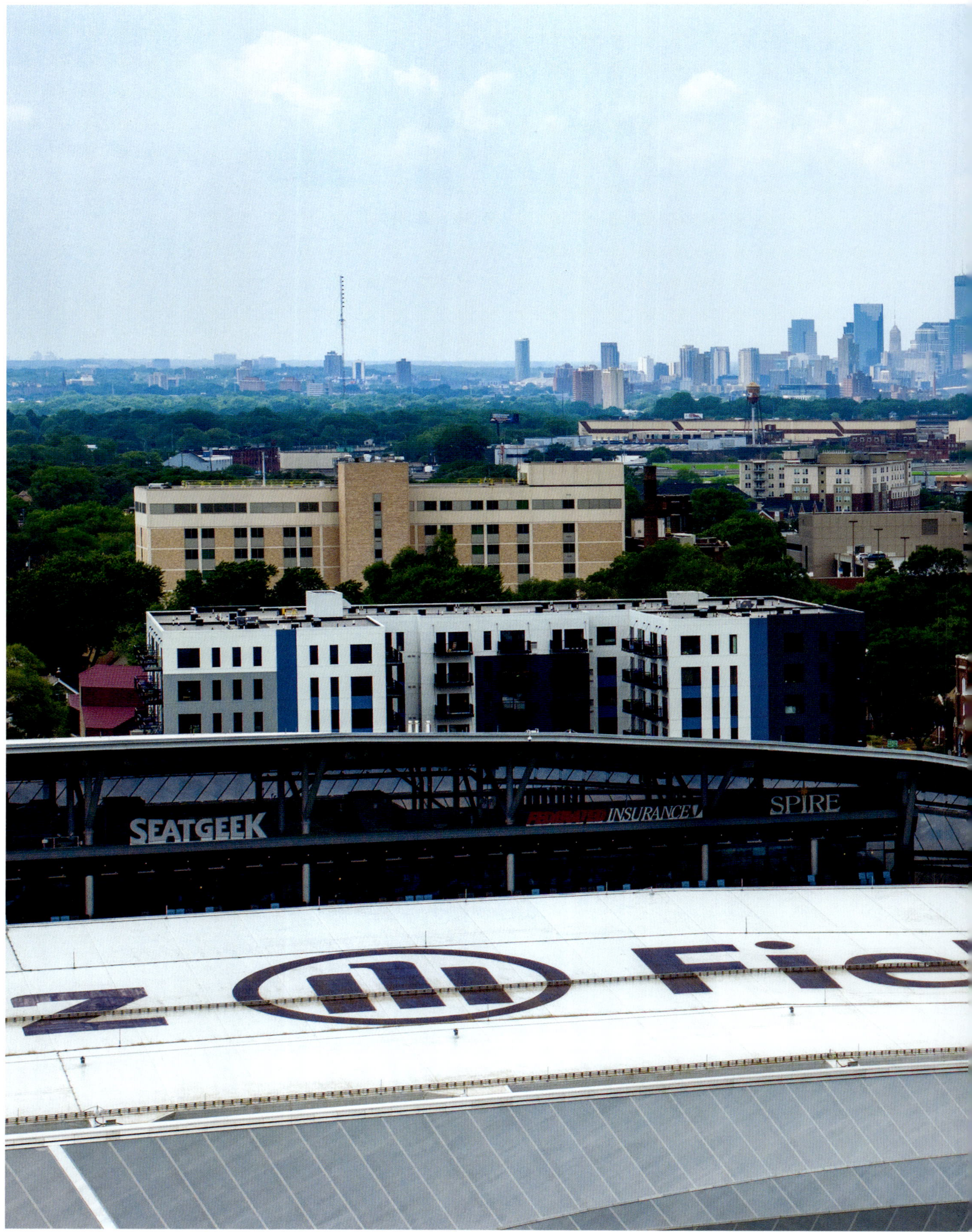

SEATGEEK
INSURANCE
SPIRE
Fie

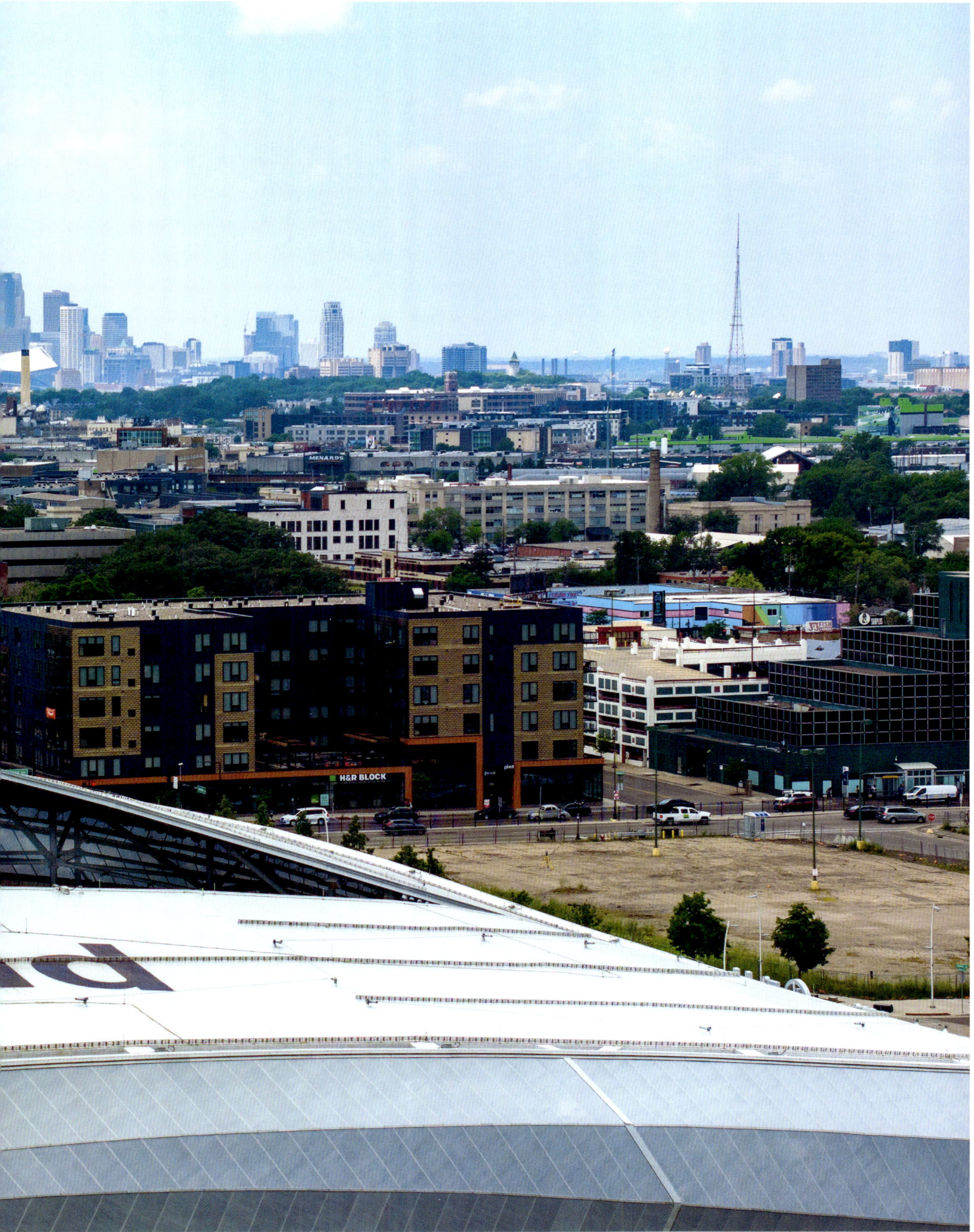

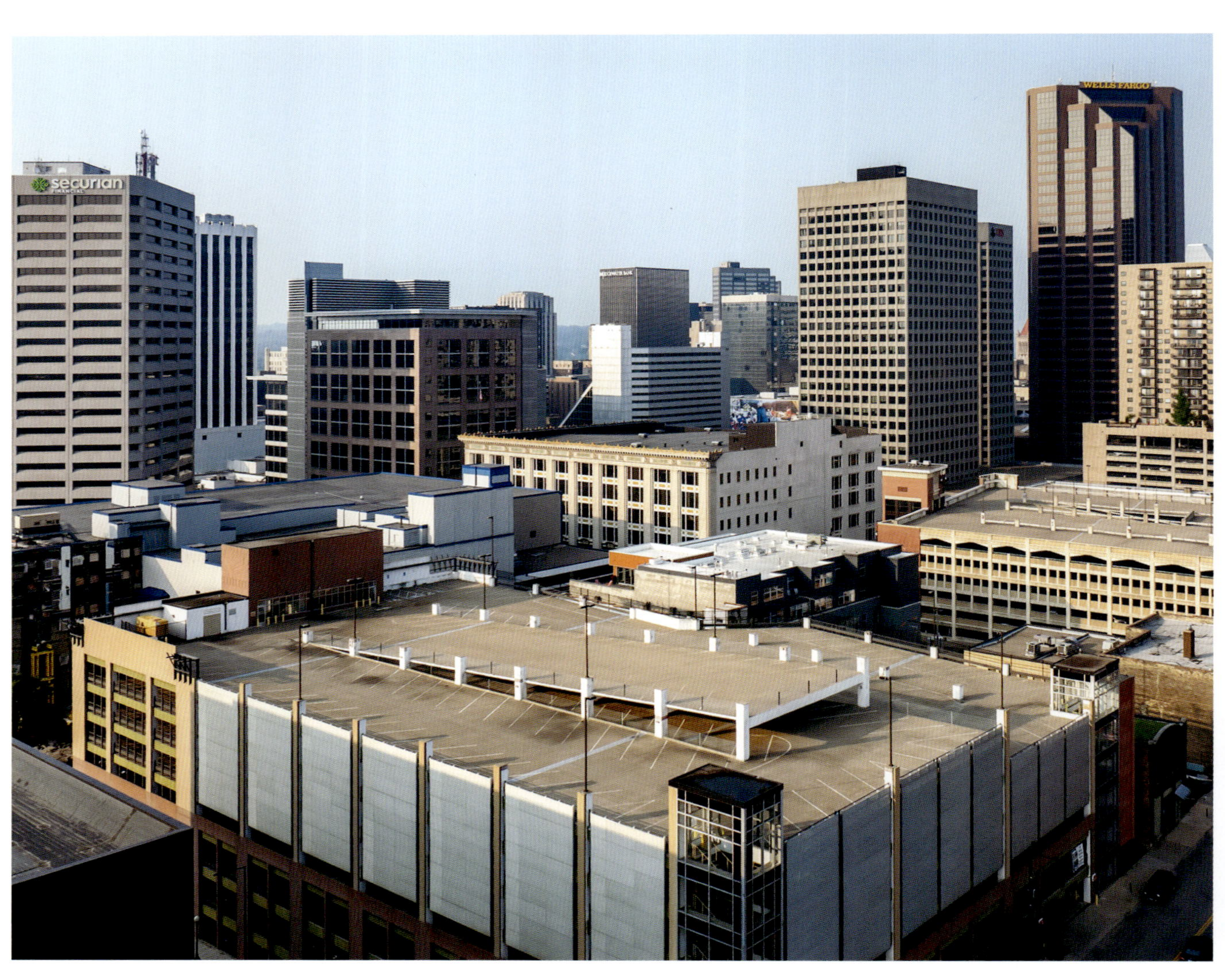

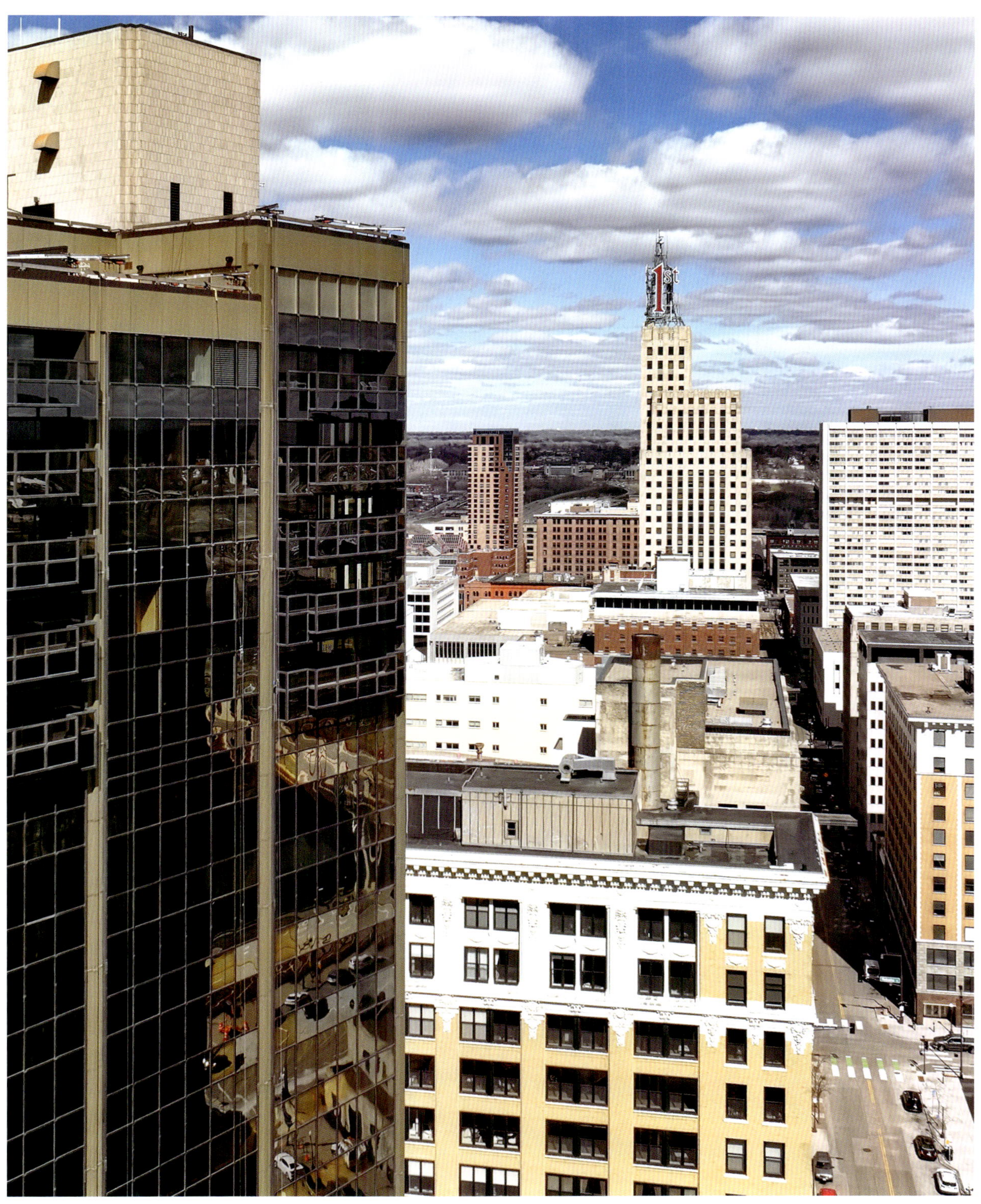

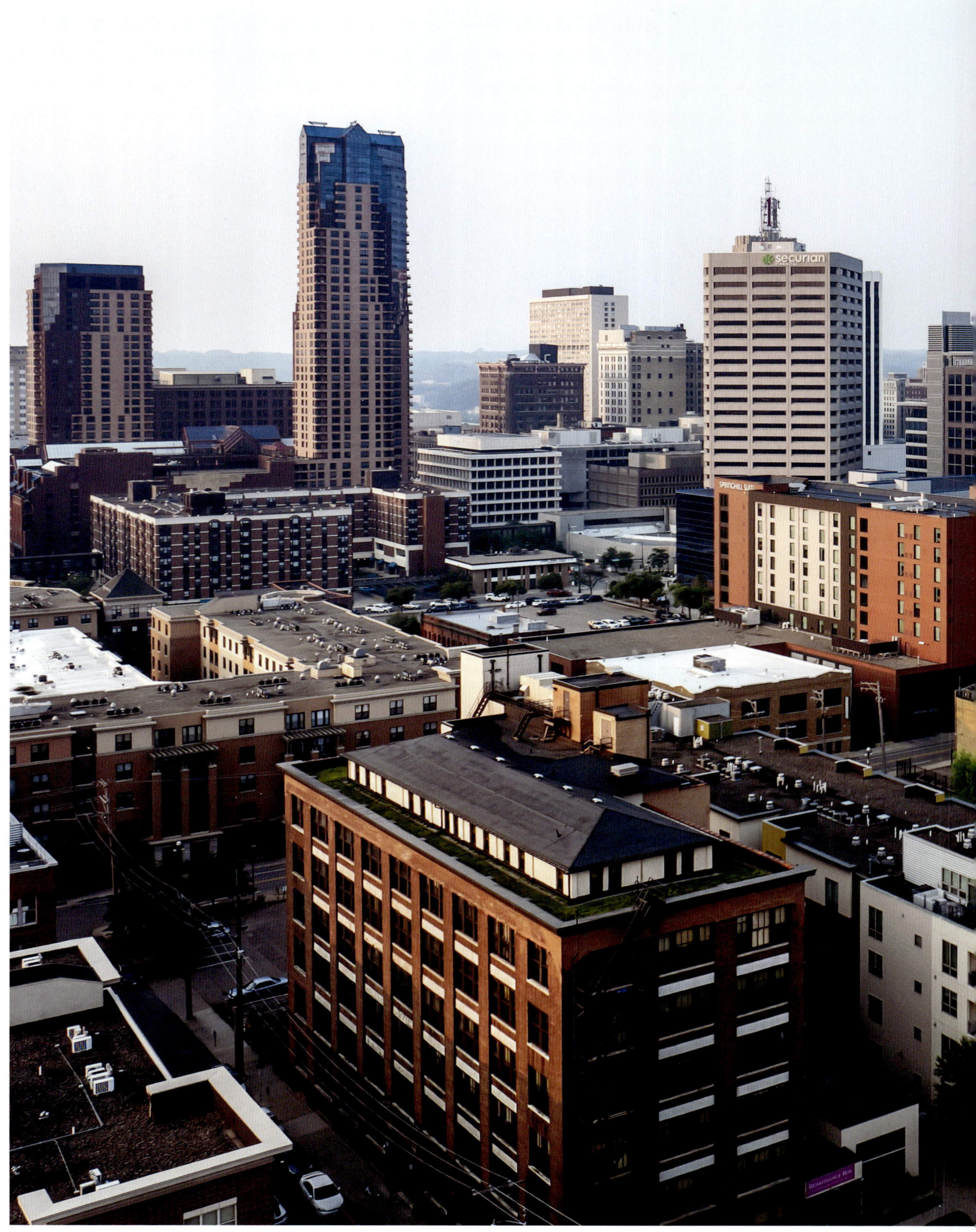

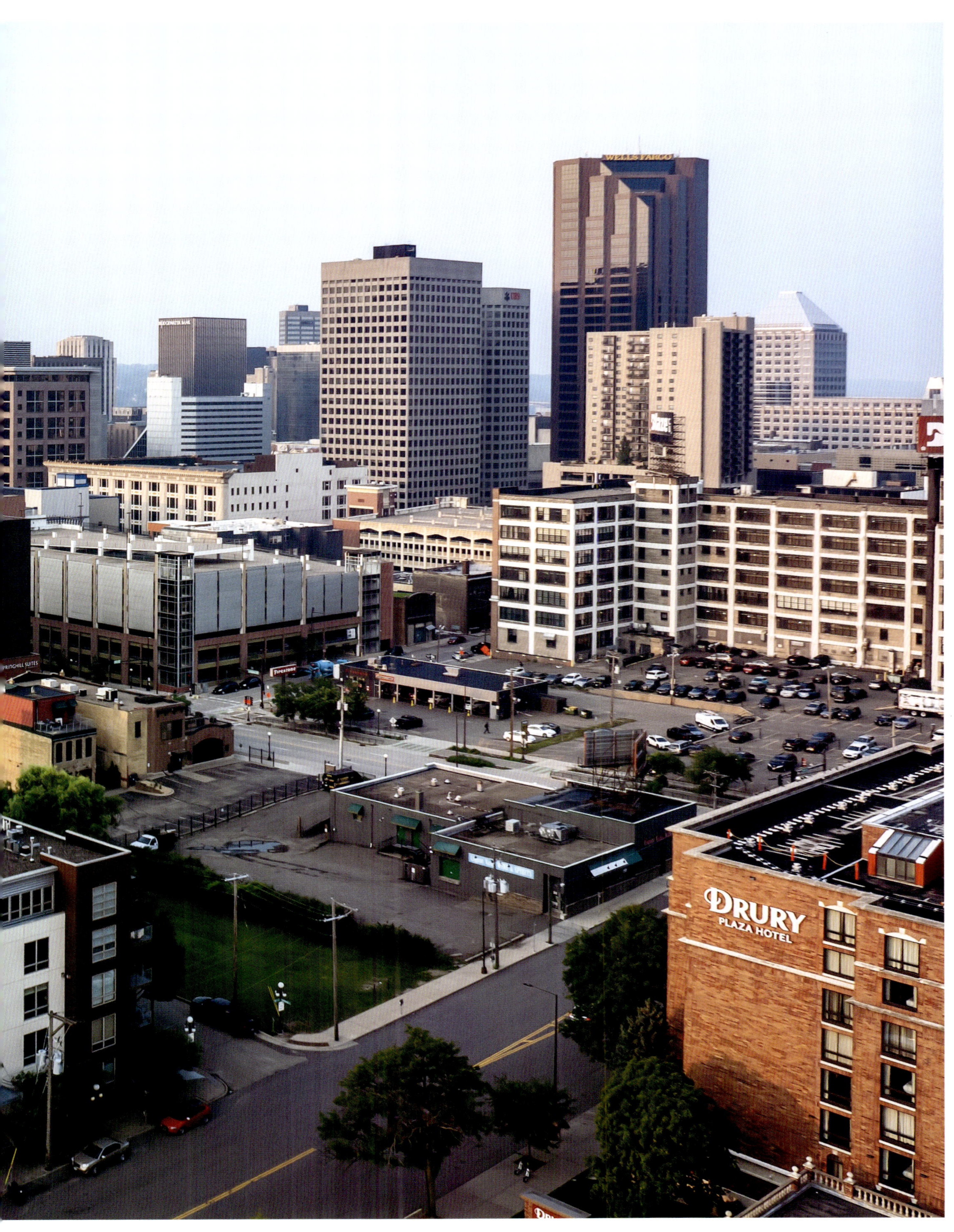

WELLS FARGO
DRURY
PLAZA HOTEL

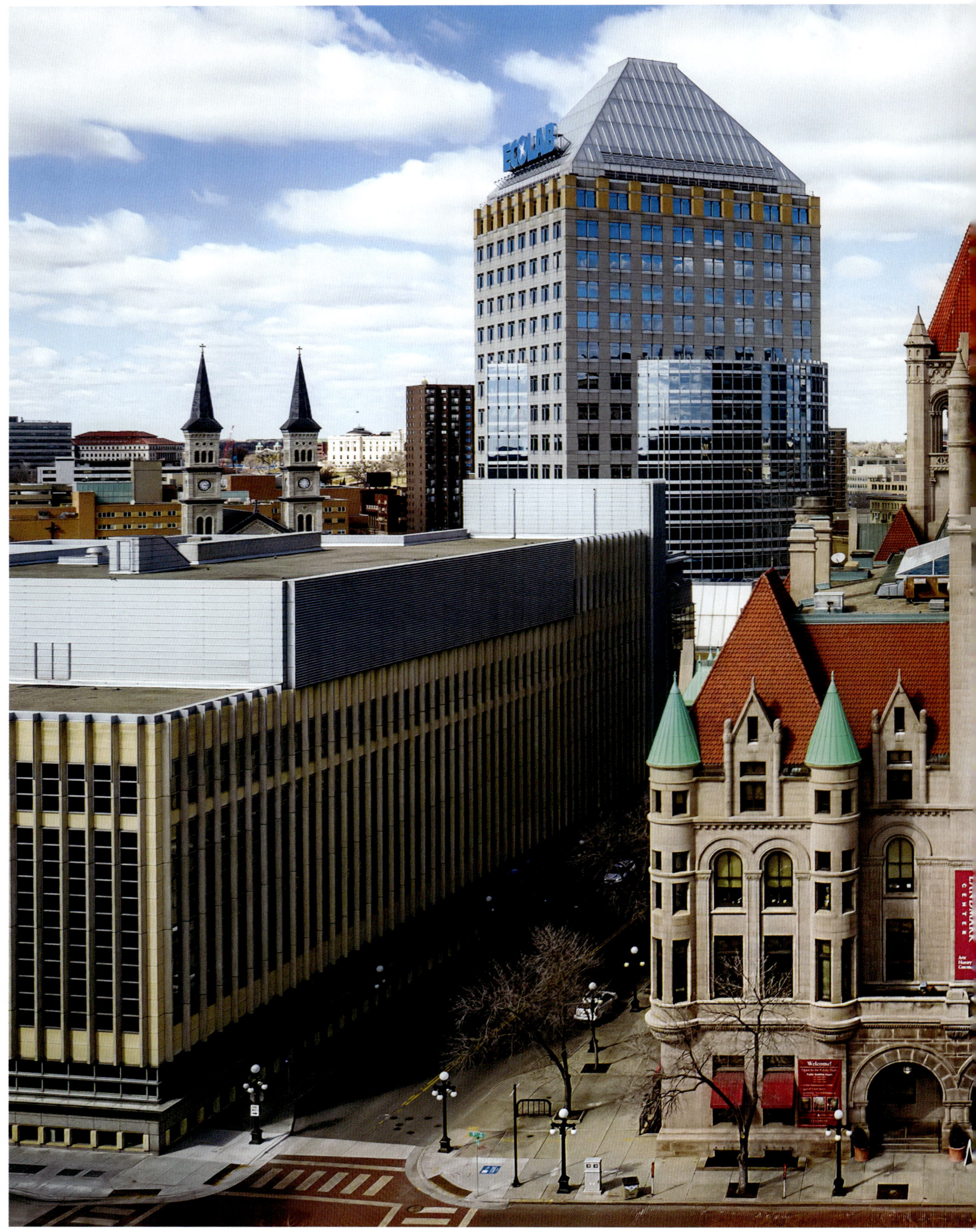

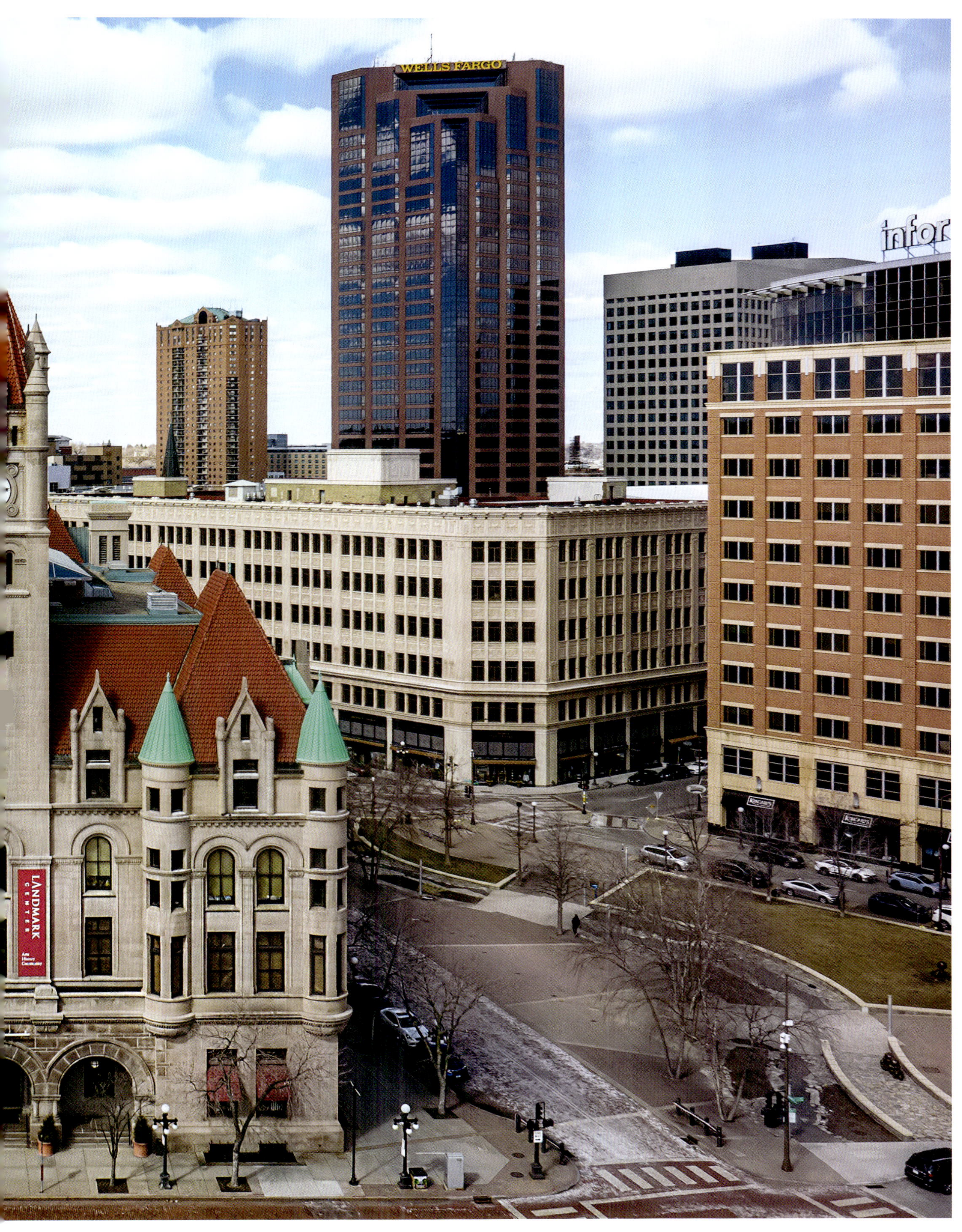

WELLS FARGO
infor
LANDMARK
CENTER

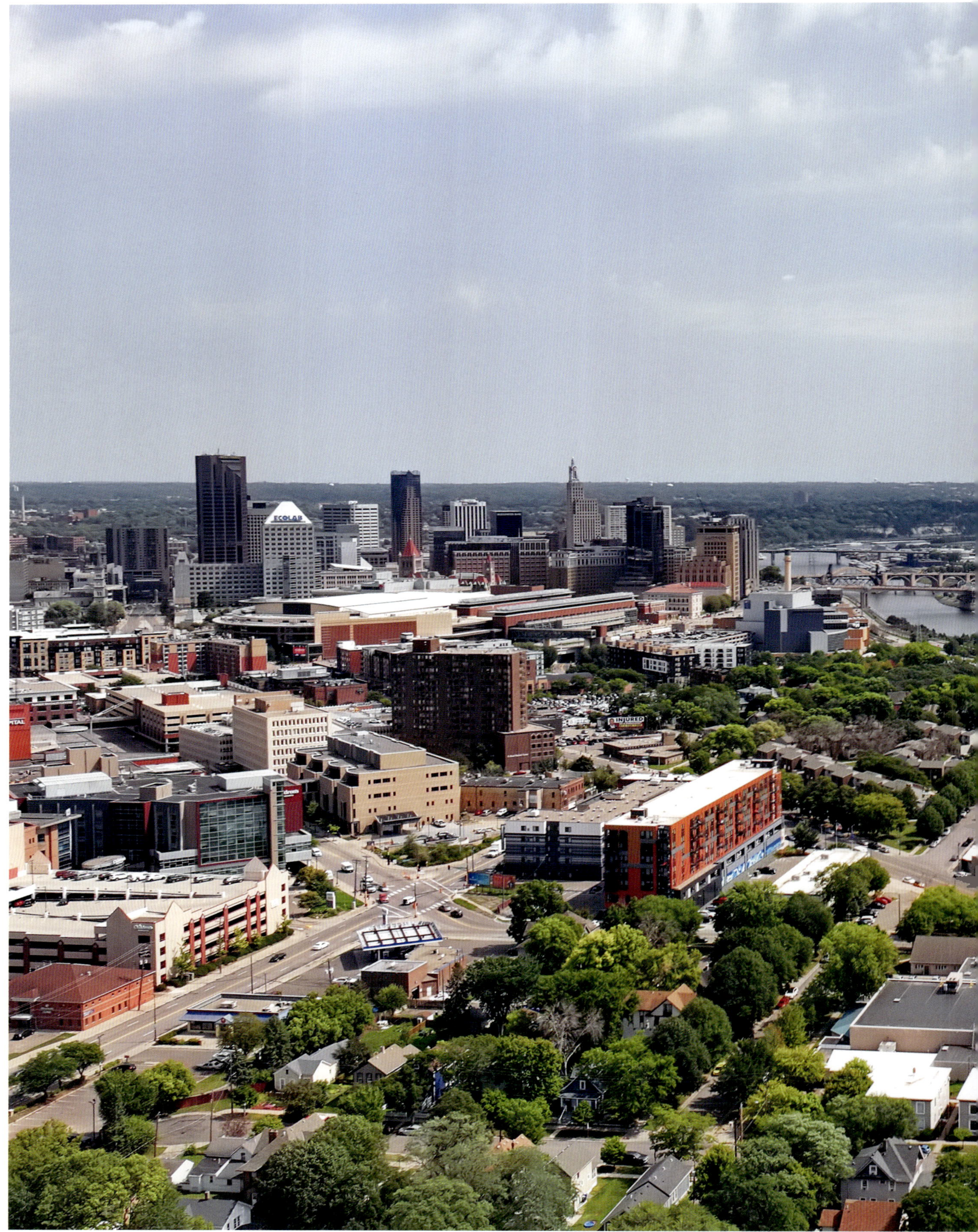

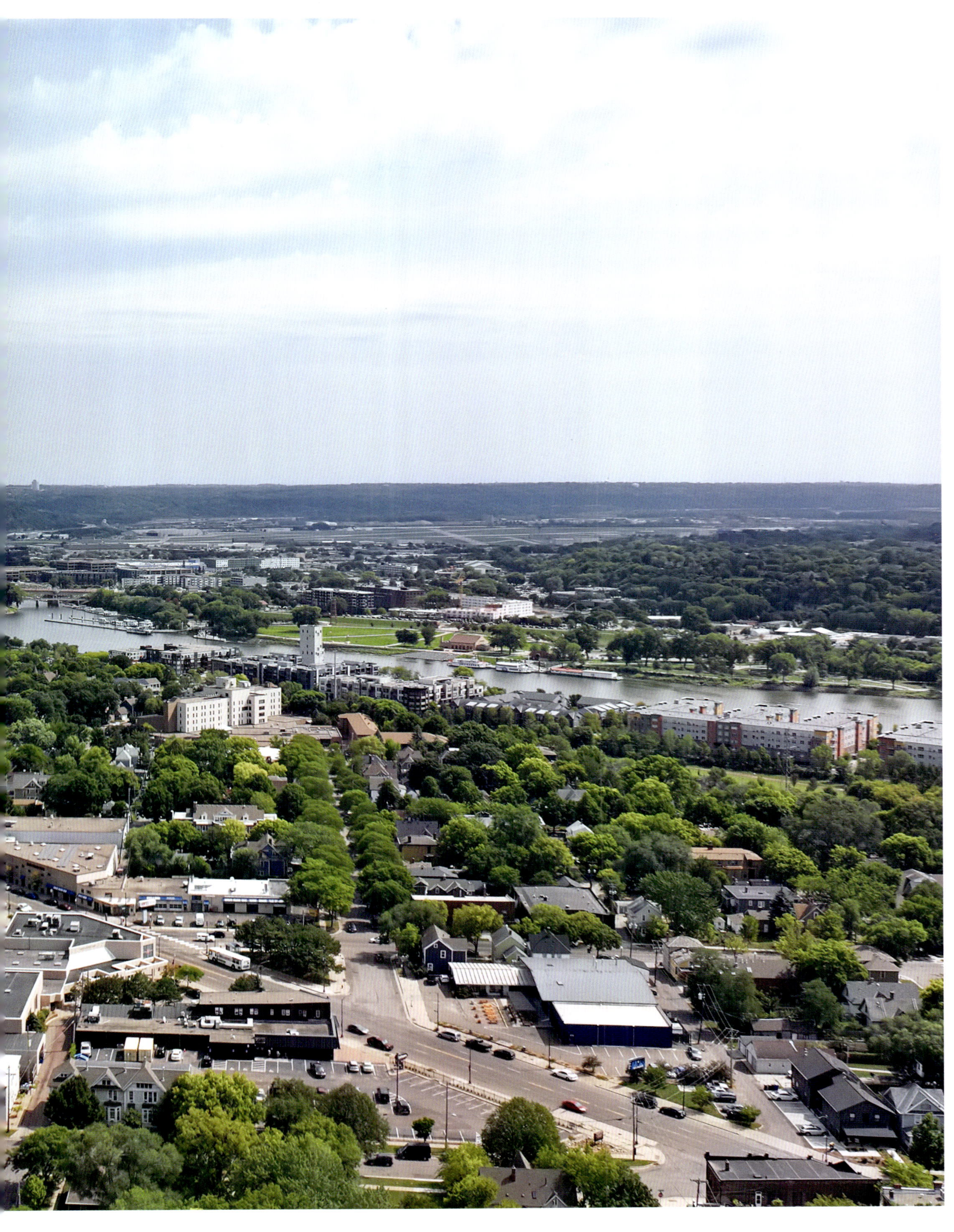

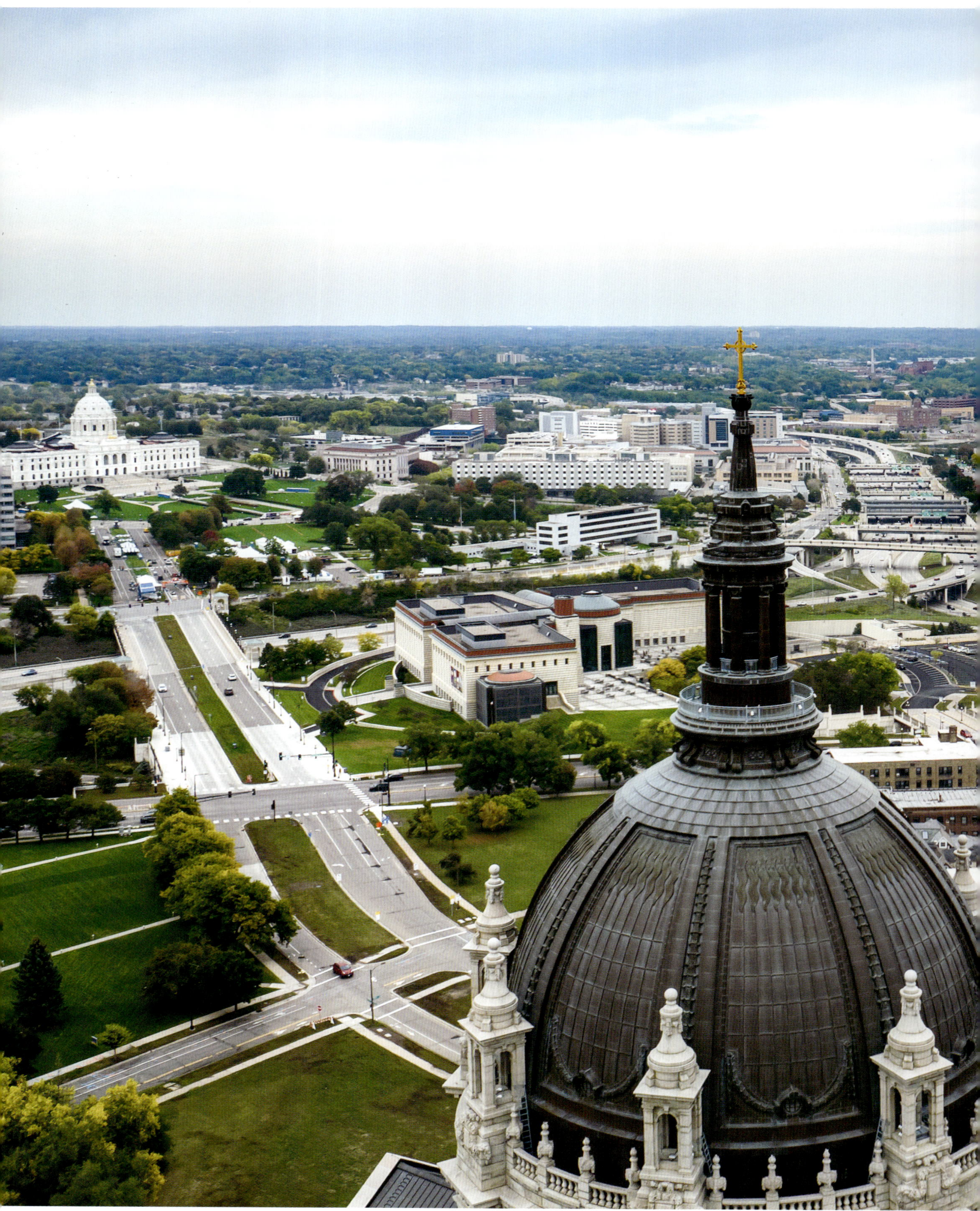

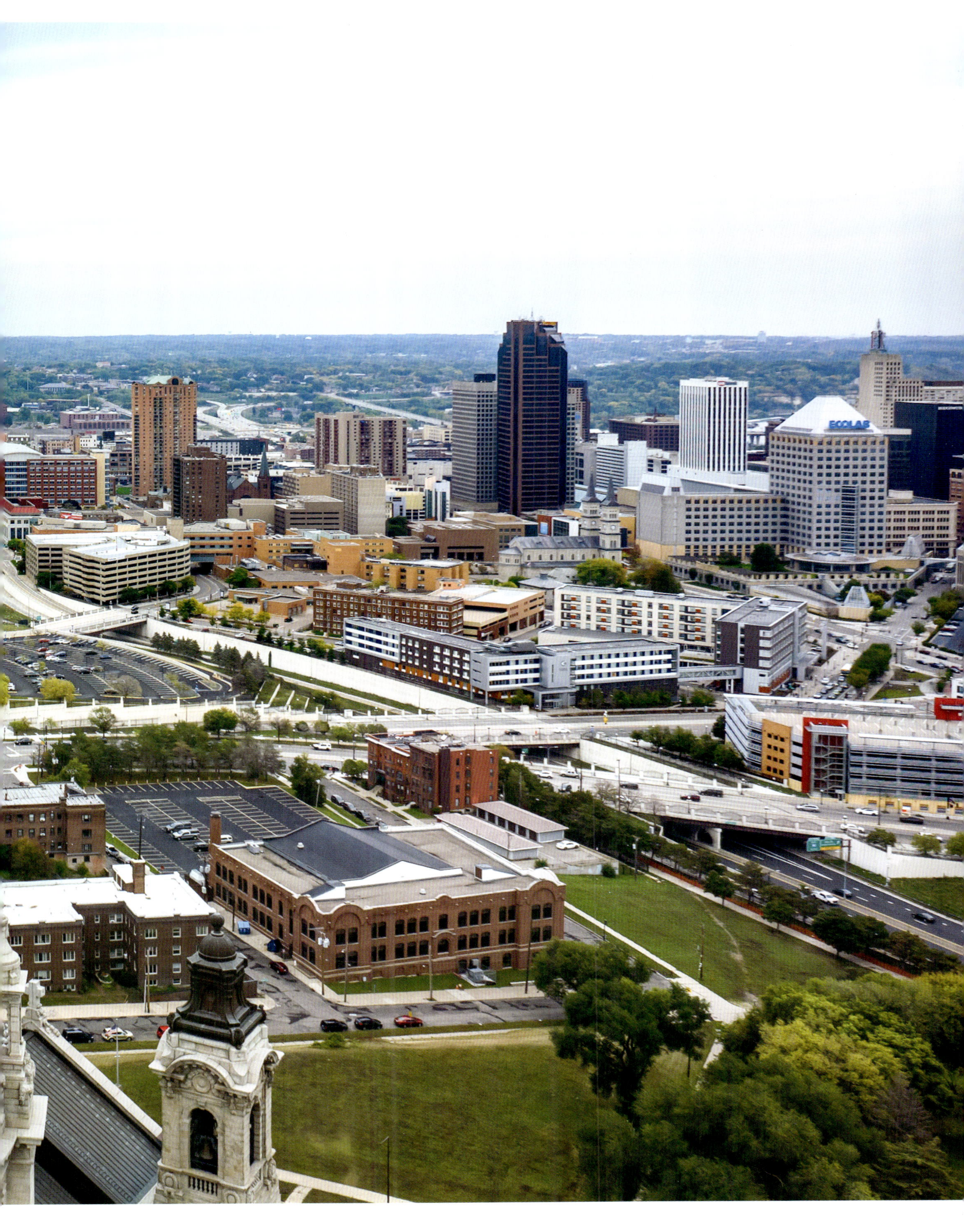

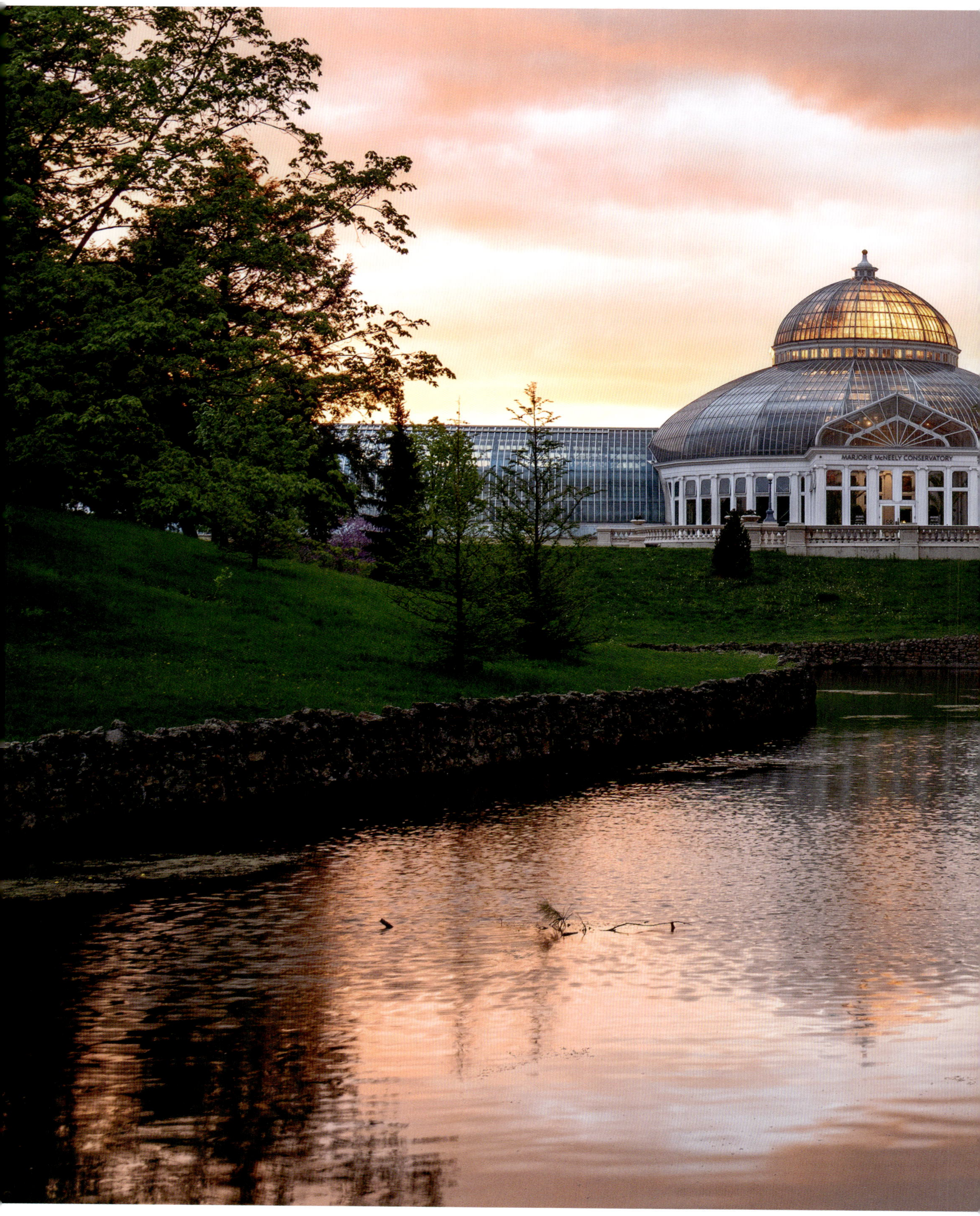
MARJORIE McNEELY CONSERVATORY

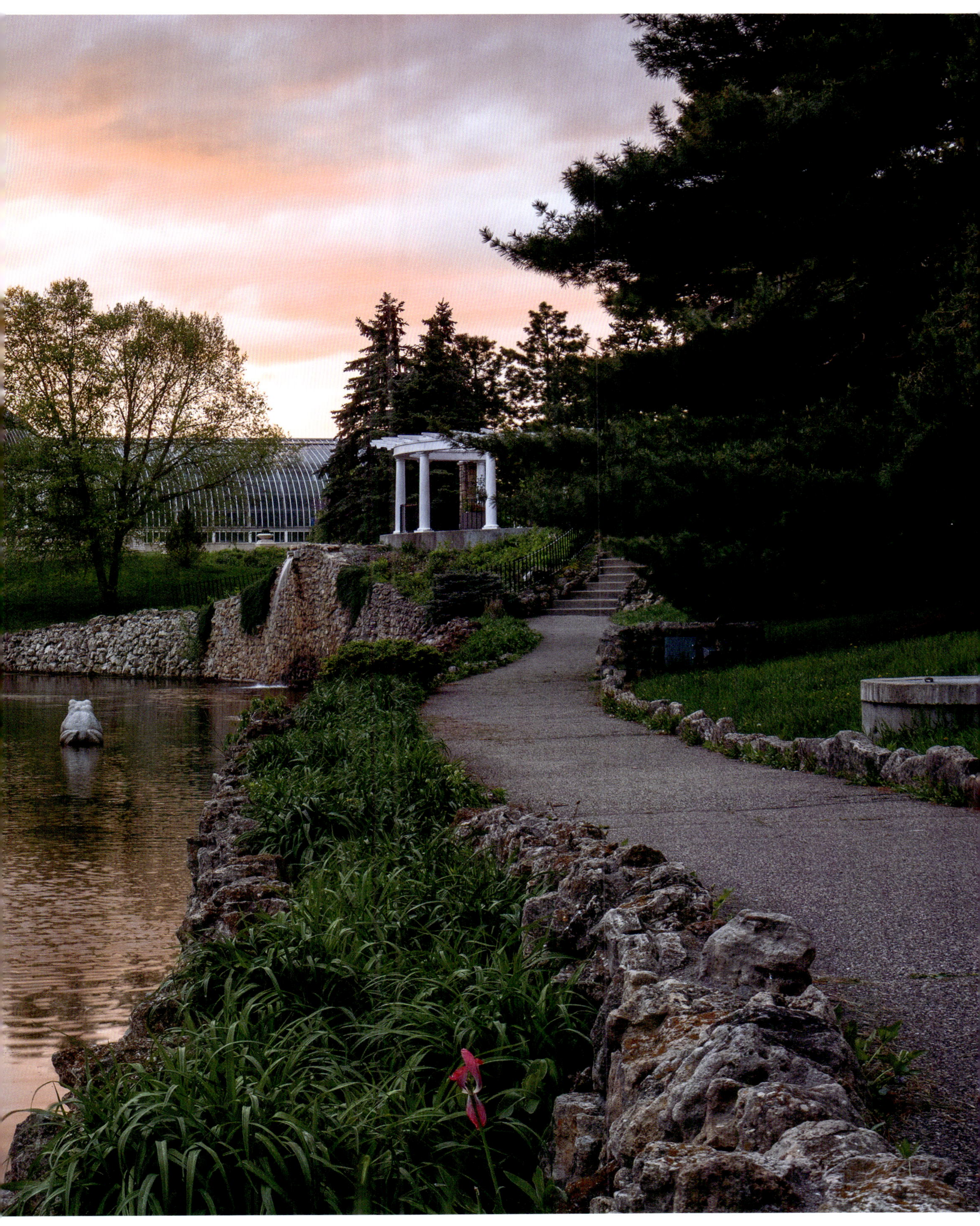

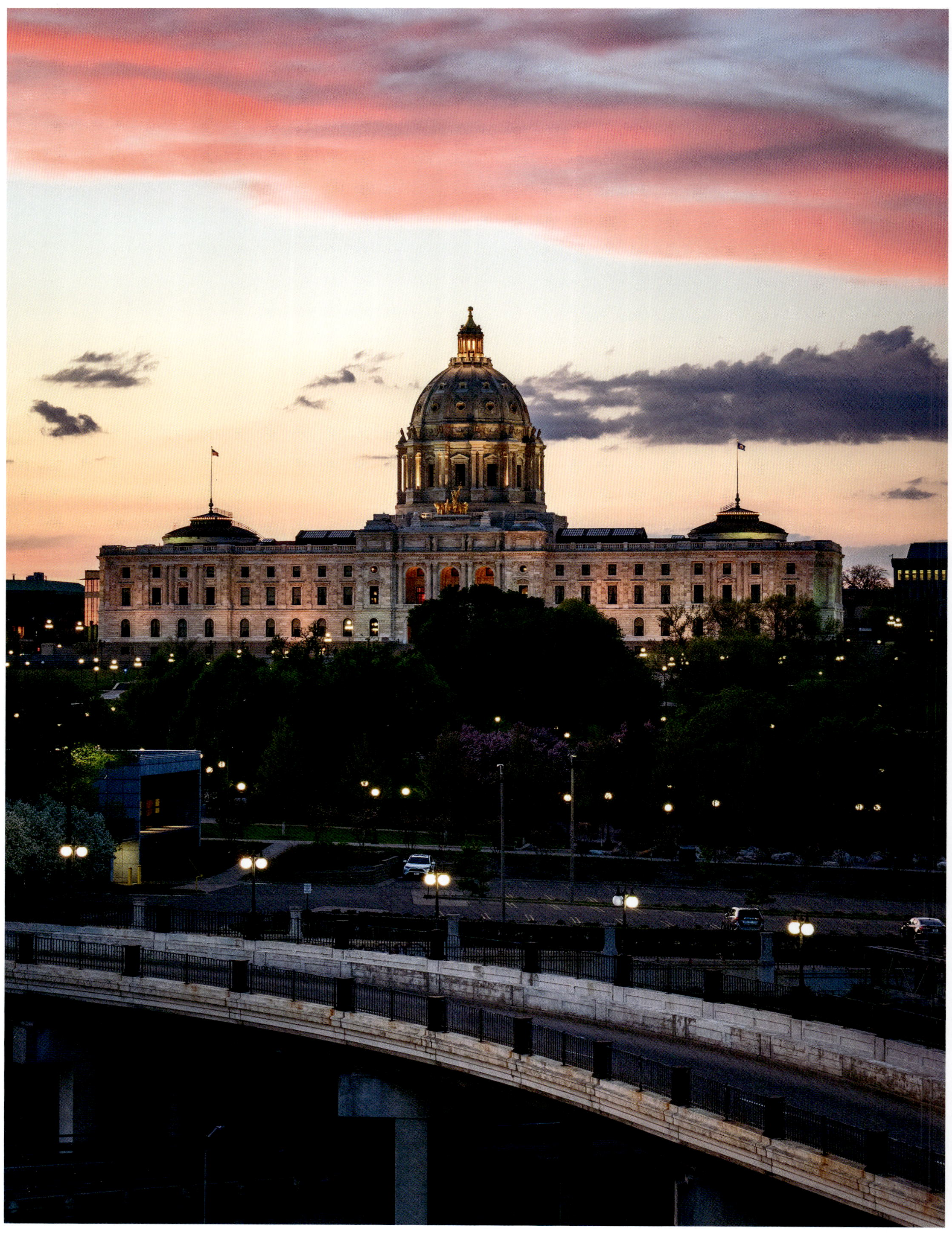

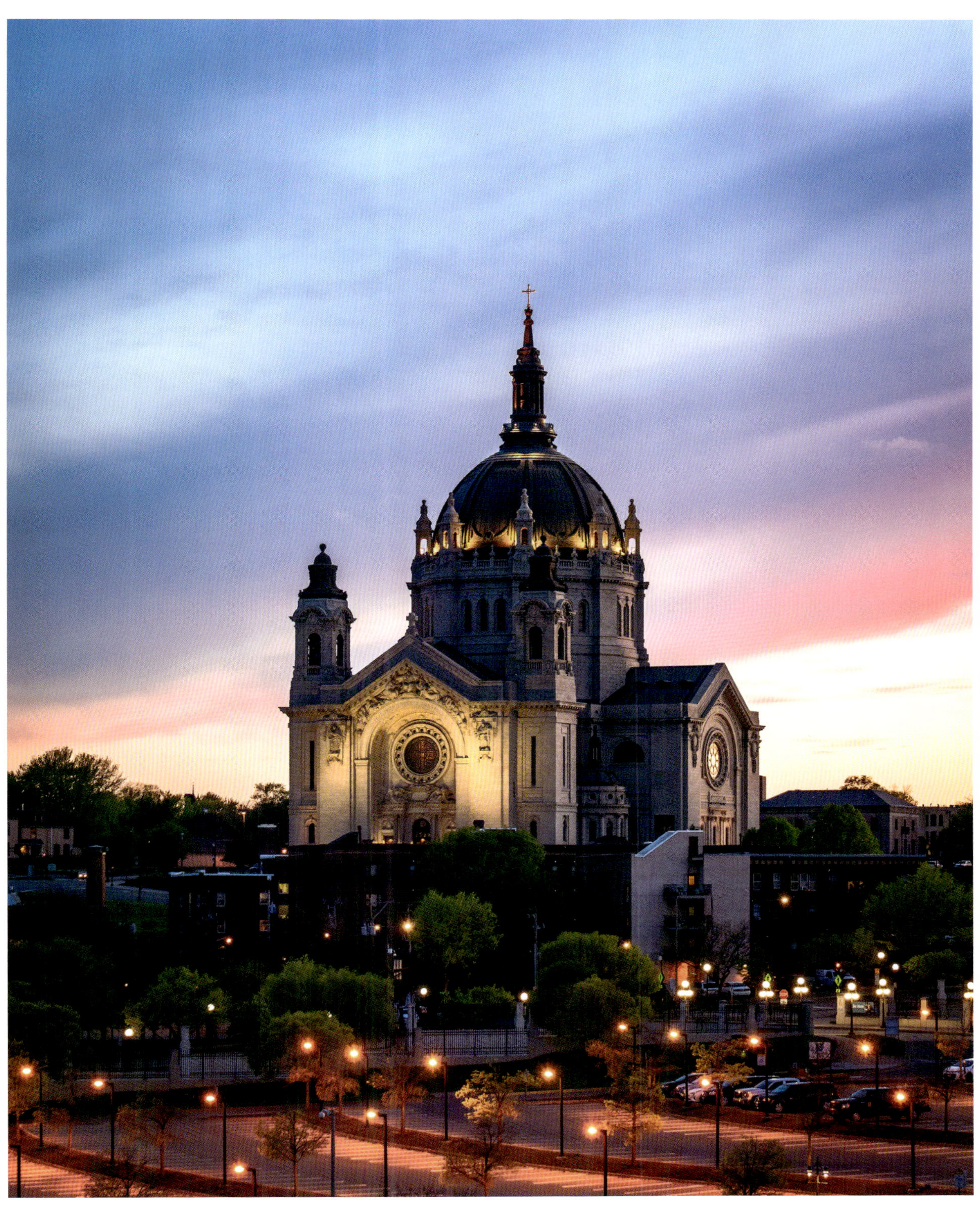

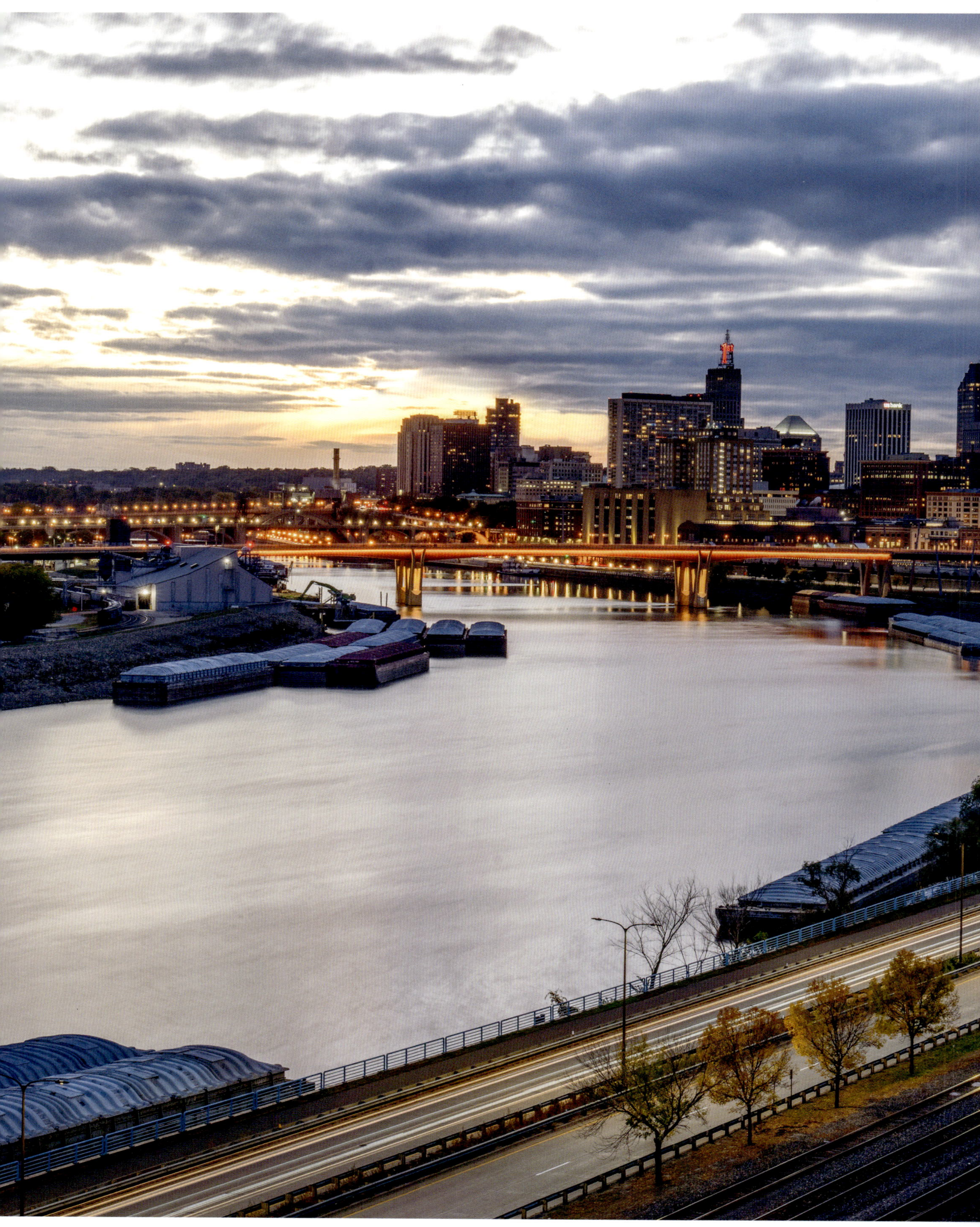

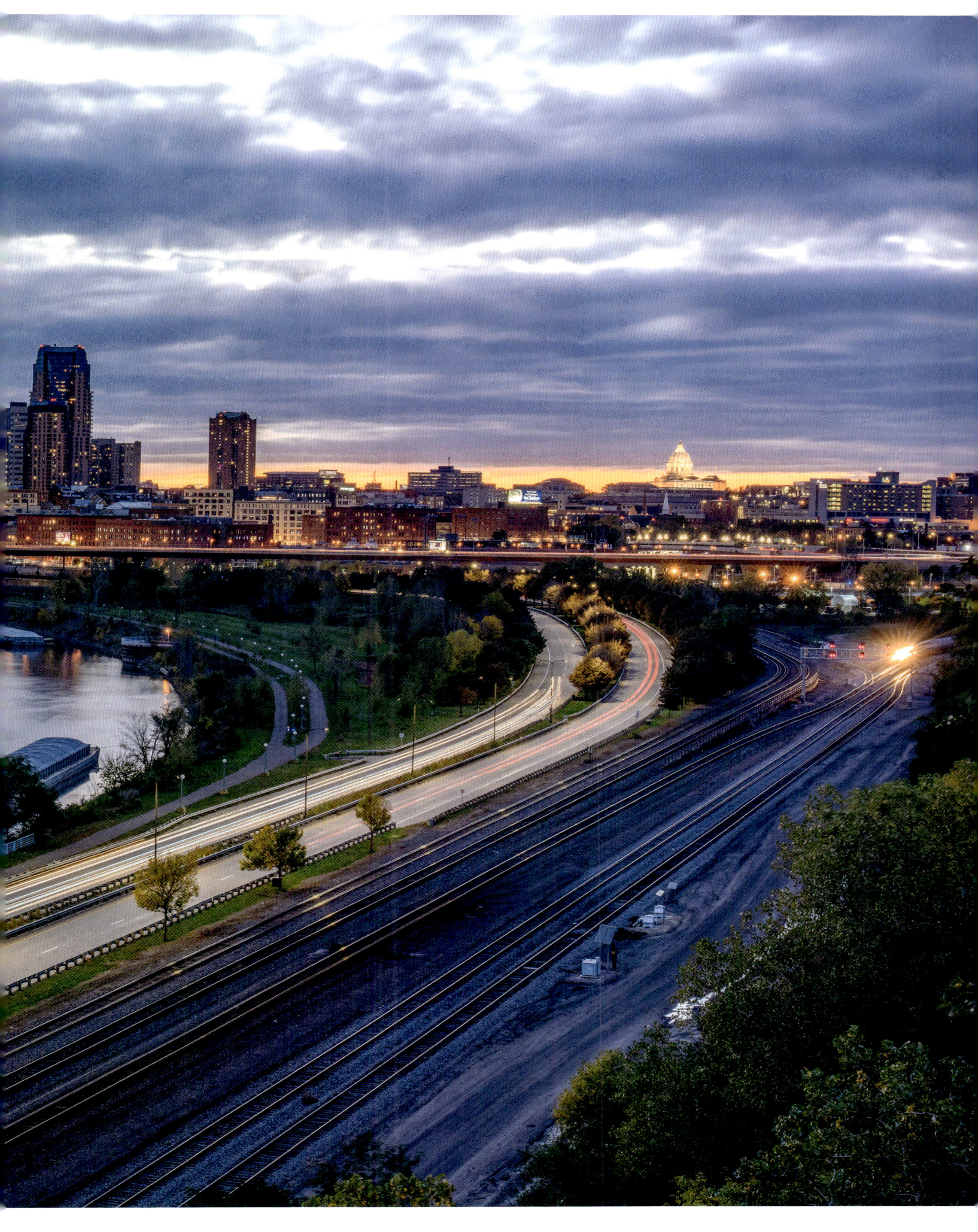

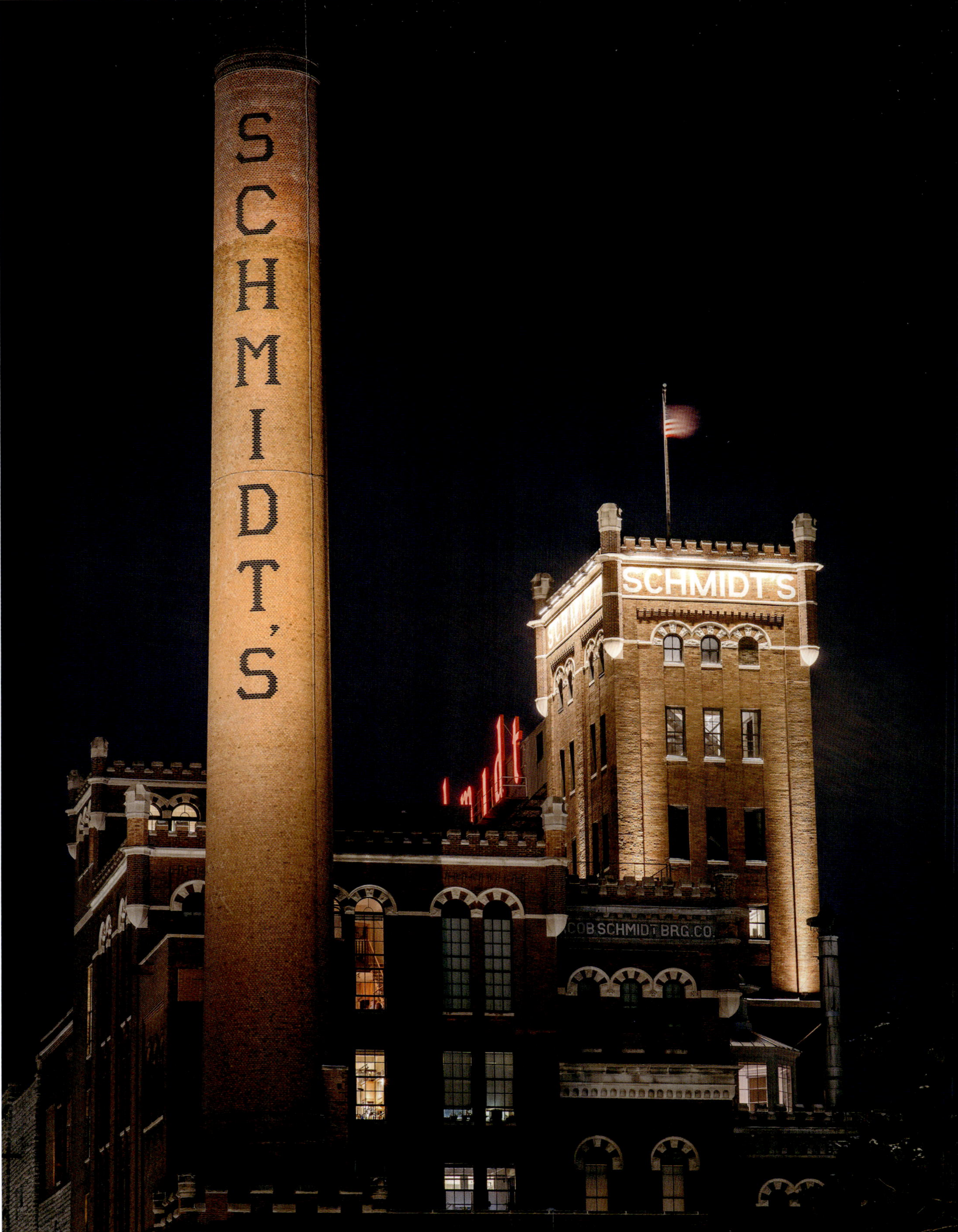

SCHMIDT'S
SCHMIDT'S
JACOB SCHMIDT BRG. CO.

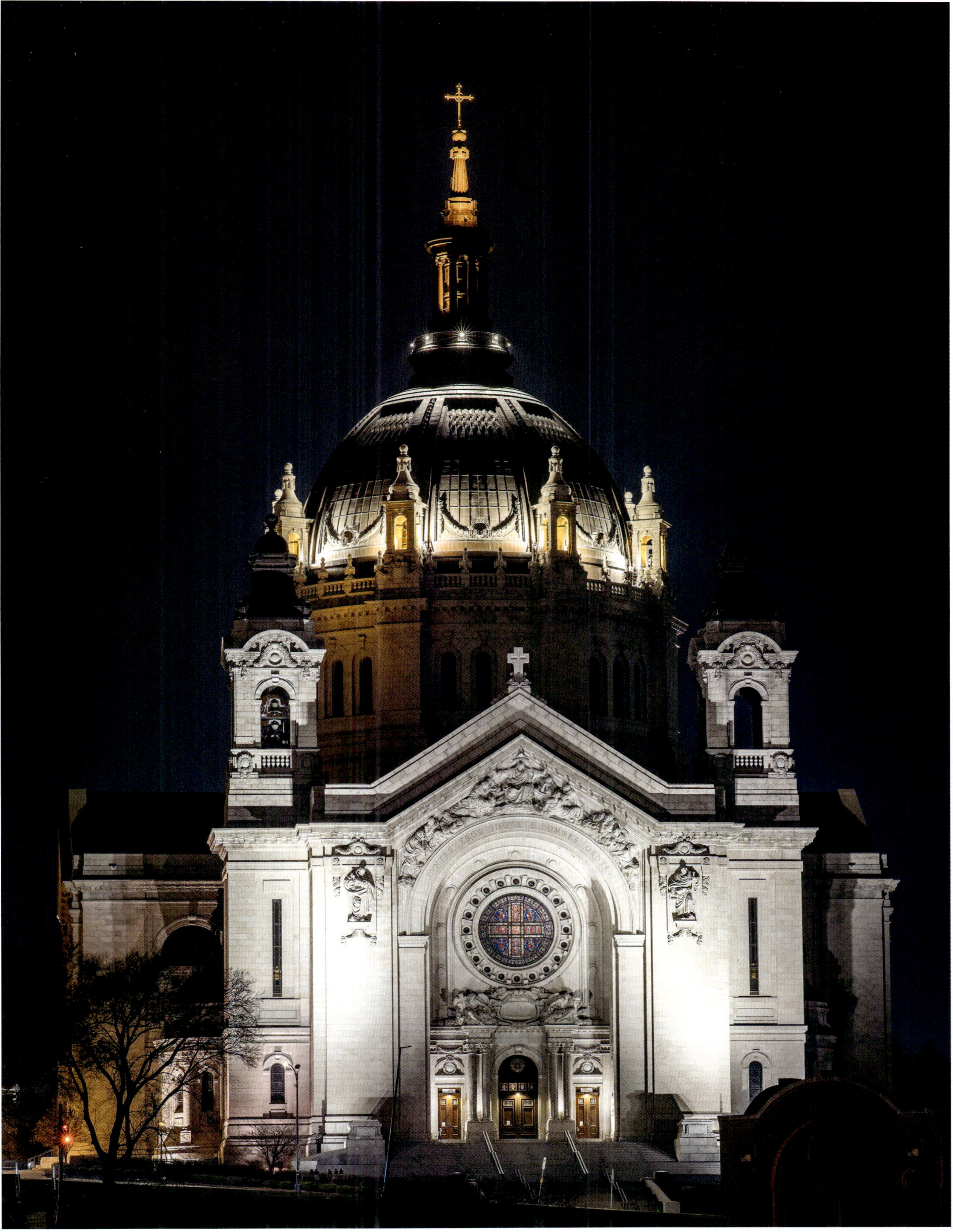

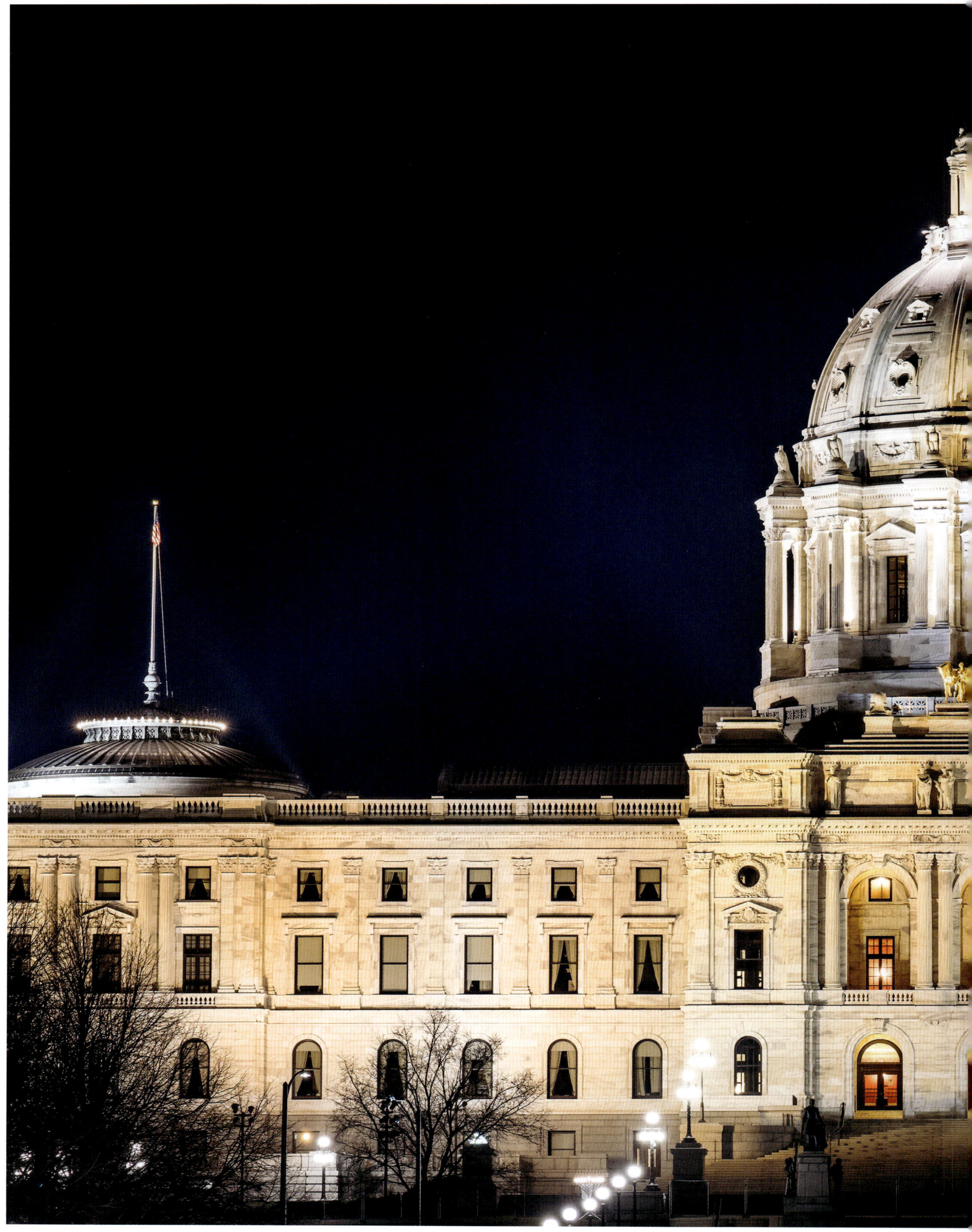

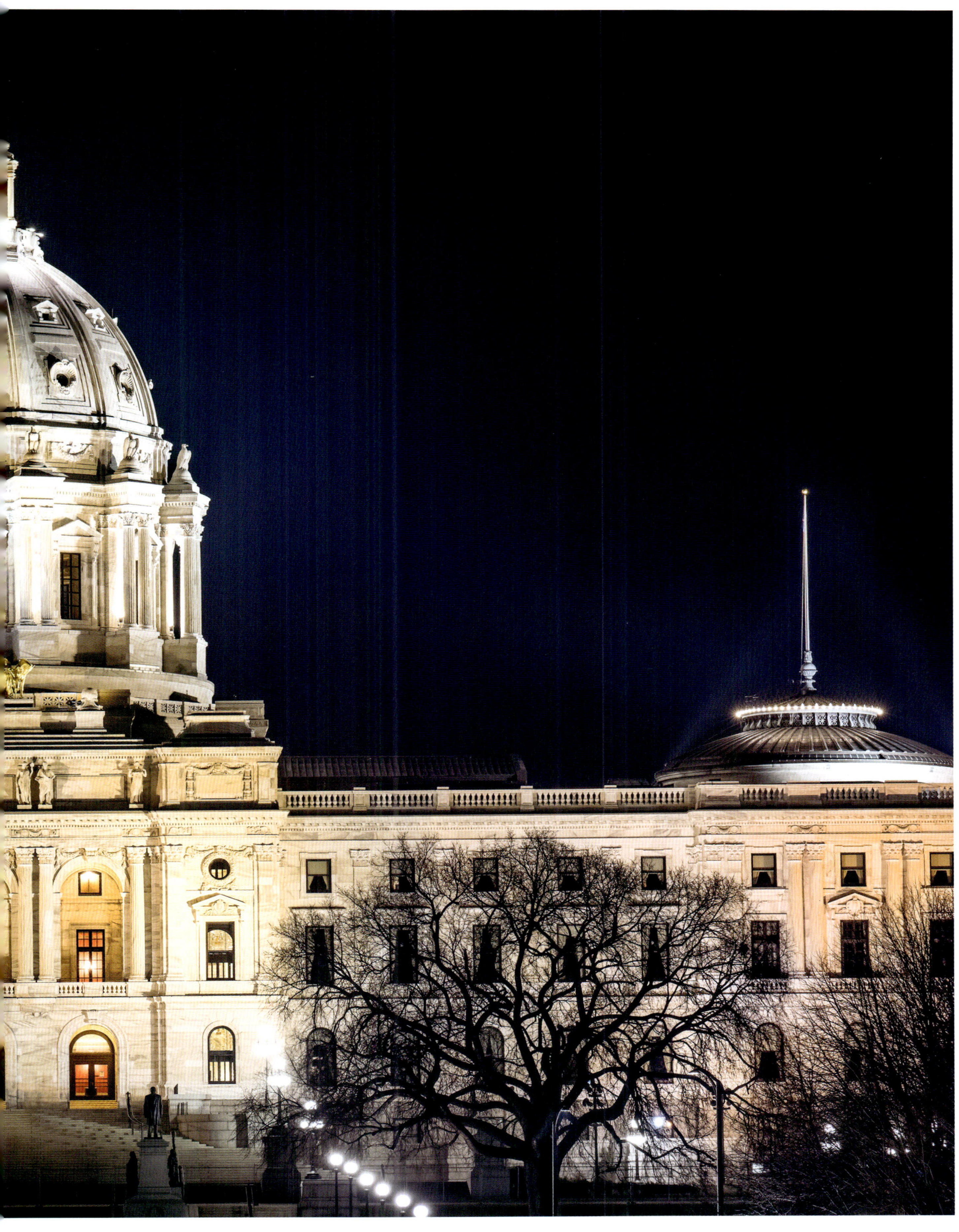

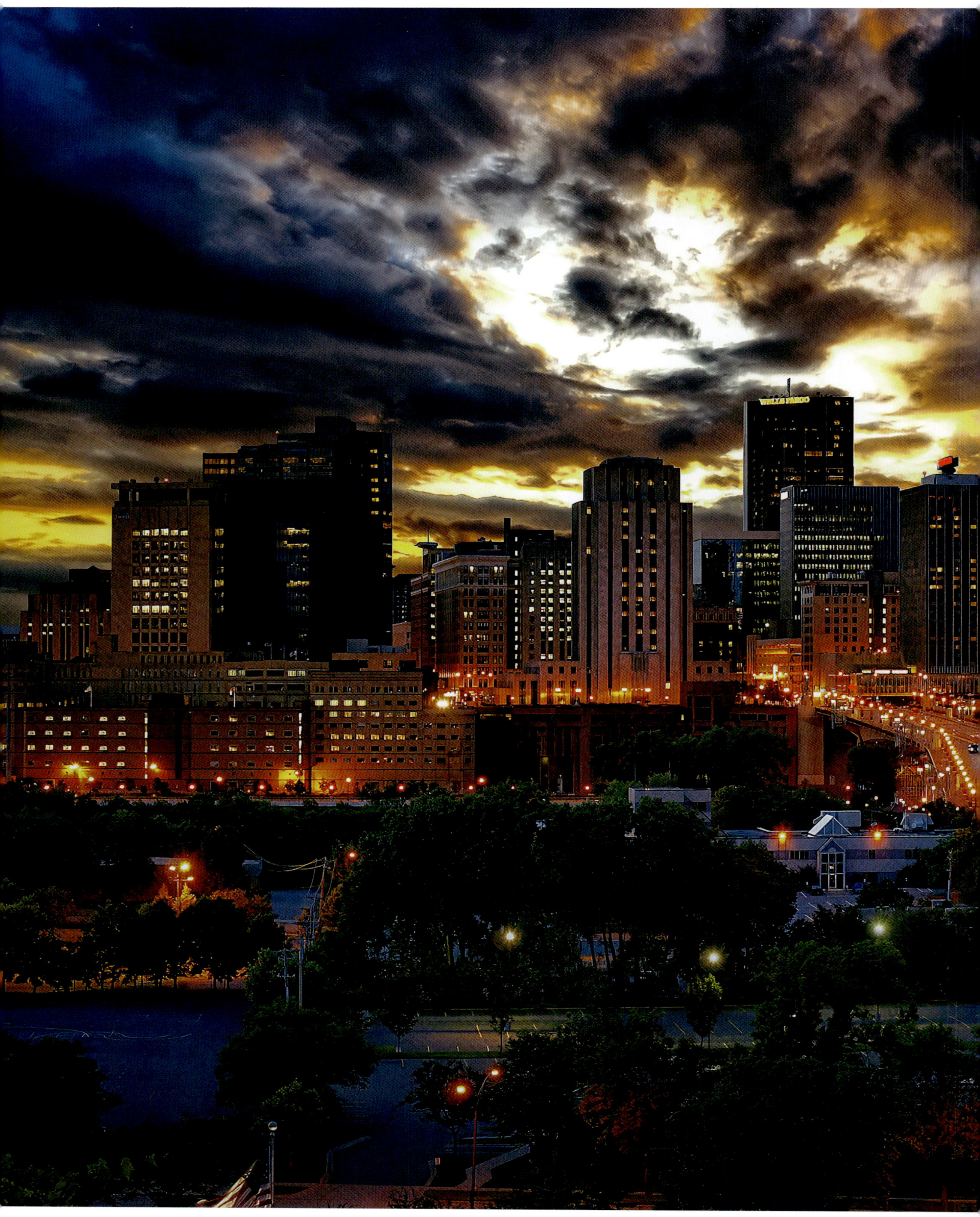

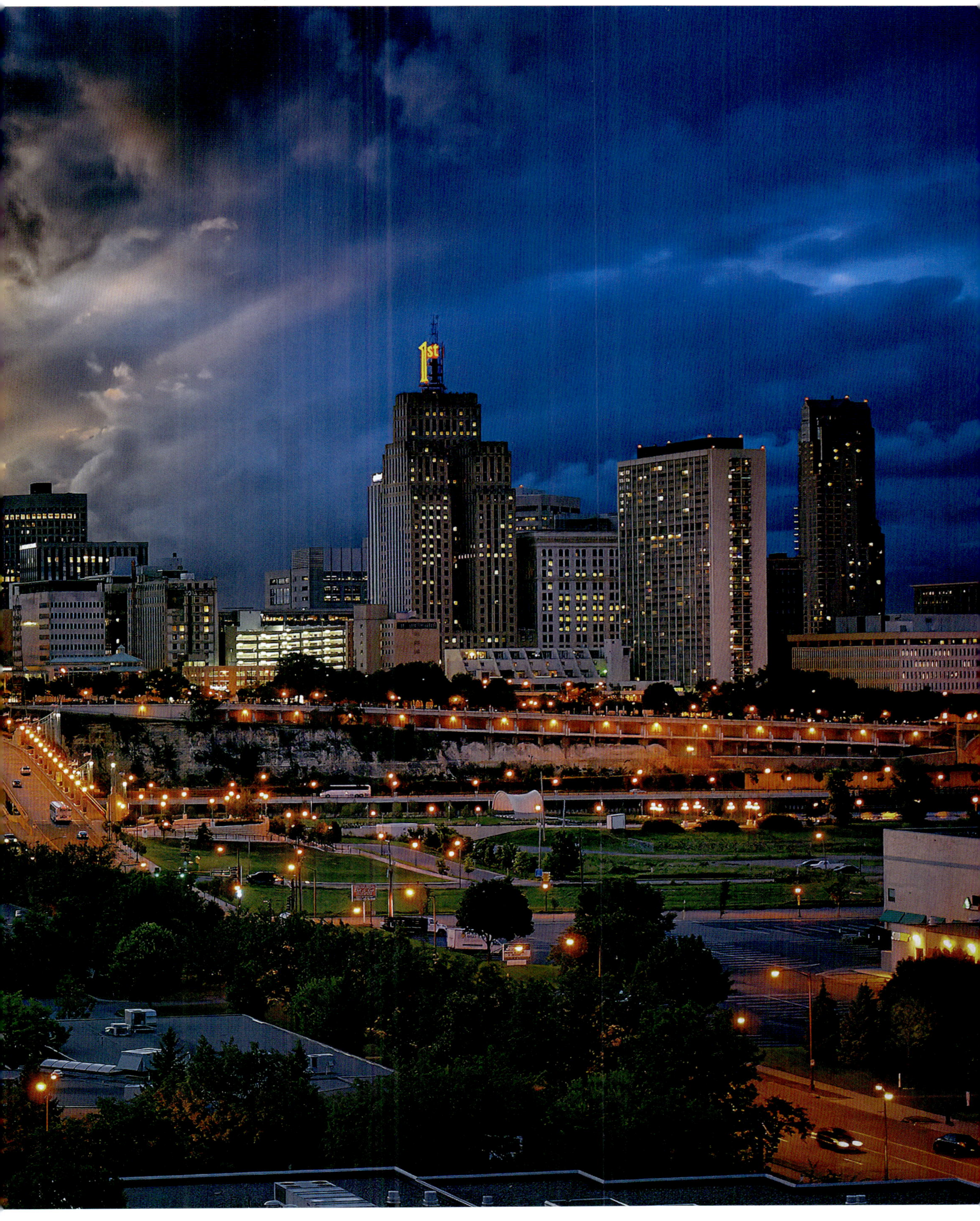

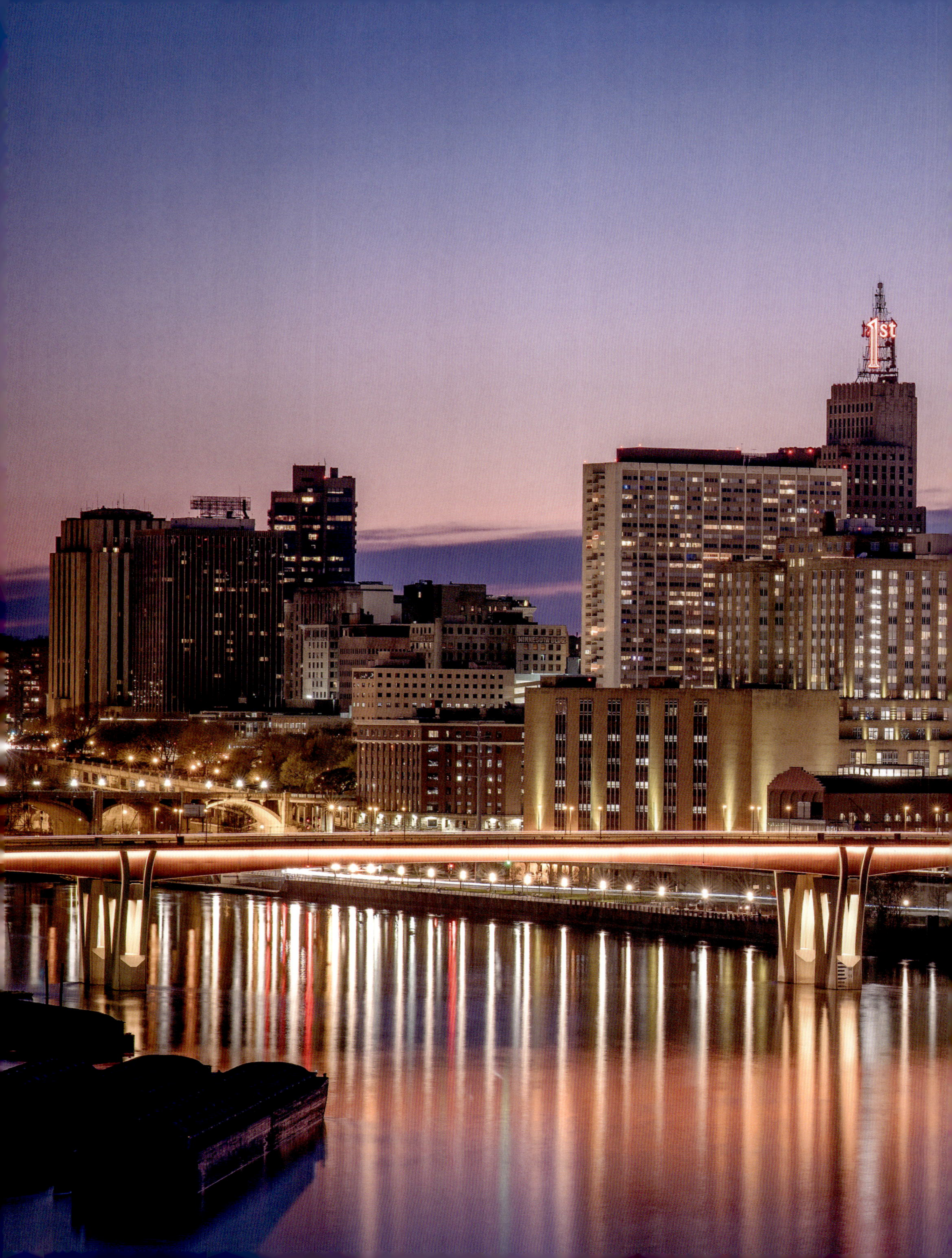
1st
MINNESOTA BLUE

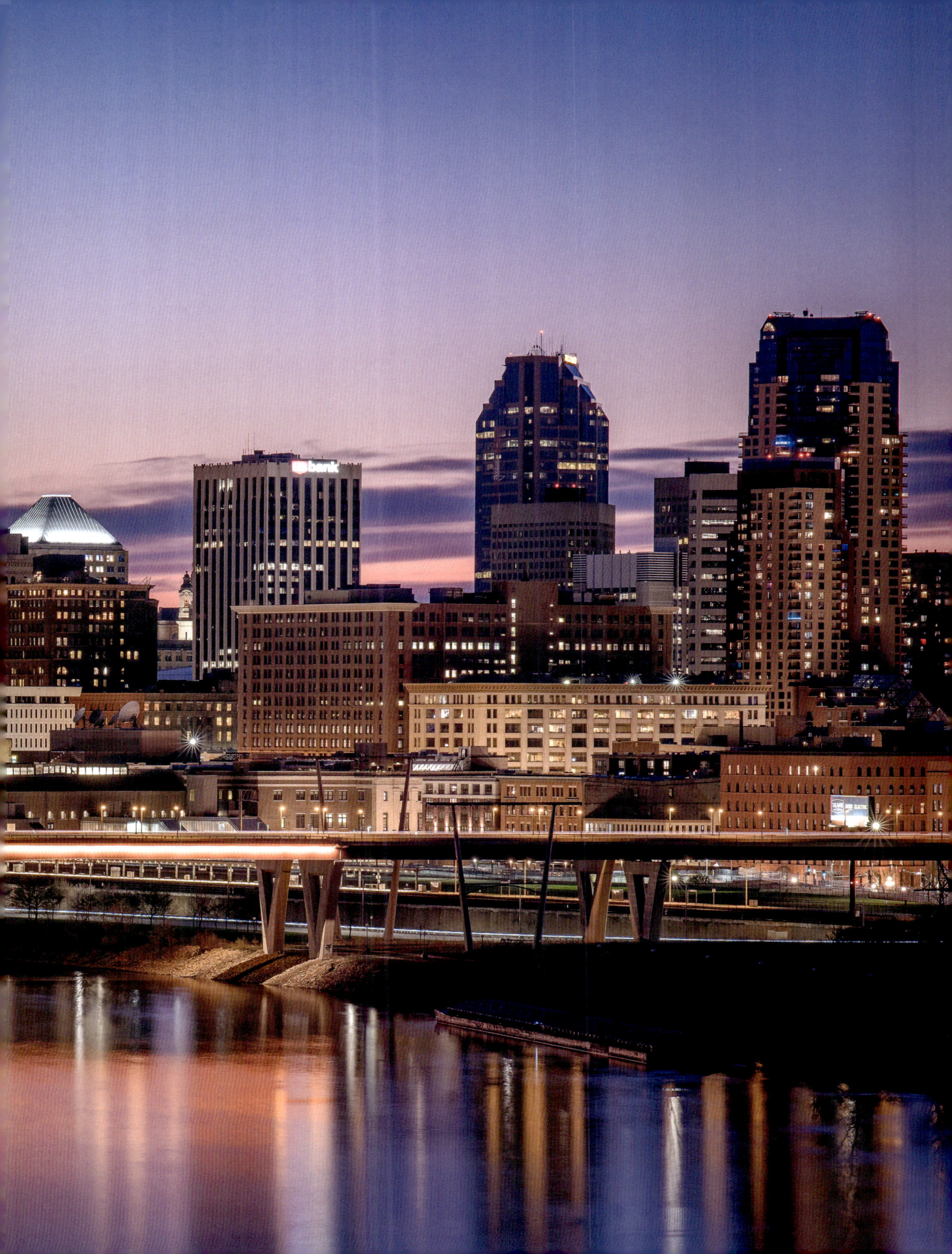

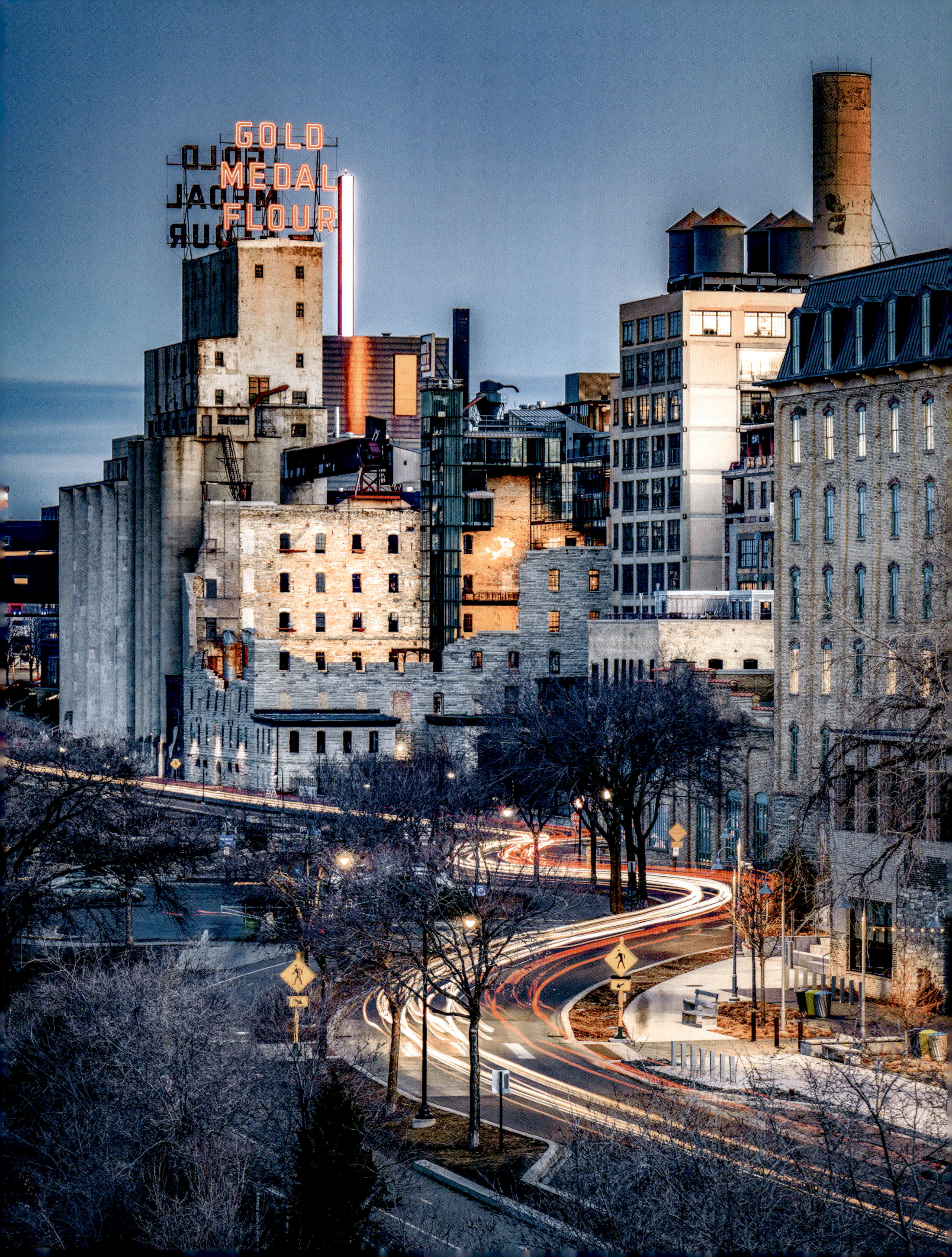

GOLD
MEDAL
FLOUR

ABOVE & ACROSS

TWIN CITIES

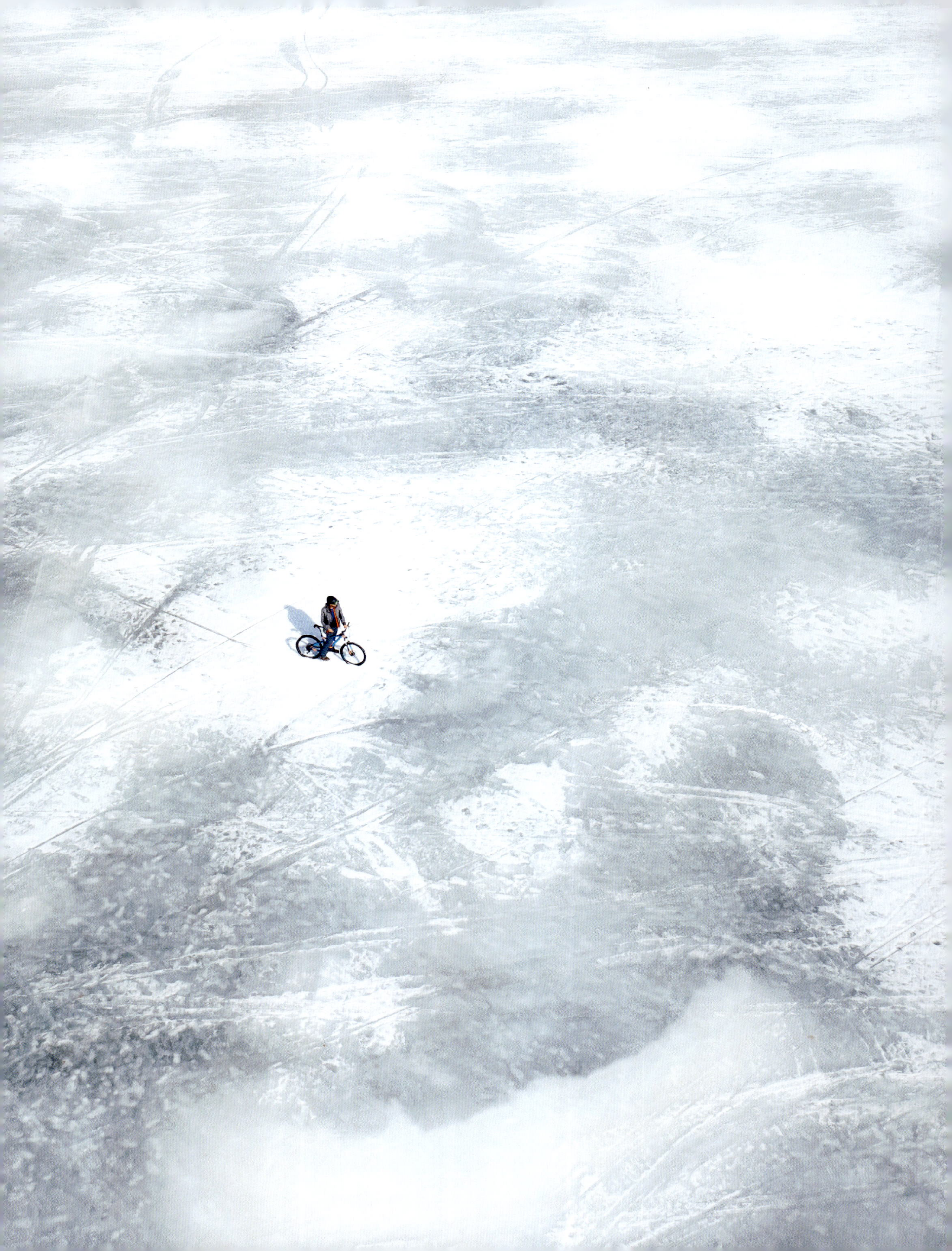

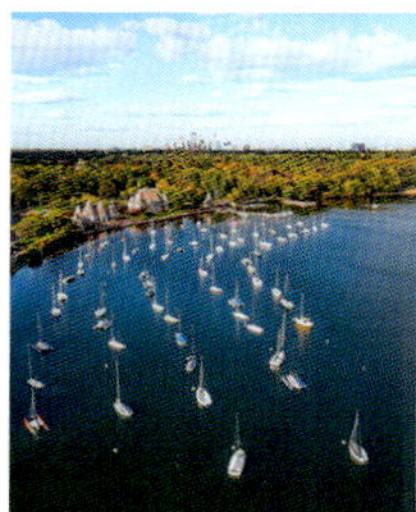

Front Cover Brian Johnson
Above Lake Harriet

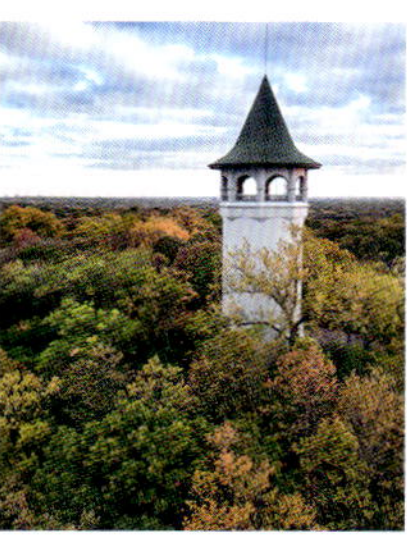

2 Brian Johnson
View of the Witch's Hat
Water Tower, Prospect Park

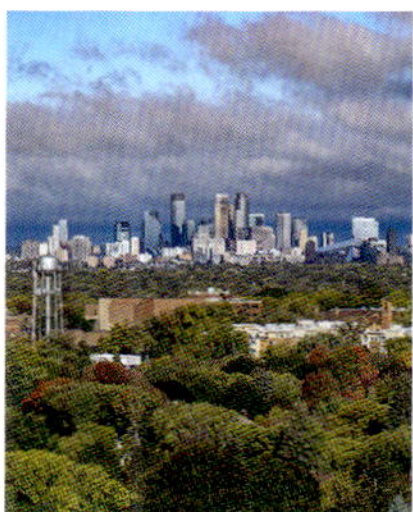

4 Michael Anderson
View of Minneapolis skyline
from Highland Park

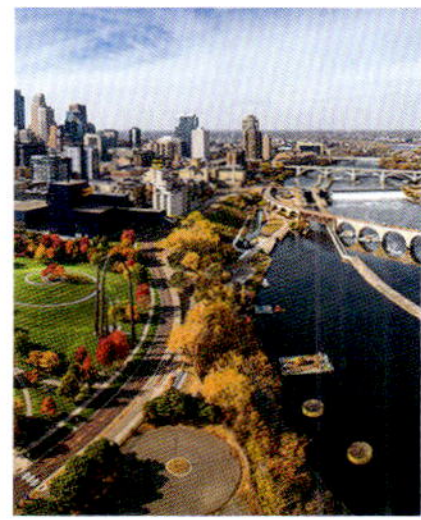

6 Jamie Hiner
View of Gold Medal Park and
the Mississippi River

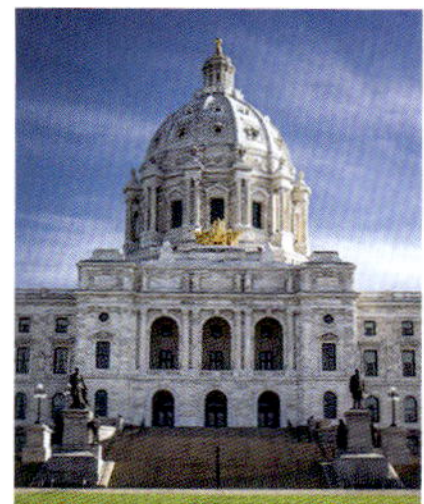

9 Mark Bergeron
View of the Minnesota
State Capitol

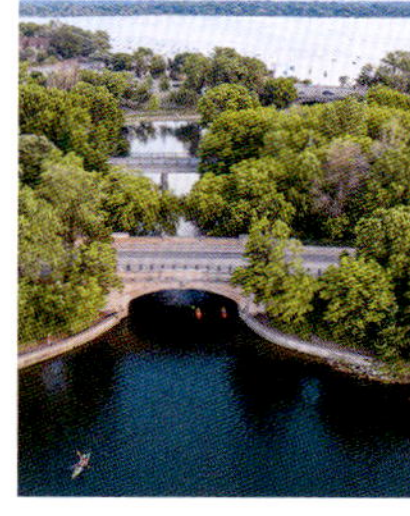

10 Omar Ghrayeb
Bridges over Bde Maka Ska

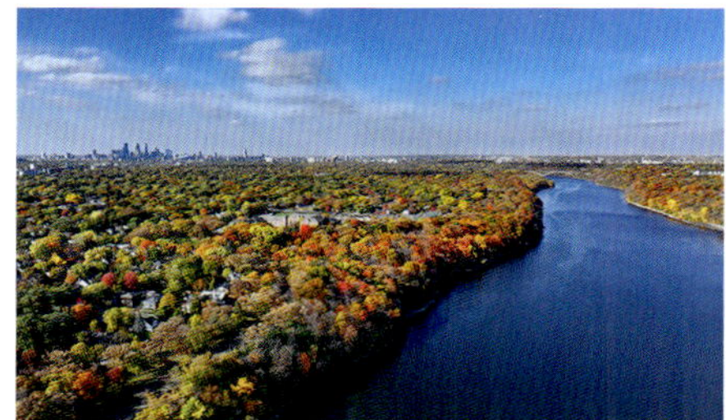

12-13 Greg Schulz
Above the Mississippi River Gorge

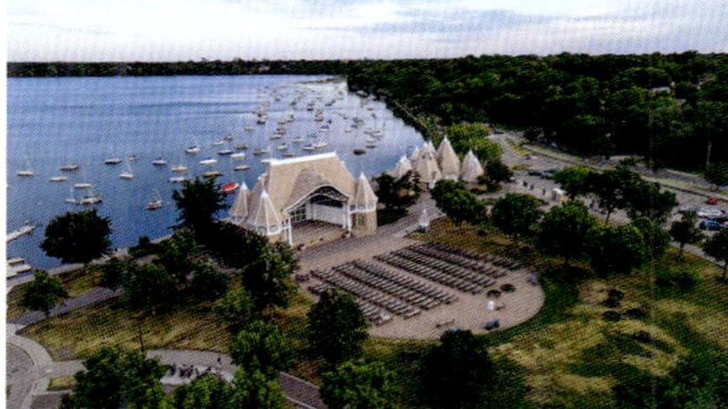

14-15 Brian Johnson
View of Lake Harriet Bandshell Park

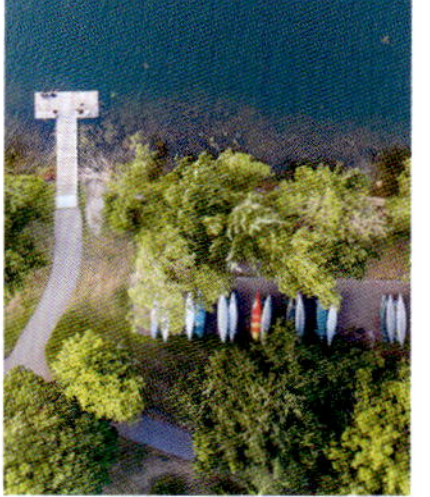

16 Omar Ghrayeb
Looking down on
Medicine Lake

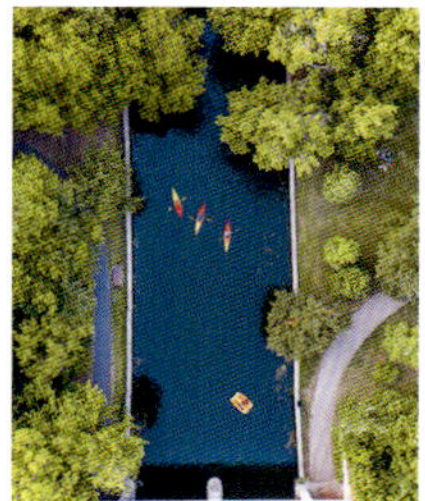

17 Omar Ghrayeb
Looking down on Lake of
the Isles inlet

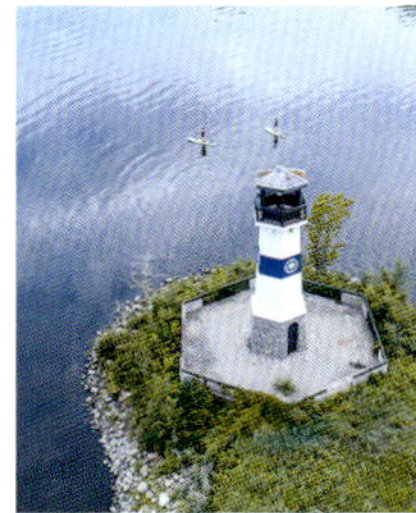

18 Omar Ghrayeb
View of Boom Island Park
Lighthouse

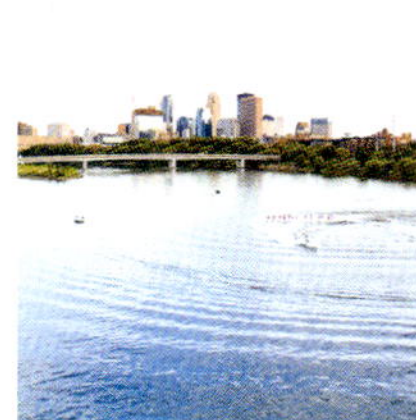

19 Omar Ghrayeb
View of Minneapolis and
the Mississippi River

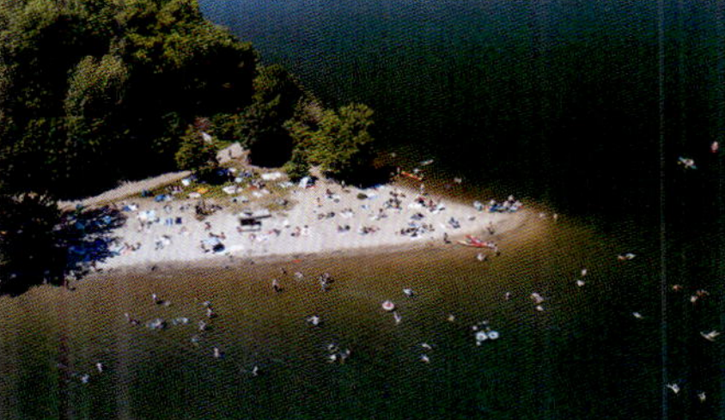

20-21 Omar Ghrayeb
Above Cedar Lake Point Beach

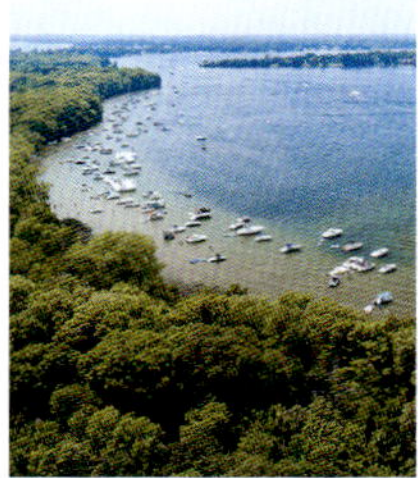

22 Omar Ghrayeb
Above Big Island
on Lake Minnetonka

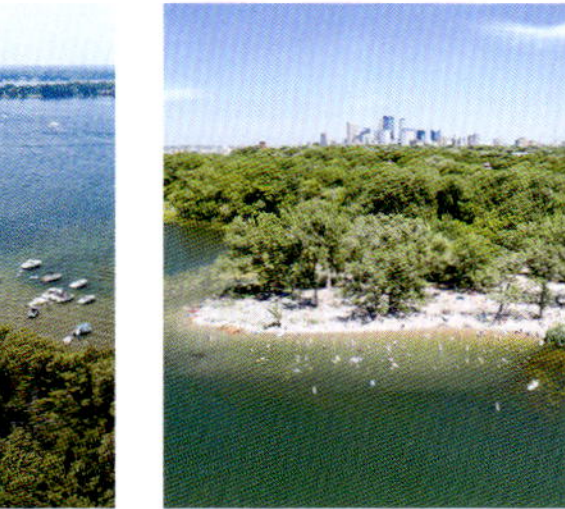

23 Omar Ghrayeb
View of Cedar Lake East
Beach and downtown
Minneapolis

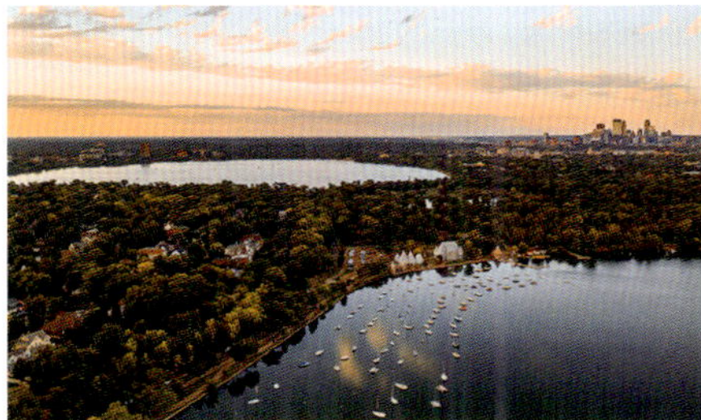

24-25 Omar Ghrayeb
Above Lake Harriet and Bde Maka Ska

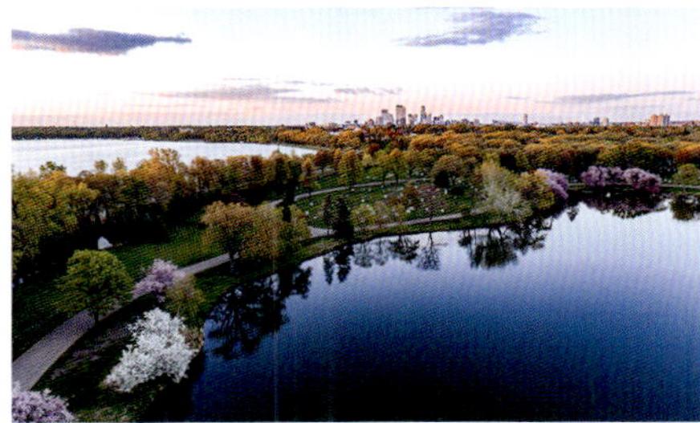

26 Omar Ghrayeb
View of Jo Pond and Bde Maka Ska

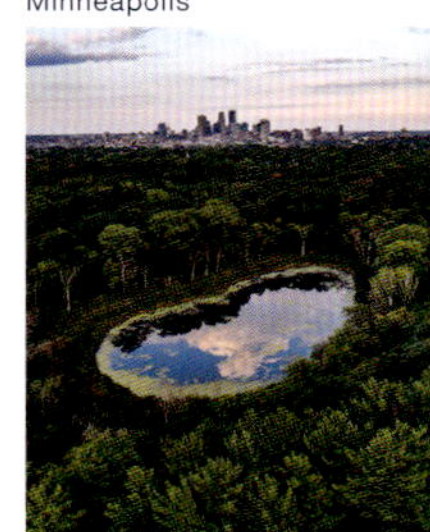

27 Brian Johnson
View of Birch Pond, Theodore
Wirth Regional Park

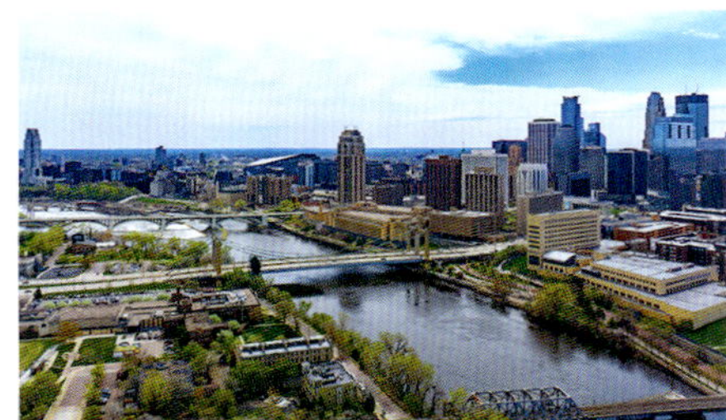

28-29 Greg Schulz
View of the Mississippi River and downtown Minneapolis

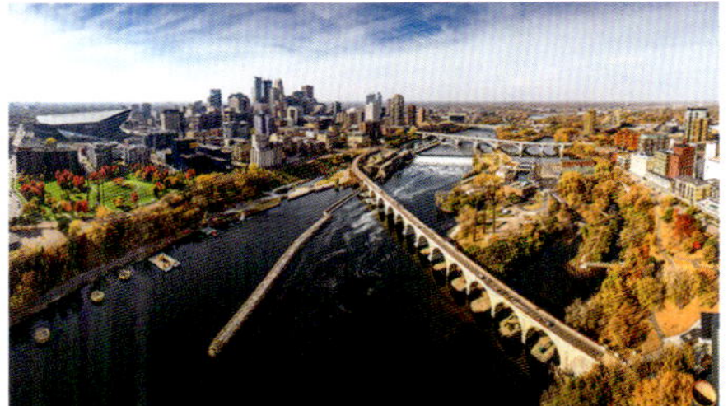

30-31 Jamie Hiner
Above Stone Bridge and the Mississippi River

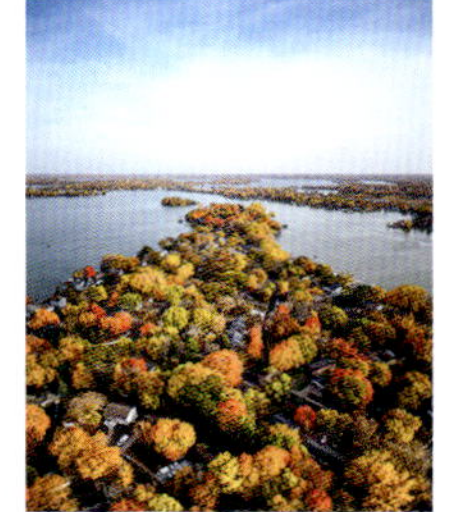

32 Jamie Hiner
Above Lake Minnetonka

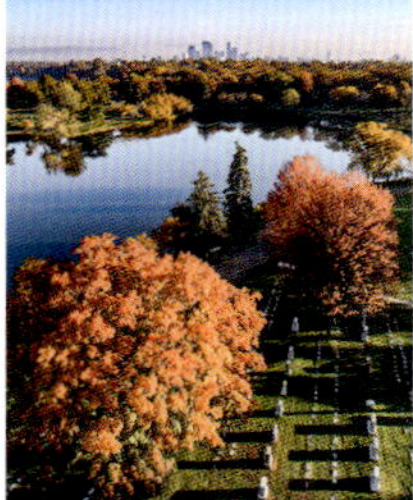

33 Brian Johnson
Above Lakewood Cemetery
and Bde Maka Ska

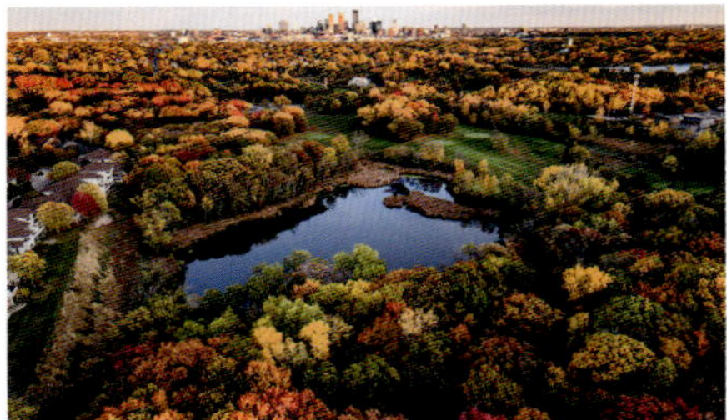

34-35 Brian Johnson
Above Theodore Wirth Golf Course

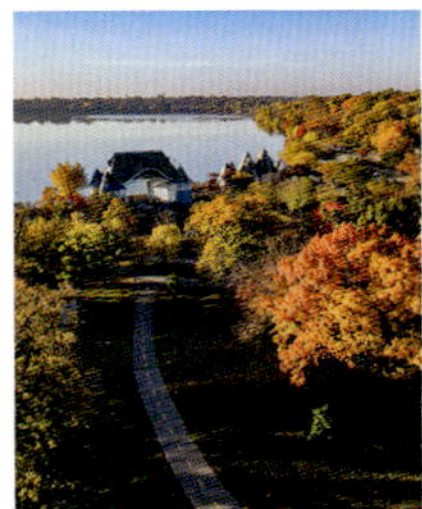

36 Brian Johnson
View of Lake Harriet
Bandshell Park

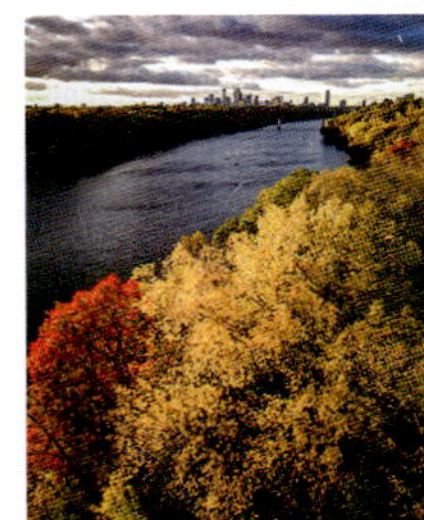

37 Brian Johnson
View of Minneapolis skyline
and the Mississippi River

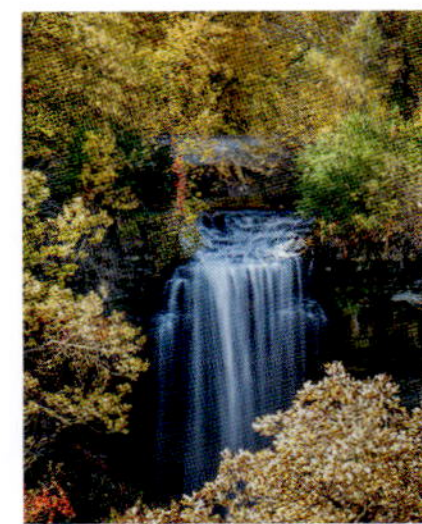

38 Michael Anderson
View of Minnehaha Falls

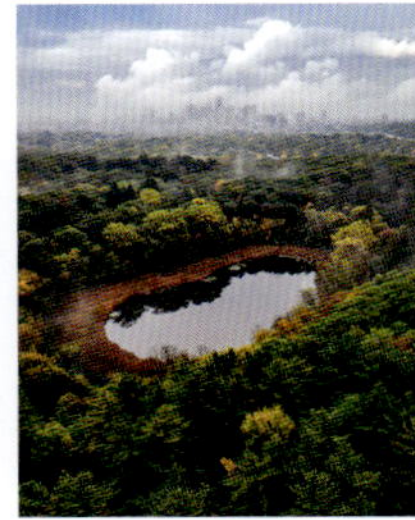

39 Brian Johnson
View of Birch Pond, Theodore
Wirth Regional Park

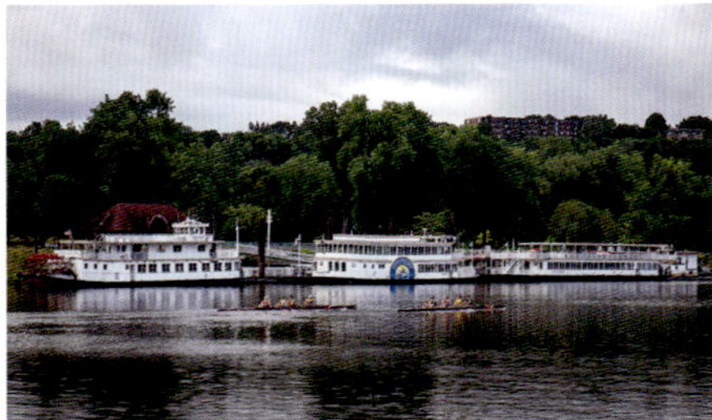

40-41 Mark Bergeron
View of Padelford Riverboats, Mississippi River

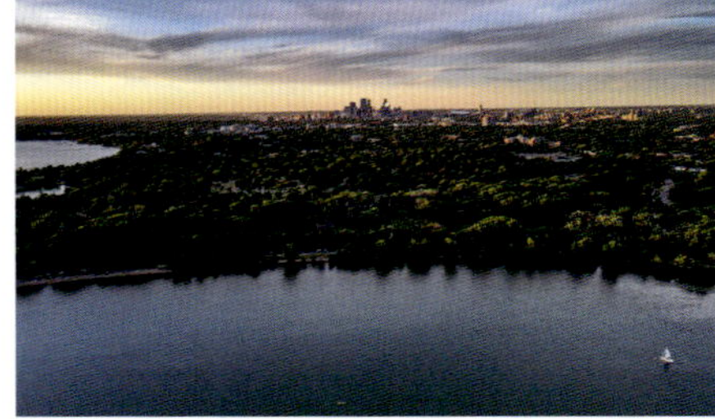

42-43 Brian Johnson
Above Lake of the Isles

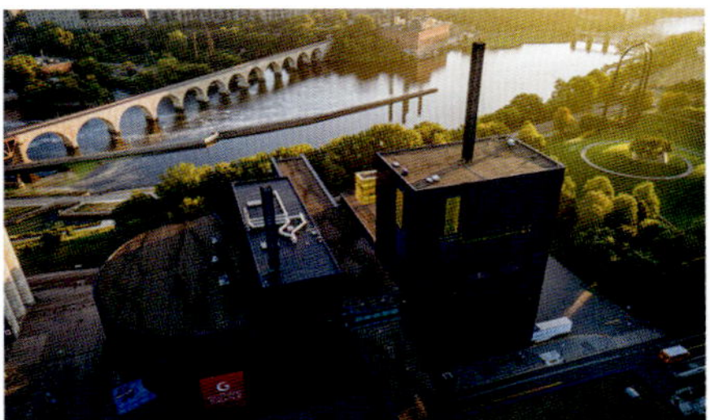

44-45 Brian Johnson
View of the Guthrie Theater and Stone Arch Bridge

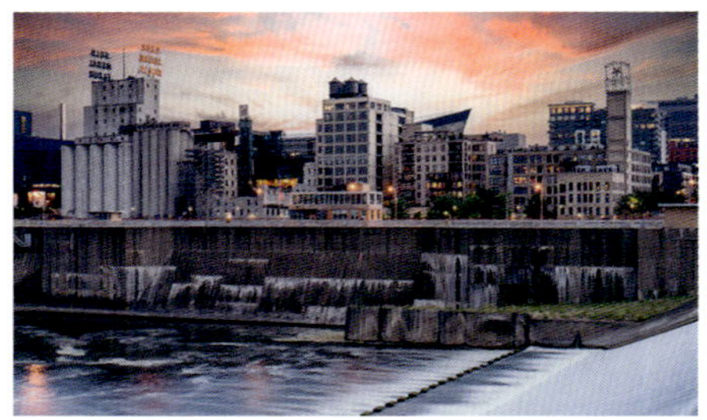

46-47 Michael Anderson
View of St. Anthony Falls

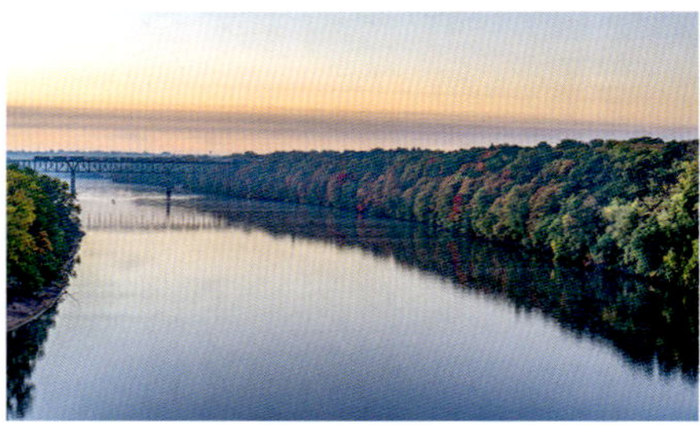

48-49 Michael Anderson
View of the Mississippi River from Franklin Avenue Bridge

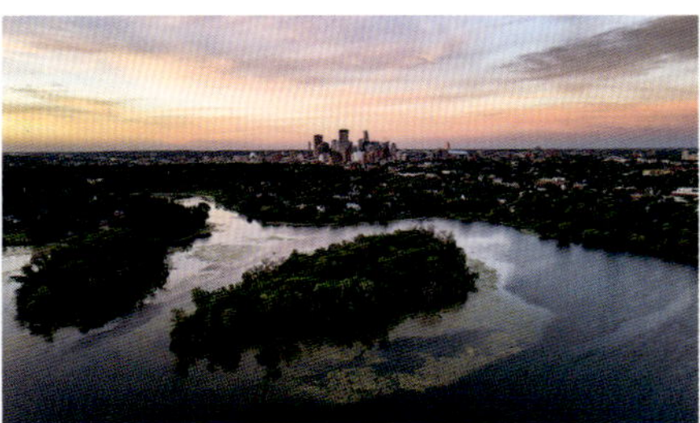

50 Brian Johnson
View of the Minneapolis skyline from Lake of the Isles

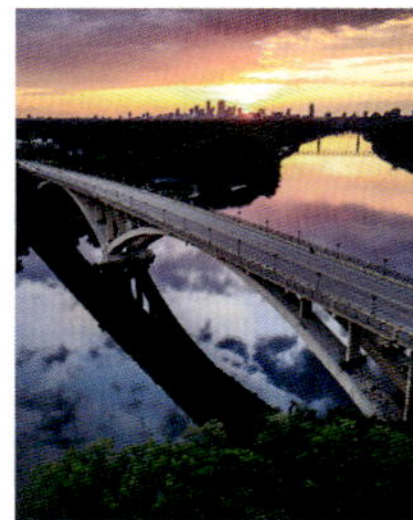

51 Brian Johnson
Above the Lake Street-
Marshall Avenue Bridge

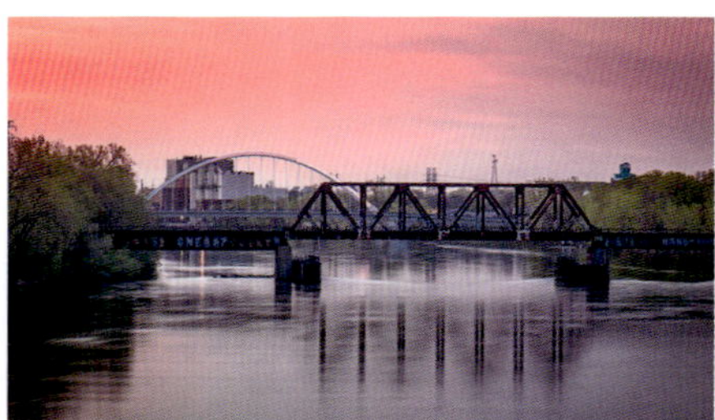

52-53 Mark Bergeron
View of Railroad Bridge and Lowry Avenue Bridge

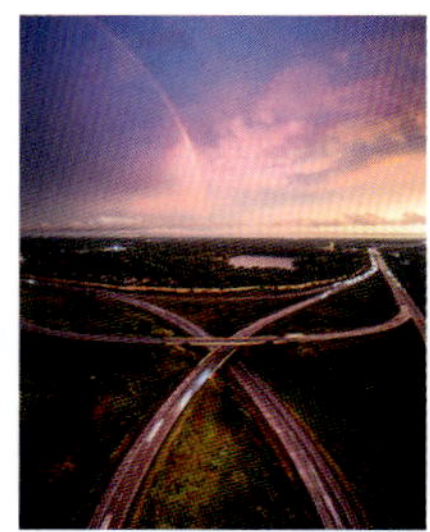

54 Jamie Hiner
Above Maple Grove

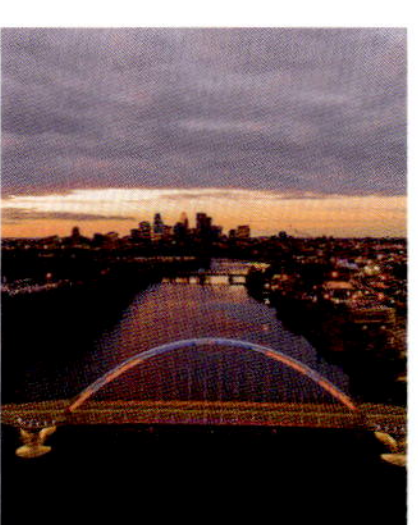

55 Omar Ghrayeb
Above Lowry Avenue Bridge

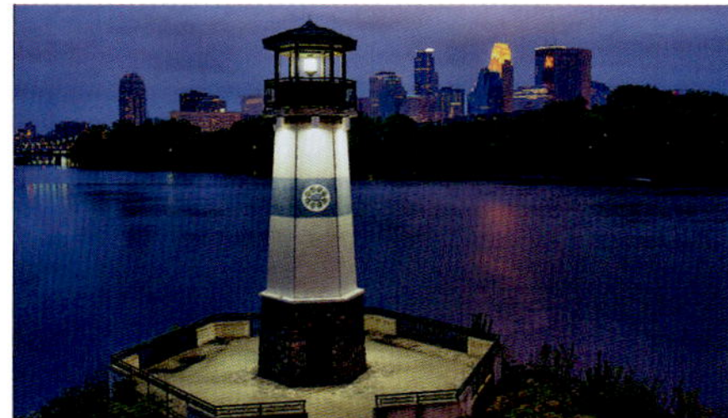

56 Dan Anderson
View of Boom Island Park Lighthouse

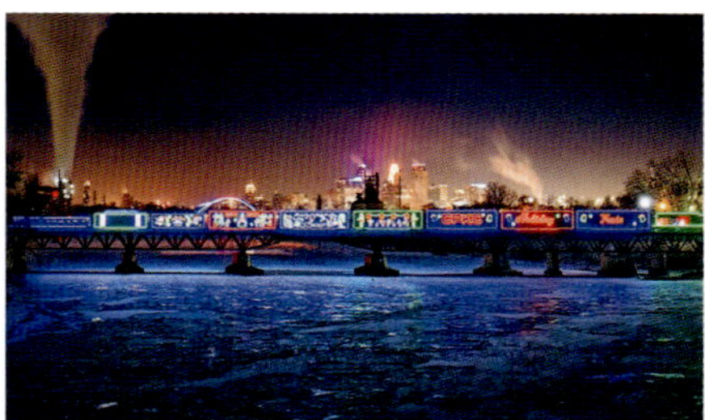

57 Dan Anderson
View of the Canadian Pacific Holiday Train crossing
the Mississippi River

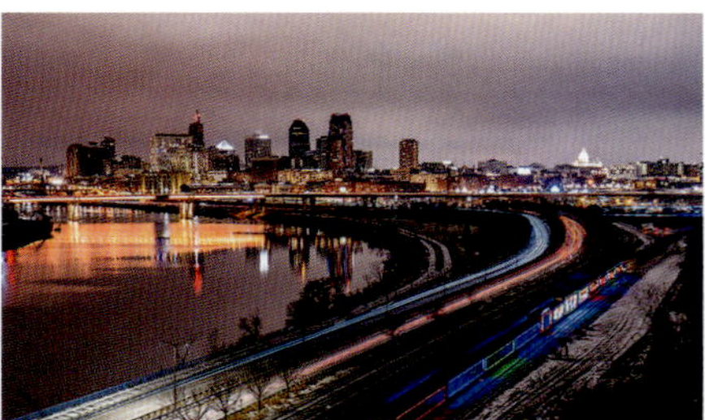

58-59 Michael Anderson
View of the Canadian Pacific Holiday Train leaving St. Paul

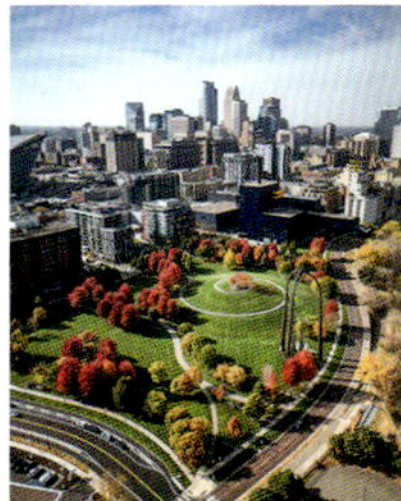

60 Jamie Hiner
Above Gold Medal Park

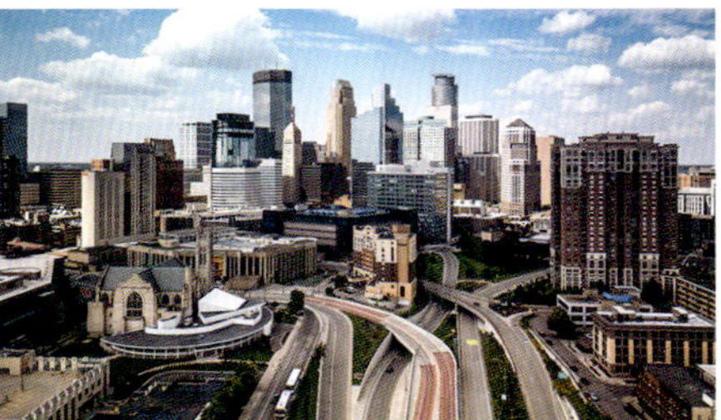

62-63 Jamie Hiner
View of downtown Minneapolis

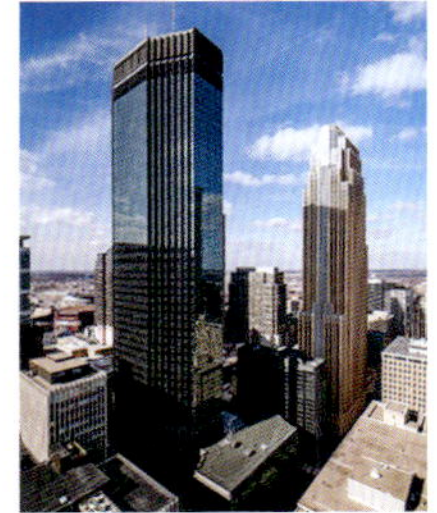

64 Brian Johnson
View of IDS Center and
the Wells Fargo Center

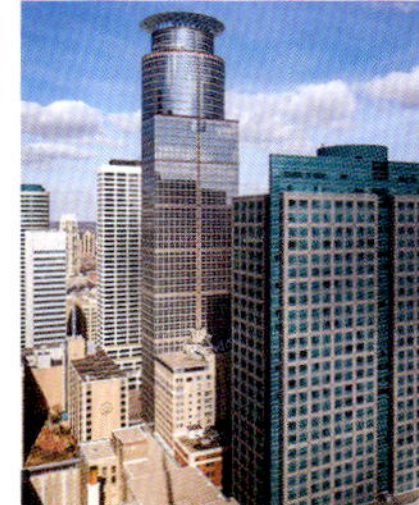

65 Brian Johnson
View of Capella Tower

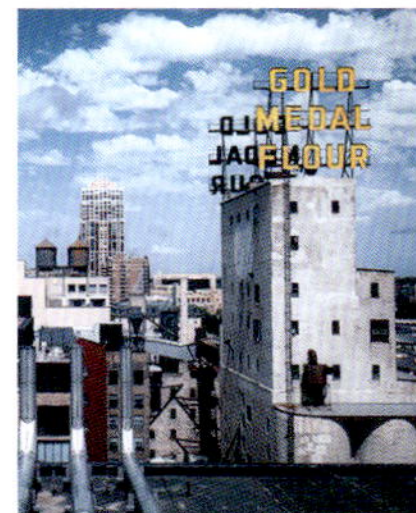

66 Malik Blaylark
View of Gold Medal Flour
sign and Mill City Museum

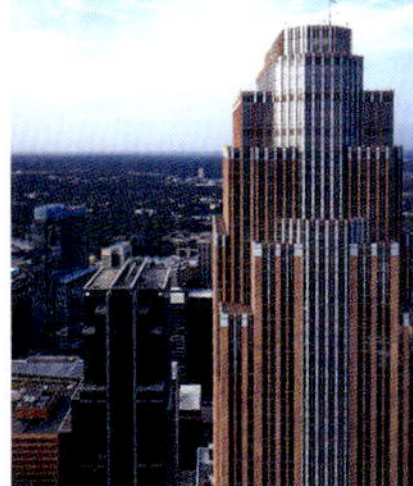

67 Malik Blaylark
View of the Wells Fargo
Center

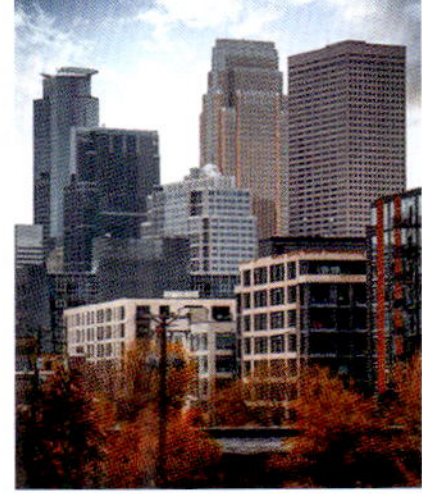

68 Zach Butler
View of Capella Tower and
the Wells Fargo Center

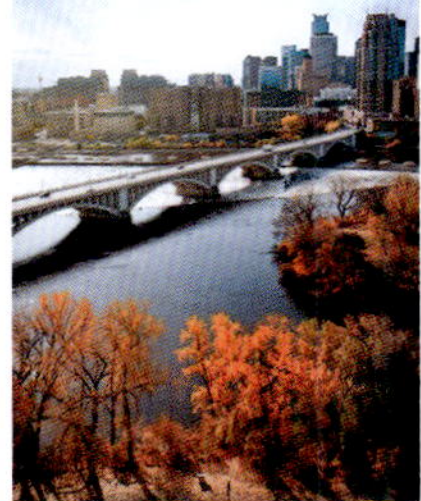

69 Zach Butler
Above the Third Avenue
Bridge

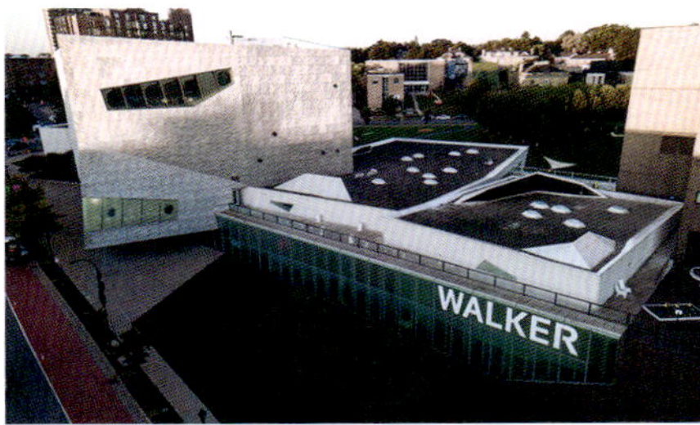

70 Brian Johnson
Above the Walker Art Center

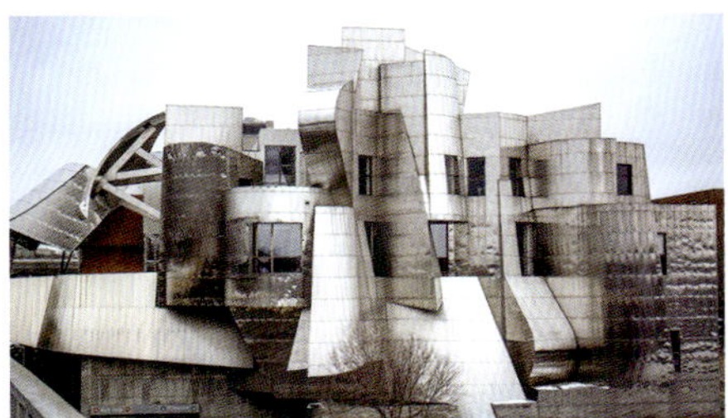

71 Mark Bergeron
View of the Weisman Art Museum

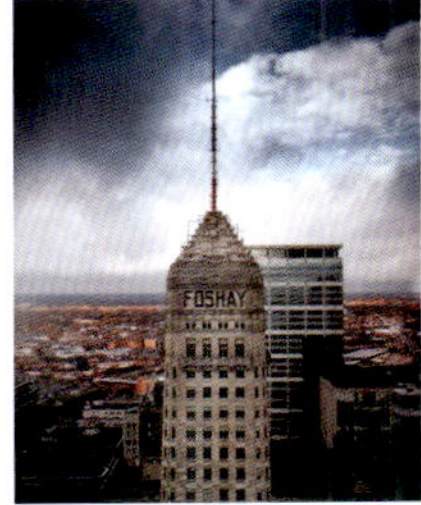

72 Zach Butler
View of the Foshay Tower

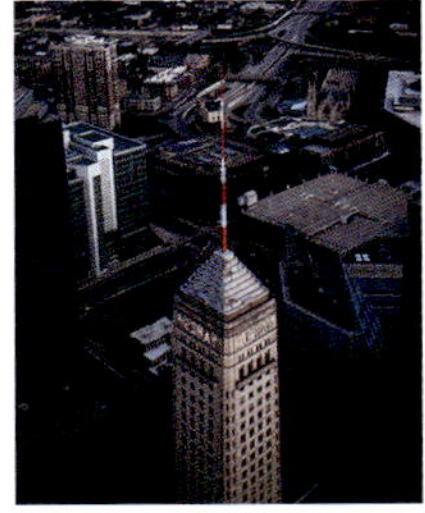

73 Malik Blaylark
Above the Foshay Tower

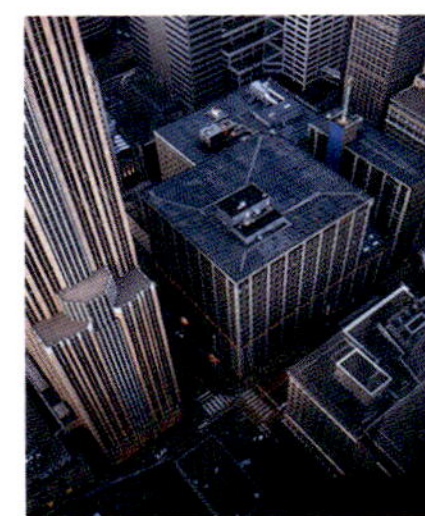

74 Malik Blaylark
Above 7th Street and
Marquette Avenue

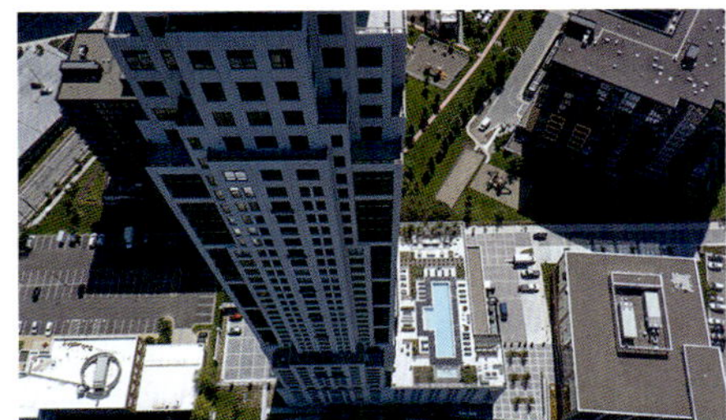

75 Greg Schulz
Above Eleven on the River

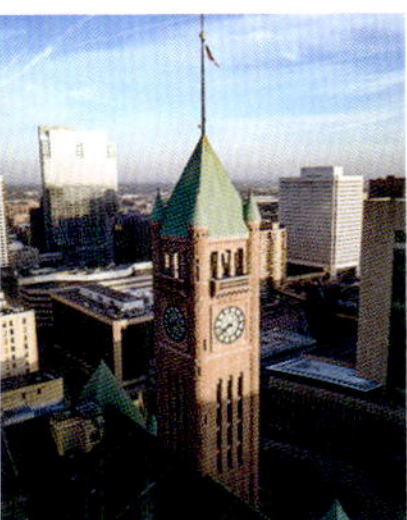

76 Brian Johnson
View of the Minneapolis
City Hall Clock Tower

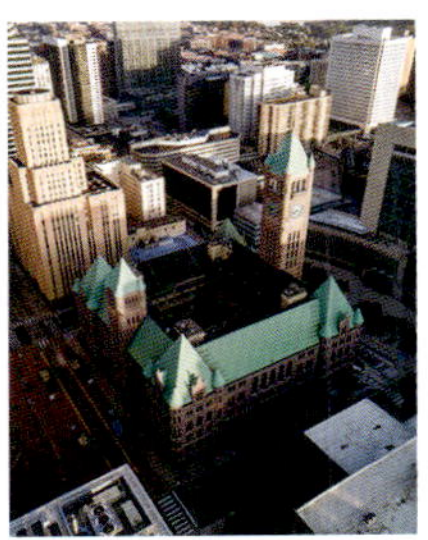

77 Brian Johnson
Above Minneapolis City Hall

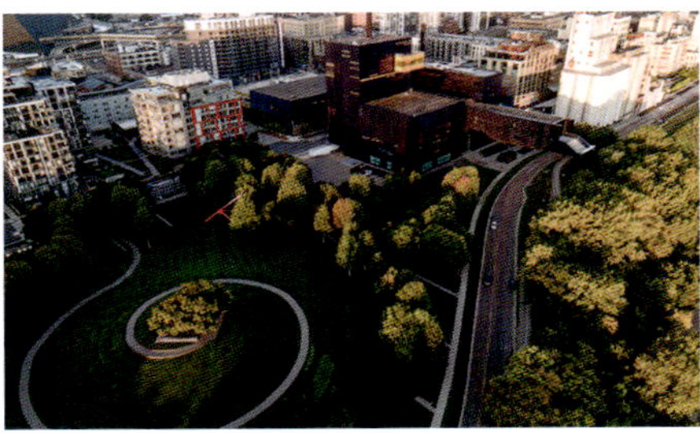

78-79 Brian Johnson
Above Gold Medal Park, Guthrie Theater,
and Mill City Museum

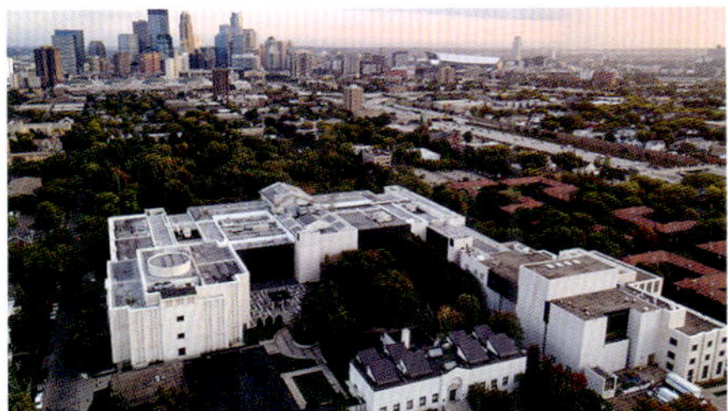

80-81 Brian Johnson
Above the Minneapolis Institute of Art

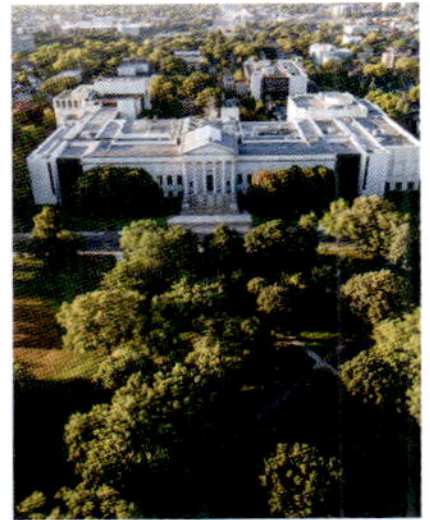

82 Brian Johnson
Above the Minneapolis
Institute of Art

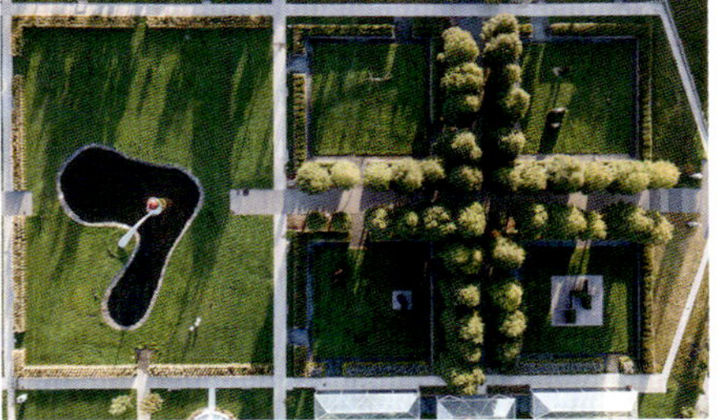

83 Brian Johnson
Looking down on the Minneapolis Sculpture Garden

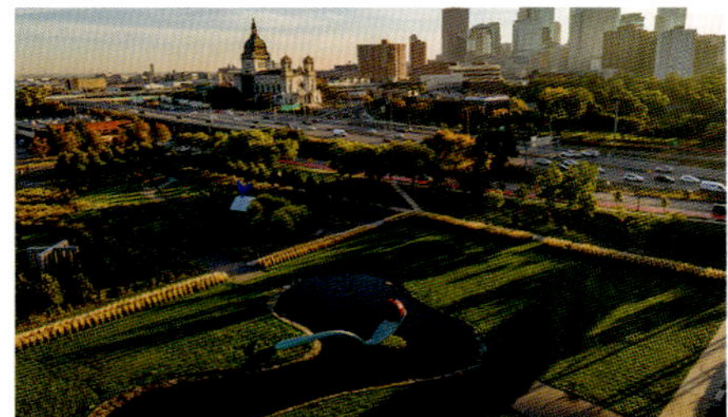

84-85 Brian Johnson
Above the Minneapolis Sculpture Garden

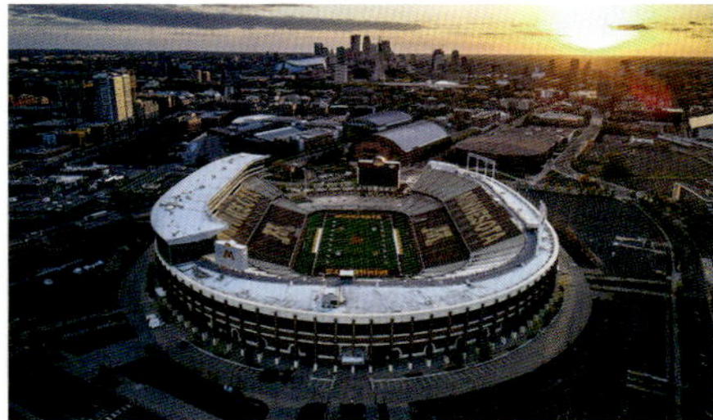

86-87 Brian Johnson
Above Huntington Bank Stadium, University of Minnesota

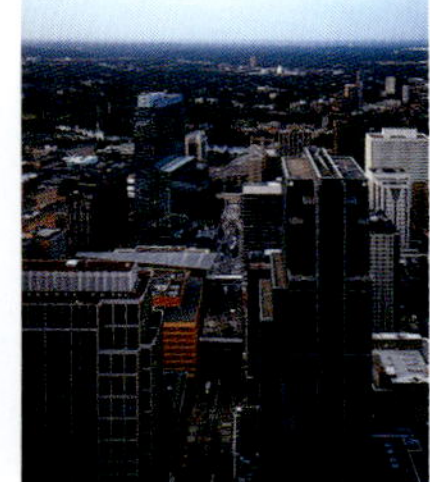

88 Malik Blaylark
Above Nicollet Mall

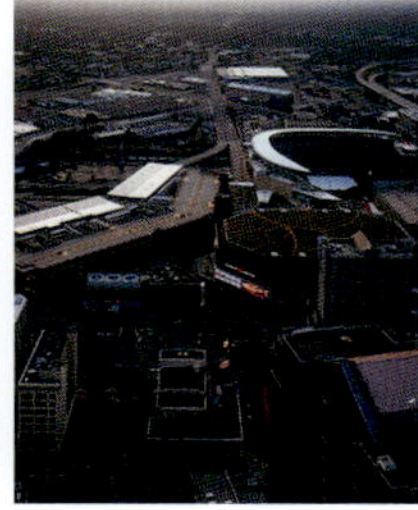

89 Malik Blaylark
Above Target Field
and Target Center

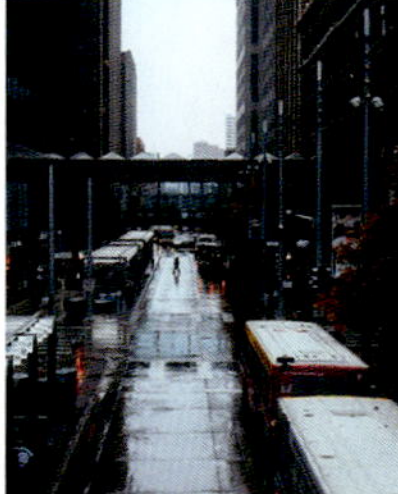

90 Malik Blaylark
View of skyway over
Nicollet Mall

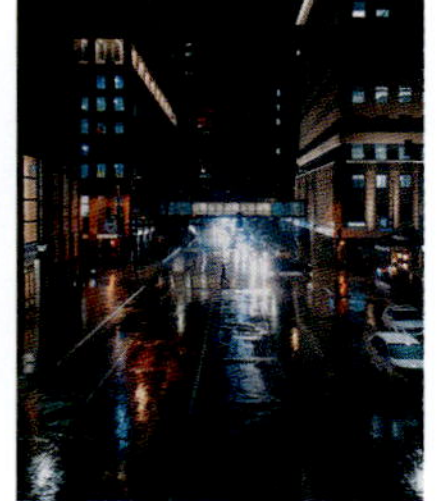

91 Malik Blaylark
View of skyway over
South 7th Street

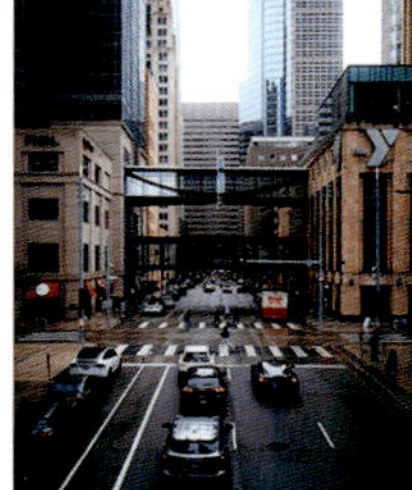

92 Malik Blaylark
View of multi-level skyway
over South 6th Street

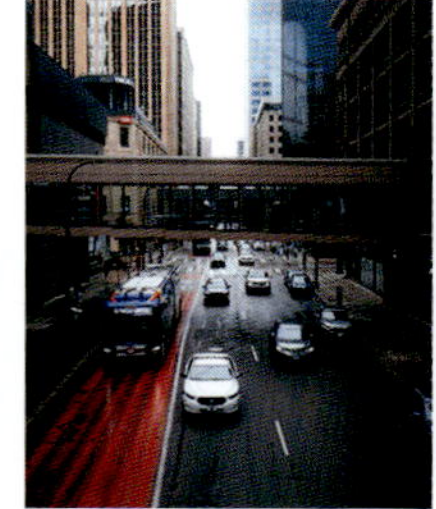

93 Malik Blaylark
View of skyway over
South 7th Street

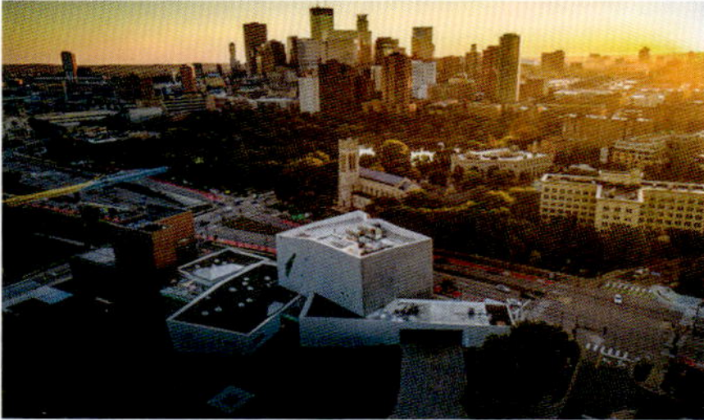

94-95 Brian Johnson
View of the Walker Art Museum and downtown Minneapolis

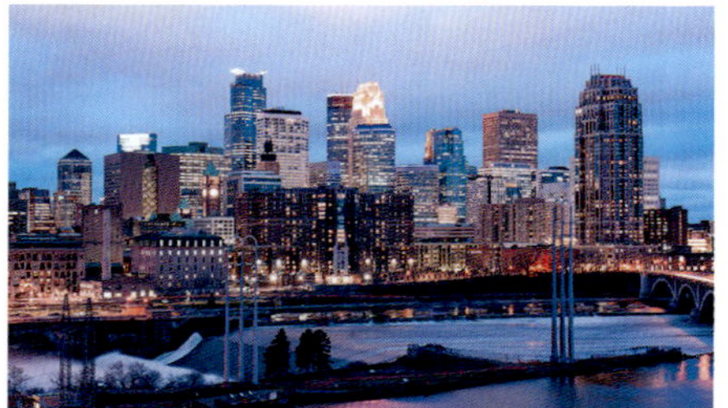

96-97 Zach Butler
View of the Minneapolis skyline from across
the Mississippi River

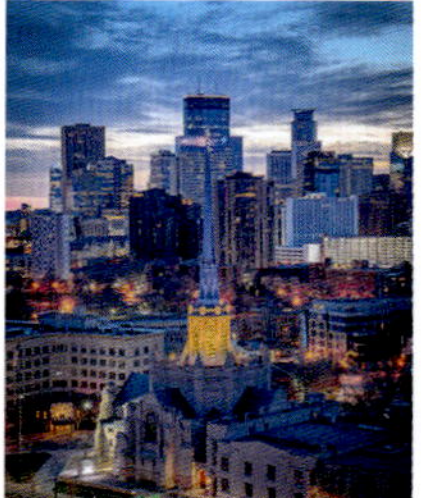

98 Michael Anderson
View of Hennepin Avenue
United Methodist Church

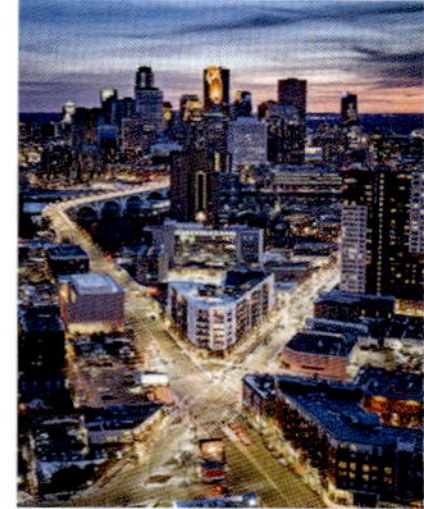

99 Michael Anderson
Above East Hennepin
Avenue and Central Avenue
intersection

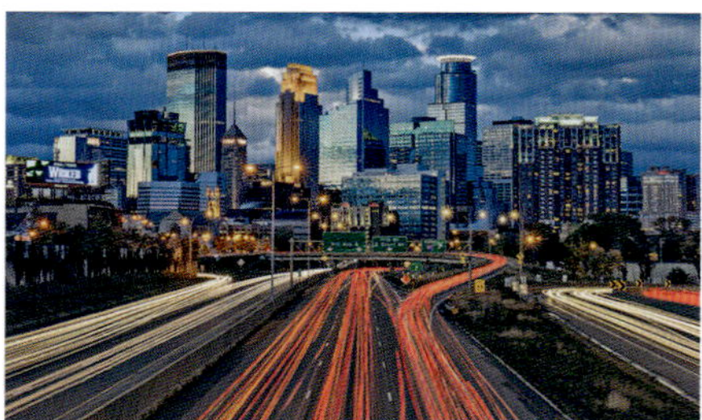

100-101 Dan Anderson
View of downtown Minneapolis

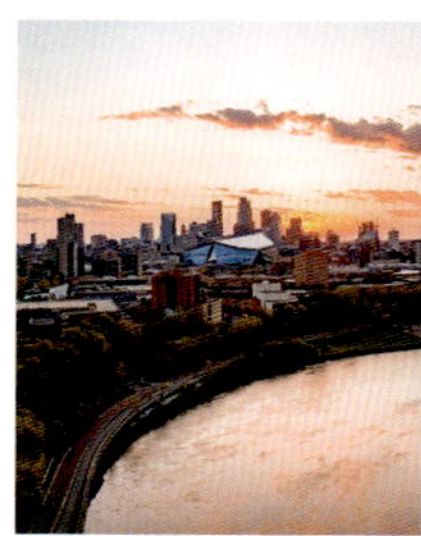

102 Omar Ghrayeb
View of U.S. Bank Stadium
from the Mississippi River

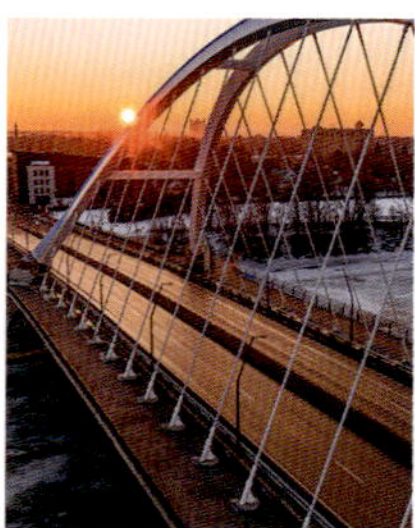

103 Omar Ghrayeb
View of Lowry Avenue Bridge

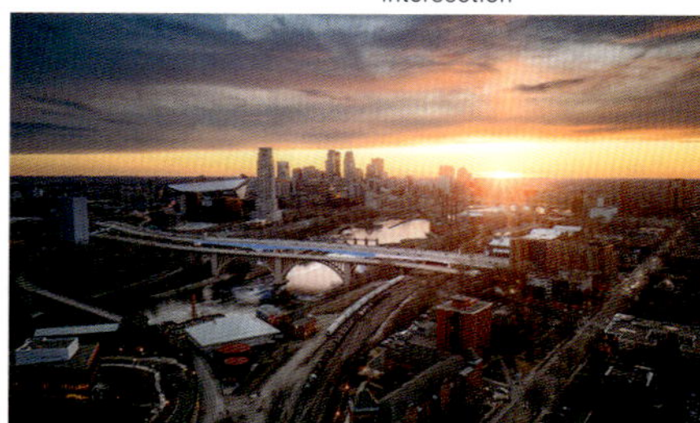

104-105 Jamie Hiner
View of downtown Minneapolis over the I-35W Bridge

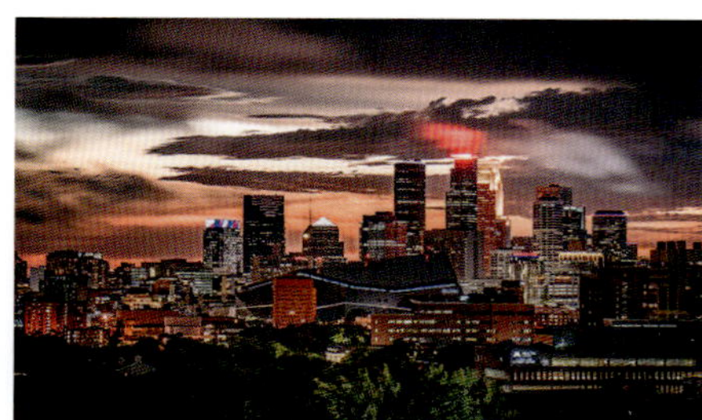

106-107 Michael Anderson
View of U.S. Bank Stadium and downtown Minneapolis

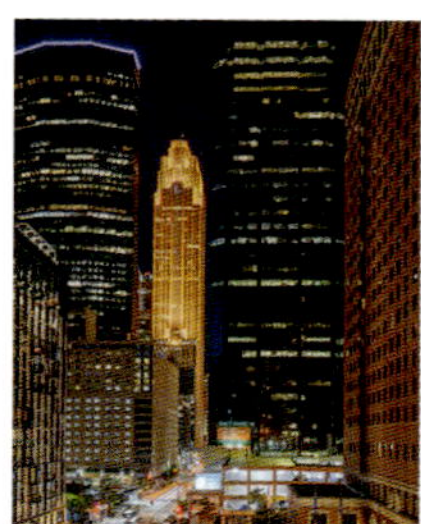

108 Michael Anderson
View of Marquette Avenue

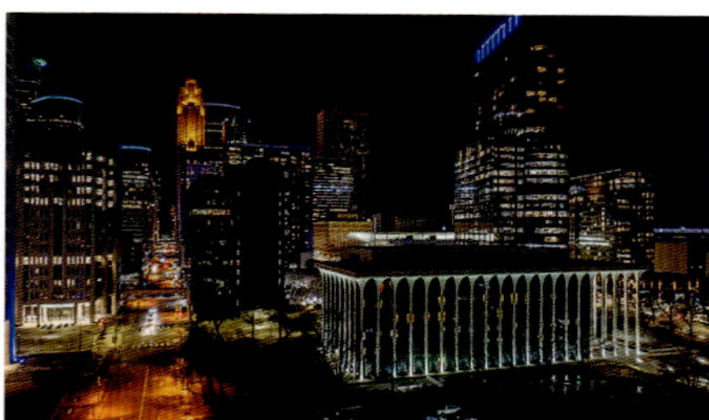

109 Greg Schulz
View of Northwestern National Life Building

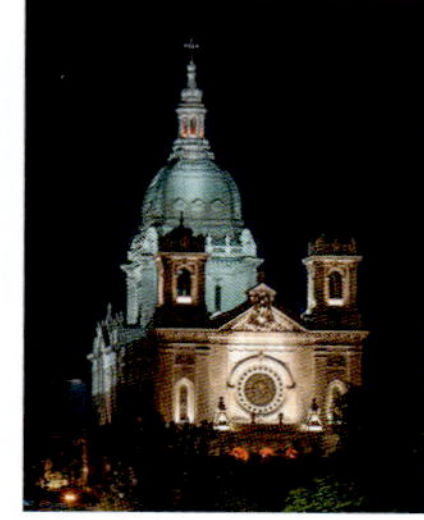

110 Mark Bergeron
View of The Basilica
of St. Mary

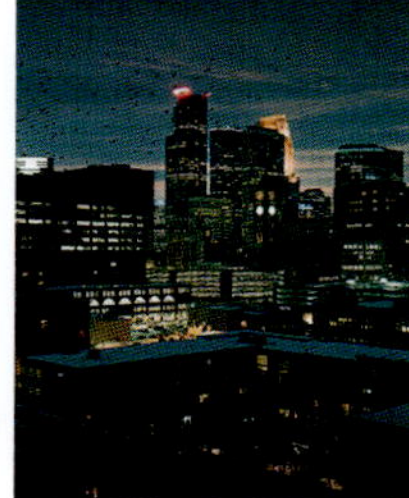

111 Zach Butler
View of Minneapolis City
Hall and Capella Tower

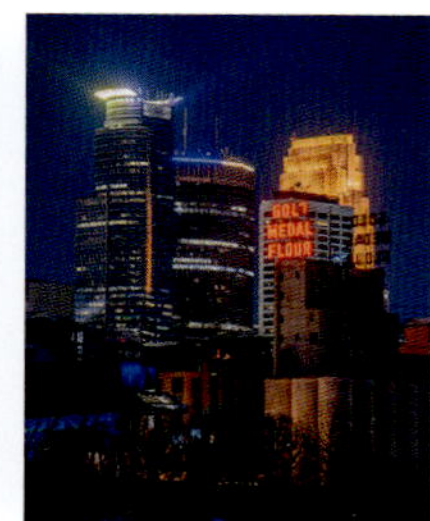

112 Michael Anderson
View of downtown
Minneapolis

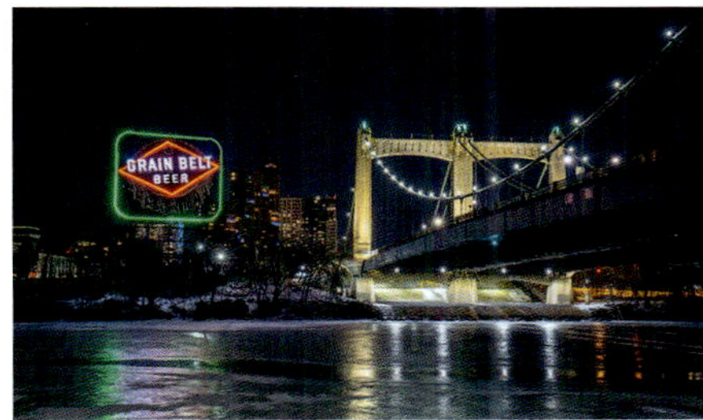

113 Michael Anderson
View of Grain Belt Beer sign and Hennepin Avenue Bridge

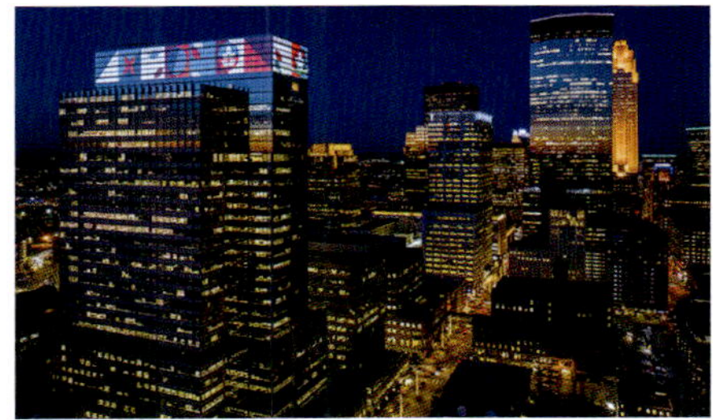

114-115 Greg Schulz
View of Target Plaza South

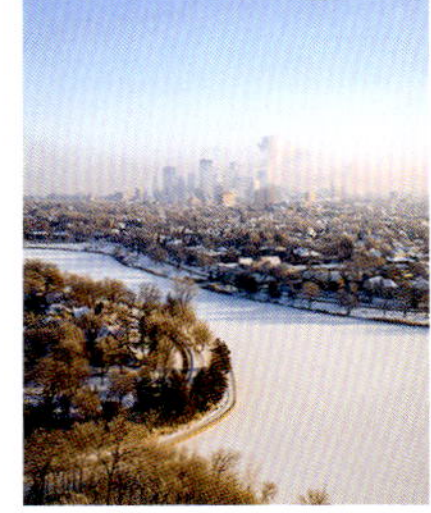

117 Omar Ghrayeb
View of the Minneapolis skyline from above Lake of the Isles

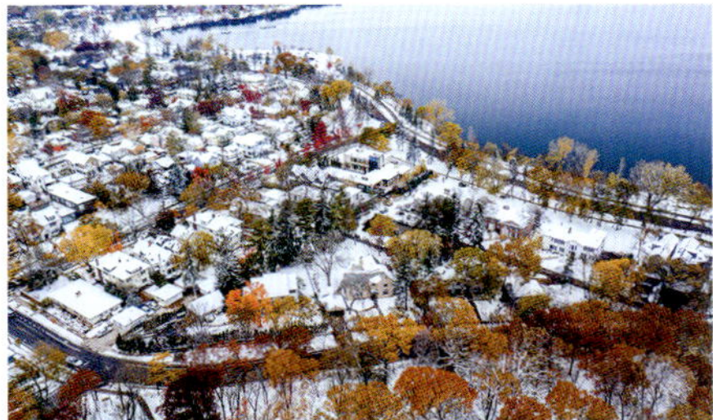

118-119 Omar Ghrayeb
Above Bde Maka Ska

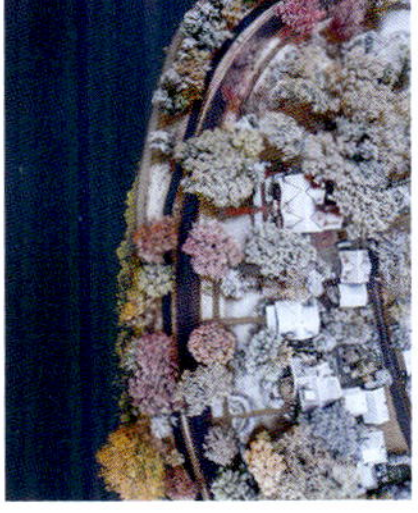

120 Omar Ghrayeb
Looking down on Lake of the Isles

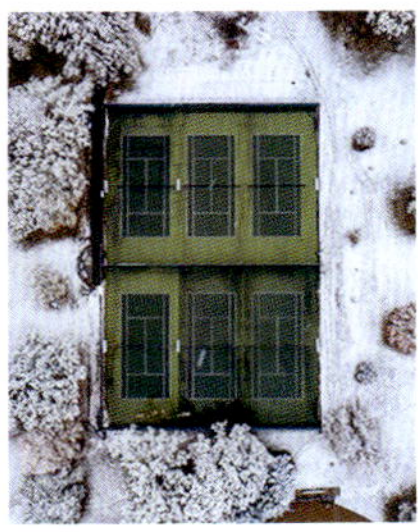

121 Omar Ghrayeb
Looking down on Kenwood Park tennis courts

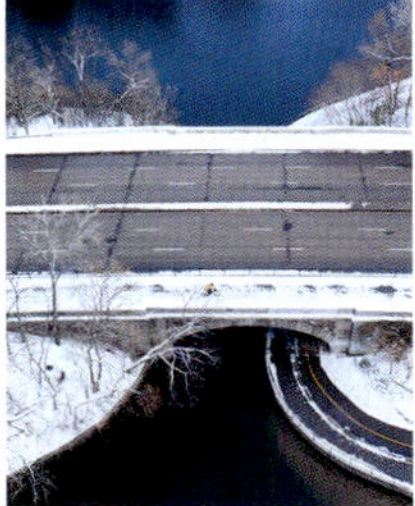

122 Omar Ghrayeb
Over Bde Maka Ska and Lake of the Isles

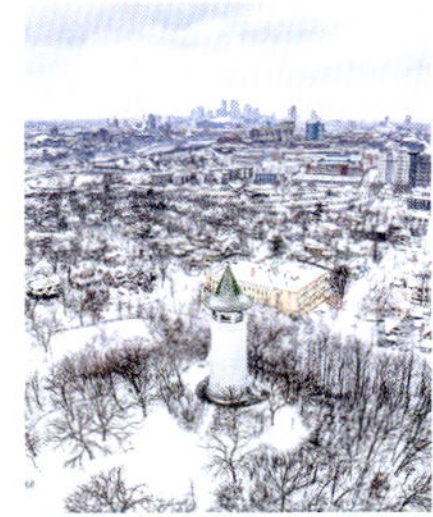

123 Michael Anderson
Above Witch's Hat Water Tower, Prospect Park

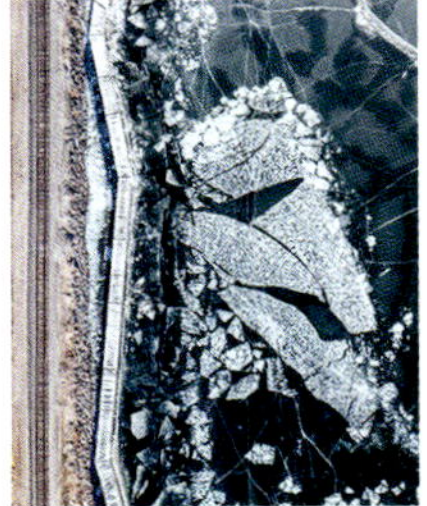

124 Omar Ghrayeb
Looking down on Lake Minnetonka

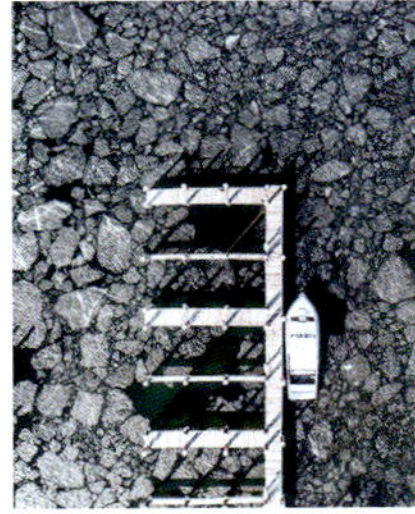

125 Omar Ghrayeb
Looking down on Lake Minnetonka

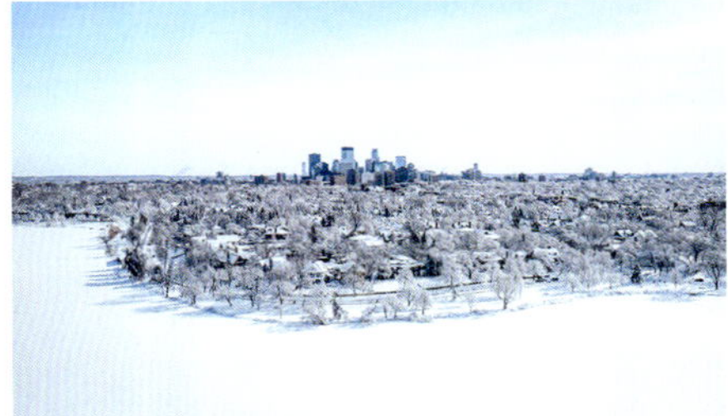

126-127 Omar Ghrayeb
View of the Minneapolis skyline from Lake of the Isles

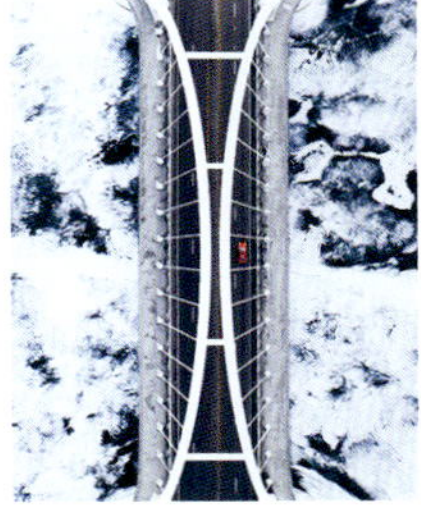

128 Omar Ghrayeb
Looking down on Lowry Avenue Bridge

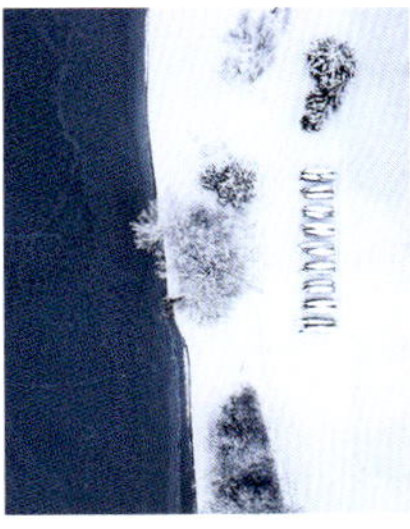

129 Omar Ghrayeb
Looking down on Lake Minnetonka

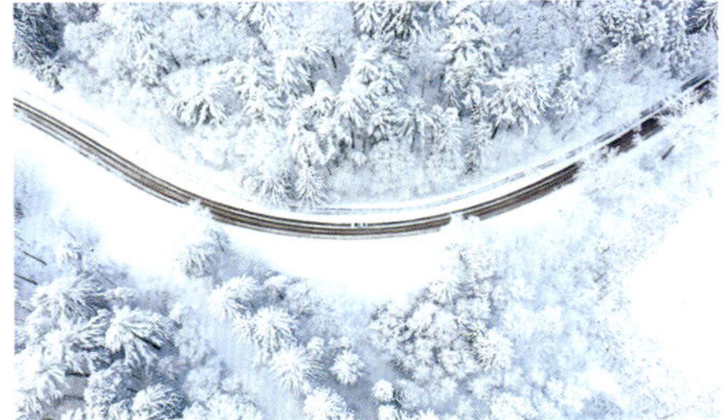

130 Omar Ghrayeb
Looking down on Theodore Wirth Regional Park

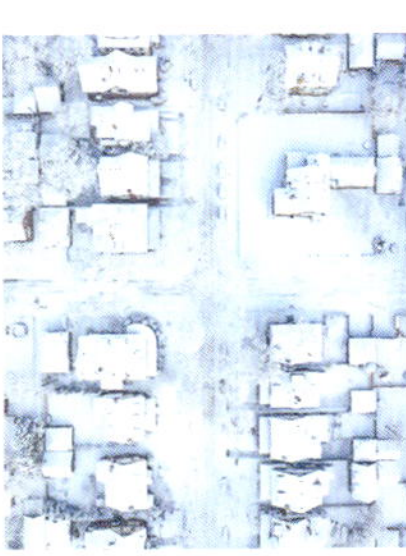

131 Omar Ghrayeb
Looking down on Linden Hills

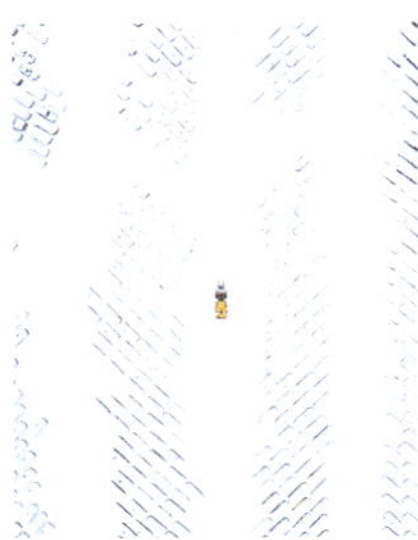

132 Omar Ghrayeb
North Minneapolis junkyard

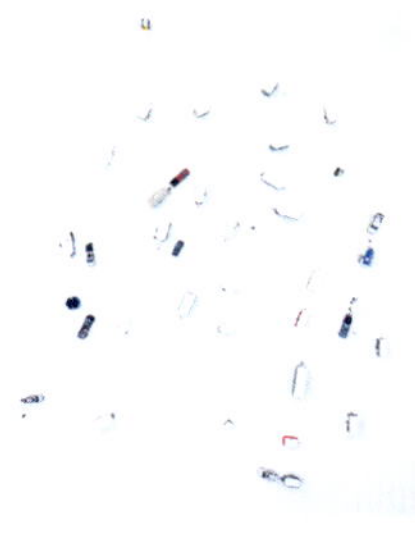

133 Omar Ghrayeb
Ice fishing huts on Lake Minnetonka

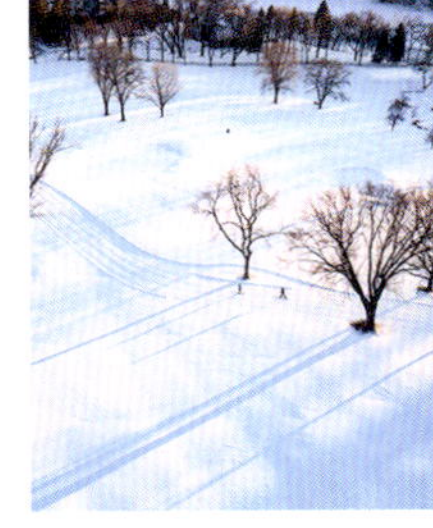

134 Omar Ghrayeb
Above Theodore Wirth Regional Park

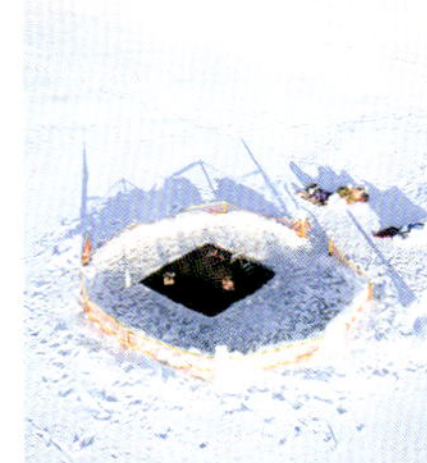

135 Omar Ghrayeb
Ice swimming on Lake Harriet

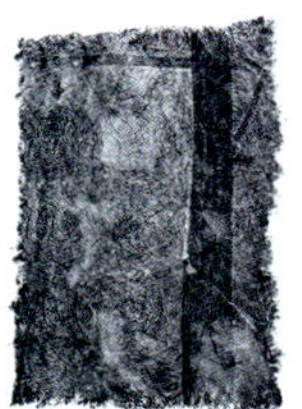

136 Omar Ghrayeb
Looking down on Lake Harriet

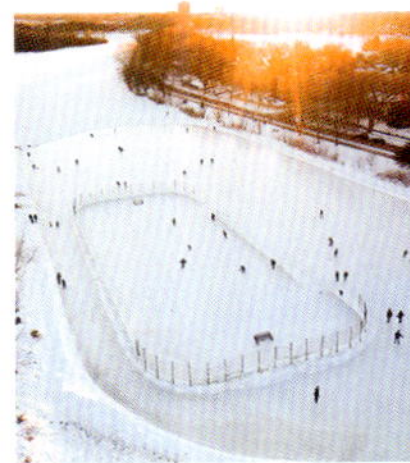

137 Omar Ghrayeb
Hockey rink on Lake of the Isles

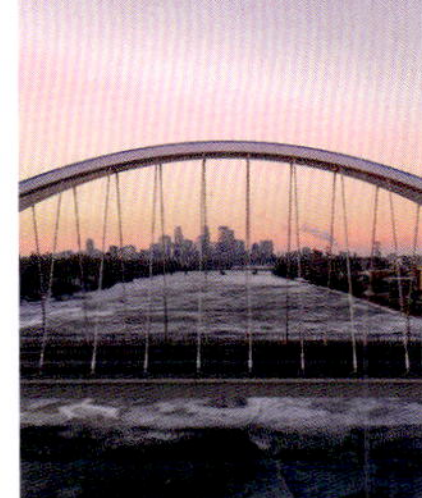

138 Omar Ghrayeb
View of downtown Minneapolis through Lowry Avenue Bridge

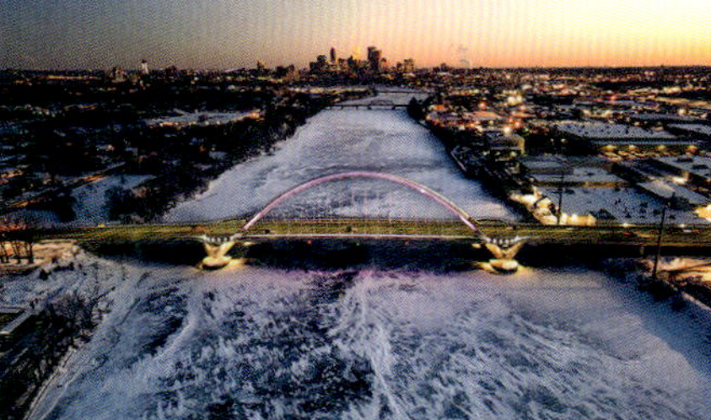

139 Brian Johnson
Above Lowry Avenue Bridge

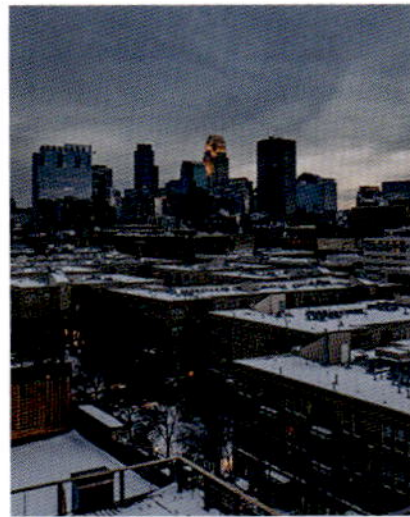

140 Malik Blaylark
View of downtown
Minneapolis from North Loop

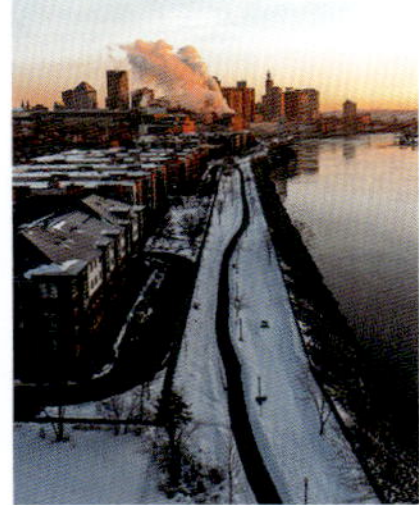

141 Malik Blaylark
View of downtown St. Paul
from High Bridge

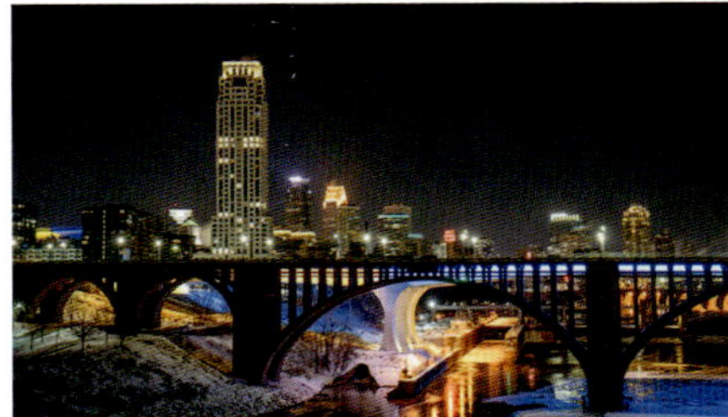

142-143 Michael Anderson
View of 10th Avenue Bridge

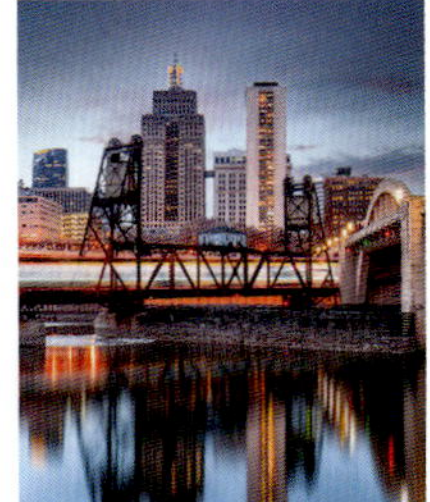

144 Zach Butler
View of First National
Bank Building

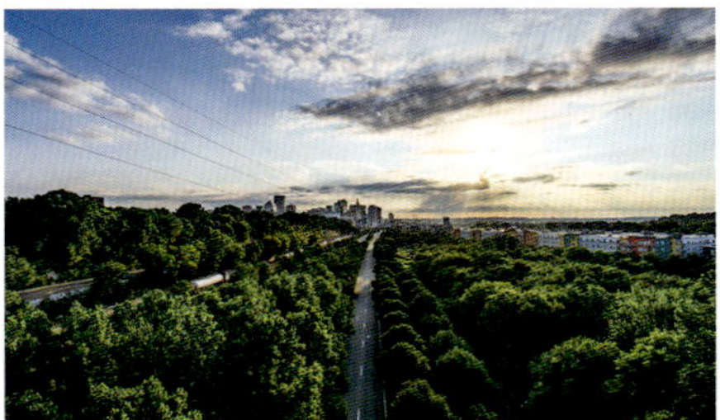

146-147 Brian Johnson
View of downtown St. Paul above Shepard Road

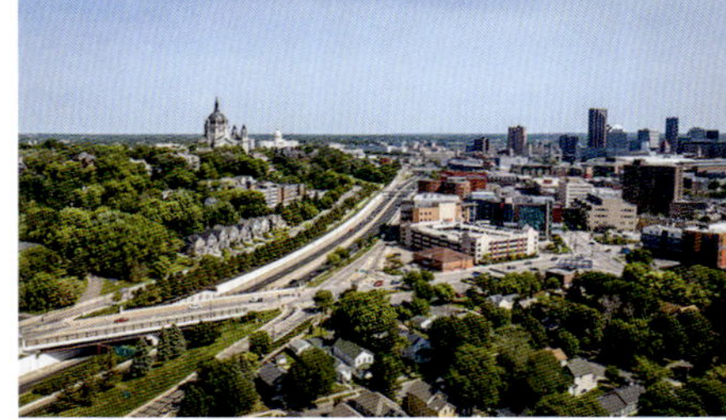

148-149 Greg Schulz
View of downtown St. Paul, the Cathedral of St. Paul,
and the Minnesota Capitol Building

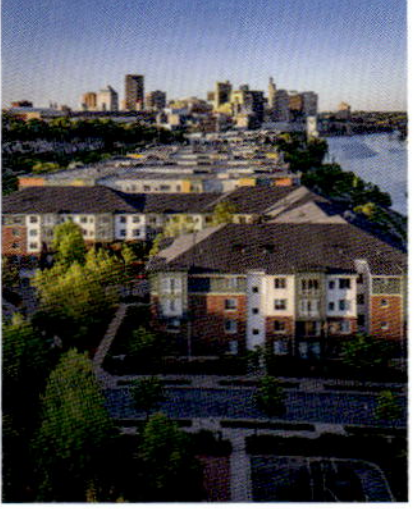

150 Mark Bergeron
View of downtown St. Paul
and the Mississippi River
from High Bridge

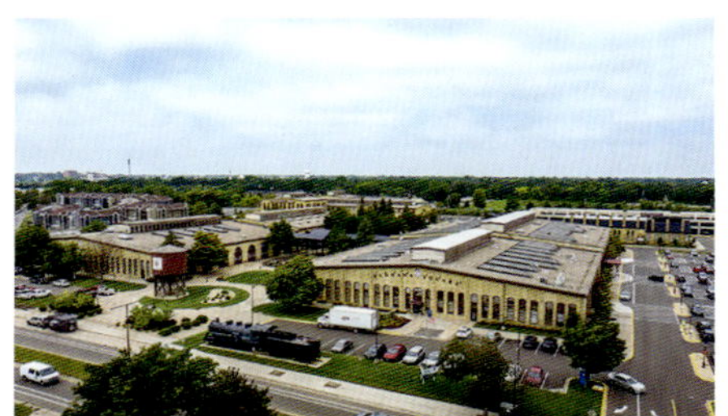

151 Greg Schulz
Above Bandana Square

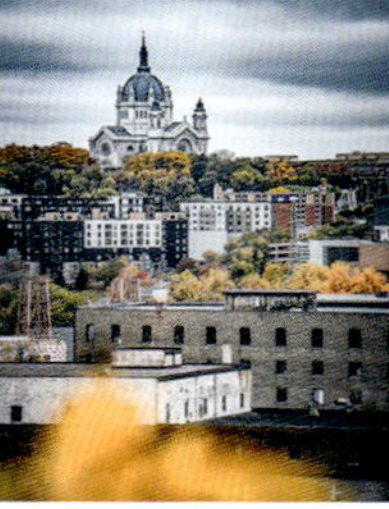

152 Micheal Anderson
View of the Cathedral
of St. Paul

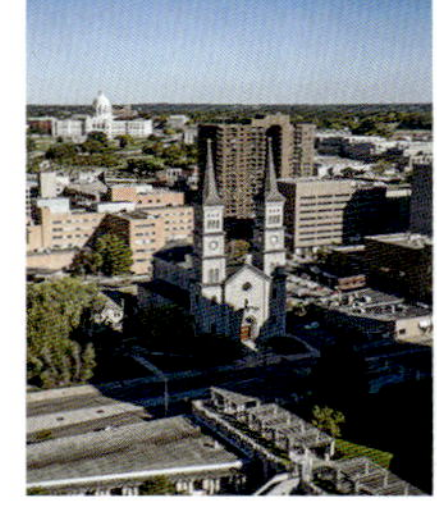

153 Greg Schulz
Above the Church
of the Assumption

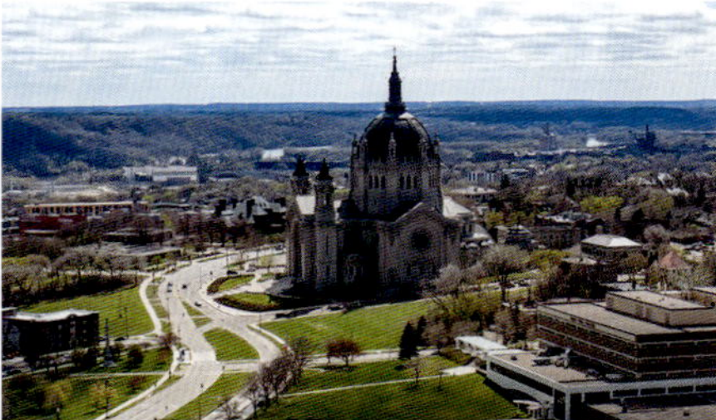

154-155 Greg Schulz
Above the Cathedral of St. Paul

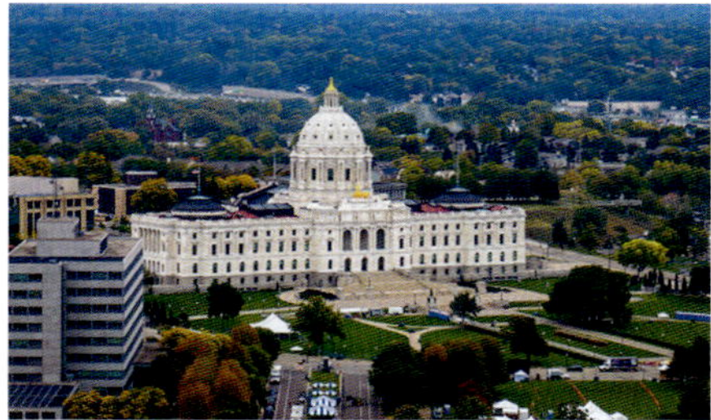

156-157 Greg Schulz
Above the Minnesota Capitol Building

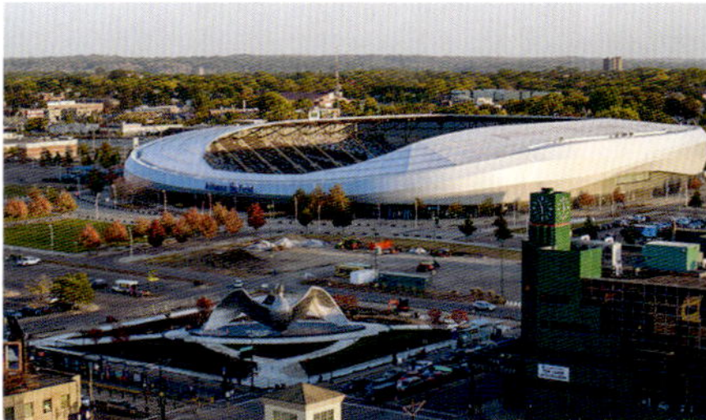

158-159 Greg Schulz
Above Allianz Field

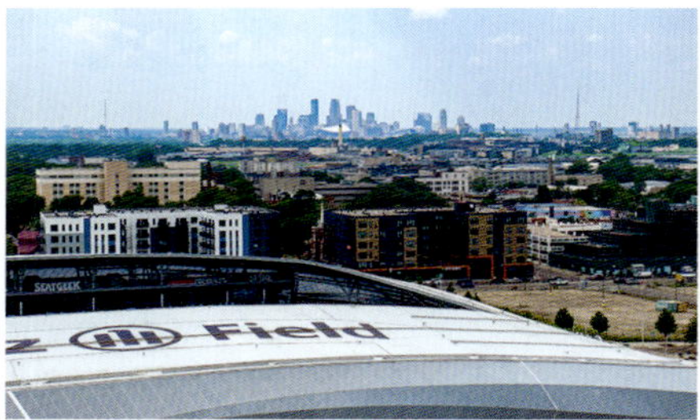

160-161 Greg Schulz
View of Allianz Field and the Minneapolis skyline

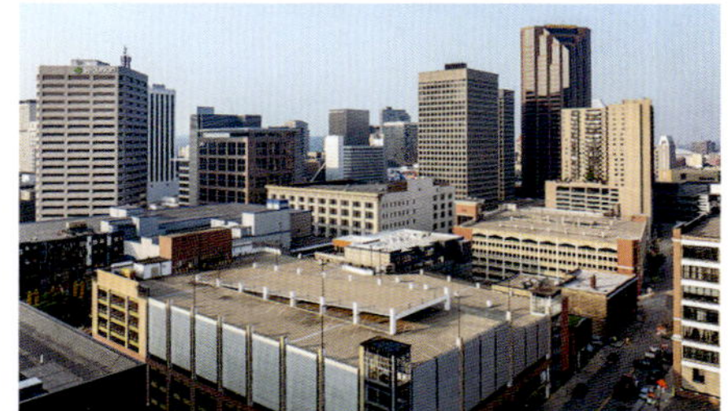

162 Greg Schulz
Above downtown St. Paul

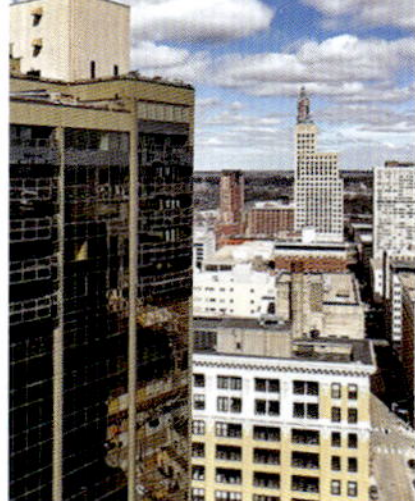

163 Greg Schulz
View of First National
Bank Building

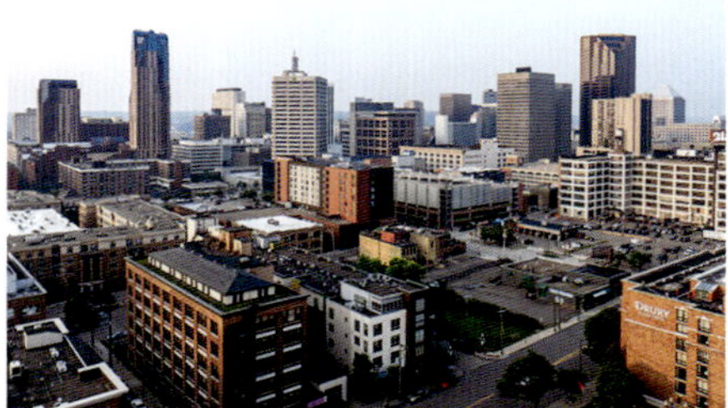

164-165 Greg Schulz
Above downtown St. Paul

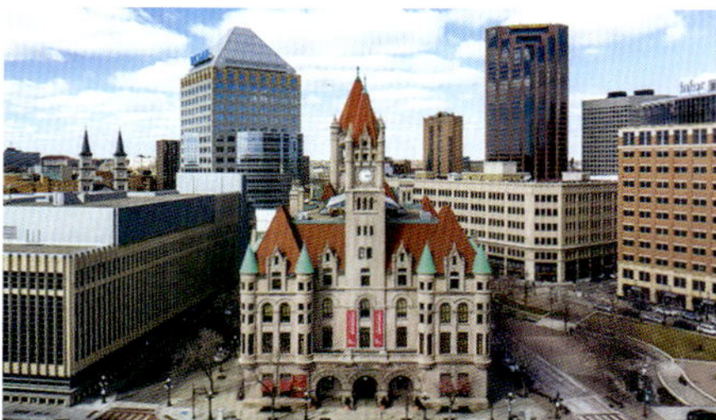

166-167 Greg Schulz
View of the Landmark Center

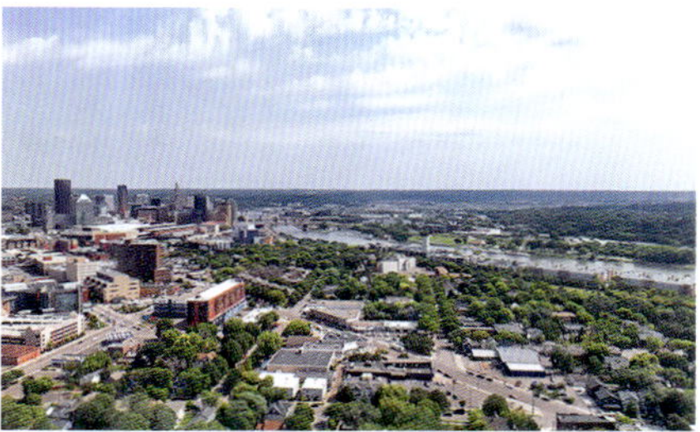

168-169 Greg Schulz
Above St. Paul and the Mississippi River

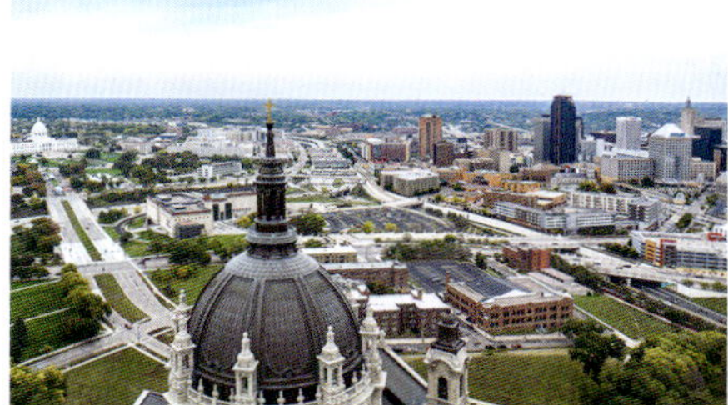

170-171 Greg Schulz
View from the Cathedral of St. Paul

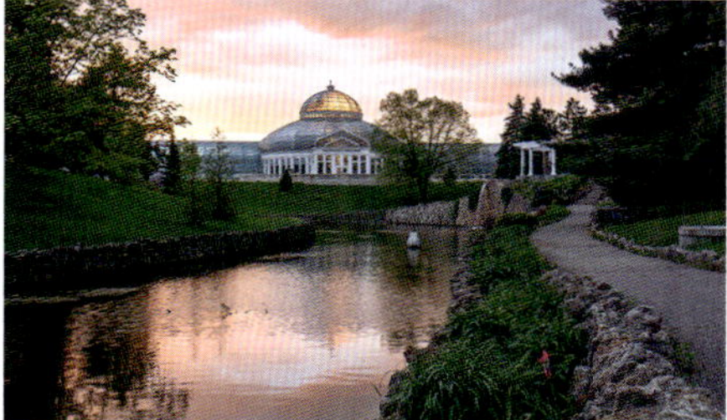

172-173 Brian Johnson
View of Marjorie McNeely Conservatory, Como Park Zoo

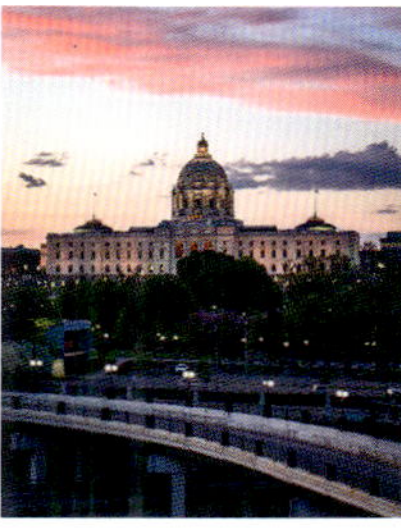

174 Brian Johnson
View of the Minnesota
Capitol Building

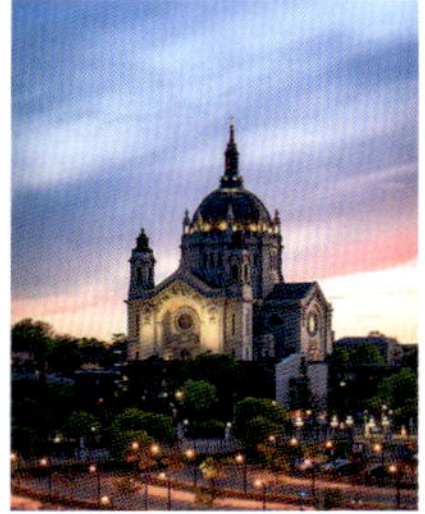

175 Brian Johnson
View of the Cathedral
of St. Paul

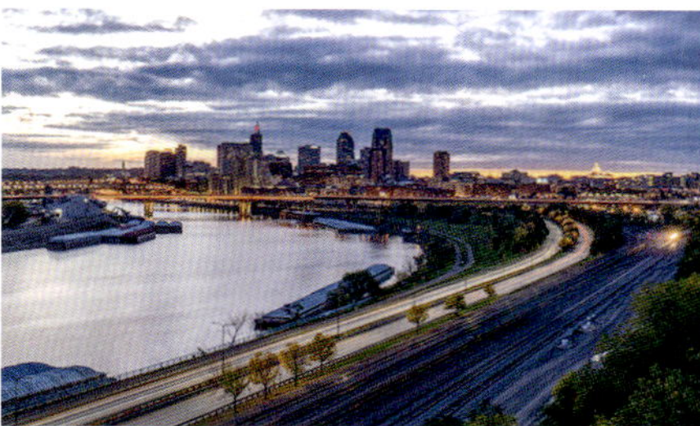

176-177 Michael Anderson
View of downtown St. Paul

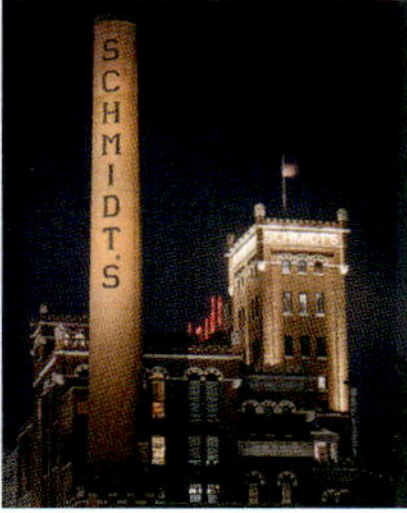

178 Mark Bergeron
View of Schmidt Brewery

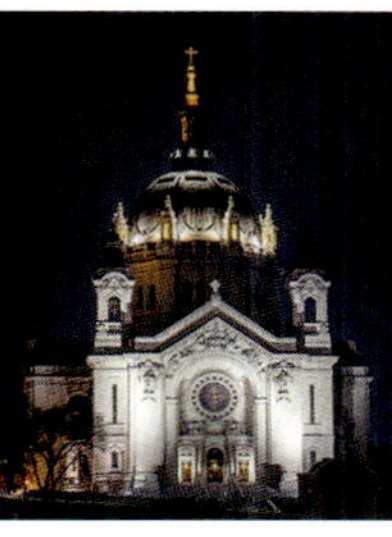

179 Mark Bergeron
View of the Cathedral
of St. Paul

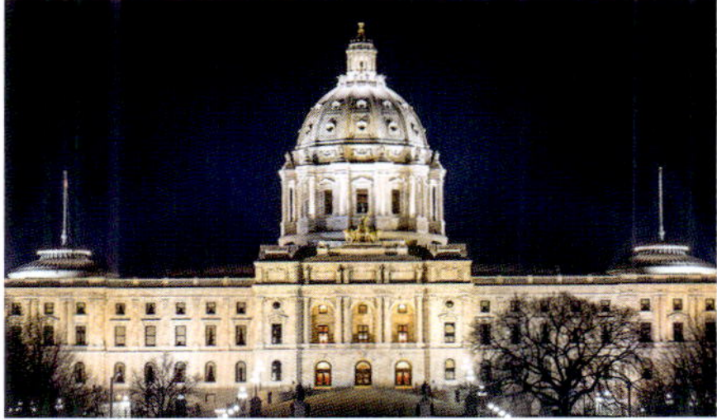

180-181 Mark Bergeron
View of the Minnesota Capitol Building

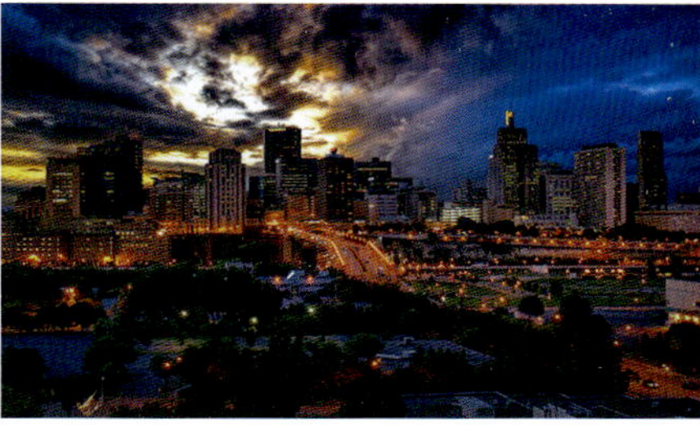

182-183 Dan Anderson
View of downtown St. Paul and Wabasha Street Bridge

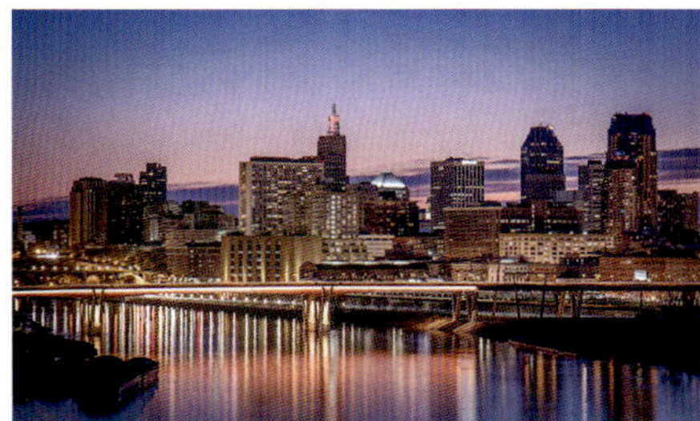

184-185 Mark Bergeron
View of downtown St. Paul and the Lafayette Bridge

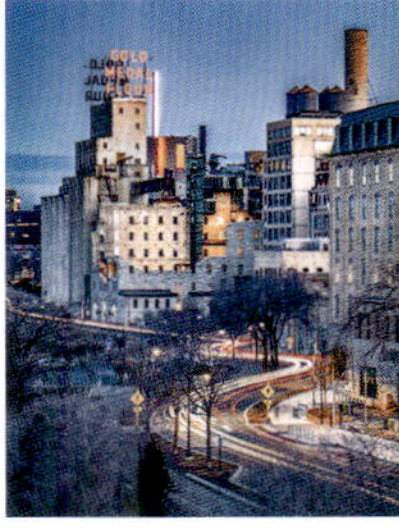

186 Michael Anderson
View of Gold Medal Flour
sign and Mill City Museum

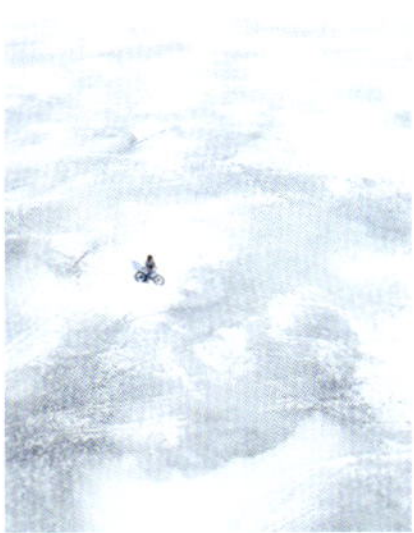

188 Omar Ghrayeb
Cyclist on Lake of the Isles

196 Omar Ghrayeb
Looking down on railway
yard, North Minneapolis

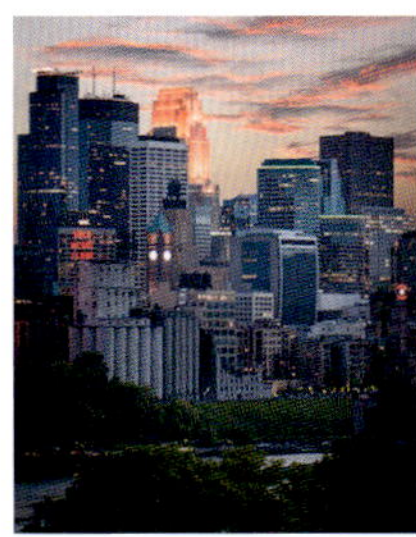

198 Zach Butler
View of downtown
Minneapolis

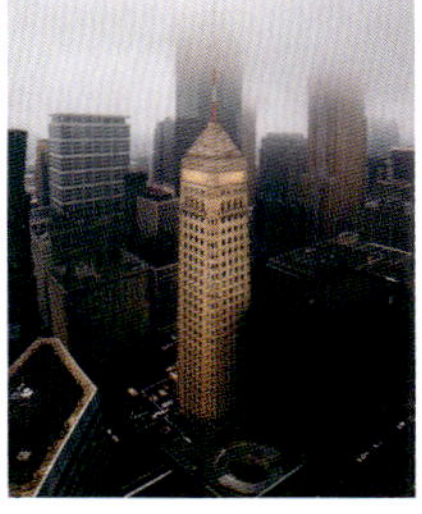

200 Jamie Hiner
Above the Foshay Tower

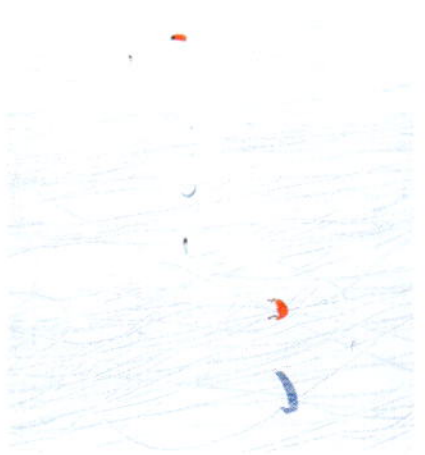

Back Cover Omar Ghrayeb
Snow kiters on Lake
Minnetonka

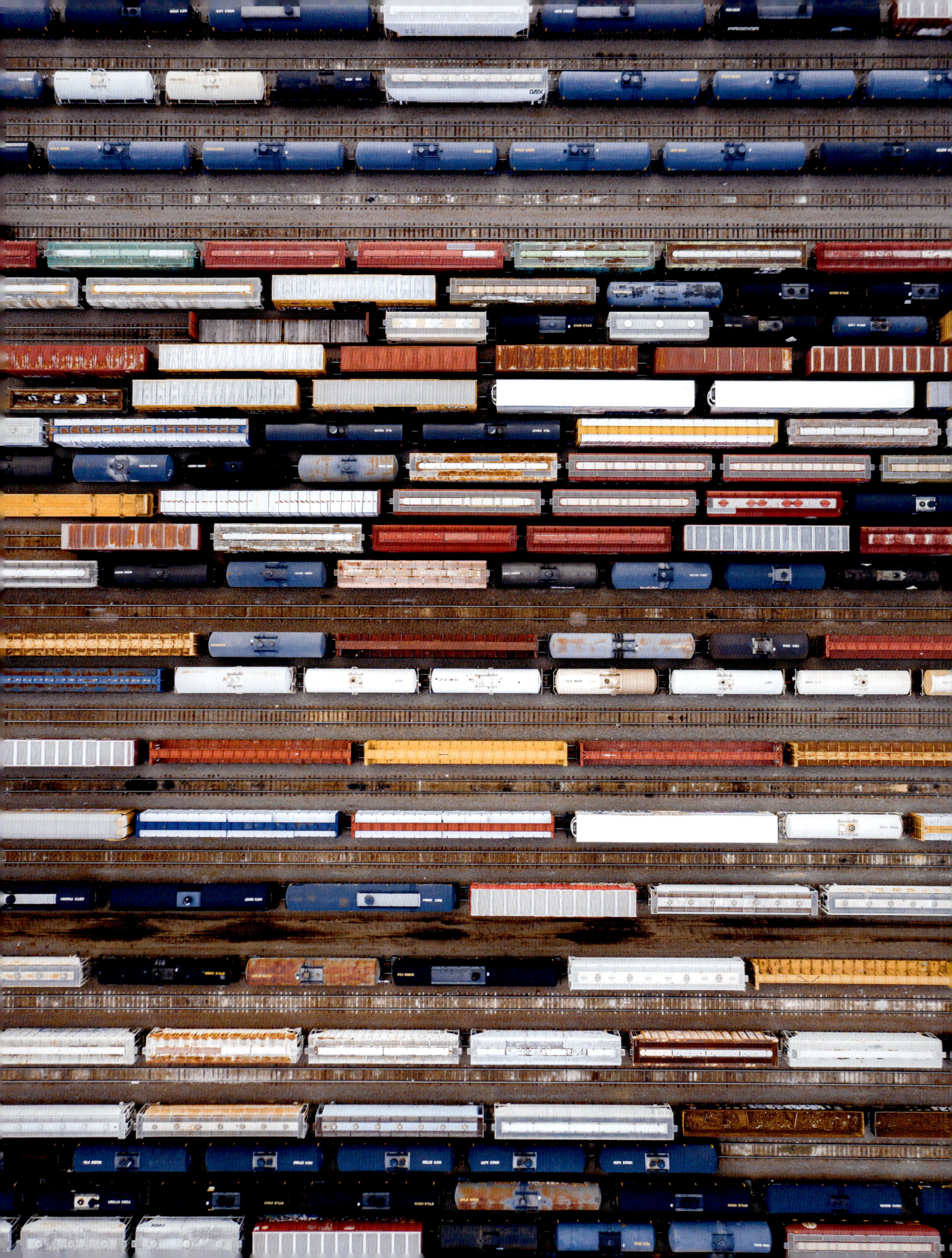

PHOTOGRAPHERS

+ BRIAN JOHNSON
Born and raised in Minnesota, Brian
Johnson discovered his love for
photography on the North Shore, and
now captures the beauty of landscapes
through local and international travels
@brian.t.imagery

+ DAN ANDERSON
Twin Cities-based photographer with
a passion for capturing the unique
landscape of Minnesota
@dan.anderson.photos

+ GREG SCHULZ
Aerial photographer living in Stillwater,
Minnesota, who specializes in architecture,
landscapes, and events, with a passion
for capturing and sharing experiences
via imagery
@picturesoverstillwater

+ JAMIE HINER
Real estate, wedding and travel content
creator with a goal of showcasing fresh
and unique perspectives
@jah_creations

+ MALIK BLAYLARK
Street photographer, travel photographer,
Youtuber, and the self-proclaimed
"Location King of the Twin Cities," raised
in the suburbs of Minneapolis
@malik.blaylark

+ MARK BERGERON
With a highly varied photographic
interest in subject matter and technique,
this life-long Midwesterner is fascinated
with fusing the creative with an analytical
approach
@markabergeron

+ MICHAEL ANDERSON
Minneapolis native specializing in
evocative landscape and cityscape
imagery from the Twin Cities
and beyond
@michaelandersonimagery

+ OMAR GHRAYEB
Lebanese-born and Minneapolis-based,
award-winning aerial photographer
Omar Ghrayeb is the creative mind
behind **OGEE VISUALS**
@ogeevisuals

+ ZACH BUTLER
Minneapolis-based architectural
photographer with a focus on cityscape,
landscape, and travel photography
@zbutler

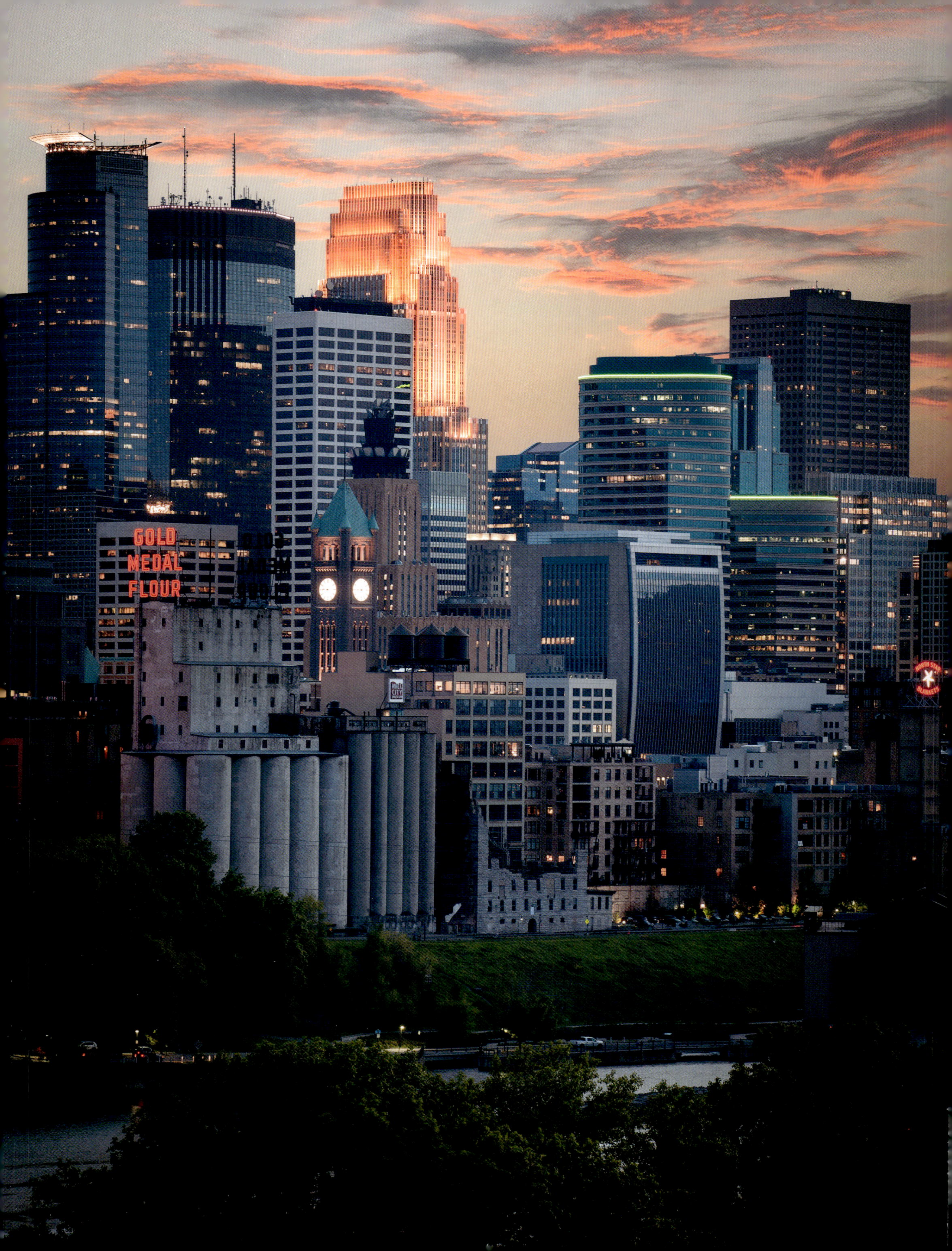
GOLD
MEDAL
FLOUR

ACKNOWLEDGEMENTS

SPECIAL THANKS

+ We would like to thank all of the photographers who have generously donated their time and allowed us to use their images to create *Above & Across Twin Cities.*

Additionally, we thank the following individuals who worked tirelessly through the production of *Above & Across Twin Cities.*

+ KATE LANDERS

+ MATTHEW JORGENSEN

+ MADDY MODERHACK

+ SAM LANDERS

+ TOM WEBER

+ MICHAEL CROY

ISBN: 978-1-951963-58-3

Printed and bound in China
First printing, 2026

Trope Publishing Co.
Chicago, Illinois, USA

The photographs from *Above & Across Twin Cities* are available for purchase. For inquiries, email the gallery at info@trope.com

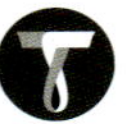

+ **INFORMATION:**
For additional information
on our books and prints,
visit WWW.TROPE.COM

ABOUT THE EDITORS

+ MICHELLE FITZGERALD
Michelle Fitzgerald is the Associate Publisher at Trope Publishing Co. and served as editor for *New York*, *Paris*, *Los Angeles*, *Rome,* and *Tokyo*, part of Trope's City Edition series, as well as the other titles in Trope's Above & Across series. A veteran of the book publishing industry, Michelle is a fierce advocate for books and is passionate about sharing them with the widest audience possible.

+ KENDRA HUSPASKA
Kendra is a Chicago-based designer and illustrator with a passion for editorial and publication design who served as editor on *Above & Across Philadelphia*, as well as *Trope Rome* and *Trope Tokyo*. As the Senior Designer at Trope Publishing Co., she has an unwavering dedication to the tactile and timeless nature of print.

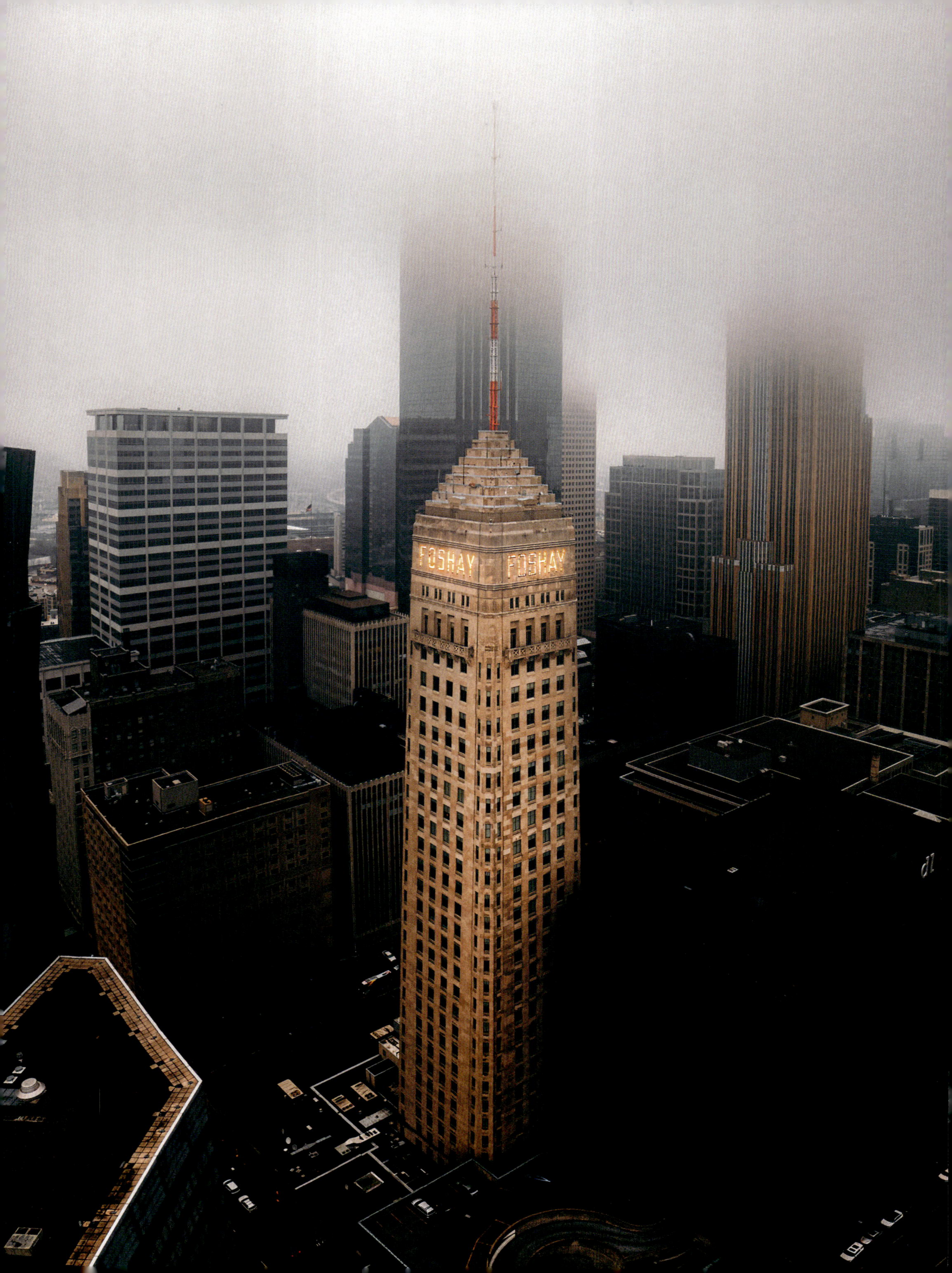

FOSHAY
FOSHAY